PERILOUS QUESTION

Also by Antonia Fraser

NON-FICTION

Mary Queen of Scots
Cromwell: Our Chief of Men
James VI of Scotland, I of England
King Charles II
The Weaker Vessel: Woman's Lot in Seventeenth-century England
The Warrior Queens: Boadicea's Chariot
The Six Wives of Henry VIII
The Gunpowder Plot: Terror and Faith in 1605
Marie Antoinette: The Journey
Love and Louis XIV: The Women in the Life of the Sun King
Must You Go? My Life with Harold Pinter

FICTION

Quiet as a Nun
The Wild Island
A Splash of Red
Cool Repentance
Oxford Blood
Jemima Shore's First Case
Your Royal Hostage
The Cavalier Case
Jemima Shore at the Sunny Grave
Political Death

PERILOUS QUESTION

Reform or Revolution?
Britain on the Brink, 1832

Antonia Fraser

PublicAffairs
New York

PublicAffairs books are available at special discounts for bulk purchases in the U.S. by corporations, institutions, and other organizations. For more information, please contact the Special Markets Department at the Perseus Books Group, 2300 Chestnut Street, Suite 200, Philadelphia, PA 19103, call (800) 810–4145, ext. 5000, or e-mail special.markets@ perseusbooks.com.

The Library of Congress Control Number: 2013933913
ISBN 978–1-61039–331–7 (HC)
ISBN 978–1-61039–332–4 (EB)
First Edition

10 9 8 7 6 5 4 3 2 1

In Memory of

HAROLD PINTER and FRANK LONGFORD
who were not afraid to ask perilous questions

CONTENTS

List of Illustrations ix

Author's Note xi

PROLOGUE: A new King, a new people 1

CHAPTER ONE: The clamour 13

CHAPTER TWO: I will pronounce the word 30

CHAPTER THREE: Believing in the Whigs 50

CHAPTER FOUR: The gentlemen of England 69

CHAPTER FIVE: Russell's Purge 86

CHAPTER SIX: King as angel 99

CHAPTER SEVEN: Away went Gilpin 115

CHAPTER EIGHT: Confound their politics 132

CHAPTER NINE: What have the Lords *done*? 151

CHAPTER TEN: A scene of desolation 167

CHAPTER ELEVEN: The fearful alternative 184

CHAPTER TWELVE: Bouncing Bill 202

CHAPTER THIRTEEN: Seventh of May 217

CHAPTER FOURTEEN: Prithee return to me 236

CHAPTER FIFTEEN: Bright day of liberty 249

EPILOGUE: This great national exploit 260

References 279

Sources 289

Index 297

Photo insert between pages 146–147

LIST OF ILLUSTRATIONS

Page 1: William IV by Sir Martin Archer Shee, 1835, aged 70. (© Royal Academy of Arts, London; John Hammond)

Page 2, top: Adelaide of Saxe-Meiningen, c.1831, by Sir William Beechey. (© National Portrait Gallery, London)

Page 2, bottom: Mary Countess Grey with two of her daughters. (Private collection)

Page 3: Charles 2nd Earl Grey, by Sir Thomas Lawrence. (Private collection)

Page 4, top: Arthur Wellesley, 1st Duke of Wellington, by John Simpson, c.1835. (Apsley House, The Wellington Museum, London / © English Heritage Photo Library / The Bridgeman Art Library)

Page 4, bottom: Sir Robert Peel by Henry William Pickersgill. (© National Portrait Gallery, London)

Page 5, top: Old Sarum by John Constable (1776–1837). (Private collection / The Stapleton Collection / The Bridgeman Art Library)

Page 5, bottom: High street market, Birmingham. Engraving by William Radclyffe, 1827, from a drawing by David Cox. (SSPL / Getty Images)

Page 6, top: Thomas Attwood. Engraving by C. Turner, 1832, after portrait by George Sharples. (Private Collection / The Bridgeman Art Library)

Page 6, middle: 'The Preston Shoe Black in Parliament Showering a few of his Brilliant Ideas out at the Expence of Some of the Rotten Members'. (By permission of the People's History Museum)

Page 6, bottom: Captain Swing, c. December 1830. 'An original portrait of Captain Swing', published by Orlando Hodgson, 1830. (© The Trustees of the British Museum)

Page 7, top: Lord John Russell and Lord Holland. Portrait by George Hayter (attributed to). (The Congregational Memorial Hall Trust (1978) Limited. Image supplied by The Public Catalogue Foundation)

Page 7, bottom: Lord and Lady Holland in the Library at Holland House. 'Holland House Library' by C. R. Leslie. (Private collection)

Page 8, top: William Cobbett. Etching by Daniel Maclise, 1835. (© National Portrait Gallery, London)

Page 8, bottom: Thomas Babington Macaulay. Drawing by I.N. Rhodes, 1832. (Private collection)

Page 9, top: 'An After Dinner Scene (At Windsor)' by John Doyle. Lithograph published by Thomas McLean, 12 October 1831. (© National Portrait Gallery, London)

Page 9, bottom: 'Handwriting Upon the Wall' after John Doyle. Published 26 May 1831. (Shelf mark: Reform Bills 2 54. The Art Archive / Bodleian Library, Oxford)

Page 10, top: 'House of Commons' by James Stephanoff, 1821. (© Palace of Westminster Collection, WOA 276)

Page 10, bottom: 'The Reformers' Attack on the Old Rotten Tree; or the Foul Nests of the Cormorants in Danger.' Cartoon published by E. King, May 1831. (By permission of the People's History Museum)

Page 11, top: The City of Bristol on Fire, 30 October 1831, from a sketch taken from Brandon Hill by C.H. Walters (Bristol Record Office: BRO 43207/20/3/1)

Page 11, bottom: 'Bombarding the Barricades or the Storming of Apsley House'. Hand-coloured etching published by J. Bell, February 1832. (© The Trustees of the British Museum)

Page 12, top: 'Dame Partington and the Ocean (of Reform) by John Doyle. Lithograph published by Thomas Mclean, 24 October 1831. (© The Trustees of the British Museum)

Page 12, bottom: 'New Reform Coach' by John Doyle. Lithograph published by Thomas McLean, 17 June 1832. (© National Portrait Gallery, London)

Page 13, top: 'The Dog Billy Led Astray by a German B----'. Woodcut published by G. Drake, 1832.

Page 13, bottom: Shoemakers' banner. (By permission of the People's History Museum)

Page 14, top: John Gilpin!!! by John Doyle. Lithograph published by Thomas McLean, 13 May 1831. (© National Portrait Gallery, London)

Page 14, bottom: Scorton 1832–Celebrating the First Reform Act. Artist unknown. (Kiplin Hall)

Page 15: The banquet given in the Guildhall, 7 July 1832, to celebrate the passing of the Bill. Painting by Benjamin Robert Haydon. (Private collection)

Page 16: 'A memento of the Great Public Question of Reform'. Designed and engraved for the *Bell's New Weekly Messenger*, 15 April 1832. (By permission of the People's History Museum)

AUTHOR'S NOTE

I wrote this book to satisfy my own curiosity: what were they like, the people who fought for (or against) the Reform Bill of 1832? What was it like, the reality of the precise, short period – July 1830 until June 1832 – in which it all took place? I wanted to investigate the flavour of the times, rather than write a history of Reform. During the period I was working on this book, British politics sometimes seemed to be tracking my early-nineteenth-century course, as topics like voting and the House of Lords regularly came up for discussion, to say nothing of popular demonstrations; any parallels are however for the reader to draw. Essentially, I was interested to pursue the perennial mixture of idealism and self-interest which permeates the politics of great events.

With this in mind, wherever appropriate I have quoted the contemporary accounts and comments – with special attention to the dramatic debates in both the House of Lords and the House of Commons. I have borne in mind the words of F. W. Maitland, which are at the heart of writing history: 'We should always be aware that what now lies in the past, once lay in the future'; that is to say, we know the Reform Bill will pass, but the people who fought for it did not. And it was a fierce fight. There is a memorial in a Harrow church to a Member of Parliament, John Henry North, who died at the age of forty-four in 1831 as a result of 'a mind too great for his earthly frame in opposing the Revolutionary Invasion of the Religion and Constitution of England' which was Reform. Not everyone suffered a nervous breakdown and died of it, but many people, unaware of the outcome, were beset with anxiety; the large majority of them deserve honour for the role they played.

In my researches, I have been enormously helped by the many existing great works on parliamentary Reform – histories of the subject are listed in the Sources and acknowledged individually, with gratitude, in the References. My work would have been impossible without them. I have also much pleasure in acknowledging specific help from the following:

I wish to thank Her Majesty the Queen for permission to quote from Queen Adelaide's Diary in the Royal Archives; also the Hon. Lady Roberts, Librarian and Curator of the Print Room, Royal Collection, Miss Pam Clarke, Senior Archivist, Royal Archives and Mrs Jill Kelsey, Deputy Archivist, Royal Archives.

I give special thanks to: Professor Carl Chinn, Professor of Community History, University of Birmingham; Phil Dunn, People's History Museum, Manchester; Miranda Goodby, Potteries Museum & Art Gallery, Stoke-on-Trent; Dr Bendor Grosvenor for permission to reproduce the Fuseli drawing of Lord Brougham; Christopher Hunwick, Archivist, Northumberland Estates and Secretary, Historic Houses Archivists Group; Rosa Jarvie and Laura Lindsay, Christie's; Centre for Kentish Studies, Maidstone, for permission to quote from the Stanhope MSS, and Danielle Watson, Public Services Assistant; the Duke of Marlborough for permission to reproduce the portrait of the Marquess of Blandford, and Heather Carter, Head of Operations, Blenheim Palace Estate Office; Sheila O'Connell, Curator of British Prints before 1880, British Museum; Victoria Osborne, Curator, Fine Art, Birmingham Museum & Art Gallery; David Raymont, Librarian, The Actuarial Profession; Margaret Richards, Archive Assistant, Arundel Castle; Professor John Rogister; the Duke of Rutland for permission to quote from the Rutland MSS, Peter Foden, Archivist, Belvoir Castle and Emma Ellis; Colin Shearer, Collections Manager, Holkham Hall; Caroline Shenton; Mrs Anne Smith, Curator & Archivist, Sherborne Castle Estates; Earl Spencer for permission to reproduce the portrait of Viscount Althorp and his prize bull; Dawn Webster, Curator, Kiplin Hall; Mrs Pamela Woolf, Wordsworth Trust; Adam Zamoyski.

I thank the following for advice and encouragement in many different ways: Dr John Adamson; Professor Helen Berry, University of Newcastle; Lord (Asa) Briggs; Professor Robert Bucholz; Professor

Sir David Cannadine; my son Orlando Fraser; Sir Martin Gilbert; Victoria Gray; the late Professor Eric Hobsbawm; Louis Jebb; Linda Kelly; Alan Mallinson; Sir Geoffrey Owen; Dr David Parrott; Professor Munro Price; Frank Prochaska; Professor Miles Taylor; Hugo Vickers; Katie Waldegrave.

The staff of the British Library, British Museum, Institute of Historical Research, London Library and the National Archives were all most helpful. My agent Jonathan Lloyd and publisher Alan Samson with Lucinda McNeile were as ever extremely supportive as was Linda Peskin at the computer. My daughter Flora Fraser shared her expertise on the period. I am grateful to Paul Foote and Stephan M. Lee for research and corrections, remaining errors being of course my own. Caroline Hotblack provided valuable picture research, and Linden Lawson admirable copy-editing.

Lastly this book is jointly dedicated to my husband Harold Pinter and my father Frank Longford, who did not live to see it published but would undoubtedly have had individual and vigorous views on the subject of Reform.

Antonia Fraser

27 November 2012

Note: For the sake of the reader, I have attempted from time to time to give the modern equivalent of sums of money in 1830. Such calculations can only ever be approximate. The Bank of England Inflation Calculator for 2011 (based on figures supplied by the Office of National Statistics) gave the figure £9,371.71 for £100 in 1830. (http://www .bankofengland.co.uk/education/inflation/calculator/flash/index .htm)

I have therefore in principle rounded this figure up to £10,000, both to allow for further inflation and for convenience in providing what is only a rough picture.

'The perilous question is that of Parliamentary Reform, and as I approach it, the more I feel all its difficulty.'–
Earl Grey, 13 January 1831

A NEW KING, A NEW PEOPLE

'A Patriot King is the most powerful of all reformers ...
A new people will seem to arise with a new King' –

Lord Bolingbroke, *The Idea of a Patriot King*, 1738

The struggle for the Great Reform Bill of 1832 took place at the cross-roads of English history. One road wound down from the long eighteenth century which, it could be argued, only ended with the victory of Waterloo in 1815. Another road led forward to the reign of Queen Victoria which began in 1837 and a nineteenth century which finally terminated with the beginning of the First World War in 1914. This was the Britain from which the imagination of J.M.W. Turner drew inspiration; in a famous picture of the 1830s, *The Fighting Temeraire*, a ship distinguished at the Battle of Trafalgar twenty-five years earlier, was shown being tugged away at sea, to be broken up; in another exquisite sunset landscape, a new industrial town existed as a dark, even menacing blur in the corner.

Communications were being transformed. This was the time when the first railways were nosing their way round Britain. Mrs Harriet Arbuthnot, confidante of the Duke of Wellington, waxed lyrical at the opening of the Liverpool–Manchester Railway: 'I don't think I ever saw a more beautiful sight than at the moment when the car attached to the engine *shot off* on its journey.'[1] To others they seemed a more baleful presage of disaster, as when the diarist Thomas Creevey reflected, on a five-mile journey from Croxteth at twenty miles an hour, that it was impossible to divest himself of 'the notion of instant death'.[2] The police force, a new concept of managing public order other than by military reaction, was founded in London in 1829. At the same time slavery in the British Empire had not yet been abolished, nor were Jews admitted to Parliament. Penal reform was becoming a topic of discussion although it was a rare citizen who questioned capital punishment – the Whig grandee Lord Holland was one of them – yet the bodies of the executed were still publicly visible: as the artist Benjamin Robert Haydon exclaimed, 'What a day! I saw a man just hanging at Newgate.'[3]

During the struggle, the famous names of the coming reign were already present, albeit in very junior capacities. Here was the nineteen-year-old Charles Dickens as a cub reporter in Parliament and a youthful Thomas Babington Macaulay, first elected MP in 1830, making his name. A promising student at Oxford attended the debates in the gallery: his name was William Ewart Gladstone. Victoria herself, who was twelve in 1830, struck an observer as 'a young, pretty, unaffected child'; Sir John Hobhouse added: 'What will become of her?'[4]

Among the politicians at Westminster, Daniel O'Connell made his first appearance from Ireland – the man who would be known as The Liberator. At the same time the leading Whig politician, Charles 2nd Earl Grey, had worshipped at the liberal shrine of Charles James Fox in the 1780s and as a young man had been the cavalier of Georgiana Duchess of Devonshire, centre of the glittering Whig world of that time. The Tory Prime Minister, the great soldier the Duke of Wellington, whose mother had taken part in the coronation of George III in 1761, was in his sixties, as indeed was Grey.[5] The reign of George IV might have lasted only ten years, although he was Regent during his father's madness before then; that of George III stretched back to 1760. There were even old men to be found like General Dalrymple who remembered the trial of Lord Lovat following the Jacobite Rebellion of 1745. Compared to this the Marquis of Huntly, the 'charming Scot' who as a young man had danced in Highland dress before Marie Antoinette, was a comparative newcomer.[6]

During the struggle, there would be frequent references to the troubles of Charles I with his Parliament and the English Civil War which followed. Then there was the last traumatic period in English reforming history, the so-called Glorious Revolution of 1688, when the Whig oligarchy imposed their choice of the Protestant William III upon the throne and ejected the Catholic James II. The diarist Charles Greville referred to Prince Talleyrand, born in the 1750s, a veteran survivor of international politics, as 'that great Treasury of bygone events'.[7] In 1830, when Talleyrand was appointed French Ambassador to London, there were many such treasuries. One prominent young Whig, Lord John Russell, was descended from the ducal Bedford family which had been so active in the oligarchic cause in the late seventeenth century. It was 140-odd years since 1688 – not a great length of time in human generations.

More recently the American War of Independence and the founding of the American nation, with its written Constitution, provided other memories to draw upon and another example of change. To some the American struggle was 'the torch which lighted the world for the last fifty years'.[8] To others it was proof that constitutions did not have to 'grow like vegetables': they could be fashioned outright.[9] But there was also the folk memory of a rebellious people.

The particular drama of the Great Reform Bill began with the death of one king and the fall of another. In June 1830 George IV, King of Great Britain, died at the age of sixty-seven. A month later the Bourbon King of France, in the shape of Charles X, was toppled. An insurrection resulted in the substitution of a cousin, Louis-Philippe, Duc d'Orléans, under the more populist title King of the French.

King George, the eldest son of the huge family of George III and Queen Charlotte, had been ailing for some time. By the spring of 1830 it was evident that he could not expect to live much longer. In April he was said to have attacks in which he went black in the face, although he still managed to call for a page to provide him with a huge piece of beef, while drinking ale, claret and brandy in succession. It was hardly surprising that the King had become enormous: 'like a feather bed,' wrote Princess Lieven, the astringent Russian Ambassadress, in May, 'while his legs, also swollen, are hard as stone; his face is drawn and the features pinched'. The Irish writer Maria Edgeworth was told by Sir David Wilkie that painting the King in the last stages of his life was 'the most difficult and melancholy business'; it took three hours to get the 'old dying dandy' into his robes, whereupon he looked like 'a great sausage stuffed into the covering'. On 26 June, as Earl Grey informed Princess Lieven, 'the poor King sank at last under his accumulated miseries, and died about 3 a.m.'.[10]

The Times weighed in with an obituary which caused exclamations of disgust in loyal quarters, with its reference to a life, 'the character of which rose little higher than that of animal indulgence'. A fortnight later the newspaper, under its powerful editor Thomas Barnes, returned to the attack: 'There never was an individual less regretted by his fellow-creatures than this deceased King. What eye has wept for him? What heart has heaved one throb of unmercenary sorrow?' – the latter jibe being a reference to his last mistress, Lady Conyngham, physically a match for her royal lover (she too was immensely fat), and with similarly lavish tastes in jewellery.[11] It was left to the Duke of Wellington to give a more charitable verdict. Here was 'the most extraordinary compound of talent, wit, buffoonery, obstinacy and good feeling,' he told Harriet Arbuthnot, ' – in short a medley of the most opposite of qualities with a great preponderance of good – that I ever saw in any character in my life'.[12]

The man who succeeded George IV was in almost every way a complete contrast. This was to be a time of change and the difference in the characters of the two monarchs symbolized it from the start. You could even say that the variation in regal name had something portentous about it. The Royal Chaplain who inadvertently prayed for 'Our Lord King George' might surely be pardoned: there had been sovereigns named George for the last 114 years since the death of Queen Anne. It was left to the new King to say emphatically: 'William, if you please.'[13]

The Duke of Clarence, now William IV, had been heir presumptive to the throne for the last three years, ever since the death of another, older brother, Frederick Duke of York. He was sixty-four, born in the same year as Lord Grey. As the third son, he was put into the Navy early in life and spent his youthful, formative years in that environment. Admiral Nelson was one of his heroes – William had acted as a witness at his wedding in the West Indies, and a relic of the shirt in which the great man died was preserved at his home at Bushy Park.

Perhaps that early naval life was responsible for his bluff good nature; this was accompanied by a certain uninhibited freedom of expression, however, which had clearly survived unimpaired by naval discipline. There was also something of the busybody about him, as had been displayed during his short stint as Lord High Admiral during his brother's reign: in the end William had resigned rather than submit to 'the laws enacted by Parliament' as his brother expected.[14]

William was friendly, and, in contrast to what a contemporary called the 'haughty reserve' of the late King George, friendly to people around him, regardless of degree. His tendency to wave and laugh at the crowds who greeted him, to walk spontaneously among them making light-hearted conversation in a way George IV would never have contemplated, shocked the staider members of society but aroused delight in lowly observers. This informality and love of a risqué joke – especially in after-dinner speeches – aroused similarly mixed reactions. When told that a certain person could not attend Court because he did not have the right breeches, the King quipped happily: 'Then let him come without his breeches.'[15] There was something childlike – bon-enfant – about his enjoyment of his new position.

The seclusion of George IV's last years had been a marked aspect of his reign: he had not visited London for a year, nor Brighton since 1827. The result had been a Court described as 'the most sombre and melancholy that ever was known'.[16] One of the first actions of William IV was to throw open the previously closed terraces of Windsor Castle to the people; unlawful names might be carved on the walls as a result, but he gained immense affection. Similarly free access to the royal parks was granted and dinner was given for the poor people of Windsor.

It was not quite clear how intelligent the new King was. As Duke of Clarence he had gained a reputation for being 'foolish and indelicate' in his utterances, but that might have been the effect of unusual talkativeness in a royal prince. In May 1830 Lord Anglesey predicted gloomily that he would be 'wild, arbitrary, prejudiced and unmanageable' but admitted that he might be popular. He had a tendency, as one of his closest aides noted, to cling strongly to opinions which he had imbibed early and 'long eagerly maintained', but again that was not so unusual in a gentleman of rank in his mid-sixties.[17]

There was however one aspect of his character which would prove to be of considerable significance in the years to come. In spite of this obstinacy in public, William had one weakness. He was uxorious, that is to say he was inclined to be influenced by the woman in his life, and expected to live in close proximity to her. None of the royal marital distance for him; he shared the conjugal bedroom, something sufficiently unusual to cause comment. When the messengers came to tell the new King of the old King's death at Bushy Park in the early hours of the morning, William was said to have retired to bed afterwards with the cheerful words: 'I've never been to bed with a Queen before.' Perhaps the story was apocryphal, but the sentiment, as in many apocryphal stories, expressed the man.[18] The Court created around this happily domestic couple might lack excitement compared to that Whig paradise of hospitality, Holland House. According to the diarist Greville, Queen Adelaide sat around embroidering flowers of an evening while William dozed – something to which he had a general tendency – occasionally waking to say strongly: 'Exactly so, Ma'am', before going to sleep again. But fashionable Whig despair – Lady Grey commenting on the 'unendurable' boredom of two days at Windsor – did not mean that the strength of the central royal union could be ignored.[19]

This need for intimacy had been true of his earlier, prolonged relationship outside marriage with the actress Mrs Jordan, who bore him a brood of children. Mrs Jordan was dead, although the FitzClarences, William's acknowledged bastards, were an important component of the new Court. The death of Princess Charlotte – George IV's only offspring – in childbirth had, however, led to a desperate search for a new royal heir (or heiress). There was an extraordinary lack of heirs within the prolific family of King George III and somewhere lurking in the order of succession was the grim figure of his fifth son, Ernest Duke of Cumberland, a notoriously reactionary character. The fourth son, the Duke of Kent, duly married in 1818 and his wife produced a daughter, named Victoria, born in May the next year. William also married in 1818: his own bride, nearly thirty years younger, was Adelaide, daughter of the Duke of Saxe-Meiningen. Adelaide had borne William two children, both daughters, but neither had lived longer than a few months. The elder, known as Princess Elizabeth, would of course have succeeded in advance of her cousin Victoria: her mother referred to her as 'our poor little Queen Bess' when she died, for she would have come to the throne as the second Elizabeth. It should be noted that at the time of William's accession, Queen Adelaide was only thirty-eight: an age at which she at least had not despaired of providing an heir, as her Diary reveals.[20]

Once upon a time there had been glamour about the late King as a young and dashing Prince – Florizel, as he had been nicknamed years ago. No one could pretend that the new royal couple had anything glamorous about them: William had looked engaging enough as a boy; he was now stout, rubicund and not very tall. His Queen gained compliments from the charitable, but mainly for her graciousness: to Maria Edgeworth she was 'a good natured-looking good sort of body'. More spiteful observers such as Greville noted that her complexion was not very good – 'this dreadful spotted majesty' – in an age when even critics of the English aristocracy admitted the peerless quality of the ladies' creamy skins.[21] She also had a strong German accent, scarcely surprising given her background, but offering a potential target for satirists.

It was an important component of the new Queen's character that, born in 1792 when the Terror was approaching in France, she had been brought up in a war-torn Germany. Meiningen was a tiny state, its capital a little larger than the town of Hertford, as a contemporary biographer of William IV wrote, with a population of about 5,000.[22] From this perspective, great events brought nothing but dread. All Adelaide's childish memories were of the horrors of Revolution – and the hideous consequences for sovereigns such as Louis XVI and Marie Antoinette if Revolution was allowed to devour its prey. The fate of Marie Antoinette, born an Archduchess of Austria, was something which haunted princesses in German royal nurseries. In addition to these fears, Adelaide had a dread of encouraging dissipation at Court, in Puritanical reaction to the previous reign. Ladies who had been urged to show their *décolletages* by George IV in his lubricious prime, were now told sharply to cover up. She did not receive the wife of Earl Ferrers because she was known to have been his mistress before marriage.[23] In short, here was a kindly, decent but unsophisticated woman, whose choice would have been a quiet life in their delightful house at Bushy Park, now catapulted into the centre of political events.

Greville did better with William IV. The King looked like a respectable old admiral, he wrote in his Diary. But an observer at the coronation saw on the contrary a wizened little old man with an extremely red face.[24] The emphasis on William's age was not a coincidence. Three Hanoverian princes – George IV, the Duke of York and the Duke of Kent – had died within the last decade, the first two in their sixties and the third in his early fifties. (This was a period when the median age of death for males was somewhere in their forties.) Throughout the early years of the reign of William IV, anxious reports of his health abounded, and as the various crises arose, the anxieties grew greater. Then there was the threat of madness in the son of a father whose reign had been so conspicuously marked by it. Rumours persisted that William too had tendencies that way – and of course his behaviour both eccentric and excitable, his wild bombastic speeches, did nothing to discourage them.

Naturally the constitutional powers of a British Sovereign remained in theory exactly the same in the case of both William and his elder brother. But one obvious consequence of a hereditary system was that character would vary considerably from monarch to monarch; and with that variation – due to the quirk of fate by which George IV died on 26 June 1830 and William IV succeeded – came the prospect of change. Lord Bolingbroke, in his famous study of 1738, *The Idea of a Patriot King*, suggested that 'A new people will seem to arise with a new King': nearly a hundred years later, there was at least that possibility.[25] Queen Adelaide might note in her Diary that at Windsor the room of the late George IV remained just as it was: 'a sad sight' with even the cushions of the mighty chair in which he died untouched.[26] But the sad sight would soon belong to the past.

*

The death of a hereditary monarch had another predictable consequence. This was the need for an immediate General Election according to the legal requirement of the time. The Prime Minister, the
so-called Iron Duke of Wellington, the victor of Waterloo, had led the
Tory Government since January 1828; previously, a spate of deaths
had robbed the Tories of George Canning and Lord Liverpool. In
this connection, it was relevant that when various governments had
been proposed to George IV of a more co-operative nature politically, Grey's name had been put forward: but George IV did not fail
to manifest his extreme dislike for the Whig leader, his contemporary,
once rival in love, and supporter of Queen Caroline, the wife he tried
to divorce in 1820; to say nothing of the fact that Grey had opposed
a large financial grant to him as Prince of Wales. 'Anyone but Grey,'
George IV told Wellington in 1828.[27] That personal debarment no
longer existed with the King's death. William IV had on the contrary
been suspected of Whig sympathies before his accession although he
quickly took pains to reassure Wellington of the continuance of his
favour, that everything should go on as before.

Nevertheless the Tory Government was no longer the force it had
once been, ruling the country one way and another for sixty years,
with one short break twenty-five years earlier. The passing of the
Act for Catholic Emancipation in 1829 had reft the party despite its
admirable intentions – even *The Times* admitted that George IV had
behaved well in giving his assent to the Bill. The quip that Wellington,
to cover the total change of policy of his Government (in the interests of pragmatism), simply and successfully ordered the Lords like
a lot of soldiers: 'About turn! March!' was very far from the truth.[28]
A powerful group had emerged known as Ultra Tories who despised
the Government for their submission, as they saw it, to pressure over
principle. The Tory Duchess of Rutland took to her bed 'with alarm
about Bloody Mary, Guy Faux, and the Duke of Norfolk' – the latter
being the premier peer, but a Catholic of ancient lineage who was
now able to give a celebratory dinner for his new rights.[29] Then there
were Tories such as Sir Robert Peel, the Home Secretary, who had in
the end supported Catholic Emancipation – once again he was seen

by opponents in his party as sacrificing his principles, an accusation against a man conscious of his own rectitude which might well influence his future political behaviour.

The campaign for Catholic Emancipation had been extraordinarily divisive. Put simply, in England, Wales and Scotland, it proposed the right of Catholics to vote in elections and stand for Parliament. Its opponents declared loudly that Protestant England itself was being attacked – the all-important power of the Anglican Church being thus eroded. In Ireland, the situation was more complicated. Here, Catholics within certain property qualifications had been allowed to vote and stand as candidates since 1793; hence Daniel O'Connell had been elected at a by-election in 1828, but as a Catholic had been unable to take his seat at Westminster.

This divisive effect is well illustrated by the seemingly bizarre behaviour of certain Ultra Tories such as the Marquess of Blandford. The young heir to the Duke of Marlborough, Member of Parliament for the family seat of New Woodstock since 1826, had been a vociferous opponent of Catholic Emancipation. Accusing Wellington and Peel of betraying the Protestant Constitution in response to the menaces of 'Jesuits and Jacobins', he decided that a House of Commons which could pass such an act must be in need of – what else but Reform? His aim was to reduce the dreaded incoming Roman Catholic influence. Now in his late twenties, Blandford was in private life a handsome scallywag who had begun early by leading riots against the Headmaster of Eton, and gone on to even more disreputable activities where women were concerned. In political terms, Tories found him 'perfectly headstrong' and utterly resolved to make Reform 'a cause of his own'. He introduced a bill to that effect in February 1830.[30]

The word 'Reform' itself did not have a particularly long history in public usage, the word 'reformation' being more generally employed. Its origin in regard to parliamentary Reform has been traced into the Association movement of Christopher Wyvill, in the 1780s, attacking the American War.[31] There had been a movement towards parliamentary Reform by the Whigs at the end of the eighteenth century, numbering in its advocates that young Charles Grey who was now the venerable Whig politician. But over all these nascent movements had fallen the darkness of the French Revolution in its later horrifically violent stages, so painful to those who had hailed it originally: it is indeed impossible to exaggerate the shadow it cast over subsequent decades. Decent people who had seen its consequences so hideously demonstrated shuddered away from the mere notion of change. Others with equal conviction saw the Revolution quite differently: this was what happened when change was denied for too long.

Now, however, it was surely impossible for Reform not to feature in the coming reign. It was not only a cause for maverick (if well intentioned) young Tories like Blandford. The young Whig Lord John Russell had produced his own bill earlier and there had been other bills in the 1820s. After years of languishing, the topic was once again assuming some kind of national importance. And by a strange coincidence, the second French Revolution, that which had ejected Charles X and crowned Louis-Philippe as King of the French a month after the accession of William IV, was there once again to exercise its cross-Channel influence, for better or for worse.

To some, the baleful consequences of ejecting a monarch would be only too clearly visible in the period ahead: the dispossessed Charles X fled first of all to Lulworth Castle, near the Dorset coast, and then set up his court at Holyrood Palace in Scotland. Here was a king chased out by his people. Sir Robert Peel referred to 'this wild liberty' established by France, which he hoped the English would never be tempted to pursue, in contrast to the 'well-tempered freedom' they actually enjoyed. Princess Lieven, a professed enemy of revolutions at home and abroad, observed that 'the democratic turn taken by things in France disturbs me greatly', although she admitted that everyone in England was showing 'the keenest interest in the new order of things in France'.[32] It was relevant that the Duke of Wellington, the hero of the nation, had defeated the French at Waterloo; as a young man in the Navy the new King had fought bravely on the English side.

The Whig grandees on the other hand were by inclination and heredity pro-French; many of them had spent long periods in Europe, including France, Louis-Philippe being known to them personally.

Lord Holland was the nephew of the Whigs' hero, Charles James Fox, who had died in 1806, and guardian of his still vivid flame. He hailed 'the glorious changes' in France: 'who could have imagined that all would have been effected, and so heroically and happily effected, in three short days and that the forbearance, magnanimity and wisdom of the people after victory should have been as great, glorious and perfect as it was during the contest.' Alluding to his Whig past, when he admired the early stages of the French Revolution, Lord Holland added in this letter to his son-in-law the significant comment: 'It makes one young again.' The Whig-inclined *Times* made a donation to 'necessitous Parisians'.[33]

Perhaps the most ominous reaction was that of a Radical tailor called Francis Place and his associates.* In a committee room, considering the new General Election, they were confronted by a gentleman holding a French publication printed in Paris 'announcing the people's victory after three days' fighting'. Sir John Hobhouse, a Radical MP since 1820, was heard first: raising his hat above his head, he cheered loudly. The whole room was electrified, whereupon a host of loud voices joined him in cheers 'as heartily as ever they were given aboard a man-of-war at the moment of victory'.[34]

This was not in fact a moment of victory – rather the beginning of a fight, the outcome of which was extremely uncertain. More generally, it was felt to be a time of danger, if excitement. It was not only the fear of revolution – the re-emergence of the *tricolor* in France was followed by a revolution in nearby Belgium – it was the uncertainty which the prospect of change always brings, and the inevitable human reaction against it. Throughout this period the word 'perilous' was in frequent use, whether by King, politicians – or those who struggled for change.

---

* Radicals were generally understood to be to the left of the Whigs, using the modern phrase; that is, more revolutionary in both the political and social sense. But they were not a formal political party in the same way.

CHAPTER ONE

THE CLAMOUR

'I dread trade, I hate its clamour' –

Captain the Hon. John Byng,
riding through England in the 1790s

'I defy you to agitate a fellow with a full stomache,' wrote William Cobbett, the Radical politician, who had visited both France and America and spent time in the Army (not to forget two years in Newgate Prison for denouncing the flogging of militia men).[1] In the Britain of the General Election of 1830, held following the death of the Sovereign, there were a great many fellows whom, according to this dictum, it would be easy to agitate. From another social sphere, the estate manager at Belvoir Castle in the Midlands reported to the Duke of Rutland on the subject of local incendiarism that, although these fires might very often be the work of rascals and vagabonds, 'still they are more likely to take place among a starving Population'. The relationship of hunger and poverty to riot in Britain was after all nothing new: twenty years earlier Lord Byron in his maiden speech in the House of Lords had commented on the revolt of the unemployed weavers in Nottinghamshire in similar terms: 'nothing but absolute want' could have driven a once honest and industrious body to such excesses.[2]

A series of appalling harvests followed by severe winter weather had bedevilled the country. In 1830, according to Greville, the thermometer at Greenwich was lower than it had been for the last ninety years.[3] Britain was already in the throes of economic distress following the end of the Napoleonic Wars when the returning soldiers sought employment, all too often in vain. Most notoriously in the past, such dire conditions had led to the so-called Peterloo Massacre near Manchester in 1819 when a group led by the Radical orator Henry Hunt had demanded political Reform as a solution to the problem; there were an estimated eleven deaths at the time at the hands of the military, and over 400 injured; subsequently there were executions and transportations overseas for life.

Henry Hunt, born in Wiltshire, from a well-off farming family, was arrested and sentenced to two and a half years in prison in a gaol which he nicknamed 'the Ilchester Bastille'. Much later he would describe the scene to Parliament: how the Yeomanry pressed down on 'the unresisting people, hundreds of whom were wounded, thrown down, trampled upon, or otherwise injured. The groans of the wounded, the horrid shrieks of the women, and the despair of the maddened wretches thus ferociously assaulted formed the most dreadful scene that could be imagined.'[4] Despite the outraged protests of those of a dissident turn of mind – notably the poet Shelley – contemporary thinking in general had not moved on where the treatment of popular protest was concerned. 'Advice how to attack a Mob' by a General Trevor of 30 November 1830 was full of military good, if aggressive, sense for armed men against the unarmed, such as 'attack those in the flank and break their line'.[5]

Agricultural distress arrived in a new form, as machines came to supplant men; and the men sought revenge (or relief) by breaking up the new machines. The campaign took its name from its leader, Captain Swing – was he a man or a myth? It began in East Kent, where landowners might expect to find the following menacing message left overnight:

> Revenge for thee is on the Wing
> From thy determined Captain Swing.

Writing in 1831 with the title *Swing Unmasked; or the Causes of Rural Incendiarism*, E.G. Wakefield suggested that Swing might be 'one of our natural enemies, the French Jacobins, who has invented a wonderful fireball for the ruin of Old England'. Wakefield wrote from his personal observation of the enthusiasm of 'poor [English] creatures' for news of the 'glorious French Revolution' in the press; and these poor creatures were after all not so very distant from the coastal regions of

France. Alternatively Captain Swing might be a rascally farmer wanting the abatement of his rent. Or again perhaps he was a disguised papist or Methodist bent on the destruction of the Church (Catholic Emancipation was still sufficiently novel to arouse these kinds of fears) or even a well-dressed agent hoping to raise the price of corn. Whatever the identity of Swing, Wakefield's conclusion was not so very far from Cobbett's aphorism quoted above: he believed that the only thing to do was to 'remove the misery'.[6]

Outbreaks of this type of unrest, dreaded by the inhabitants of great – or greater – houses, spread through southern England, areas of the Midlands and East Anglia. These 'poor creatures' taking refuge in violence which seemed mindless to outsiders but curiously logical to themselves – they would replace the machines as the machines had replaced them – had no part in the parliamentary election. Their cries, and with rising frequency their deeds of protest, were not originally rooted in a desire for parliamentary Reform, but for relief from the fearful economic realities of their situation. Where elections were concerned, just over 3 per cent of the population voted in 1830, some 400,000-odd people out of a population of approximately sixteen million: all were, of course, male.[7]*

There were 658 seats allotted to the United Kingdom altogether, Ireland being given seats in the Westminster Parliament (to which Catholics would now be admitted for the first time) by the Act of Union in 1801. The great majority of these seats were in England; Ireland had 100, Scotland 45 and Wales 24. The constituencies were of various types including county, borough or burgh and university constituencies, and generally had more than one Member: thus the total number of constituencies for the 658 seats was 379. Within the simplicity of these figures, however, is concealed a system of fiendish variety and intricacy, just because it had originated so many centuries ago and evolved according to perceptions of another time. Walter Bagehot, writing in the 1870s, summed it up: 'A system of representation made

---

* No women had the vote; hence the contemporary phrase 'Universal Suffrage', for which some were beginning to clamour, actually meant 'Universal Male Suffrage'. Here the phrase 'Universal Suffrage' will be generally used in this early-nineteenth-century sense.

without design, was fixed as eternal, and upon a changing nation.' Naturally such a system laid itself open to abuses. As one modern authority has pointed out, 'generations of attorneys grew fat on the niceties of electoral law', and certainly there were many disputed returns after any General Election.[8]

In the other Chamber, the House of Lords, the seats were strictly hereditary. Although new peerages could be created: that was theoretically the prerogative of the Sovereign. Not all Irish peers sat in the House of Lords after the Union of 1801; twenty-eight peers were elected among their number. This meant that others could stand as MPs (Viscount Palmerston, possessor of an Irish peerage, was an example of this). The Scottish peers had a similar system after the Union of 1707, electing sixteen to sit in the Lords. The eldest sons of English and Scottish peers, enjoying so-called courtesy titles like Viscount Althorp, heir to Earl Spencer, could also be elected as MPs, although of course the death of the father would automatically hoist the son, happily or unhappily, into the Lords.

When Oliver Cromwell had supported the abolition of the House of Lords in the middle of the seventeenth century – only temporarily, as it turned out – he had referred to its Members as 'lumps of gilded earth'. The vivid if contemptuous phrase expressed the fact that the Lords derived their existence from being landowners, and very often great landowners at that. The current parliamentary system, by which patrons of 'pocket boroughs' nominated individuals to enjoy the seats which were considered in effect to belong to them, meant that Members of the Lords were an important force in any election. 'May not I do what I like with my own?' exclaimed the Duke of Newcastle in a notorious bout of indignation when the abolition of certain seats of which he had the patronage was proposed.[9] Perhaps this simple ducal identification of a parliamentary seat with any other piece of property was an extreme point of view; nevertheless the connection of property and representation was fundamental. It did, of course, definitively exclude the propertyless, the poor creatures, whether compliant with their fate or rebellious.

So-called 'rotten boroughs' – an eighteenth-century usage – were those where, due to the decline in local population over the years, a minuscule number of voters elected two Members of Parliament; Newtown on the Isle of Wight was one glaring example, with fourteen houses and twenty-three voters. Under the circumstances, nomination for seats by a powerful local patron was a strong possibility. Money often changed hands and, given the open ballot, patrons could check whether their interests had been properly served. One argument in favour of the 'rotten boroughs', however, was that they enabled bright young men of no particular fortune to rise through the system and dazzle in Parliament.

A witty cleric called Sydney Smith understood how to deal with that argument – as with so many issues of this time. He made fun of it. Sydney Smith was now sixty; having edited the first issue of the *Edinburgh Review*, he left for London where he enjoyed exceptional popularity as an Anglican preacher and became the darling of Holland House. After that, Smith expounded his progressive views from a Yorkshire parish: he was, for example, a staunch advocate of Catholic Emancipation. From there, through patronage, he transferred to Combe Florey in Somerset. On this issue, he compared rotten boroughs to the pains in the stomach of a rich man risen from poverty, who exclaims: 'I am not rich in consequence of the pains in my stomache but in spite of them: I would have been ten times richer and fifty times happier if I had no pains in my stomache at all.' Smith added: 'Gentlemen, those rotten boroughs are your pains in the stomache – and you would have been a much richer and greater people if you had never had them at all.'[10]

As for the money, Edward Stanley would state in Parliament later, without fear of contradiction, that 'it was as notorious as the sun at noon-day, that boroughs were bought and sold in the market by their proprietors'.[11] The system also lent itself to corruption and bribery (which led to drunkenness) and the sums of money could be astronomical. There was a notorious Northumberland county election in 1826 in which four candidates battled for two seats. Young John George Lambton (created Lord Durham in 1828) managed the election campaign of his brother-in-law Lord Howick, eldest son of Lord

Grey, and tempers grew so hot that he fought a duel with one candidate, Thomas Wentworth Beaumont, on the sands beneath Bamburgh Castle. The election cost Beaumont £80,000 in vain, Howick £20,000 and the Tories £30,000 each (roughly £8 million, £2 million and £3 million in today's money).[12]

It was however the geographical distribution of the seats in 1830 which would present the most incongruous sight to a modern eye. Despite an extraordinary rise in the population, there had been virtually no alteration in the original medieval scheme since 1760 and before that the Act of Union with Scotland in 1707. Furthermore, one vital feature of late-eighteenth- and early-nineteenth-century England had been totally ignored, and that was the phenomenon now termed the Industrial Revolution. Macaulay, then a young MP, managed to have semi-religious feelings on the subject as he expatiated on the wonders of industry by quoting the Bible: 'By their fruits ye shall know them.' So manufacturers must be judged by cotton goods and cutlery, engineers by suspension bridges and steam tunnels. Indeed, he contrasted 'the speed, the precision with which every process is performed in our factories' with the 'awkwardness, the rudeness, the slowness, the uncertainty' of the judicial system. Finding in industry what others of the time found in Nature, he struck a contemporary as being like a traveller who ventured through 'rich and picturesque scenery' by railroad. Others were more conventional in their reaction. 'Every rural sound is sunk in the clamour of cotton works; and the simple peasant . . . is transformed into the impudent mechanic,' wrote the Captain the Hon. John Byng, later Viscount Torrington, riding through the Midlands in the 1790s; and again, 'I dread trade, I hate its clamour.'[13]

But the clamour was there. It was heard, for example, in cities like Birmingham. In her novel *Emma*, published in 1816, Jane Austen had Mrs Elton exclaim with regard to Birmingham: 'I always say there is something direful in the sound.' Genteel distaste was one thing; the rush towards employment, often in small industries, where employers and men were closely connected, meant that the population there had virtually doubled in the twenty years between 1811 and 1831 when it was over 145,000; a new fast stagecoach service meant that news of the clamour from other places could easily reach the rising population of Birmingham. Sheffield had multiplied nearly threefold to 110,000; Manchester from 95,000 to 310,000, Bradford and Leeds had both soared. As for Scotland, Glasgow was a phenomenon in itself, with the greatest surge of all.[14] It should be emphasized that with the exception of the under-represented Glasgow, there were no parliamentary seats attached to these teeming, choking, productive industrial cities, or what Lord Melbourne would later describe in Parliament as these 'great emporiums of commerce', full of men of 'opulence, of spirit, of intelligence' who had arrived at an almost imperial grandeur and 'metropolitan magnificence'.[15]

In the meantime there were the infamous 'rotten boroughs' such as Old Sarum, where two MPs represented – quite literally – a lump of stone and a green field. No wonder visitors flocked to see this miraculous site! John Constable was sufficiently fascinated by this wild landscape which had once been a medieval city to commemorate it – Sir Thomas Lawrence admired the result and told him he should dedicate it to the House of Commons. Gatton in Surrey was only slightly less miraculous: here there were six houses in the borough, and 135 inhabitants in the parish – 'those celebrated and opulent and populous Towns', as the painter Haydon sarcastically called them. This particular borough of Gatton was sold several times, the price in the summer of 1830 said to be £180,000 (approximately £18 million in today's money).[16] There was no miracle where Dunwich in Suffolk was concerned: it had in effect fallen into the sea, but still it returned two Members of Parliament. Places with a long and ancient history frequently had a disproportionate amount of seats to their inhabitants, witness Cornwall, where there was a total of forty-four Members for a thinly scattered population. In general, there was a pronounced bias towards the south over the north of England.

It was not that efforts had not been made to remedy at least the most egregious of these perceived abuses. East Retford was a so-called freeman borough, and where bribery was concerned, local freemen were said to have established a tariff of twenty guineas a vote – roughly the agricultural wage for the year in certain parts of England. Candidates duly paying up in 1818 and 1820, there had been no contest; but the emergence of two candidates in 1824 had led to extraordinary expenditure. Efforts had been made, notably by the Reform-minded Lord John Russell, to award its seats to Birmingham, bereft of representation. But this East Retford initiative had not succeeded.

All in all, a system had grown up like a monstrous warped tree on the landscape, the sight of which could no longer be ignored in an age of change in so many other areas. The General Election of 1830 was, however, still conducted in the shadow of this monstrous growth. One aspect of the system was the proliferation of election days: no particular date was designated, the returning officers for the various constituencies suiting the local needs. Furthermore, where there was a contest, polling could go on for days. In 1830 polling – all of which was done, and had to be done, openly – began on 29 July and ended on 1 September (there were contests in about a third of the constituencies). The new Parliament was summoned for 14 September, for a maximum seven-year term under the terms of the Septennial Act of 1716.

In an age before the full intricacies of party organization as it is now experienced, the designation of Tories and Whigs was not always clear-cut, as has been stressed with regard to the Ultra Tories. These, however, were the party designations – Tory and Whig – which were familiar. The word 'Conservative' was only just beginning to be mentioned: in 1832 Daniel O'Connell would call it 'the new fangled phrase now used in polite society'; 'Liberal' was not yet in use for a political party. In a shifting situation, one analysis of the results of the 1830 Election uses the term 'friends' and 'foes' of the Wellington Ministry instead: as a result of this calculation, the Government could count on a majority of about 42, with 333 potential 'friends' to 291 'foes'.[17]

An important fact about the Whigs was that very few survived who had experienced office during that brief spell of government a quarter of a century back. There were of course surprises, and the emergence of one name: the election of a vigorous, brilliant, eccentric, striking-looking lawyer called Henry Brougham. A Whig, he defeated the Tory interest for a Yorkshire seat (previously he had sat for smaller constituencies). He would surely – with all his manifest virtues, all his possible vices – be prominent in the coming session of Parliament. Nevertheless it would seem to the superficial observer in the autumn of 1830 that the Whigs constituted a hereditary party of opposition, the Tories one of government.

There certainly seemed no particular reason to suppose that this Parliament would not continue like a docile carthorse to plod on under the direction of the Duke of Wellington – although the victory of a very different type of animal might have been construed as an omen: this was a racehorse named Birmingham who won the St Leger at odds of forty to one. This race meeting at Doncaster was a traditional holiday for Yorkshire workers.

In early October – 'for good or for bad', as he put it – Earl Grey and his wife left their beloved northern estate of Howick in Northumberland for Westminster. Throughout the period which lay ahead, Grey's yearning for his country home, his country life and the exceptionally happy domestic environment which he had been granted despite the amatory adventures of his youth, was to be a feature of his conduct. 'A small comfortable house, a little land to afford me occupation out of doors, my Mary, and my children are all that are necessary,' he had written as early as 1801.[18] Born in 1764, Grey had married Mary Ponsonby at the age of thirty. Here was a strong character of the new Whig mould: Mary Grey had great charm but was certainly not wildly, romantically rakish as the previous generation, Georgiana Duchess of Devonshire and her sister Harriet Countess of Bessborough, had been. Yet in reflecting to the diarist Thomas Creevey on her successful marriage, Lady Grey showed her characteristic tolerance, reflecting that 'mine is a very lucky case': had she, 'in the accident of marriage', been married to a man for whom she felt no respect, 'I might have done like them, for all what I know.' A devoted mother to her large family, Lady Grey was also capable of expressing her own opinions. Although she yawned at the Court of William IV, Lady Grey had also been critical of George IV: he seemed 'to hate all public men', she reflected.[19]

Grey the contented family man was indeed a sight that moved visitors; perhaps he was unconsciously atoning for that time when, among other adventures, the reckless young aristocrat whose patrician, thoroughbred look was 'doted upon' by Lord Byron, had begotten an illegitimate child by Georgiana Duchess of Devonshire.[20] In October 1830, for example, there would be a gathering of sons, sons-in-law, daughters, daughters-in-law – and twenty-three grandchildren. This was where he wished to be.

He particularly enjoyed suggesting reading matter to his children; and Grey the patriarch did not draw the usual distinction of that time, that class, between the education of his sons and his daughters; significantly, the latter were intelligent, well-instructed young women whose gifts he would come to employ in his own political cause. And one should note that his appreciation for female company had not diminished with the years if the satisfaction these days, one supposes, was a purely emotional one. An attractive if reputedly saucy woman such as Lady Lyndhurst could rely on the favour of Grey in society, while his visits and correspondence to the Russian Ambassadress Princess Lieven were an important part of his private life. Indeed, even his ally Lord Holland admitted that Grey was susceptible to the flattery of fair ladies.[21]

Nowadays Grey's noble appearance was generally felt to be an important part of his image. Somehow it was easy to believe that here was a matching nobility of temperament between the outer and the inner man. Certainly contemporaries could never resist alluding to it, whether as a measure of admiration for the superiority of the man, as condemnation for his haughtiness: the critical Greville suggested that his reputation actually owed much to this 'tall, commanding and dignified' spectacle which he presented. Thomas Attwood, the important middle-class reformer from Birmingham, revealed afterwards: 'I looked at his unsullied character' – as reflected in his appearance – 'with something approaching reverence.' Grey was regularly accused of vanity, which may have been a way of alleviating the jealousy of the less noble-looking observer. The Tory Lord Ellenborough, in his Diary, called attention to Grey's fits of petulance, while admitting that in the main he was 'grand and statesmanlike'.[22]

Where Grey's looks were concerned, the romantic black curls had long ago receded but they had left a splendid dome of a head on which every painter – and every caricaturist – seized with enthusiasm. But his figure was still slender, that figure which had caused him to be nick-named 'Lanky' at Eton; and the depiction of Grey in his tight-fitting white pantaloons was another feature of the art, formal or informal, of the time. Pessimistic by nature – as early as November 1820 he was wishing for 'nothing so much as a peaceable retirement for my declining years' – Grey was nevertheless strongly idealistic where parliamentary Reform was concerned, the dominating passion of his public career. When he declared at the Opening of Parliament in 1830 that 'through my whole life, I have advocated Reform', it was fundamentally true even if Wellington had put it rather more crudely that summer: Grey, he told Harriet Arbuthnot, was both arrogant and very obstinate, with 'all kinds of fantastic notions about Reform in Parliament'.[23]

A man of ancient birth and great wealth based largely on land, Grey subscribed strongly to the view that these privileges – as one might call them in modern terms – also carried duties. He had, for example, an idealistic view of the aristocracy as a class which predisposed him in its favour, while the harsh realism of public life had taught him where to pick and choose among their number. On that subject, it is how-ever fair to say that Grey, when in doubt, picked a member of his own family. His nepotism became notorious – although it is also fair to add that Grey was not the only statesman surrounded by his close rela-tions, and in the interlocked relationships of the Whigs, and indeed the Tories, a relation might perfectly reasonably be considered the best man for the job.

Grey had proposed Reform as early as 1792, when the Society of the Friends of the People was formed, although that had divided the Whigs at the time. In the autumn of 1830, he believed that it was a cause whose time had come. While still at Howick, he had heard that the Duke of Wellington was not unlikely to appear in the new charac-ter of a parliamentary reformer in the next session. Grey reflected that this really would make the session, as his friend the high-spirited *bon viveur* Lord Sefton would say, 'Good fun!' For a convinced pessimist, this was an extraordinarily optimistic statement; nevertheless it represented his state of mind as the great Grey caravan bowled down from the north to London.

The Duke of Wellington, leader of the Tories, was at sixty-one five years younger than Grey. Fifteen years after Waterloo, it would be impossible to exaggerate the nationwide esteem in which he was held. His great eminence – an eminence which he had earned – made Greville believe that he could speak to the Sovereign as an equal. As Alexis de Tocqueville, an intelligent French observer touring Britain, wrote: 'glory clothes a man in such magic that seeing him in the flesh and hearing him speak I felt as if a shudder ran through my veins.' And of course physically he was unmistakable – another gift to artists – with what the painter Haydon called his greyhound eyes and his eagle nose.[24] But there was another aspect to Wellington's character, other than the leadership qualities of the great soldier and the realistic statesman (who had carried through Catholic Emancipation against his own convictions). This was a certain detachment from ordinary concerns, a social reliance on 'none but military dandies and fine ladies', as the critical *Times* put it.[25] If Wellington's personal eminence meant that he could talk to the Sovereign as an equal, it also led to that type of isolation which haunts the very grand.

Where politics were concerned, it was relevant that Wellington had only been a Member of the House of Commons for a short period, fragmented by military campaigns; and that brief span had ended over twenty years ago with his elevation to the peerage. Perhaps lack of knowledge of the day-to-day grind of Parliament was responsible for the fact that he was a curiously uneasy public speaker. 'As embarrassed as a child reciting its lesson,' said the otherwise awestruck de Tocqueville. He was also – fine, upstanding, unmistakable figure as the Iron Duke undoubtedly was – becoming rather deaf. Used to making decisions – and very successful decisions – on the battlefield, Wellington was not naturally inclined towards intellectual debate with persons he considered to have inferior judgement and character.

The Birmingham-born George Holyoake, looking back on his long 'Agitator's life', noted that Wellington treated his men as he did his muskets: 'he kept them dry and clean and ready for action'. But since men were a great deal more complex than muskets, Lord Grey had a point when he declared that Wellington did not understand 'the character of the times'.[26] Where dealing with the riotous was concerned, he was a strong, unabashed believer in force and had the self-confidence to express it. In 1830 he observed to Greville with grim pride that his own regiment alone could take on all the population of London, and he told a deputation from Manchester with similar menace that 'the people of England are very quiet if they are left alone, but if they won't be quiet, there is a way to make them'.[27] When Wellington was told that there might nonetheless be conflict with the people, he reportedly exclaimed: 'Ah, bah!' It remained to be seen how this robust philosophy would fare if the people positively declined either to remain quiet or to be silenced with a dismissive word.

Petitions to Parliament – formal written requests of a specific nature from the public – were an important feature of early-nineteenth-century politics and a weathervane where public preoccupations were concerned. Petitions to change an existing law or introduce a new one had an ancient history and were generally addressed to a particular Member (including a peer) to be drawn to the attention of the House. It was significant that there had been no petitions exclusively on the subject of Reform for the five years from 1824 to 1829 when Catholic rights, the slave trade and the Corn Laws were popular subjects; but in 1830 this subject began to feature again. The number of petitions from the public rose dramatically: there were 645 in 1830.[28]

As he set about to address the House of Lords on the subject of the King's Speech after the Opening of Parliament on 2 November, Wellington certainly did not rate this modest manifestation of popular enthusiasm as worthy of note. Nor for that matter did the turbulent Swing-type protests – traumatic or thrilling, depending on your point of view – appear to have influenced him.

*

In Birmingham, on 11 October 1830, a dinner was held to celebrate the recent French Revolution at a place soon to be celebrated for its intimate connection to Reform. This was Beardsworth's Repository, the chief centre for the sale of horses in the Midlands; John Beardsworth allowed political friends to make use of it free of charge; it was capable of holding, as on this occasion, nearly 4,000 people.[29] The food was lavish: 3,500 lbs of beef, veal, ham, legs of pork and mutton, and the whole feast was under the auspices of the Birmingham Political Union, founded with Thomas Attwood as its first President in December 1829. Associated with him was his close friend Joshua Scholefield, an iron manufacturer and banker, 'a small rotund man with fire and purpose', who became Deputy Chairman.

Undoubtedly, the foundation of the Union owed something to the peculiar circumstances of Birmingham, where the prevalence of small industries and workshops led to 'a freer intercourse between all classes', as Richard Cobden would later describe it to John Bright; he compared Birmingham favourably in this respect to Manchester, where the great capitalists formed an aristocracy and 'an impassable gulf' separated workmen from employers.[30]

Attwood was at this point in his late forties, a county banker, with a house at Harborne in the pastoral country just outside Birmingham; a man of great solidity of character who was at the same time an inspiring leader and orator. He held the passionate conviction that the interests of masters and men were in fact one: 'if the masters flourish, the men are certain to flourish with them'. Attwood's devotion to his beliefs may be judged by the fact that he had pondered the foundation of the Birmingham Political Union all one night in his library at Harborne and, in the grey light of the early morning, went down on his knees and prayed that the Birmingham Political Union should only prosper if the 'liberty and happiness of the people were enhanced'.[31]

With a broad Brummagem accent, dropping his aitches, he could hardly have presented a greater contrast to the languid patrician tones of Whigs such as Lord John Russell, with his archaic pronunciation – cucumber as cowcumber, for example. Attwood nevertheless spoke in a notably clear voice, and had the ability to sink to a theatrical whisper if the drama of the occasion demanded it. When Attwood sat for Haydon, the painter noted that his whole appearance spoke of vigour, his carriage being upright, his forehead high, white and shining, his very hair seeming to grow upwards, and the blood rushing into his face when he talked on his favourite subject. George Holyoake wrote of the characteristic strength of the Midland mind, despite being provincial, 'whereas the London mind has brightness': Attwood was a supreme example of that Midland strength.[32]

Attwood was not only vigorous, he was also opinionated, his particular hobby horse being the reform of English finance by enlarging the money supply (county banks had been forbidden to enlarge their note issue in 1826). It was a strange paradox that this man, the epitome of the new, intelligent, vocal middle class (many of them without votes), had begun life as a Tory. It was his hobby horse which had led him to the conviction that parliamentary Reform was necessary to achieve his primary aim. Attwood's character was, however, to be of vital importance in one aspect of the campaign for Reform. This was his absolute determination not be defined as advocating popular violence, even if the cause was good. That is to say, he was prepared to tolerate defensive action on the part of people if attacked, but not overt aggression. It was a point jovially expressed in a verse sung by the Union which referred to the trade in guns and swords for which Birmingham had been famous; now new weapons were being forged:

> We now make arms against foes at home
> But these are intellectual.[33]

On this particular occasion, for example, Attwood made the point that while the French had recently been justified in using force, the English would not be. The motto of the Union was 'The Constitution, nothing less, nothing more'. It was the measure of Attwood that at the end of an emotional speech he appealed to his hearers in unequivocal terms. He had been accused, he said, of setting in motion 'a tremendous principle which no human power could control; that I should like a Frankenstein* create a monster of gigantic strength, endowed with life but not with reason, that would hunt me to destruction. Is that so?' But Attwood derided the concept of peril. 'Where is the man among you who would not follow me to death in a righteous cause?' He received the rapturous answer: 'All, all.'[34]

This public-spirited fellow was in fact perfectly capable of wooing the multitude: on one campaign he was reputed to have kissed 8,000 women, which, if true, left the exploits of the shining Whig Duchess Georgiana, kissing a mere butcher, in the shade. By January 1831 the Birmingham Political Union would have 8,000 members. And it was a remarkable indication of the current disarray of the Tory Party that the maverick Lord Blandford, that Ultra Tory who wanted Reform for his own anti-papist purposes, had, shortly after its foundation, been made an honorary member of the Union. 'A strange bedfellow,' commented Attwood drily, this Ultra Tory Marquess, whom his fellow Tory John Wilson Croker would jovially hail as 'Citizen Churchill'.[35]

Attwood's demand for peaceful change was in contrast to events taking place elsewhere in the country. The first threshing machine was destroyed at a village near Canterbury on 28 August 1830. By 14 October *The Times* was referring to an 'organisational system of stack-burning'. When William Cobbett visited Battle in East Sussex two days later he was accused of having 'much excited the feelings of the paupers'. The rector of nearby Hurst Green found his house surrounded by a ring of rioters.[36] On 22 October the first trial of the machine-breakers was held at Canterbury. The judge, however, showed the changing measure of the times by imposing unexpectedly light sentences – a caution and a mere three days' prison; he did so, he said piously, in the hopes that 'the kindness and moderation evinced this day . . . would be met by a corresponding feeling among the people'. Another straw in the wind was the reaction of William Henry Gambier, tackled at six in the evening by a mob from Maidstone. (Unlike some of the mobs, they did not have blackened faces.)

* He referred to the best-selling novel of Mary Shelley published twelve years earlier.

'We are starving,' declared their leader John Adams, a journeyman shoemaker. Gambier, son of the local rector at Langley, replied that 'the present King was desirous of doing all that could be done and I had no doubt that Parliament had the same disposition, and that they should wait until Parliament met'.[37]

Of course the riots were not confined to east Kent and Sussex, but spread as riots do, word of mouth acting as the clarion along with posters intentionally framed to cause alarm. Nor were the great estates immune from such threats. The Goodwood estate of the Duke of Richmond, a Tory politician of liberal turn of mind, experienced the visit of Captain Swing, as did estates spreading into the west. Agricultural machinery acted as a magnet; hence there were riots too in East Anglia. It remained to be seen whether Gambier had been correct in his prophecy about Parliament and, for that matter, about the intentions of the new King.

It was therefore in an atmosphere of menace but also anticipation that William IV set forth in his state coach, accompanied by all the panoply of a royal procession, from St James's Palace to Westminster on 2 November.

CHAPTER TWO

I WILL PRONOUNCE THE WORD

'If danger is all around us ... the way to go is by securing
the affections of your fellow subjects, and by redeeming
their grievances and my Lords, I will pronounce the word:
by reforming Parliament.' –

Earl Grey, House of Lords, 2 November 1830

The Parliament to which King William IV travelled was, like the electoral system which provided half of its occupants, astonishingly old-
fashioned and not intended by its architects for its present purpose.
The House of Commons had in fact begun life as the medieval St Stephen's Chapel and was certainly much better arranged for a chapel
than a parliamentary Chamber. First, its size was inadequate: under
sixty feet long, approximately thirty-three feet wide, only 400 out
of the 658 MPs could be accommodated at any one time. Of course
the addition of the Irish MPs at the Act of Union had only added to
the problems. It was famously dark and, one might add, infamously
ventilated.

A gallery reporter (later a newspaper editor and historian), James
Grant, who published his recollections of Parliament in 1836, wrote:
'I shall not soon forget the disappointment which I experienced on the
first sight of the interior of the House of Commons.' He had been told
already that the place ill accorded with the dignity of what had been
termed 'the first assembly of gentlemen in the world'. All the same he
was not prepared for what he called a second edition of the Black Hole
of Calcutta (the notoriously tiny dungeon where British prisoners had
been held seventy-odd years earlier).[1]

Desperately hot in summer, the Chamber was airless in winter.
Not surprisingly, the unhealthy atmosphere led to coughing, splut-
tering and other developments likely to interrupt the speakers on the

floor. The historical novelist Lord Lytton, who began life as an MP known as Edward Bulwer, let his pen loose on the subject: 'wheezing and sneezing, and puffing and grunting, till at last the ripening symphony swells into one mighty diapason of simultaneous groans! . . . Sounds so mournful, so agonising, so inhuman and so ghastly were never heard before!' There was only a momentary silence when the solemn voice of the Speaker called for 'Order'; immediately the hideous chorus of noise resumed.[2]

Apart from the Lords and Commons, who had a right to be there, if no right to comfort, there was public access – as indeed there always had been to the Palace of Westminster. It might be compared to a modern shopping mall, a place where Pepys, for example, went to buy favours for his lady friends and which also contained an excellent wine shop. As for the Chamber, a hearty financial trade was run by which the principal doorkeeper was able to retire with a fortune after thirty years, through charging half a crown a visit. And with public access came the occasional surly encounter when Ministers found themselves insulted on what they might have legitimately regarded as their own ground. Sometimes this public intrusion was unintentional: so muddling was the layout that people could genuinely stray, as with a Scottish Highlander, in full tartan rig, who advanced on the front benches 'as if to rest himself on the brow of the heath-clad mountains of Caledonia'. He was only surprised that others were so crowded in the South Gallery, when he himself had plenty of room. Tipped off in the end by a friendly MP, 'Donald' was said to have run away at full tilt without looking back.[3]

As for the ladies – many of whom, as important hostesses, a role in its own right, were keenly interested in politics – they were not officially admitted to the floor. Grant does tell of an incident when a member of 'The Sex', as females were then generally designated, got into a side gallery. The Speaker was said to be delighted at 'a politician in petticoats' and referred with similar gallantry to 'the fair intruder'. This was an unexpected vision. There was, however, a curious arrangement, tacitly accepted, by which 'The Sex' could peer down the hole around the lantern which lit the House, otherwise known as the Ventilator;

this meant adopting a particularly uncomfortable position and also enduring clouds of candle smoke; furthermore, the watchers could never see the Speaker's face, only hear his booming roar of 'Order'. In Grant's opinion, the only women who stuck it out did so for the sake of husbands, brothers – or lovers; although at least one lady, Elizabeth Leveson-Gower, from a great Whig family and married into the magnificently plutocratic Grosvenors, who later wrote travel books, made it clear that she did so out of a social conscience, despite 'acute discomfort' (she was particularly interested in the contrast of wealth and poverty in Ireland).[4]

The condition of the gallery reporters, whose work would be vital to any debate which involved the country as a whole, was only one degree better. The secrecy which Parliament had attempted to impose on its proceedings had become eroded towards the end of the eighteenth century, partly due to the efforts of the libertarian John Wilkes. Journalists had been admitted freely since 1778, and the taking of notes had been tolerated five years later. Hansard's *Parliamentary Debates*, giving a full account of speeches, procedure and voting in both Houses, were printed as such from 1829 onwards, the result of a co-operation between the reports of the Radical William Cobbett and the printer Thomas Hansard; the former selling out to Hansard when he faced bankruptcy.

But total accuracy was hardly achievable. Squashed-together reporters were frequently unable to hear properly. *The Times*, already known as 'The Thunderer', was vociferous in complaint on this issue. Reporters were nevertheless expected to endure long hours in order that their reports should be printed, and the newspapers carried out to the provinces in the new fast coaches. They were also obliged to clear out during voting (a practice only abolished in 1853).[5] Limiting each paper to one reporter might help with the crowded gallery, but of course made the responsibility of recording events still more onerous.

In spite of the privations of reporters and ladies and Highland intruders, there is no doubt that the main sufferers were the wheezing, snuffling MPs themselves. The fact that the public gallery was only fifteen feet above the floor, supported by pillars reaching down to the benches below, made for additional claustrophobia.[6] All this meant that Members of both Houses, when preparing for any kind of struggle, were lucky if they were endowed with real physical stamina, as was the Leader of the House of Commons, the John Bull–like figure of Lord Althorp (like other viscounts, he was commonly addressed as Lord). Lord John Russell, on the other hand, undersized and with an under-sized voice about which reporters complained, needed great rations of emotional courage. In these testing conditions, long speeches late at night and forward into the dawn – four hours was not unusual – called forth admiration. As William Cobbett would say later, you needed perfect health and also great bodily strength.[7] He might have added that the old – or older – would be additionally tested.

The official Opening of Parliament was preceded by various secret and not-so-secret meetings, as the politicians jockeyed for position. In general, there was an extraordinary lack of cohesion inside the parties and ill-defined boundaries between them on the subject of Reform, due to the constantly changing nature of political loyalties during the pre-vious decade. Where the Tories were concerned, there were Canning-ites, named for their dead leader, prepared to listen to reason on the subject of Reform, followed by the similarly inclined Huskissonites, named for yet another dead leader who died in a rail accident in Sep-tember. There were Tories like the eccentric Blandford, with his own reasons for backing Reform, and other so-called Ultra Tories, deeply offended by the Catholic debacle, as they saw it, of the previous year in which both Wellington and Peel had participated.

Where the Whigs were concerned, this lack of differentiation brought with it the possibility of fruitful overtures to the other side. One young MP who believed in this was Edward Stanley, just thirty, later styled Lord Stanley as heir to the Earl of Derby, and an MP for the last eight years. Academically brilliant – he had won the Syracuse Latin Prize at Oxford – Stanley would later be known as 'the Rupert of Debate': his oratorical style, both dashing and ferocious, to say nothing of his hot temper, reminded hearers of the great seventeenth-century cavalry leader Rupert of the Rhine. Stanley's (Derby's) future career was another indication of the fact that party politics were not set in stone at this point. This fair-skinned, red-headed Prince Rupert would in fact change sides later, become a Tory and enjoy a long and distinguished political career. At this point, however, he was described as 'foremost among the youngsters', along with Sir James Graham, and counted among the Whigs. Like another aristocrat, Lord Lansdowne, he took to wearing the old Whig uniform of a blue coat with brass buttons and a buff waistcoat.[8]

Graham himself was a few years older, and had been a Whig MP since 1826; a man of considerable organizational abilities, he was described by a more erratic contemporary, Lord Durham, perhaps for this reason, as 'an official drudge, a gentleman and a saint'.[9] Certainly, as a wealthy landowner he had become celebrated for the management of his large Cumberland estate and his prosperous tenantry. Economic reform was something that concerned him deeply.

These two Whig 'youngsters' now engineered a secret approach to the Tory Home Secretary, Sir Robert Peel, via Charles Arbuthnot, the husband of Wellington's confidante Harriet and a useful intermediary. Peel was surely a key figure in what the younger Whigs hoped to achieve. Unlike Stanley, he was proudly middle-class, the son of a rich manufacturer from whom he had recently inherited the baronetcy, along with an estimated fortune of £1.5 million (£150 million in today's money).[10] Peel was born in 1788, that is to say twenty years after Wellington and Grey. Now in his early forties, he had been at Harrow as a schoolboy and watched his older contemporaries going off to the Napoleonic Wars. He was also, incidentally, a man of strong cultural interests whose collection of pictures meant perhaps as much to him as anything inanimate (he was an original Trustee of the National Gallery). His love for his beautiful wife Julia meant that he too, like the Whig lords, was inclined to pine for the country when she was absent. But Lord Lytton would also refer to Peel's 'pure and cold moral character': this meant that Peel, intelligent and well educated as he was, was not a man to mount a charm offensive, if such were needed.[11] When Wellington talked to Lord Stanhope of Peel's 'scrupulous veracity of all men he had ever known' he was not necessarily depicting the ideal convivial politician.[12]

Even Peel's appearance was somewhat offputting; despite his florid good looks and dignified posture there was something uncomfortably stagey about the way he banged the box in front of him when speaking and then turned round for the applause of his supporters, which was seized upon by satirists. Was it perhaps an air of complacency which perturbed his listeners? G.W.E. Russell, reporting the Whig tradition, wrote that he 'utterly lacked – perhaps he would have despised – that almost prophetic rapture which we recognize in Burke and Chatham'.[13] Peel's rallying dinners were actually said to do more harm than good. Where Reform was concerned, Peel was certainly not a bigot either by experience or inclination. But he was not of course the leader of the Tory Party – that was the role of the Duke of Wellington.

There were other eve-of-Parliament discussions which centred on the reforming proposals of the new MP for Yorkshire, Henry Brougham. In his fifties, he was thus of a different generation from the rising Whigs such as Stanley and Lord John Russell. His rise to prominence had been as a result of his own irrepressible efforts: thirty years earlier the young lawyer had been among those who founded the seminal journal of enquiry, the *Edinburgh Review*. Irascible, multi-faceted, Brougham was both intellectual and dazzling in his oratory – as a result of which he had earned an enormous living at the Bar, strictly necessary to his lavish way of life. Lord Holland paid an extraordinary tribute to him: his style of oratory, he wrote in his Diary, was 'almost preternatural and miraculous', based on 'the variety and versatility of his genius . . . his roundness of retort and reply'. Such a character inevitably lent itself to caricature, and his amazing bottle-nose helped matters singularly, as did the piercing eyes under projecting brows and the 'uproarious condition' of his dark grey hair, which aroused the admiration of Haydon (it also, incidentally, made his head popular as a tavern sign).[14]

But even without such an eccentric appearance, Brougham would have made his mark. For one thing his self-confidence was boundless; one exchange with Grey seemed to sum him up. The two great men were crossing a ford at Howick which turned out to be flooded. Under the circumstances, Grey asked Brougham: 'Can you swim?' To which

Brougham replied magnificently in the strong northern accent which characterized his speech: 'I have neverrre swum but I have no doubt I could if I trrried.' Brougham's enormous knowledge was also legendary and he had no objections to sharing it. After one such breakfast meeting broke up, Samuel Rogers remarked: 'This morning Solon, Lycurgus, Demosthenes, Archimedes, Sir Isaac Newton, Lord Chesterfield and a good many others went away in one postchaise.' A more sardonic observer quipped: 'if only he knew a little about the law, he would know everything.'[15]

Brougham's wife completed the unconventionality of the picture. A widow with a pleasing income and an equally pleasing house in Hill Street, she was not up to the high standards for conversation and intelligence that the Whigs expected from the ladies in their circle: the diarist Creevey described her as being 'like an overgrown doll at the top of the table in a bandeau of roses, her face in a perpetual simper without utterance'.[16] Brougham's confidence was undimmed by this tacit disapproval; for it was the confidence of a man who had won his place on merit amid others who had benefited by inheritance. This was a time obsessed by the study of phrenology, the science by which the shape and markings of the skull denoted character; it was generally agreed that the organ of combativeness on Brougham's skull was mightily developed.

It was hardly to be expected that such a man would prove an easy colleague, let alone a pack animal. In their rising anxieties for Reform in principle, the Whig notables were not necessarily inclined to favour Brougham's particular reforms. At the end of September he had spoken out boldly on the subject at a public dinner in Leeds: 'I will leave in no man's hand, now that I am Member for Yorkshire, the great cause of Parliamentary Reform.' In sum this proved to be his threefold plan: to enfranchise those that were known as the 'great towns', to extend the vote to various householders and limit the small boroughs to one Member.[17]

Hardly revolutionary, with no mention of such vexed topics discussed in Radical circles as Universal Franchise or the Secret Ballot (all voting would still be done in public), it was nevertheless more advanced than anything the Whigs had explored previously and it made them nervous. The Whigs were like a body of men with an enormous dog of famous attacking power at their side; admire the dog as they might, they were never absolutely sure where he would place his huge jaws next. And did the dog perhaps have an agenda all his own, including leadership of the pack itself?

The Opening of the new Parliament therefore found all those concerned in it apprehensive, and not a great deal of cohesion in either party. If many of the Tories were surly, the Whigs, like all people who have been out of office for a long time, did not necessarily believe their moment had come; Grey's actual political leadership, such an important element in any Whig Renaissance, was in any case untried. As Byron had written with the pen he wielded from time to time as a knife:

> Nought's permanent among the human race
> Except the Whigs *not* getting into place.[18]

Meanwhile ferment in the country was spreading, not diminishing. On the eve of Parliament *The Times* reported that Canterbury had been 'the scene of the utmost confusion'. Labourers were seen throwing stones at troops and 'the cry for bread and labour is loud, machines are daily destroyed and no man can say what the end will be'. The Duke of Rutland wrote to Frances Lady Shelley: 'It is my firm belief that we are nearer to a tremendous explosion than we ever have been.' He referred to the poison 'so deeply and widely circulated in the minds of people', adding: 'Some friends of mine ascribe it to the schoolmasters!' There had been a recent meeting at Leicester in which a speaker who predicted the sweeping-away of even 'a vestige of Nobility' from the country was greeted with the enthusiastic response: 'the sooner it is done the better'.[19]

One of those following this turbulent scene with acute interest was the Radical tailor Francis Place. Here was a man who thoroughly understood the life of the poor; his father being bailiff at the Marshalsea court, he was actually raised in a debtors' prison. Earning his living from a young age as a journeyman tailor, Place became Secretary to the Leather-Breeches Makers' Trade in 1792 at the age of twenty-two. Strongly built, Place maintained his physical fitness on the verge of sixty by walking twenty or thirty miles a day.

His other marked characteristic was his avidity for learning, extraordinary by the standards of his time and class. Place established a vast political library – 'the headquarters of English Radicalism' – in his house. It was described at the beginning of the twentieth century by an old man who still remembered being shown it, as 'a sort of gossiping shop for such persons as were in any way engaged in public matters, having the benefit of people for their object'. Another contemporary wondered at the sheer organization of the library: 'books, pamphlets, journals, memoranda of every kind – political, philosophical, physiological, and every other "cal" which can be imagined, all arranged in such perfect order that he can put his hand on any book or paper he may want in a moment'.[20] Where Brougham's skull showed combativeness, with Francis Place, in phrenological terms, 'the bump of order' was very strong indeed.

He certainly did not find the coming Parliament orderly enough, having referred in May to the 'rascally' House of Commons, which excited him to 'indignation, hatred and abhorrence' whenever he thought of it. His Westminster dwelling nevertheless made him an important man in the political sphere, since Westminster was one of the few electoral seats with something approaching manhood suffrage, based on freehold. Just as Attwood was originally interested in currency reform, Place had an attachment to Malthusian doctrines of population control, with a particular prejudice in favour of contraception to enable the people to reduce their own numbers. Hence Reform for him had become a primary element of justice for the working classes and his prodigious organizational talents were now to be dedicated to it, despite his theoretical dislike of the Whigs.

Francis Place was at this point not in an optimistic mood. On 1 November he wrote to Henry Hunt, the Radical known for good reason as 'Orator' Hunt, on the subject of the Duke of Wellington: 'The Duke thinks this is not the time to meet the wishes of the people. He does not understand things and has therefore decided to make no concessions.' Personally Place hoped that Wellington would stick to this disastrous course (thus provoking confrontation). Whatever happened, according to Place, it was merely 'a question of longer or shorter – change will come'. And he issued a prophecy: 'No corrupt system ever yet reformed itself.' It was now time to see whether Place was right.[21] Was there really no possibility of orderly change?

William IV, always assiduous in carrying out his constitutional role (unlike his elder brother), arrived at Parliament with a clear-cut duty to perform. It was customary for the King's Speech, which declared the Government's policy for the coming session, to be pronounced by the Sovereign himself in the House of Lords. Once on the throne, he was watched by Queen Adelaide and her ladies. The sight was impressive in itself – the scarlet cloth, the beautiful chandeliers and above all the 'general air of good manners, an easy good taste and, so to say, an aroma of aristocracy', as Alexis de Tocqueville would describe it.[22] On this occasion the aroma of aristocracy was not enough to atone for the fact that the King's Speech made no reference at all to any kind of plans for parliamentary Reform, such as had been vaguely expected – witness Lord Grey's playful notion earlier of the 'good fun' to be had. Indeed, on the day itself, according to Lady Grey, there was still a story being spread that the Duke 'would yield to the wish of the nation' despite his dislike of Reform; in short he would do anything rather than resign.[23]

William did emphasize his continued good connections – 'diplomatic relations and friendly intercourse' – with the French court, to which he had sent cordial messages.[24] Louis-Philippe, the new King of the French, had been anxious for recognition and the aged Prince Talleyrand had recently been sent to London as his Ambassador. Nevertheless many of the hereditary Lords he addressed were well aware that the Bourbon ex-King was in exile in Britain, and in such an atmosphere there was a possibility that Louis-Philippe would abandon his own hereditary Chamber of Peers much as Oliver Cromwell had done two centuries earlier (although, as it turned out, with less permanent effect). Less happily from the point of view of the Whigs, King

William talked of the recent revolt in Belgium, whereby the Belgians threw off Dutch rule and seemed to suggest the possibility of English intervention. 'I am endeavouring in concert with my allies to devise means of restoring tranquillity,' he said; these words had a sinister sound to the Whigs as the traditional party of peace – and also, incidentally, to Radicals such as Thomas Attwood and Francis Place who were inexorably opposed to any such war.

The real drama of the occasion began with Lord Grey's speech. His hearers now listened to him with profound attention as, whatever their views, they respected his style of oratory, which recalled to hearers the 'stately splendours' of the eighteenth century, and admired the characteristic upright pose of the tall, elegant figure as he walked up and down the centre of the Chamber, his hands folded in front of him 'on his person', for eight or ten minutes. As Creevey had observed a decade earlier: 'There is nothing approaching this damned fellow in the kingdom, when he mounts his best horse.'[25]

Grey began by complaining about what had been said: where the Low Countries were concerned, in this 'direct course' against the behaviour of the people there was 'language directly opposed to the principle of non-interference'. Grey then passed more solemnly to what had been left unsaid: there had been no discussion of the violence which now dominated the domestic scene. His pronouncement was unequivocal: 'If danger is all around us . . . the way to go is by securing the affections of your fellow subjects, and by redeeming their grievances. And, my Lords, I will pronounce the word – by reforming Parliament.'[26]

'Through my whole life,' he continued, 'I have advocated Reform, and I have thought that, if it were not attended to in time, the people would lose all confidence in Parliament, and we must make up our minds to witness the destruction of the Constitution.' It was noteworthy that Grey, the wealthy aristocrat who believed in the hereditary principle including the duties it imposed, was here invoking quite a different force: 'the people'. And by implication these people were supposed to have wishes which had to be respected. If Francis Place was right, and Wellington really thought this was not the time to meet 'the wishes of the people' – could this blanket dismissal really be in prospect? – then Grey placed the Whigs by implication in direct opposition. Yet it should be stressed that the idea of the rule of the people as such – what is now known as democracy – was anathema in the early nineteenth century.

Indeed, the very word 'democracy' caused a shudder at this juncture while the phrase 'the people' implied, generally speaking, a mob and not a very friendly mob at that. After all, the original democrats had been the republicans of the French Revolution who had emerged in opposition to the aristocrats, and the connection was held to contaminate it.* Sir Herbert Taylor, King William's influential private secretary, would confide to Grey that his master 'dreaded the Democracy [his capital letter] towards which he conceived the institutions of the country to be gradually approaching'.[27]

What Lord Grey was proposing was however a strictly limited measure of Reform. He was on more stable ground – if conservatism means stability – when he announced that he was against Universal Suffrage: 'Perhaps in the early part of my life,' he admitted, 'I have urged this question with the rashness of youth.' So the Reform that the Whigs were asking for at this juncture referred to an electorate whose claims were based on property. But he continued with another reference to the people – how the recent July French Revolution had been brought about by an attack on 'the people's liberties'. The inference was clear: the people's liberties must be respected ere worse befell the country.

The Duke of Wellington rose to his feet shortly after. His crucial words came towards the end of a long speech.[28] He agreed, he said, with Lord Grey that his Government and he himself as Prime Minister were not prepared for any measure of Reform. 'Nay, he on his own part, would go further, and say, that he had never read or heard of

---

* J.R.M. Butler, in his seminal study *The Passing of the Great Reform Bill*, first published in 1914, largely written in 1912, wrote of this period that the word democracy occupied the position which 'Socialism holds today'.[29] It was understood to mean 'something vaguely terrible which might "come" and would "come"'. A more recent comparison might be to the word Communism in the USA in the McCarthyite era.

any measure up to the present moment which could in any degree satisfy his mind that the state of representation could be improved or be rendered more satisfactory to the country at large at the present.' He would not even enter into a discussion, but did not hesitate *'to declare unequivocally'* what were his sentiments upon the matter. The Duke was fully convinced, he said, that the country possessed at this time a legislature which answered all the good purposes of legislation, and this by a 'greater degree' than any legislature ever had answered in any country whatever.

The Duke evidently felt that even now he had not gone far enough, so he went on to say that the legislature and the system of representation 'possessed the full and entire confidence of the country – deservedly possessed that confidence'. In fact if he had the duty of forming a legislature, he would try to form one to produce the same results. The reason? The electorate consisted of 'a large body of the property of the country in which landed interests had the preponderating influence'. Under the circumstances the Duke was not prepared to bring forward any measure of the description alluded to by Lord Grey – he did not mention the fearful word Reform.

As if this was not sufficiently clear, Wellington proceeded to speak even more emphatically: 'He was not only not prepared to bring forward any measure of this nature, but he would at once declare that as far as he was concerned, as long as he held any station in the government of the country, he would always feel it his duty to resist such measures when proposed by others.' At first the Lords sat in silence: a stunned silence. Then the murmuring began as the implications of the Prime Minister's message began to sink in.

Did the Iron Duke himself have some inkling of the stark – and starkly confrontational – nature of what he had just said? There is some evidence that he did. 'I have not said too much, have I?' he asked the Foreign Secretary, Lord Aberdeen, at his side. 'You'll hear of it,' replied Aberdeen. But to someone else on his way out who asked what the Duke had said, Aberdeen was more explicit. 'He said that we were going out,' the Foreign Secretary observed.[30]

*

Almost immediately the first part of Lord Aberdeen's prophecy came into effect. Everyone could soon hear the noise of outraged reaction to the Duke's speech. The fires, the hooliganism, the sheer unpredictable behaviour of mobs, especially in London, alarmed not only the Government but also the royal establishment. This constituted a particular problem at this juncture since the King and Queen were destined by immemorial custom to attend the Lord Mayor's Banquet in the City on 9 November.* Under the circumstances – the glass windows of the great houses being a particular hazard – the Government advised the King not to attend.

This direct obeisance to popular violence was hailed for what it was by Francis Place: 'This is the first time, observe, that apprehension of violence by the people against all administration has induced them openly to change their plan of proceeding.' And Place went further – just as Wellington had done. 'This is the first step of the BRITISH REVOLUTION,' he wrote.[31] By 7 November the theatres were closed for 'very fear'; in the commercial world, the jewellers and silversmiths shut up shop and sent their goods to the banks while the merchants barricaded their warehouses. Consols (consolidated annuities) were a redeemable government stock set up in 1751 whose price was an important indication of how the stability of the State was regarded. After Wellington's speech they fell sharply. In Europe – to the annoyance of the English – there was publicly expressed wonder (which was certainly imbued with *Schadenfreude*, given the recent revolutions there) that the King of England could not venture out in his own capital to dine with the Lord Mayor. In the meantime the Birmingham Political Union under Attwood's leadership petitioned the King to dismiss his Ministers.

As Wellington's totally unexpected, rigorous speech crystallized certain wavering attitudes concerning Reform – the Huskissonite Tories found themselves in alliance with the Whigs – so the unlooked-for cancellation of a very public occasion confronted the ruling classes with the possibility, however remote, of losing control. Nowhere was this felt more strongly than in St James's Palace, where the King

* It was a custom abandoned by King Edward VII at the beginning of the twentieth century.

and Queen resided – the frugal William IV regarding Buckingham Palace as too expensive. Mrs Arbuthnot reported that the King was 'very much frightened, the Queen cries half the day with fright'. This robustly Tory lady added in her passionate style: 'And all *about nothing.*' These violent people did not want Reform; '*what they want is plunder*' or, to put it bluntly, 'those who have nothing want the property of those who have something'. The faithful acolyte then summed up the great Duke's point of view succinctly: Wellington felt that the beginning of Reform was the beginning of Revolution.[32]

Wellington himself remained characteristically calm, telling the Knight of Kerry crisply on 6 November that he did not have the leisure to discuss parliamentary Reform; at the same time strict precautions were taken at his splendid London residence, Apsley House, with its many windows facing Hyde Park. Armed men were stationed at the more vulnerable windows such as the Duchess's bathroom and the Duke's bedroom. Instructions were clear: no one was to fire unless the gates were actually broken open and an intruder entered the garden over the railings. Wellington also bore with his usual contemptuous equanimity the jeers of the crowd, and shouts of 'No Polignac' – a reference to the French Prime Minister of the recently departed government. He told Princess Lieven 'that Reform could no more be carried without him than the Catholic Question; that he would have nothing to do with it, and consequently that nothing would be done'. Grey in turn commented to the Princess on the 'blind presumption of the man'.[33]

Obviously such a situation could not long obtain, with Hunt and Cobbett addressing the crowds at the Rotunda at Blackfriars Bridge – a famous Radical meeting place – 'in the most seditious manner'. On 9 November a large mob paraded in the City, went on to Temple Bar and, armed with wood taken from a convenient fence in Chancery Lane, proceeded to beat the police with gusto. The police regrouped and, collecting more men, beat them back. This particular episode of rioting ended without fatal injuries – but with many broken heads. Around the House of Lords itself there were cries of 'No Tyrants!' Of course on paper all the strength was with the military: Harriet

Granville, the Whig hostess, heard that when a member of the crowd shouted 'Liberty or Death!' at a soldier, he replied with menace: 'I am very sorry I cannot give you Liberty, but I can give you Death if you like it at this very moment.'[34] And that was certainly true enough. But the balance was shifting.

There was an increasing number of liberal-minded Tories.* A significant intervention in the House of Lords came from the Duke of Richmond on 8 November. This Tory grandee had a rich country life on his Goodwood Estates, where he dispensed princely hospitality and was celebrated for the breed of sheep which he had made the pride of the Sussex downs; his racing interests were crowned by his Stewardship of the Jockey Club. Richmond, a man of fine appearance, was 'personally liked' according to Greville (even if his intelligence was not rated very highly). Regardless of this possible defect, he struck another contemporary as the finest specimen of the purely English nobleman that he had ever met.[35]

Descended from Charles II via a royal mistress, Richmond had been a brave soldier, ADC to Wellington in the Peninsular War and present at Waterloo; he had also been MP for Chichester for seven years before succeeding to his father's dukedom. He was professedly anti-Catholic (he was Provincial Grand Master of the Freemasons from 1819 onwards) and had left the Tory Party in protest against Catholic Emancipation. To him, however, Reform was a very different issue.

Now Richmond responded robustly to the Ultra Tory Marquess of Londonderry (a famously splenetic orator in his party's cause): 'he believed, when the hour of danger came, that the people would rally round the Throne', but the only way to bring about that surge of support was to form a government which really possessed their confidence. If that were achieved 'he would stake his character and his very existence – that the Sovereign might go as he pleased into the heart of his City of London without the assistance of police or the protection

* Although the word 'liberal' was not quite so pejorative as 'democratic' in the early nineteenth century, it did not always have the modern connotation. It will however be used from time to time as an adjective.

of guards, and be borne along amid the joyous cheers of a loving and delighted people'. As to Reform: he was no friend to it and would be last to yield to the clamours of the mob; but he agreed with those who thought that some Reform was necessary, and he was prepared to concede the demands of the people.[36] Richmond, by implication, was already drawing an important distinction between the 'mob', a hateful revolutionary lot, probably drunk, certainly violent, and 'the people' who had certain not unreasonable needs.

On this same day there was a markedly intemperate debate in the House of Commons. Lord Althorp, who had recently been chosen as the leader of the Whigs there, described the cancellation of the royal visit as 'one of the most extraordinary and alarming events he had known'. Brougham spoke, probably with more truth, of 'the most awful mercantile inconvenience'. For the Government, Peel aimed to chill the blood as he described the thousands of handbills which had been circulated with inflammatory messages. One, calling for 'Liberty or Death!', was signed by 'An Englishman calling for an armed response'. Another reported that a thousand cutlasses had been removed from the Tower for the use of PEEL'S BLOODY GANG and urged all London to come armed for a meeting on Tuesday.[37]

Then Peel moved from the general to the particular. He read aloud an anonymous letter to Wellington foretelling attacks on 'your Grace's person'; at which there was cheering and laughter from the Opposition benches. 'Good God! a sarcastic cheer!' said Peel, 'and from an officer in the army too' – the reference was to a Colonel Davies, whose cheering had been particularly loud. Davies later leapt to his feet to explain the cheer. Impudently, he suggested that he had cheered out of sheer relief at finding that it was the unpopularity of Wellington, not that of the King, which had caused the cancellation. Was it really the Prime Minister's intention, he asked, to bring down the King's popularity to the same level as his own? Sir James Graham hammered in the Whig message when he pointed out that only a week previously the King had gone to the theatre without any problem; it was Wellington's declaration against Reform which had started it all. In short, this declaration had made him 'the most unpopular Minister that was ever known in England'.

The King remained extremely supportive of Wellington, and even bravely offered to take him back from the Guildhall in his own carriage, which would have exposed the royal person to abuse intended for the politician; yet one thing had to be faced. The obstacle of Wellington's unflinching denunciation remained. As even the loyal Mrs Arbuthnot admitted: 'The grand difficulty is the question of *reform*.'[38]

It was hardly to be expected that the Whigs outside Parliament would remain quiescent during these tempestuous times. Whether it was a dinner given by Brougham or a providential meeting between leading Whigs when riding in the park (the contemporary equivalent of jogging) or the biggest Opposition meeting yet held at the house of Lord Althorp on 13 November, there was a universal feeling that the chase was on. For one thing the Huskissonite Tories had been obliged at last to recognize that their views were closer to the Whigs than those of their parliamentary leader and gave an official welcome to Reform, so long as the terms were kept general. The Whig motion agreed on 13 November was certainly general enough, as it took into consideration 'the state of representation of the people in Parliament' with a view to unspecified action 'to remedy such defects as may appear therein'.[39]

Two days later, in a vote in the House of Commons on this mild motion, the Government was defeated – coincidentally there was a fire at Wellington's country palace of Stratfield Saye in Hampshire, among other ramping depredations of a Swing type. Immediately Lord Grey, with his penchant for addressing a female audience in private, wrote to Princess Lieven about the vote: 'You desired me to send you anything *piquant*. What do you think of this?' The vote actually went against the Government by 233 to 204 votes; the county Members voting 47 to 15 against. As for the Ultra Tories, in the key defection three-quarters of them voted against their own Government. The MP John Wilson Croker, trenchant and brilliant in equal measure, wrote succinctly in his Diary: 'We are out.' Young Lord Durham, Grey's handsome, impetuous son-in-law, put it even more crudely: 'We gave them a good licking.'[40]

Wellington maintained to the end that aloofness from popular reality which, it might be argued, had been responsible for the crisis in the first place. On the night of the vote he was at Apsley House giving a dinner. At 10 p.m. he asked the Marquess of Worcester, heir to the Duke of Beaufort, to go down to the House and find out the majority – the majority for the Government, that is. Worcester was bowling down St James's in a cabriolet when a friend called out to him:

'You are too late, the division has taken place.'

'Well, what are the numbers?'

'233 to 204,' was the simple reply.

Worcester, satisfied, duly turned back to Apsley House. He related the exact totals to the Duke, still imagining the vote had gone in the Government's favour. Wellington in turn jumped to the same erroneous conclusion and exclaimed: 'What! No more? I don't understand it.'[41]

The delusion persisted. The Countess of Jersey was a powerful Tory hostess whose *hauteur* frightened all but the bravest hearts – Disraeli would introduce her as 'Queen Sarah' in his novel *Endymion*. She went on to a reception at Princess Lieven's and denounced a guest there for suggesting that the Government had been defeated. When she finally learnt the truth, Lady Jersey burst into tears. There is evidence that Wellington himself was taken aback. Princess Lieven boldly asked him:

'Why did you let it come about unless you meant it to end like this?'

'Devil take me, no!' Wellington replied.

He was 'absolutely surprised' when told they were beaten. When the Princess questioned Peel about it at dinner, the consummate politician indicated that Wellington had been far too explicit: 'one may do everything, but one should not say everything'.[42]

The next morning, early, Wellington resigned. In the afternoon the King sent for Lord Grey to form a government. As *The Times* put it: 'There has not been, within our memory, a resignation of an entire

Cabinet, upon which public opinion may be said to have borne so directly and so powerfully.' What a change in that opinion His Grace the Duke had experienced within a single fortnight, 'which he had the misfortune to produce by his own words'.[43]

CHAPTER THREE

BELIEVING IN THE WHIGS

'The Tories believe in the divine right of Kings and the Whigs
believe in the divine right of noblemen and gentlemen' –

Thomas Dolby, *The Cyclopedia of Laconics*, c. 1832

The Whig world from which the new Government sprang was one
of wealth and privilege. The Duke of Devonshire was perhaps the
wealthiest of all, with an income of over £400,000 a year (roughly £40
million); but in acreage owned many of the individual Whigs were
fabulously well endowed. This was an age when the average man left
nothing, or at least nothing probate statistics considered property.[1]
Compared to this, the wealth of the Whigs set them apart even if
there were exceptions like Lord John Russell, a younger son, who was
dependent on salaries and legacies. But Lord Grey was a substantial
landowner, for all that the demands of a large family produced financial difficulties from time to time. Lord Althorp would inherit £160,000
(£16 million) from his father at the end of this period, together with
enormous land interests spread across various counties, producing a
vast income. Lord Holland's immense London properties added value
to his fortune.

The Whig world was also one where a concept of public duty co-
existed with a healthy sense that the Whigs need not abandon all
thoughts of self-advantage in order to fulfil their noble ideals. No
more than any other political party – or politician – were the Whigs
free from ambition. Since worlds of wealth and privilege inevitably
incur the opprobrium of those who dwell outside them, there were
many sneers on this subject. The Tories, ran one contemporary
saying, believed in the divine right of Kings; the Whigs believed in
the divine right of noblemen and gentlemen – that is to say, the Whigs.
Like many sneers, this contained a particle of the truth but not the

whole truth. Another tale summed up that complacency which Whigs did tend to feel: a little girl asked her mother, 'Mamma, are Tories born wicked, or do they grow wicked afterwards?' To which the mother replied, 'They are born wicked and grow worse.'[2]

It would however be fairer to say, as the convinced Tory Croker observed to Brougham long after the struggle was over, that there were two antagonistic principles at the root of all government – stability and experiment. The former was Tory and the latter Whig. A Whig like the Anglo-Irish Lord Duncannon, for example, grew up with a philosophy of a duty to govern, along with the feeling of a right to do so. Perhaps Charles James Fox, the Whig hero who had died in 1806, put it best when he talked of 'something being due to one's station in life, something to friendship, something to the country'.[3]

That was the good side of the Whig philosophy; of course it had another side, as when the grandee Lord Holland, who had been at Harrow, criticized the self-educated – among whom so many of the Radicals including Francis Place would have to be included. They were, he thought, 'peculiarly conceited and arrogant and apt to look down on the generality of mankind from their being ignorant of how much other people knew, not having been at public schools'. There were satires aplenty on the subject of the Whigs; a verse about the 'Young Whig' declared:

> He talks quite grand of Grant and Grey;
> He jests at Holland House;
> He dines extremely every day
> On ortolans and grouse.[4]

Returning to their good qualities, the Whigs were loyal to each other, never leaving a friend in the lurch according to Emily Cowper, mistress and later wife of Lord Palmerston. The celebrated Francis Jeffrey of the *Edinburgh Review* drew attention to their 'frankness, cheerfulness, and sweet-blooded courage'. The painter Haydon summed up the general feeling of reluctant admiration: there was 'nothing like 'em when they add intelligence to breeding'.[5]

Obviously men who shared these ideals formed a powerful net-work. It was all the more powerful for the intricate connections of blood which bound them together and led, inevitably, to that charge of nepotism already mentioned in connection with Grey.* It was per-fectly accurate to describe them as 'the Great Grandmotherhood', given the fact that the (Althorp) Spencers, Russells, (Duncannon) Bessboroughs and Devonshires all had descent from Lavinia Countess Spencer in common. As Lord Melbourne admitted, the Whigs really did all seem to be cousins.[6]

Such connections were continued into the younger generations: Duncannon's son married Lord Durham's daughter (who was her-self a granddaughter of Lord Grey, since Durham had married Lady Louisa Grey in 1816), Duncannon and Althorp were first cousins, as were Althorp and the Duke of Devonshire. An addiction to family connections was as much part of the Whig philosophy as sport – racing and cricket – agriculture on their great estates or indeed that enlight-ened Francophilia. It was the latter which had years ago made them among those gravely disappointed in the outcome of the French Rev-olution. Sydney Smith chose to refer to the absolute monarch Louis XIV as 'that old Beast', which was amusing, but left the problem of Robespierre's terror-enforced rule unsolved.[7]

Whigs were characterized not only by their wealth but also their great houses; some of these, such as Devonshire House and Lans-downe House, were in London. Most famously Holland House lay in Kensington, just outside the official boundaries of London. Lady Hol-land herself waxed eloquent on the subject of the 'fresh air, verdure and singing birds' to be found surrounding the Jacobean dwelling after 'the dense vapours, gas lights and din of London'; the 'evil-smelling and dismal' atmosphere of the capital, due to the effects of coal and steam, being a favourite source of complaint at the time among great ladies.[8] In this semi-rural – but highly political – paradise, guests often found it convenient to spend the night after dining, with the increased intimacy that involved. Furthermore King William, whose visits to

---

* Karl Marx would refer scornfully to the Whigs as 'Tartuffes of politics', their 'family-nepotism' opening them to the charge of hypocrisy.

London houses were subject to etiquette, could dine freely at Holland House as being technically in the country.

In another way there was an outsider quality to Holland House. Years ago the beautiful, bold Elizabeth Vassall, already the wife of another man, had captured the heart of the young Lord Holland. His lines 'All eyes are Vassals: Thou alone a Queen' summed up his life-long devotion to this mesmerizing and capricious woman, then the wife of Sir Godfrey Webster.[9] Divorce and remarriage followed but not before an illegitimate son, named for his celebrated Fox great-uncle, had been born to the couple.

To her husband, Elizabeth Holland remained Cleopatra: ('I loved you much at forty four/I love you better at three score,' he wrote). To others she was genuinely terrifying: Sydney Smith suggested that London apothecaries should prepare a special draught of medicine for those frightened by Lady Holland. Nevertheless, many young men of promise such as Macaulay benefited from her patronage and she was adept at picking such for her salon. Macaulay described her to his sister as 'a great lady, fanciful, hysterical and hypochondriacal', at once 'ill-natured and good-natured, afraid of ghosts and not of God'; he compared her to Queen Elizabeth when old. The word 'womanly', she once told the young MP, was one she hated since it was always used as a term of reproach. Macaulay commented that it was hardly likely to apply to her . . . All the same Lady Holland had an acute political eye and also, one might say, an eye for the main chance: her immediate reaction to the accession of Louis-Philippe was to enlist Talleyrand, the new French Ambassador, to supervise the sending of the chic muslin caps she required from France.

At Holland House there was a subliminal feeling that the usual rules did not apply; perhaps it originated with Lady Holland's dubi-ous position as a divorced woman (not being received at Court, for example). This might apply to the hospitality itself: the hostess, treat-ing her *homme d'affaires* the librarian Dr John Allen as 'a negro slave', made and unmade seating arrangements according to whim; fifteen people regularly sat at a table intended for nine – although it was prob-ably more important to the guests that the cheeses at Holland House were proverbially excellent. As for Holland himself, contemporaries agreed that he was a man of rare charm; even if his Foxite physical appearance, with his heavy brows and equally weighty figure, made him resemble 'a turbot on its tail' when he wore a white tie. Devoted as he might be to the memory of Fox, he was an equally loyal supporter of Lord Grey. Indeed, he penned his own self-effacing epitaph, found after his death:

> Nephew of Fox, and friend of Grey,
> Enough my mead of fame . . .

In sum, the sheer exciting enterprise of society at Holland House, as well as the host and hostess, made it a vital element in the Whig world.[10]

Other Whig houses were in the country proper, ready for the round of sporting visits at the appropriate seasons which could also be the occasion of political planning. There was for example Bowood, the house of the Marquess of Lansdowne in Wiltshire; Woburn, the seat of the Duke of Bedford; the great houses of Lord Fitzwilliam at Wentworth Woodhouse and Lord Spencer at Althorp in Northamptonshire; and there was Holkham, lived in by the intelligent, liberal-minded agriculturalist Thomas Coke of Norfolk. These houses were of course centres of political influence in another sense, in that the owners would through their position be nominating MPs to seats.

The Whigs also benefited from the development of the Club system in London following the Napoleonic Wars.[11] The busy, enjoyably exclusive gatherings which took place at Brooks's Club, originally a gambling club, could not fail to be extremely influential given the long years of Whig Opposition. Of course the clique within it incurred hostility, as cliques do: Francis Place, for example, referred with scorn to the 'half dandy, half idiot fashionable people' who sometimes condescended to notice their so-called inferiors.[12] It was significant in this context that the Carlton Club (originally the Tory Club) was only founded in the atmosphere of potential Tory defeat of March 1832; it had the laudable ambition 'to be the best in London', an implied answer to the success of the Whig powerhouse Brooks's or White's

Club nearby whose membership was frequently said to be politically 'indiscriminate'.*

Not every Club was avowedly political; the Athenaeum, for example, the inspiration of John Wilson Croker, had a different aim: Croker considered that 'literary men and artists' required 'a place of rendez-vous also', so that, with the exception of bishops and judges, there had to be a publication of sorts to qualify for membership. In principle this was the beginning of what has been described as 'the Golden Age of the Clubs' fanning out from the intense interest of the Whigs in such associations.[13] It was the principle of association which was being underlined, just as the working classes and even middle classes – notably Thomas Attwood – were beginning to discover the same principle in the formation of unions.

As Grey came to form his Government, the first real drama which occurred centred on Henry Brougham. There were two complications. The first concerned the high income which Brougham earned, not supplemented by landed wealth. Offered the post of Attorney-General in the House of Commons, he declared himself unable to accept on the grounds that he might one day lose his seat, and thus be condemned to penury. Then there was the question of the leadership of the House of Commons: the Whigs were adopting one of their new heroes in Lord Althorp at their head – as with many English heroes, an unlikely one – and it was not felt helpful to have Brougham diminishing his authority. This put the emphasis on the post of Lord Chancellor in the House of Lords: highly paid and with a lifetime pension at the end of it, this position of immense distinction would surely suit Brougham. But would it suit the Whigs to have the dazzling but unstable Brougham thus elevated – would it suit the King and country? It could be argued that this was not necessarily a political role and there is evidence that some efforts were made towards retaining the Tory Lord Chancellor, Lord Lyndhurst.[14]

This remarkable self-made man, born in America but brought up

* The Reform Club, whose name speaks for itself, was founded in the aftermath of the struggle in 1834.

in England, the son of the painter John Singleton Copley, added to a handsome appearance a speaking voice whose 'rich, melodious tone' reminded some hearers of Mephistopheles in *Faust*. Lyndhurst was famous for the cunning of his persuasive arguments coupled with a fabled air of sincerity; he was certainly a brilliant lawyer, even if the sincerity was sometimes in doubt. Lyndhurst was also one of those who had spoken up against Catholic Emancipation, describing the Roman Catholic religion in 1827 as 'one of encroachment'. Yet for a moment in mid-November it seemed that Lyndhurst might be retained especially as he, like Brougham without inherited wealth to back him, feared to lose his £10,000 a year salary as Lord Chancellor.

There was furthermore a private complication in the shape of Lady Lyndhurst. There were two aspects to Dolly Lyndhurst's public reputation. On the one hand her striking looks were generally admired: extremely handsome and so dark, according to Creevey, that she was 'very near a woman of colour', Dolly was compared to portraits by Leonardo da Vinci. On the other hand her character was rather less favourably judged: 'an underbred creature,' thought Maria Edgeworth; all the better-bred ladies hated her. There were rumours of affairs, including a scandalous one with the royal Duke of Cumberland, and a current one with Lord Dudley, and even an unpleasant implication that Lyndhurst was not totally put out by such a situation. Among her admirers was said to be Lord Grey who, despite his domestic bliss, was never one to cut and run where a predatory pretty face was concerned and frequently sat, apparently enchanted, by her side at receptions. Lord Ellenborough recorded in his Diary that it was a misfortune for Lyndhurst to have such a wife 'and be led by her . . . to acts which discredit him'. As to Dolly's feelings for Lyndhurst, Greville reported that she detested him as a husband while desiring him as a partner.[15]

It was the loyal if discreditable Dolly who now spent all day on 17 November attempting to persuade Lord Grey, via his son-in-law Lord Durham, to retain Lyndhurst as Lord Chancellor. Yet despite being described as 'the fool of women' – which great hostesses like Princess Lieven certainly believed – it was strange how Grey was never actually persuaded to do anything he did not want to do in the first place. The Princess congratulated herself, for example, on securing the position of Foreign Secretary for Lord Palmerston; but Grey, while listening to her blandishments, had every intention of doing this anyway. Once his long-term ally Lord Holland had turned down the Foreign Secretary-ship on grounds of health (he suffered from gout) and the Marquess of Lansdowne preferred to be Lord President of the Council, the choice of Palmerston with his many useful Tory contacts was a conciliatory measure to the Reform-minded Tories.

In the same way Grey recognized that Brougham's appointment to the post was a convenient solution on two grounds: first it secured Brougham's loyalty (as well as his finances). Second, it left the bat-tleground which would be the House of Commons to the general-ship of Lord Althorp. So Brougham took his seat on the Woolsack as Lord Chancellor under the title of Baron Brougham and Vaux; the latter addition, ascribed to descent from the Vaux family, was consid-ered pretentious, even dubious by some; but then Brougham always attracted a measure of ridicule along with the admiration. More to the point, when he took his seat on 22 November, those present included the royal Dukes of Gloucester and Sussex (the latter a known friend to Reform) and Prince Leopold, widower of Princess Charlotte and a contender for the new Belgian throne. There was now an established feel to the wayward Brougham.

Grey's Cabinet, when it was formed, had as its bedrock the Whigs – and the Whig cousinship. He had promoted, it transpired, a formi-dable number of his close relatives and connections. It was not totally unjust that Lord Lytton, in a colourful passage, contrasted the fuss when King William appointed his illegitimate son as Constable of the Tower with the acceptance of Grey's nepotism: 'My lord Grey! What son-what brother-what nephew-what cousin-what remote and unconjectured relative in the Genesis of the Greys has not fastened his limpet to the rock of the national expenditure? Attack the propriety of these appointments, and what haughty rebukes from the Minister will you not receive.'

The Earl of Ellenborough, a Tory peer, noted drily in his Diary that three of Grey's sons-in-law were members of the Government: Durham, Charles Wood, who acted as his Private Secretary throughout this vital period, and George Barrington.[16] Then there were Grey's brothers-in-law: Edward Ellice, husband of Lady Hannah Grey, as a Government Whip, and George Ponsonby, Lady Grey's brother, on the Treasury Board; to say nothing of his son and heir Lord Howick, Under Secretary of State for War and the Colonies. Ellenborough, who began his Diary in 1828 when he joined Wellington's Ministry, noted that altogether they were costing the State £16,000 a year (roughly £1.5 million in modern money). Understandably, the self-created Brougham repeated the charge in his memoirs.

One might point out the similar surge forward of Sir Robert Peel's relatives – William, Jonathan and Edmund Peel all stood in the 1830 Election, as did his brother-in-law George Dawson: in short this was the mentality of the age. Yet even Grey's supporters, such as *The Times*, believed there was a case to answer. Harriet Martineau in her history, published only a few years after Grey's death, thought that this was the only derogatory charge which could be made against him.[17] Grey himself would have replied that this was the responsibility of his class; just as he personally drew attention to the acres owned by his Cabinet – in excess of anything previously recorded – as giving them an enormous stake in the country.

A better defence of this particular Cabinet would be its deliberately conciliatory nature at a time when the national mood was so aggressively against anything in the nature of compromise. This was an attempt at a coalition, in short, with Tories like the Duke of Richmond as Postmaster General alongside impassioned Whigs such as Lord Durham as Lord Privy Seal. Canningite Tories were included, such as Lord Goderich – who had briefly been a Tory Prime Minister – at the Colonial Office. Lord Melbourne was Home Secretary, Lord Althorp Chancellor of the Exchequer as well as Leader of the Commons. But then Charles Grant, a former Canningite, was President of the Board of Control for India. Of the thirteen-strong Cabinet, it was noteworthy that Grant was the only member without a title of any sort (Sir James Graham, First Lord of the Admiralty, was a Baronet). There was a Duke, a Marquess, two Earls, four Viscounts and one simple Baron in the shape of Lord Holland.

Where appointments for Scotland and Ireland were concerned, Scotland drew upon the intelligentsia in the shape of the celebrated Francis Jeffrey of the *Edinburgh Review* as Lord Advocate, with Henry Cockburn as Solicitor-General. Edward Stanley, heir to the Earl of Derby, was Chief Secretary for Ireland with the Marquess of Anglesey, incidentally another Canningite, as Lord Lieutenant.

The man chosen as Foreign Secretary, the forty-six-year-old Henry Temple, Viscount Palmerston was also a Canningite Tory; in some ways he was innately conservative. In Ireland, for example, in 1828 he believed in the 'sword and musket' as the best method of preserving tranquillity, and elsewhere the execution or transportation of rioters.[18] Palmerston had sat as the Member for Cambridge University – not an especially liberal constituency – roughly for the last twenty years. One of the Russell family who spent his lifetime in the political world recollected Palmerston's 'slipshod and untidy style' of oratory, sentences larded with 'hums' and 'hahs', sentences eked out with phrases such as 'You know what I mean' and 'all that kind of thing'. In private however the Duchess of Dino, Talleyrand's niece, found his conversation 'dry but not wanting in wit'.[19]

Palmerston was clever, with a rich, raffish personality, emphasized by his long-time connection to the beautiful Whig hostess Emily Countess Cowper (Melbourne's sister). Once described as 'grace put in action, whose softness was as seductive as her joyousness', Emily Cowper finally married Palmerston some years later, following her widowhood. Above all, Palmerston believed in the need for Reform. In October 1830 the Tory John Wilson Croker visited him with regard to a place in Wellington's threatened Ministry and asked Palmerston directly:

'Are you resolved, or are you not, to vote for Parliamentary Reform?'

'I am,' he replied.

'Well then,' retorted Croker, 'there is no use talking to you any more on this subject. You and I, I am grieved to see, shall never again sit on the same bench together.'[20]

In spite of Croker's huff, Palmerston remained an important potential link to the Reform-minded Tories.

Another man conservative by nature yet a part of the Whig world was Palmerston's future brother-in-law William Lamb, Lord Melbourne, who became Home Secretary. Melbourne's aristocratic appearance – 'refined and handsome' in the words of Haydon – was supported by the careless elegance of his dress. It was said that 'no one ever *happened* to have coats that fitted better'.[21] Melbourne's private life was no more straightforward than that of his sister Emily; but his wayward wife Lady Caroline Lamb, erstwhile mistress of Lord Byron, had died in 1828, four years after their official separation. As William Lamb he had been a Member of the House of Commons until 1829 and, as a Canningite, acted as Chief Secretary for Ireland for a year in the Wellington Government until his father died and he joined the Lords. It will be seen that Melbourne, like Palmerston, had the possibility of acting as a bridge with his former colleagues. He was certainly not a passionate reformer – more of an aristocratic pragmatist who thought that Reform was preferable to a collapse of the regime, as had happened recently in France.

In the climate of expectation – or dread – which followed the formation of the Whig Government in mid-November 1830, disturbances in the country grew rather than diminished. Aggression was expressed in many different ways. For the political unions, in their infancy, it took the form of meetings. There was nothing straightforward or indeed programmed about their growth – at one point the Duke of Wellington, for example, had to be told that they actually had existed when he was Prime Minister.[22] The Birmingham Political Union was obviously a formative influence and there would be many copies. At the same time the early unions – whatever their detractors might say – were essentially non-violent, this being a central tenet of Attwood's creed. Open-air banquets, open-air meetings, speeches, declamatory speeches – all these were symptoms of popular discontent rather than revolutionary calls to arms. Lord Grey complained about 'the large assemblages' near the new 'great town' of Manchester, under the direction of the local trade union, to protest against the low rate of wages offered by the master manufacturers; but he did not suggest that their methods were crudely violent.[23]

The more ferocious disturbances in the country did not necessarily have a central unifying theme and were dealt with in a variety of different ways. For example on 24 November the Duke of Buckingham felt impelled to organize a 'feudal levy' among his tenants, in order to repel rioters at Itchen Abbas in Hampshire, who were surrounding his Avington House estate; forty or fifty prisoners were taken. On the same date, magistrates in Norfolk dealing with rioters of the Swing variety thought fit to comment on the need for landowners to provide employment, with the implication that there was more to rioting than the mere need to show violent resistance to lawful authority.[24] This attempt at understanding was in direct contradiction to the resolution of the Cabinet on 4 December that magistrates should be urged to show no weakness. Lord Melbourne sent a circular to his local magistrates dictating that on no account should they pander to the poor. At the end of the year he reiterated this stalwart sentiment: 'to force nothing but force can be successfully opposed'.[25] Meantime machine-breaking was becoming rife on the Norfolk-Suffolk coastline. Nor were the disturbances confined to the south: near Carlisle there was a huge fire caused by some disaffected weavers.

The Royal Hospital in Chelsea, home to military pensioners, had various 'out-pensioners' on whom it could call; these were now supposed to volunteer to supplement the efforts of police, existing military forces and feudal levies. Two warships – sloops – were sent to the Tyne in case the current 'insurrectionary spirit' extended there. One solution to this militant spirit, favoured at the time, was the encouragement of emigration: tacitly it was accepted that lack of employment – and thus potential starvation – might not necessarily be cured by force. The revolutionary nature of the times, in which among others Wellington and his former Foreign Secretary Lord Aberdeen profoundly believed, received graphic illustration when a 'shabby-looking' man with a pistol and a knife was found trying to get into the House of Lords with the apparent aim of assassinating Wellington (the Iron

Duke maintained his usual cool on hearing this news).[26] The crowds in St James's were believed to be uniformly hostile – or at any rate, only the hostile gave voice.

Punitive measures of the sort Melbourne approved continued: at a special commission which sat at Winchester, to try charges of Swing-type insurrection, there were 285 people up for trial; of these 101 were capitally convicted, six destined for execution and sixty-nine to be transported for life. On the other hand, on 18 December there was a meeting at Beardsworth's Repository in Birmingham, at which a petition of rights was to be entrusted to the Earl of Radnor to present to the House of Lords; this was certainly mild enough. By the end of 1830 there were apparently two possible courses that the country could take.

Everything for the moment hung on the future of Reform. 'Lambton, I wish you would take our Reform Bill in hand.' Thus Lord Grey, casually on the steps of the House of Commons, addressed his son-in-law 'Radical Jack' Lambton, Lord Durham.[27] And so a Committee of Four was formed: Lord Althorp; Lord John Russell, Paymaster General but still just outside the Cabinet; Lord Duncannon, who became First Commissioner of Land Revenue (that is, Woods and Forests) early next year; and Durham himself. In their different ways, these men would all be essential to the committee's progress.

John Spencer Viscount Althorp was one of those extraordinary characters who might be described as the quintessential Whig of his time – except that his sheer eccentricity made him quite unlike anyone else. He was now forty-eight and had been a Member of the Commons, sitting first for Okehampton, then established in Northamptonshire, for twenty-six years; although, as the eldest son, the threat of succeeding to his father's title of Earl Spencer hung over him, so that the health of the frail Lord Spencer was a matter of practical concern throughout this period.

'Honest Jack' Althorp's private life had been curiously romantic for such an apparently stolid man. He had made what was in effect an arranged marriage to an heiress named Esther Acklom, endowed not so much with beauty as with a fortune of £10,000 a year; but then her intelligence and wit won him over: the couple had fallen in love with each other. Esther's early death, leaving no children, meant that Althorp resolved never to marry again; what was more, he gave up his beloved hunting (he had been Master of the Pytchley) as a tribute to her memory and resolved to wear black for the rest of his life. Poignantly, he referred to the alterations to their estate they had planned together: 'I miss more than I can say *her*, to whom alone I could tell their success or failure, with a certainty of her feeling as much or more interest in them than myself.'[28]

Althorp's real interests were undoubtedly rooted in the country. He was the founder of the Yorkshire Agricultural Society; at his property at Wiseton he built up a herd of shorthorns, begun by buying a bull called Regent in 1818. Now his prize bulls, with names like Roman and Ivanhoe (Sir Walter Scott's novel was published in 1819), were the widower's pride and joy, a substitute for the happy married life he no longer enjoyed; he was painted with one of them, his bluff farmer's appearance making him appear a suitable member of the herd. For Jack Althorp had nothing visibly of the aristocrat about him. The *Morning Post* would ridicule him thus:

> Most rustic ALTHORP, honest, stupid, dull
> Blunderer in thoughts, thy ev'ry act a bull.

But such crude lampoons missed one great quality of this man, clumsy speaker, most rustic by inclination as he might be. 'Honest Jack', as the nickname indicated, was seen by one and all as trustworthy and as such could command respect at the very least over the most difficult issues.

This perceived innate decency explained his mastery of the House of Commons, where he had been chosen as Leader in March 1830, despite his deficiencies as an orator ('a better speaker in every vestry in England' was one contemporary comment). Francis Jeffrey commented on this decency in his correspondence with Lord Cockburn: 'There is something to me quite delightful in his calm, clumsy, courteous, inimitable probity and well-meaning and it seems to have charm for everybody.' As a more hostile observer – a Tory – ruefully expressed it: 'Oh, it was his damn good temper did all the mischief.'[29] Even the bull he most resembled was John Bull, a cartoon figure beginning to evolve as the type of honest, incorruptible Englishman.

Yet the trustworthiness was only part of the picture. Jack Althorp, if he did not let it show, was actually a clever man: perhaps this very diffidence qualified him to be the type of John Bull; he had gone from being a popular but undistinguished schoolboy at Harrow (he excelled at boxing, a sport he continued to patronize in later life), to gaining a first-class degree in Mathematics at Cambridge; Althorp's capacity for intellectual curiosity took a practical turn when he set about learning chemistry in order to apply it to agriculture. Thus intricate legal clauses in committee presented no difficulties to him, even if he always felt like a man about to be hanged before speaking in the House of Commons.[30]

By Althorp's own account, Cambridge had been important to him in another way since it was here that he began to discover the political philosophy – that of the Whigs – which would be his other passion in life. He told Sir Denis Le Marchant* that it was at Cambridge he found the Whigs so much more to his taste than the Tories. Althorp's Whig connections helped him fit easily into the House of Commons. A few months in Italy during the brief peace at the beginning of the century made him, in his own words, 'a determined liberal'. It was a comfort to Althorp that he had never voted against the Whig hero, Charles James Fox.[31]

Part of Althorp's trustworthiness lay in his very lack of ambition – another very English quality. In November 1830 Althorp wrote to his fellow committee member Lord John Russell about his own motives for taking office: 'I have not been able to escape, and have been obliged to sacrifice myself; for to me it is an entire sacrifice.'[32] The man to whom he wrote the words was a politician of a very different ilk. Politics was in the blood of Lord John Russell: in 1819, at the time he was adopting the cause of parliamentary Reform, he published a life of his famous radical ancestor, that Lord Russell who had been executed by Charles II for standing up – as he saw it – for the rights of liberty

---

* An important eyewitness to these events, as Private Secretary to Lord Brougham, since he kept a Diary.

against the Crown. Ten years younger than Althorp, Russell had not joined in that short-lived Whig administration of 1806, only becoming an MP for Tavistock in 1813.

People could not help commenting on Russell's appearance: with his large head and broad shoulders and notably small body, he caused astonishment when he stood up. His high, stammering voice with its drawling Whig accent added to the picture he presented, which was the reverse of impressive. Russell also lacked the easy warmth of many of the Whigs; as Lytton analysed it:

> He wants your vote but your affections not
> Yet human hearts need sun as well as oats
> So cold a climate plays the deuce with votes.[33]

Yet as a character Russell had not only intellectual brilliance but extraordinary determination: perhaps that determination he showed in pursuing those causes in which he believed, such as parliamentary Reform, was inspired not only by the Whig principles of the great Russell family, but by his need to overcome physical weakness.

There were other obstacles. As a younger son, Russell was not independently wealthy, unlike many of his colleagues. The new salary, as Paymaster General, of £2,000 a year, with a house, was important to him in a way that simply did not apply to most of the others who, whatever their debts and financial encumbrances, started from a solid base of huge estates. Educated at Westminster and the University of Edinburgh – at a time when Whig aristocrats generally trod the path which led from Eton or Harrow to Oxford or Cambridge – the passion which would lead Sydney Smith to dub him Lord John Reformer was there early; a European tour with Lord and Lady Holland when he was sixteen brought him further into the heart of Whig circles, with their agreeable mix of hedonism and idealism. Russell had a fiery intelligence which he had already used to attack the Test and Corporation Acts.

The third member of the committee, John William Ponsonby, Viscount Duncannon was heir to the Earl of Bessborough, hence able to sit in the House of Commons. Like his exact contemporary and first cousin 'Honest Jack' Althorp, he had been a Member since his early twenties, for the last four years representing County Kilkenny. (Duncannon's mother was Harriet, known as Hary-O, sister of Georgiana Duchess of Devonshire, who once summed up her tumultuous private life involving long absences from her family and the birth of illegitimate children with the words: 'You know I can never love anything *a little*.')[34] Duncannon's Anglo-Irish property and connections meant that he would be able to maintain good relations with the Irish MPs, since he had notably liberal views on Ireland; as a block vote these would be of growing importance in the London Parliament under their leader Daniel O'Connell. He was not a good speaker, as everyone agreed, an appalling stammer handicapping him in public from the start, so that he was cruelly nicknamed Dumbcannon; but in contrast, behind the scenes, with his calm temperament and unruffled manner he was an excellent manager of men – in short, perfect material for a Chief Whip.

And then there was Durham himself, to whom Grey had confided the Bill in that casually patrician manner. There was nothing calm about Durham's temperament; if Russell would prove to be the crucial intelligence of the quartet, then Durham was its passionate heart. His temper, which he was apparently unable – or unwilling – to check, made him a difficult adversary and an even trickier colleague. As the parliamentary journalist James Grant discreetly commented in his memoirs, 'he was well known to be of irritable temperament'.[35] It was relevant that Lord Durham had been fatherless since the age of five; he would come to regard his father-in-law Lord Grey as a father figure, but of course that relationship implied bad as well as good on the 'son's' side, rebellion as well as respect. Conversely on Grey's side – and this would prove to be crucial in his attitude to Durham – there was considerable tenderness for the wild, Byronically romantic boy, and keen sympathy for any personal sufferings he might have.

Undeniably Durham was an attractive figure, 'handsomely formed', with his jet black eyes and eyelashes so long that there was something slightly feminine about him. Heir to the prominent mining family in northern England – which made him Grey's neighbour – Durham was now thirty-eight, a decade younger than Althorp and Duncannon; he had been a Member of the House of Commons for the Durham seat since the age of twenty-one, before his elevation to the peerage.

For all Grey's paternal feelings, it cannot be said that Durham won many golden opinions from outsiders. Princess Lieven described him as 'the haughtiest aristocrat' in England, surely a considerable achievement. He could be petty, even vindictive when crossed; one charge against him was that he was an autocrat in the home, who cuffed his servants and spoilt his children, and a democrat abroad: a version of the German saying *Hausteufel, Strassenengel*: devil in the house, angel in the street.[36] Yet he was not known as 'Radical Jack' (in contrast to 'Honest Jack' Althorp) for nothing. His feelings for Reform were passionately expressed but they were sincere. They were also unchangeable.

Perhaps the fairest verdict was that of the equable Lord Holland in his Diary: 'No two men are more unalike than Durham when in a good humour and Durham in his angry, tetchy and I am afraid one must add usual mood.' One historian of this period felicitously compared Durham – 'in temper and impetuous heart' – to Achilles:[37] this latter-day flawed hero had greeted the recent French Revolution as 'glorious' because the liberties of the people had prevailed; now was the time for this formidable but temperamental campaigner to hurl himself on the topic of Reform in his own country.

While the Whig lords gathered to plan and plot, elsewhere the friends of Reform were also beginning to hope. The Unitarian attorney Joseph Parkes wrote to Francis Place on 5 December: 'I think the Whigs *must* and therefore will do something real; and when the wand of Reform once touches the body of Corruption she [*sic*] will soon vanish.'[38] Nevertheless Parkes argued for continued demonstrations – just in case the Whigs were tempted to forget their obligations.

As for Albany Fonblanque, he was a brilliant political journalist of French Huguenot descent, a keen student of political philosophy as well as current events. He had been employed on the staff of *The Times* and the *Morning Chronicle*, where his superior writing was contrasted by Macaulay with the 'rant and twaddle' of other journalists. Now he took over control of the *Examiner*, which he would edit for the next seventeen years; this was a weekly literary paper which under Leigh Hunt and his brother John had acquired an additional reputation for political independence. A keen reformer, Fonblanque bade farewell to 1830 explicitly in these terms: 'We have closed the year ONE of the People's cause.'[39]

This was a bold claim. The new King William IV might have made one of his outspoken and explosive comments if he read Fonblanque's description of the early months of his reign. But in a certain manner it was true: the events of the autumn of 1830, the clamour for Reform coming in very different ways from both people and Parliament would have been unthinkable twelve months earlier. A great deal now depended on the committee which began to meet at Lord Durham's London house in Cleveland Row, Mayfair.

In the meantime there was an attitude of joyful expectancy: it pervaded all classes. The Birmingham Political Union expressed gratitude to the King for dismissing Wellington, and placed entire confidence for the future 'in the wisdom and patriotic firmness of His Majesty'. 'It is quite extraordinary how this question [of Reform] is gaining every day,' wrote Georgiana Ellis, daughter of the Whig aristocrats the Earl of Carlisle and Georgiana Cavendish, to her sister on 1 December 1830: 'It is scarcely any longer a question of whether you are for, or against, Reform, but what sort of Reform you prefer.' With that enthusiasm, Georgiana Ellis contrasted the low spirits of Sir Thomas Baring, who for twenty years had devoted his time and fortune to the good of the poor in his neighbourhood, and now found them 'all going against him'.[40]

CHAPTER FOUR

THE GENTLEMEN OF ENGLAND

'Upon the gentlemen of England, then, I call ...' –
Lord John Russell, House of Commons, 1 March 1831

'A happy new year to you,' wrote Lord Grey to his wife Mary on 1 January 1831. 'I am afraid I must look neither for happiness nor peace during its continuance, if my possession of office should continue so long.' This doleful prediction on the part of the Prime Minister was not shared by the energetic Committee of Four now struggling with the details of Reform; they acted in a state of rising excitement. But they decided on conducting all their cogitations in great secrecy. One clever ruse was to ignore the customary professional help of clerks and use instead the skills of the Prime Minister's wife and well-educated eldest daughter Georgiana – 'the Grey ladies' – to copy out documents.[1] Loyalty and discretion were thus ensured; the great work went forward while the female secretarial help remained, as so often, unknown to history.

A draft of their proposals was shown to the Prime Minister on 14 January. A scribbled paper with many crossings-out was read by Lord John Russell and Lord Grey at Panshanger, near Hertford. A convenient Whig retreat, this was the newly created Regency Gothic country house of Earl Cowper, husband of Emily, Palmerston's mistress. It shows the complexity and uncertainties of the developing project, ending with a series of rough calculations. Thus 'fifty boroughs no longer to send Members to parliament' becomes 'fifty-two' then 'fifty-three'. 'Fifty-one' to send only one Member becomes 'fifty-five' and so forth and so on.[2]

The real role of Grey at this point was, however, to cement his relationship with his new Sovereign; William IV's hopefully benign agreement to his Government's proposals for Reform would shortly

69

be of the greatest importance. Their correspondence throughout January, while the committee toiled away in secret, shows considerable wariness on the part of the King. On 12 January for example he pointedly congratulated Grey on 'strenuously' supporting him against all attempts to undermine 'the established rights of the Crown'; similarly Grey had, he believed, resisted the efforts to destroy 'those institutions under which this society has so long prospered'. The King went on to contrast this happy domestic state with that of foreign countries who were suffering so severely from the effects of 'revolutionary projects' and 'what are called Radical remedies' – he meant of course France and the Low Countries.[3]

By way of reply, Grey wrote to Sir Herbert Taylor, the King's private secretary, expressing his own credo on the subject (a point of view from which he would never seriously deviate in the coming long months). 'The perilous question is that of Parliamentary Reform, and as I approach it, the more I feel all its difficulty. With the universal feeling that prevails on this subject, it is impossible to avoid doing something; and not to do enough to satisfy public expectation (I mean the satisfaction of the rational public) would be worse than to do nothing.'[4]

The next day Taylor wrote back to Grey on the King's behalf in what was another clear statement of position: deliberately citing Grey's own use of the word 'perilous', he said that the King was not surprised his Prime Minister should approach parliamentary Reform with dread; 'nor is His Majesty blind or indifferent to public feeling, or to public expectation'. Conceding that some 'reasonable reforms' might be necessary to check 'the restless spirit of innovation' which was abroad, nevertheless the King believed these elements were being exaggerated in their importance.[5]

Meanwhile there was an ever-present danger of a clash between the House of Commons and the House of Lords which should be viewed 'as a great national and political calamity'; in this case Reform might notably increase the influence of the House of Commons at the expense of the Lords, a most disagreeable possibility. As to the evils of the present system, these were more theoretical than practical; after all, it seemed to work perfectly well. Most emphatically of all: 'His Majesty cannot consider public meetings as a just criterion of the sentiments of the people.' Establishing his personal objections to election by Secret Ballot (inconsistent with the 'manly spirit and the free avowal of opinion' which distinguish the English people) and to Universal Suffrage ('one of those wild projects which have sprung from revolutionary speculation'), the King even wondered whether the whole movement for Reform was not 'a specious cloak for the introduction of Republicanism'.

This was certainly not a Sovereign who was going to make it easy for anyone to solve the perilous question. Another reference to it by the King, a few weeks later, showed that Grey's phrase had caught his fancy, even if the monarch and his Prime Minister did not as yet agree on the correct answer.[6] By 24 January Grey was warning Durham (who was ill) that 'there is likely to be more difficulty than I thought'.[7] The Court, when not at Windsor or St James's Palace, was established at Brighton, in the fantastic seaside pavilion in which George IV had taken such pleasure. It was to Brighton that Grey came on Sunday 30 January to show the King the Bill. It was, as Grey's first biographer wrote, 'a day of potential crisis', since William could in theory refuse his agreement. The King passed the test, however, from the Whig point of view, and accepted the totality of the Bill as it was (without the Secret Ballot or Universal Suffrage). As Grey wrote to his wife the next day: 'He has approved everything.' Grey was equally succinct to his confidante Princess Lieven: 'The King had our plan of Reform fully explained to him, and he understood it perfectly.'[8]

One preoccupation which further linked Grey to his Sovereign was the planning of King William's coronation. The King was actually reluctant to have a ceremony at all; but, in the event of being unable to avoid it, he was absolutely determined on economy. Here he was in deliberate contrast to his elder brother, whose coronation ten years previously had cost a total of £238,000 (£23-odd million in today's money); the sum spent by all three earlier Georges put together had only come to a total of £25,000 (£2.5 million).[9] A coronation, however, featured a Queen as well as a King – if there was one available. Everyone shuddered at the thought of the hideous incident in which Queen Caroline had attempted to gatecrash the coronation of George IV; there had not been a Sovereign's wife more conventionally involved for seventy years, since Queen Charlotte in 1761. In other ways Parliament were having to get used to the presence – and expense – of a Queen again.

What were her legitimate claims on the State? A matter of principle to MPs, such a topic was of more vital concern to Queen Adelaide herself, liable to bedevil her relationship with any administration, especially a Whig one. She was after all surrounded by Tories at Court; foremost was her favourite, Earl Howe, her handsome, urbane Lord Chamberlain, described by another ecstatic lady as 'so gentleman-like and unpretending'. Sneers about the precise relationship of Lord Howe and the young(ish) Queen were not wanting; when there was a rumour of her pregnancy, wicked Greville made a bad-taste joke: '*Howe* miraculous!'[10] Howe was thirty-four, the same generation as his mistress (unlike the King). He had been a Tory Lord of the Bedchamber in the previous administration. However it was not at all clear at this point what significance should be put upon the public allegiance of an explicitly Tory royal official: a Whig Government with a Tory Opposition, like a happily wedded Queen, was a novelty.

It was to her private Diary that Adelaide confided the distressing details of the royal couple's farewell to Wellington when he resigned as Prime Minister: 'How grieved we were at what had happened.' His own visible emotion touched the Queen: 'I saw tears in the hero's eyes, a rare sight which rejoiced me.'[11] Publicly the Queen positively paraded her deeply Tory sympathies. When she agreed to be the godmother to the grandchild of the Marquess of Londonderry, the most outspoken, even rancorous, Tory denouncer of all manner of Reform, Adelaide drove in state to the christening, donating a mother-of-pearl bowl and a comb to the infant and £45 (£4,500) to the nursery.[12] Previously she had been the witness at the marriage of Londonderry's sister Lady Caroline to the MP Thomas Wood.

Londonderry was a great magnate in the north, where his coal mines rivalled those of the Lambton family. A former Army officer and then

THE GENTLEMEN OF ENGLAND

an ambassador, he was the half-brother of the Tory Foreign Secretary Lord Castlereagh, who had committed suicide. Londonderry, now in his fifties, was famously rash and uncontrolled in his behaviour despite his former diplomatic career. His nickname was 'Fighting Charlie': the kind of man who fought duels and would not hesitate to settle a coal strike by a face-to-face confrontation with the miners' leader. Some of his contemporaries thought he was actually deranged. These qualities had not prevented him from making a most advantageous second marriage to the heiress Frances Vane-Tempest, inspiring the poet Thomas Moore to reflect that the stars must be at fault when 'a wealthy young lady so mad is/As to marry old dandies that might be their daddies'.[13] From the Queen's point of view, Londonderry was a personal attachment which she had every right to maintain – but such connections would not necessarily be seen as such in the rising climate of political change and clash.

Then there were the King's illegitimate children by the late Mrs Jordan, to whom the Queen was notably charming. They were headed by George FitzClarence, already clamouring for some proper recognition of his status as a king's son (even one born on the wrong side of the blanket); Greville was no doubt right when he suggested that the bastards longed to bring back the good old days of Charles II with his dozen illegitimate children, on whose infant heads dukedoms were regularly scattered.[14] There were the new King's younger brothers and sisters, most of whom, with the notable exception of the Duke of Sussex, had by nature deeply Tory sympathies. All of these were liable to inflame the Queen's feelings if she felt herself wrongly used – and she would then do her best, not surprisingly, to inflame the King.

Various questions arose. Conventionally, a Queen of child-bearing age – and Adelaide was only thirty-eight at her husband's accession – had provisions made for her regency, if the King died leaving her either the mother of the heir or potentially so because she was pregnant. There were also provisions to be made for her welfare as a widow. In fact the first clash came over Adelaide's welfare as a Queen. There was opposition to her outfit allowance from Charles Grant, the Canningite MP for Inverness-shire who had joined the Government as part of its coalition element and was currently President of the

Board of Control. Previously regarded as congenitally lazy, on this occasion Grant showed a stubborn energy, threatening to resign if the Queen's outfit allowance continued to be mooted. It was Palmerston, the new Foreign Secretary and a man of the world where ladies were concerned, who observed: 'This might be, I will say it, *Disastrous*.'[15]

In the end the crisis was solved when the King and Queen gave way. Adelaide showed 'good sense and good humour', as tactfully reported by Sir Herbert Taylor; but suspicions about the intentions of the Government towards matters royal were not allayed. Where the coronation was concerned, it was decided that Parliament would not grant the Consort a new crown, as had happened with previous queens: there had to be some more economical solution.[16] All this inevitably deepened the tension between Court and Government. There was not yet a vicious spiral whereby the press attacked the Queen for her Tory political influence over the King, while the King was moved by chivalry to show her public sympathy in the face of such attacks. But the possibility was there.

The press in the early nineteenth century was certainly no respecter of royal persons. The attacks and satires of the previous reign might pale compared to those to which Marie Antoinette had been subjected in France in the pre-Revolutionary days; but they were still vicious. As 1831 dawned, the press in general was entering a new period of popular influence, much as the unions were exploring the possibilities of popular opinion as a force. In consequence, a clever Tory like John Wilson Croker, who referred to journalists as 'needy adventurers', foresaw a time when a member of the Cabinet would be trusted with that important duty of state, 'the regulation of public opinion'. Every large provincial town had its newspaper despite the fourpenny stamp tax, which meant selling it at seven pence a copy when an agricultural wage averaged at something like nine shillings a week.[17] Illicit lending meant that readers avidly interested in Reform extended far beyond the number of papers actually sold.

One of the most respected provincial papers at this stage was the *Leeds Mercury*, which had been bought from its printer-proprietors in 1801 by Edward Baines; by now Baines had so built up its fortunes that it was regarded as a responsible advocate of moderate Reform, with sales in excess of 5,000 (and a readership of course far in excess of that). His son Edward Baines junior, who would take over the proprietorship, first emerged as a journalist defending the cause of peaceful protest at Peterloo. The *Nottingham Journal*, for example, was characterized as a Tory newspaper yet it too proved a strong proponent of Reform; whereas the *Manchester Guardian*, founded in 1821 following Peterloo, had shown liberal sympathies from the first.[18]

The press was not allowed to exist unrestrained. William Blackstone, in his celebrated *Commentaries on the Laws of England* in the later eighteenth century, had called the free press essential to the nature of a free state, but this freedom did not count when there were 'previous restraints upon publication'. It has been calculated, for example, that there were eighteen convictions for seditious libel and seventy-five for blasphemous libel between 1821 and 1834.[19] In contrast to the respectable provincial papers and the established London papers such as *The Times* or the *Morning Chronicle*, which all had to pay a stamp tax, there were a host of unstamped extreme Radical sheets and newspapers written by John Wilson Croker's 'needy adventurers'. But they were adventurers in the cause of Reform who, in papers like the *Gorgon* and the *Poor Man's Guardian*, founded by Cobbett, reached the ear of the public. The Radical philosopher James Mill summed up the situation: the press, he said, could be a grand instrument for the diffusion of knowledge – or error: a judgement which, it might be argued, has stood the test of time.[20]

Thomas Barnes, editor of *The Times* since 1817 (early journalistic efforts had included the exciting life of a theatre critic), would have definitely ranged himself and his paper among the former instruments.[21] An extraordinarily handsome man in youth – he was described as having 'a profile of Grecian regularity' by Leigh Hunt, which may have helped him in his early life as 'a complete voluptuary' – Barnes was now in his mid-forties. He had put on weight since that Grecian youth, the curls were iron grey; but he still cut an impressive, broad-shouldered figure, with an agility maintained by frequent swimming in the Thames between Chelsea and Parliament. Barnes also made it his business to have strong links to politicians: for example, he saw a lot of Brougham, *The Times* having backed Queen Caroline when Brougham defended her. They frequently took informal breakfasts together for the exchanging of information. This was in contrast to another organ of opinion favouring the Whigs, the *Morning Chronicle*, which, under its editor John Black, had deplored the Peterloo Massacre, but attacked the conduct of the then Queen.

On 26 January 1831 Barnes in *The Times* made it quite clear where his newspaper stood. 'We repeat our earnest counsel to the people to be strenuous, indefatigable and uncompromising in their demands for Reform.' Three days later he repeated this encouragement of popular intervention in even stronger terms: 'Unless the people – the people everywhere – come forward and petition, ay, *thunder* for reform, it is they who betray an honest Minister – it is not the Minister who betrays the people.' For the time being, however, *The Times* remained supportive of the new monarch; in mid-February it announced that 'no credence should be put in the rumours that an illustrious personage [that is to say the King] was insincere in his attachment to the popular cause'.[22]

Lord Grey, in his letter to the King, had promoted the idea of 'the rational public', in contrast presumably to the irrational mob. Certainly the cogitations of the Committee of Four, however removed from the public gaze, were held against a background of virtually countrywide violence, rational or otherwise being a matter of opinion. Parliament was due to sit again at the beginning of February. There was an inauspicious beginning in which Lord Althorp presented to the Commons a Budget which, with its proposed transfer tax on exchange of funded property, aroused cries of furious protest from the City; after a notably fine speech from Sir Robert Peel the offending clause had to be withdrawn (perhaps there was a lesson here on the interrelationship of finance and government).[23] More optimistically, on 3 February Grey announced in the House of Lords that 'ministers had at last succeeded in framing a measure'; Lord John Russell would present the Reform Bill in the Commons on 1 March.[24]

In the meantime, the great estates (whose masters were very often away in Parliament but kept in touch with the message from the countryside) had to cope with the problems of seemingly random attack. At Eaton Hall in Cheshire, the estate of Earl Grosvenor (created Marquess of Westminster later this year), a gamekeeper spoke out stoutly: 'he only wished the rioters would come here; we would defend the house against 3,000 people'. Lord Grosvenor had his pistols loaded and his grooms were ready to gallop prisoners off to Flint Castle, as he told his daughter-in-law Elizabeth. In mid-February she watched fifty-one yeomen being drilled in the 'driving snow and sleet' for two and a half hours in front of the house, by her husband. Sir Stephen Glynne at nearby Hawarden was a great deal more timid; said to be 'in the greatest fright' and wondering if he could trust his 200 constables, he sent to Manchester for troops.[25] At Belvoir Castle, home of the Duke of Rutland, a leading Tory, 100 staves were acquired for the use of Special Constables in January 1831.[26]

In London the Tories, feeling their way in the unaccustomed role of the Opposition, held a series of meetings before the terms of the Reform Bill were announced. At a meeting at Peel's house in White-hall Gardens on 20 February – amid the exquisite pictures which were part of his rich collection – it was decided not to offer initial resistance to this unknown Bill (whose proposals still remained secret). If, as has been suggested, Peel was uneasy with this decision, he was certainly right to be concerned at such tactics, as future events would demonstrate. Nevertheless at a further meeting at Apsley House on Sunday 27 February, under the aegis of the Duke of Wellington, there was general agreement not to make a concerted attack from the start which might lead to a dissolution of Parliament, with a consequent General Election – all at a time of violent uncertainty regarding the future of parliamentary Reform. So the two sides mustered with their parliamentary staves at the ready, but on the Tory side there was no precise sense of when they might most efficiently wield them.

Lord John Russell rose to move the first reading of the Bill for Parliamentary Reform in England and Ireland (Scotland would be the subject of a separate bill) on Tuesday 1 March 1831.[27] The House of

Commons, which of course at its utmost could only accommodate two-thirds of its Members, was packed. Before Russell spoke, one Member showed the eagerness with which seats had been sought by asking the Speaker, Charles Manners-Sutton, whether it was in order for MPs to put their names on the back of a seat. The Speaker merely observed that the House was 'remarkably full' when he came into it, but after prayers and before voting there appeared to be more papers marking seats than Members. Members of the House of Lords crowded into their gallery, including the royal Duke of Sussex, who was known to favour Reform.

From the first moment of his long speech, Russell paid due respect to the general concern felt about the present situation. 'I rise, Sir, with feelings of deep anxiety and interest, to bring forward a question, which, unparalleled as it is in importance, is likewise unparalleled in difficulty' – an echo of Grey with his employment of that word 'perilous' which the King had picked up. Russell reminded his hearers that he had raised the question of parliamentary Reform previously as an individual; now the measure was not so much his but that of the Government: 'the deliberate measure of a whole Cabinet'. There might be 'a crowded audience' here but he wanted to refer them to the millions outside the House of Commons 'who look with anxiety – who look with hope – who look with expectation, to the result of this day's deliberations'.

Russell then went on to stress the essentially conciliatory position of the present Government. Standing in the middle between 'the Bigotry' of the one who thought no reformation necessary, and the 'fanaticism' of the other who thought that only one particular kind of Reform could be satisfactory, 'we fix ourselves on what is, I hope, firm and steadfast ground, between the abuses we wish to amend and the convulsions we hope to avert'. It was all good stirring stuff. Russell's next point invoked history: there had been a time when the House of Commons had represented the people of England – the 1628 Petition of Right had alluded to the ancient statutes of Edward I – and that happy state of affairs must be restored.

It was his appeal to reason which most clearly represented Russell's own point of view. A stranger from some distant country would be told that England's proudest boast was its political freedom. What would be his surprise, then, to be taken to 'a green mound' and told that this green mound actually sent two Members to Parliament. Or he might be shown an equally green park with many signs of luxurious vegetation but none of human habitation, which was entitled to the same privilege. Then this innocent stranger would be shown large, flourishing towns in the north of England, 'full of trade and activity' – this time he would be told that these towns were entitled to send no MPs at all to London. Furthermore, at an election in Liverpool he might be shocked by the 'gross venality and corruption'. No wonder the whole people were calling loudly for Reform. It would be easier, reflected Lord John, to move the 'flourishing manufactories' [*sic*] of Leeds and Manchester to Gatton and Old Sarum, the green park and the green mound.

Lord John Russell then proceeded to outline in great detail the plan on which the Committee of Four had agreed, and the Cabinet as a whole had endorsed. For a while his audience could hardly believe what they were hearing as his small, high, old-fashioned voice proceeded relentlessly onwards (*The Times* frequently complained about its inaudibility). Then, as the extraordinarily radical – one has to use the word – nature of what he was proposing began to sink in, his speech was punctuated with cheers: some of these were cheers of enthusiasm, others of disbelieving derision. After a while there were bouts of what Sir John Hobhouse called 'wild, ironical laughter'. The colour came and went in Sir Robert Peel's face. Towards the end of Lord John's speech, Peel actually put his head in his hands. Whatever he had anticipated, it was not this.[28]

There were two main propositions: redistribution, and clarification of the right to vote.[29] As a result of the first, all boroughs with less than 2,000 inhabitants were to be disenfranchised (Schedule A), a total of sixty boroughs; those with less than 4,000 were to be robbed of one of their two MPs (Schedule B), a total of forty-seven. The second proposition limited the right to vote in the boroughs to those £10 householders, and in the counties to 40s freeholders. This would have the effect of simplifying a byzantine system of qualifications for the vote.

There were to be twenty-seven new boroughs and 168 MPs would lose their seats; half a million (adult males) would be added to the electorate. The most violent reaction of the House came when Russell started to read out the names of the boroughs which would thus be disenfranchised, while others would be reduced. By their very nature, these were likely to have historic resonances: the past was one thing, and good for oratory, but of course actual live Members of Parliament listening to Russell found their seats blandly eliminated.

In his final peroration, Russell took on his opponents squarely. The argument to history – our ancestors granted Old Sarum representatives, so we should do the same – he firmly demolished. He even invoked the name of Edmund Burke, the great man who had once been the inspiration of Whig freedom, finally the enemy of the French Revolution. First, our ancestors granted these representatives simply because Old Sarum was a large town; which is just why they proposed to give representatives to Manchester. To quote Burke, you might just as well say that the principles of the Roman Empire under Augustus had to be the same as those of the Roman Republic under the first Brutus. The Bill, he believed, would not destroy the power of the aristocracy by removing their nominated boroughs. They would continue to enjoy large incomes and property, by which they could relieve the poor by charity, and thus evince 'private worth and public virtue'.

This kind of influence would remain; what would be removed was the influence of the idle aristocrat, cut off from the people. He appealed to them: 'the gentlemen of England have never been found wanting in any great crisis . . . I ask them now when a great sacrifice is to be made, to show their generosity – to convince the people of their public spirit – and to identify themselves for the future with the people. Upon the gentlemen of England, then, I call . . .'

When Lord John finally sat down there was disbelief, astonishment and finally a tempestuous reaction. In the general hubbub, it was some time before Sir Robert Inglis, for the Tories, could make himself heard. Unfortunately this gentleman of England was verging on the apoplectic in his response to Lord John's call. Inglis's father was a self-made man who had three times been Chairman of the East India Company and been made a baronet. Sir Robert, the same generation as Althorp, was a dedicated believer in the Tory Protestant interest as guarding the proper order of the State. Although he was against the slave trade, and had liberal views on India, he had spoken out frequently against Catholic Relief and Catholic Emancipation. As a result he had defeated Sir Robert Peel (who finally supported it) in the fight for the Oxford University parliamentary seat, which he would occupy for twenty-five years.

Sir Robert had been involved in public affairs for many years. An intelligent, cultured man, he was a Fellow of the Royal Society, acted as a Commissioner of Public Records and as a Trustee of the British Museum. Normally his 'rosy, corpulent, beaming appearance', graced with one of his splendid trademark floral buttonholes, was a harbinger of goodwill.[30] On this occasion Sir Robert was not beaming.

He felt, he said, 'a sensation of awe at the contemplation of the abyss, on the brink of which we stand'. It was the first time for nearly fifty years that someone had come to the House from the Government declaring their own incompetence at carrying out legislative functions. As for the demands of 'the people', he reacted with horror at the very idea. Had they not survived other periods of crisis, such as 1793, or the year of Peterloo? The danger had been 'met, averted and beaten down'. Therefore although he did not deny 'that there does exist at this time . . . a state of diseased and feverish excitement', it was purely temporary, due to the three days of 'Paris' (the July Revolution). In short, whatever Lord John Russell's intentions might be, the object of his Bill 'cannot be Restoration, cannot then be Reform, but, in a single word, is and must be Revolution'.

By invoking from the first the dreaded word 'revolution', Sir Robert instinctively conveyed the sheer shock and horror of what had been outlined. This shock, on which everyone agreed whatever their opinions, took many different forms. Part of it was certainly due to the closeness with which the secret had been kept. 'I hope God will forgive you on account of this Bill,' said Lord Sidmouth to Lord Grey on the day of Russell's speech. 'I don't think I can.' Sir John Hobhouse wrote: 'Never shall I forget the astonishment of my neighbours as he [Russell] developed his plan. Indeed, all the House seemed perfectly astounded.' An MP called Baring Wall, who sat for Guildford, kept exclaiming: 'They are mad! They are mad!' Princess Lieven – surely she was the favoured confidante of Lord Grey? – confessed herself 'absolutely stupefied' at the extent of the Bill, and confirmed that 'the most absolute secrecy' had been maintained until the last moment.[31]

The young MP for Derby, Edward Strutt, a Unitarian from a wealthy and high-minded manufacturing family, a convinced Whig reformer, told his wife with some satisfaction that the Bill had '*horrified*' – his italics – 'the great proportion of the House'. The Duke of Wellington was giving a dinner party, and when the first reports reached him of what was being proposed, simply declined to believe them: there must be some mistake.[32] In short, in the exultant language of *The Times*, 'the secret was kept till the blow was struck'.

The next day in the Commons Lord Stormont, heir to the Earl of Mansfield, quoted a passage from *Coriolanus* on the grounds that 'the great Poet' Shakespeare had surely anticipated this situation:

> Thus we debase
> The nature of our seats, and make the rabble
> Call our cares, fears; which will in time break ope
> The locks o'the Senate, and bring in the crows
> To peck the eagles.

The most notable feature of the debate on 2 March was, however, the rise of a new star on the Whig horizon.[33]

Thomas Babington Macaulay was just thirty when he became an MP for Calne in Wiltshire – incidentally a so-called rotten borough in the gift of the Whig grandee Lord Lansdowne, a fact which allowed his opponents to make merry; they also used it as an argument for the nomination system by which bright young outsiders were brought into Parliament. With his high forehead, hair already receding, and his heavy brows above piercing eyes, Macaulay dominated by sheer brilliance rather than physique. As Greville put it, 'a lump of more ordinary clay never enclosed a powerful mind and lively imagination'.

Sydney Smith had a wittier word for him: he was, he said, 'a book in breeches'. There was something odd about Macaulay's diction: Lytton captured it when he referred to his 'strong utterance' which occasionally split 'into a strange, wild key, like hissing words that struggle to be free'. It was the content of the hissing words which mesmerized hearers in this vital session of Parliament; Edward Littleton MP once commented that his speeches carried away the House, as he seemed to be carried away himself 'in a whirlwind of mixed passions'.[34]

Macaulay began by describing the Bill as 'a wise, noble and comprehensive measure'. He dismissed Sir Robert Inglis's challenge to show that the Constitution had ever been better with the contemptuous phrase: 'Sir, we are legislators, not antiquaries.' Then he got into his stride: 'Our ancestors would have been amazed indeed if they had foreseen that a city of more than 100,000 inhabitants would be left without Representation in the nineteenth century, merely because it stood on ground which in the thirteenth century, had been occupied by a few huts.' As to the idea of there being an evil in change just because it was change, there was also an evil in discontent as discontent. This Bill was 'a great measure of reconciliation' after recent horrors. Furthermore Macaulay expressed his conviction that the middle class wanted to uphold both the royal prerogatives and the constitutional role of the Peers. Rotten boroughs he dismissed – 'Despotism has its happy accidents' – of which of course he was one. The real point was this: 'Turn where we may – within, around – the voice of great events is proclaiming to us, *Reform, that you may preserve.*'

Macaulay was at his finest and most characteristic in the passage which followed, 'thumping out the word "Now" nine times': 'Now, while the roof of a British palace' – he meant Holyrood, residence of Charles X – 'affords an ignominious shelter to the exiled heir of forty Kings . . . Now, while the heart of England is still sound – now, in this your accepted time, now in this day of your salvation – take counsels not of prejudice . . . but of history – of reason of the ages which are past – of the signs of this most portentous time. Renew the youth of the State,' he went on. There he concentrated on the word 'save', as in: 'Save property divided against itself. Save the multitude endangered by their own ungovernable passions. Save the aristocracy, endangered by its own unpopular power. Save the greatest, and fairest, and most civilized community that ever existed, from calamities which may in a few days sweep away all the rich heritage of so many ages of wisdom and glory. The danger is terrible. The time is short.'

The immediate response to this came from the young Viscount Mahon, heir to Earl Stanhope, MP for Wootton Bassett, and at the age of twenty-five already a published author. A violent Tory but a most agreeable and cultivated man, according to Macaulay himself – later as Lord Stanhope he produced a highly illuminating account of his conversations with the Duke of Wellington – Mahon came from an eccentric family (he was the nephew of the traveller Lady Hester Stanhope). Mahon would shortly be inspired to produce a savage dystopian piece on post-Reform England. In the meantime he merely commented rather feebly that Macaulay had considered so many branches of the subject that he hardly knew which to reply to first.

It was true. In this crucial week in early March the Opposition, under Sir Robert Peel in the Commons, was reeling from the extraordinary shock of the Whig ambush. Tactics of demolition had to be applied to the perilous question. One expedient had been ruled out in advance – had it not? – and that was calling for a vote on the Bill at once, which was likely to produce a dissolution and an immediate General Election, which was not thought to be in the Tories' interest, given the state of the country.

So the two forces, pro- and anti-Reform, prepared to square up for the seven days at the first reading which would follow. There was tremendous optimism among the Whigs. Thomas Creevey reported in his Diary that his 'raptures' with the Bill increased daily, as also his astonishment at its boldness. Here was 'a little fellow not weighing above eight stone' – he meant Lord John Russell – creating an entirely new House of Commons. 'What a coup it is! It is its boldness that makes its success so certain . . .'[35] Another Whig, John Campbell, MP for Stafford, was not quite so confident. 'This really is a REVOLUTION *ipso facto*,' he wrote. 'It is unquestionably a new Constitution.'[36] (Despite the fact that Grey in the House of Lords argued firmly that it was in no way a new Constitution.) The sensation produced in the House of Commons convinced Campbell that there was not the remotest chance of this Bill being carried.

The attack did not only come from the right. The Radical MP Henry 'Orator' Hunt, who had got into the House of Commons at a by-election in December, also attacked the Bill. He justified his *sobriquet* by denouncing Macaulay for his derisory reference to the lower classes and Peterloo. This was the occasion, alluded to earlier, on which Hunt described his own experience of that fearful occasion: 'there was a real massacre. A drunken and infuriated yeomanry,' he went on, only to be interrupted by cries of 'No! No!' and 'Question'. Hunt battled forward: 'a drunken and infuriated yeomanry with swords newly sharpened' – there were renewed angry cries of 'No!' and 'Question'. 'Where is the man who will step forward and say "No!"' Hunt's voice grew louder and louder; all the same he was almost drowned by the furious cries of the interrupters.[37] All this meant that the Whigs, who had aimed at bringing about Reform by coalition, looked fair to be harried by those who felt they had not gone far enough, as well as those who felt they had gone too far.

On 3 March, Sir Robert Peel rose in the House of Commons to mount the official attack for the Tories.

CHAPTER FIVE

RUSSELL'S PURGE

'I will call this Bill, Russell's Purge of Parliament' –
Sir Charles Wetherell, House of Commons

The attack of Sir Robert Peel upon the Reform Bill concentrated on the importance of the stability of the State – that traditional and respectable Tory cry. Given that his opponents like Lord Grey were arguing that Reform would actually in some mysterious, gratifying way *preserve* the status quo, and given the tumultuous state of the country, this was indeed the case Peel had to answer. He might have covered his face with his hands towards the end of Lord John Russell's speech, but it was not in Peel's highly rational nature to give way to despair. On the night of 3 March Peel spoke for two hours, eloquently as was his wont.[1]

It has been suggested by one of Peel's biographers that this policy of restraint – no instant calling for a vote on the first reading – remained a sensible calculation despite the surprise of the proposals: in the case of such a vote, the Government would have fought back boldly, just as their Bill was in itself a bold move.[2] Nevertheless this prolonged disquisition was an enormous relief to the Whigs at the time. They feared for a snap vote, by which their campaign should be cut off in its infancy. Brougham, whose dramatic sense of self-worth meant that the story never got lost in the telling, related how the welcome news had reached him. His Secretary Sir Denis Le Marchant, who was in the House, dispatched a note which actually read: 'Peel has been up twenty minutes' – this meant that they were safe from a snap vote. But instead of opening the note, Brougham suggested they all had a drink first. Drink duly taken, and the message finally read, Brougham whirled the note round his head, shouting 'Hurrah! Hurrah! Victory! Victory!' Then he told his friends that Peel was remaining on his legs.[3]

More drinks were had all round to celebrate. In fact it had been Sir Robert Inglis, not Peel, as discussed in the last chapter: Le Marchant had made a mistake in his report, as he later admitted. But the point remained: the Tories had definitely lost the initiative. With the co-operation of the newspapers, the country would be able to follow with zest the debate which followed.

Unlike 'Orator' Hunt, Peel received cheers at various points, and not only from his fellow Tories. It was clever to begin by suggesting that the Whigs, in the light of their recent electoral victory, were still animated by party faction. Yet he doubted whether 'the old system of party tactics' was applicable to the present state of things – should they not be looking rather to 'the maintenance of order, of law, and of property?' Lamentably, Peel saw principles in operation which he believed would be fatal to 'the well-being of society'. Whenever the Government showed signs of resisting those principles, he would give them his support; conversely, when the Government encouraged them, he would offer 'his decided opposition'. Unlike the Duke of Wellington, Peel was careful not to set his face publicly against all change: he was in favour of reforming every institution that really required it, but he preferred to do so 'gradually, dispassionately, and deliberately' in order that Reform might be long-lasting. Peel was setting the tone for an Opposition which took its stand on integrity and tradition, not on a mulish determination to cause havoc.

In the meantime the Whigs remained extremely confident. Grey wrote a few days later that opposition to the Bill was 'little short of insanity in view of the strength of feeling in the country'. He told another friend: 'the public is now decidedly with us.'[4] Furthermore the Whigs were bolstered by the support of the Radicals. Francis Place, who had once dismissed 'gabbling Whigs', now felt considerable enthusiasm for what was happening. William Cobbett became 'a Bill-man heart and soul'. Of course there remained the problem of the Radicals' demands, as expressed in Parliament by Hunt – the question of the Secret Ballot and Universal Suffrage.

On 4 March there was a public meeting at the Crown and Anchor Tavern in the Strand, a well-known Radical venue (where Charles

James Fox had been celebrated in the old days); it was blessed with a huge room over eighty feet long. A series of resolutions were passed calling for Triennial Parliaments, three-year terms as opposed to the current seven, and 'the [Secret] Ballot'. But Sir John Hobhouse jumped on the table and cried out that nothing should be passed but votes of confidence in the Ministers.[5]

This was in effect the position of *The Times* when it reported Russell's speech under four headings.[6] These were as follows: changes brought about by the total or partial disenfranchisement of certain boroughs, with rights transferred elsewhere, to larger towns and counties; the change in the qualification of the votes in boroughs and counties; the changes in the mode of securing the 'purity' of electoral lists, and of taking the poll; lastly the changes of representation in Scotland and Ireland. 'Speaking in general terms,' commented *The Times*, 'we approve of the present plan most sincerely . . . The crew of a stranded ship do not examine too minutely the merits of the vessel which is to take them off the wretched island on which they are cast, to a place of plenty and safety.' Thus the paper thundered: 'To the House we should say "Pass it, pass it." To the people, "Urge in every way the passing of the bill: call for it, press it forward."'

The process of debate which followed was long and exhausting, much of it taking place at night. The young Charles Dickens was one of those in attendance as a reporter and wrote on 7 March that he was so 'exceedingly tired' from his week's exertions that he had slept on the sofa the whole day.[7] Many of the most vehement speeches were made by MPs whose seats were threatened; although Charles Baring Wall was thought in poor taste when he observed that the partial disenfranchisement of Guildford 'would leave him but half a man'.

Hudson Gurney, from the Norfolk banking family, was MP for Newtown, Isle of Wight; despite having predominantly Whig sympathies, he was unhappy at the reduction of the number of MPs for the island. He grumbled that the Bill would give additional Members to Ireland and the metropolitan districts: 'the worst of representatives . . . radicals, knowing nothing and representing no interests whatsoever'. Gurney told Sir Denis Le Marchant that there was no chance of the

House passing the Bill: 'No one but Oliver Cromwell could ever have done that.'[8] As against these predictable cavils, Edward Stanley made a powerful speech for Reform which found an echo in many hearts: even the Tory Lord Ellenborough reckoned that he had spoken 'very much like a gentleman'. Political concessions, Stanley said, which came too late, were like the Sybilline Books of antiquity: 'the longer you delayed the purchase, the higher the price you must pay, and the less advantage you receive'.[9]

There were also undoubted anomalies to be condemned, arising from the use of population figures for the distribution of seats. The Census of 1821 was used (the Census of 1831 was not yet available); the distinction between boroughs and parishes was mistakenly interpreted in different ways, in different areas, which meant that a skilful member of the Opposition could point to these obvious disparities. John Wilson Croker, in a speech generally regarded as 'clever but extremely violent', accused Lord John Russell of trying to remodel 'all the institutions of the empire by the rules of arithmetic'. (Croker could not pronounce the letter 'R' so that the hated word came out as 'Weform' – but this only added to the venom of his delivery.) Croker referred to Russell sardonically as 'our new Justinian' with his 'pandects and codex', whose Government had nevertheless made considerable errors in interpreting the 1821 Census.[10]

Croker also made play with the Whig bias shown in the obliteration or limitation of seats. For example, there were still to be two MPs for Downton, the living of the keen reformer Lord Radnor. He picked on the situation at Macaulay's constituency at Calne, which he had obtained through the patronage of Lord Lansdowne; apparently Calne, with less than 5,000 inhabitants, was to be awarded two Members, whereas Bolton, with 22,000, was only awarded one. And how strange that Tavistock, in the gift of another Whig grandee, the Duke of Bedford, Russell's very own father, had survived the cull! Croker undoubtedly enjoyed himself as he expostulated with mock sympathy: 'God forbid that we should ever see the time when the natural influence of a munificent and benevolent landlord like the Duke of Bedford is to be annihilated.'

On 7 March, a satirical sketch by John Doyle appeared entitled 'The Last of the Boroughbridges'. Doyle was a Dublin-born painter who since 1827 had become increasingly famous for his political prints, issued during parliamentary sessions, under the initials of H.B. (This career lasted a span of twenty-two years.)[11] Thackeray would praise them for their 'polite points of wit' which raised 'quiet, gentleman-like smiles', but Doyle was in fact remarkably acute at seizing the right image and reference. He would delineate John Bull as trying on his new 'Grey' breeches, with Russell as the tailor, standing by with shears; meanwhile Wellington denounced the material, purported to be 'Cord du Roy', as fustian and Peel lamented that he never thought to see his poor old friend John Bull *sans culotte*.

In this case Doyle's subject was Sir Charles Wetherell, MP for Boroughbridge and the Recorder of Bristol. Wetherell's taste for invective – often garnished with 'rich humour' and 'happy sarcasms' along the way – tended to distract from his excellent legal brain and genuine antiquarian interests. In the same way, his eccentric appearance, likened by a contemporary to that of some untidy friar with threadbare clothing looking as if 'made by accident', masked an incisive intelligence.[12] To Wetherell, Toryism had a superior excellence quite unconnected to the need for office: he had in fact been sacked by Wellington from his post as Attorney-General for the ferocity of his speeches against Catholic Emancipation.

Here this passionately Tory character was seen by Doyle as a dying man in robe and nightcap. The Duke of Cumberland and the Earl of Eldon, both deeply right-wing figures, were weeping at his bedside, with the Marquess of Chandos, Tory heir to the Duke of Buckingham, as his nurse. Wetherell bemoaned the fact that he was being dispatched out of this world with 'a dose of Russell's purge'. These had been his own dramatic words in Parliament with their appeal to seventeenth-century history. 'I will call this Bill, Russell's Purge of Parliament . . . the nauseous experiment of a repetition of Pride's Purge, republican in its basis . . . destructive of all property, of all right, of all privilege.'[13] The same arbitrary violence which expelled a majority of Members in the time of the Commonwealth was now proceeding to expose the House of Commons again to such odious tyranny. Wetherell had been greeted with tumultuous cheering. It was hardly surprising that Wetherell was a favourite of Doyle's; another sketch showed 'John Bull between Tragedy and Comedy', with Tragedy represented by John Henry North, MP (he who would die of heartbreak over Reform), dragging poor John Bull to 'the first abyss in the revolutionary Hell which is yawning for us', while Wetherell as Comedy reflects: 'Oh, I shall die of laughing.'

The question remained: was the robed and nightcapped man really dying? Perhaps Russell's purge was not so easily administered, especially to the unelected Members of the House of Lords.

Meanwhile Reform continued to be the talk of fashionable London. Lord Grey called across to Creevey at dinner at his own house: 'Do you think, Creevey, we shall carry our Reform Bill in the Lords?' The diarist remarked on the Prime Minister's renewed vitality: 'all alive – o! quite overflowing'.[14] Although in his private correspondence Grey, like many a politician before and after him, continued to bemoan his exhaustion and advancing years, where politics was concerned he was the warhorse who responded to the sound of trumpets 'and smelleth the battle afar off'. The celebrated Tory hostess Lady Jersey had a very different slant on it all. 'She is mad in her rage against our Reform,' wrote Creevey, 'and moves heaven and earth against it, wherever she goes, according to her powers; but these powers are by no means what they used to be. In short she is like the rotten boroughs – going to the devil as far as she can.'[15]

In this fervid atmosphere, political theatre flourished. By an eighteenth-century Act of Parliament, spoken drama was supposed to be limited to the so-called patent theatres: the two Theatre Royals in the Haymarket and Covent Garden. The Royal Coburg Theatre,* founded in 1818, took advantage of its position on the south bank of the river to go in a more adventurous direction. *Reform, or John Bull Triumphant* was subtitled *A Patriotic Drama*: a play in one act by W.T. Moncrieffe, it was first performed on 14 March 1831.[16]

---

* Now the Old Vic.

John Bull, the essential, decent Englishman, in a 'farmer's drab great coat', shows tolerance towards his incendiarist tenants, in contrast to his steward, named Premium: 'why they set one of my barns on fire the other night, poor deluded creatures'. Other characters include a stereotype Irishman, Patrick Murphy, in a round hat with a shamrock in it, and a Scot named Sandy Glaskey in plaid, with a thistle in his bonnet. The callous Premium threatens the tenants with transportation to the Swan River if they do not pay their rents and upbraids one in particular for indulging in the luxury of a wife and family: 'You should leave these enjoyments to your betters, sirrah.' Unfortunately for Premium, this indulgent fellow is actually John Bull in disguise: he proceeds to belabour Premium with a stick and then assures his tenants: 'Everything shall be *reformed* – you shall all henceforth have proper persons to represent your grievances.'

Throughout, the play was notable for its favourable references to 'that patriotic and good monarch' William IV, indicative of the current climate of opinion about his reforming sympathies. It ended with an invocation by John Bull himself:

> Pshaw! Let's from sorrow sever
> And shout reform forever.
> We'll dance and sing
> God Save the King
> A better there was never.

In its review of 19 March, the *Spectator* described the play as 'completely successful – and so will Reform be'.

On 7 March, the day that Doyle's witty sketch appeared, *The Times* reported that many of its correspondents were calling for illuminations, possibly that very night when the King was due to go to the opera at Covent Garden: this would be 'a public expression of rational joy'.[17] The provincial reaction was equally warm; also on 7 March the Birmingham Political Union held a meeting. Thanks to Attwood's energetic concerns on the subject, the Union had remained in principle law-abiding, an example to other unions. Now a concourse of about

15,000 people expressed its gratitude for the proposed measure – to the King and his Ministers. Henceforth the Union considered that there had been a 'compact' with Grey: he had their backing, so long as the Bill he produced remained intact. It was a version of what the *Spectator* had eloquently called for: 'The Bill, the whole Bill and nothing but the Bill'.[18] This kind of fruitful provincial reaction was of course counterpoised by the more mindless violence of the Swing-type rioters; together the two forces allowed the Government to feel that the country as a whole was resolutely on the side of Reform.

Within Parliament itself, those Irish Members under the charismatic leader Daniel O'Connell also perceived that support for the Whig proposals was in their own best interests. The situation of the Whigs regarding O'Connell was complicated. Edward Stanley, the Chief Secretary for Ireland (one of the necessary coalition Members), was totally opposed to what he saw as the Irishman's seditious influence. A trumped-up charge of conspiracy was brought against him in January 1831:[19] Stanley believed that if O'Connell was dealt with, even transported overseas, Ireland might be tranquil. The true Whigs in England, headed by Althorp, felt very differently. O'Connell's support was vital. In the end a deal was done by which a guilty plea was entered, but by the time the case would have come to court, the law officers decided that the particular statute had expired.

Now the Irish leader announced that, despite some objections, he would give the Bill 'his most decided support'. O'Connell might be seen as Dr Frankenstein by Doyle – he who had created a monster. But if he was creating a monster, O'Connell had a definite, constructive agenda, the repeal of the Act of Union, however unpopular he might be in England. Furthermore he had a thrilling voice in which to expound it. Lytton wrote of its 'sonorous swell', paying tribute to the variety of its tones:

> It play'd with each wild passion as it went
> Now stirr'd the uproar, now the murmur still'd
> And sobs and laughter answered as it willed.[20]

Numerically, there were 100 Irish MPs altogether, including one for

Dublin University and comparatively few in O'Connell's thrall. But then in the coming debate the numbers might be so tight that even the slightest support would prove significant. Certainly no political measure had ever before gained such countrywide, almost breathless attention; this was a time when labourers near Edinburgh, anxious for a full report, clubbed together for copies of the *Caledonian Mercury* and men in the Midlands eagerly awaited the arrival of the fast coaches from London bearing the latest news from Parliament.[21]

While the interval between the two readings of the Bill gave time for public support to resonate throughout the country, it also enabled the Tories, so disunited since 1829, to rally. The Duke of Wellington remained obdurate on the question of Reform: suggestions that certain clauses could be opposed, others tolerated – what Croker called 'moderate gunpowder' – were dismissed. It was in the best interests of the country, Wellington believed, that the Tories should be in a belligerent mood; they should be unaffected by popular outcries for Reform from people of little sense and even less education. Thus on 18 March the Tories actually brought about a defeat of the Government – of all things the issue was a proposed alteration of the Timber Duties – but they secured a majority of 46 votes. Described by Grey as 'an untoward event', it was a warning that all the eager labourers in Scotland reading the *Caledonian Mercury* still were no closer to representation: in electoral terms nothing had changed.[22]

Grey duly informed the King in a letter to Sir Herbert Taylor of 'the determination taken by the Cabinet last night, to proceed with the Reform Bill as if the division on the Timber Duties had not taken place', giving his technical reasons.[23] At the same time defeat on such a trivial issue did raise the spectre of defeat on a larger scale – and on the great issue of the moment. The Whigs had been warned. If they were defeated, and then asked the King to dissolve Parliament – thus provoking a countrywide General Election – would he agree? The subject had to be raised and it had to be raised delicately. When Grey felt his way via Sir Herbert Taylor, he received a highly discouraging reply. The King, reported Taylor, was deeply against dissolution due to 'apprehensions of a convulsion in this country, and chiefly in

Ireland, which have taken such a hold on his mind, that I am persuaded no argument will shake them'. In response to 'the perilous question', dissolution had become 'the obnoxious proposal'.[24]

Then William spoke for himself. In an extremely long letter dated 20 March he rehearsed all his previous support for Grey and the Bill.[25] But he declared himself resolutely opposed to 'an alternative . . . namely a dissolution of Parliament, to which it is his bounden duty most strenuously to object at this critical period'. It was the royal prerogative to dissolve Parliament. This meant presumably that it was also the royal prerogative not to do so. Was the docile William of January beginning to stir in his palace?

The debate on the second reading of the Reform Bill was summed up by Lord John Russell on 22 March.[26] He addressed himself firmly to the question of civic unrest, its cause, its cure, and gave his own take on history. Sir Richard Vyvyan, the MP for Cornwall, had referred to revolutions in 1789 and the time of Charles I; but Russell wanted to refer listeners not only to the revolutions of 'our ancestors' but also to that which occurred in France in July last. He posed a rhetorical question: 'How was it caused? Were Charles X and his Ministers *too ready* to come forward with plans for Reform?' Russell answered his own question. He himself firmly believed 'that if the people were popularly represented, they would not make that Revolution which Sir Richard Vyvyan dreaded. It gave him great satisfaction to think . . . that they had not hesitated to risk that power, to risk their fame, to risk their places, and all that was dear to them as men and Ministers, to improve, largely, liberally and generously, and he hoped successfully, the Constitution of Great Britain.' The vote was now put, actually on the motion of Sir Richard Vyvyan for delay: that the second reading of the Bill for Representation of Parliament should be held in six months' time. Thus, paradoxically, 'No' became the positive vote in favour of Reform.

The voting took place 'at exactly three minutes to three', as Hobhouse meticulously noted, early in the morning of 23 March. 'The excitement was beyond anything,' with each side confident of winning. As a result, in Greville's account, there were 'great sums' betted on the outcome.[27] When the Speaker, according to custom, put the question that Sir Richard Vyvyan's motion should be passed, the Whigs bellowed out 'No' and with equal ferocity the Tories responded with 'Aye'; there was a roar, in Macaulay's vivid phrase, like two volleys of cannon from opposite sides of a battlefield. The Speaker admitted that he did not know which side had it and put the question again. This time he declared: 'I am not sure but I think the Ayes have it.'

It was at this point, by tradition, that the Ayes left the Chamber to register their votes, which meant that those still in their seats could also be counted. The Ayes seemed to take for ever filing out; to the nervously watching Whigs, the Commons appeared horribly empty after their departure. There was extreme despondency, which gradually faded as the tellers began their work of counting the heads that remained. The tellers spoke loudly so that all could hear . . . Thus there was a shout as they acclaimed 290, a further cry of joy at 300. The ultimate figure of 302 was received with further enthusiasm. At the same time the tension was only building because, clearly, in a house of over 650 Members the possibility of defeat still loomed over them. Rumours came in from outside where the Tory Ayes were gathered: 307, 310, 305 – all disastrous.

It was only when the voice of Charles Wood, Grey's young son-in-law and Private Secretary, was heard calling out that the truth was known. Wood had jumped onto a bench by the entrance. 'They are only three hundred and one,' he shouted. Macaulay said that the shout that the Whigs sent up in reply could have been heard at Charing Cross.[28]

One vote: but it was enough. Hepburne Scott, an MP who was against Reform, captured something of the astonishing surprise. When the last man walked in and the numbers were declared, 'I felt as if my nearest relative was dead, a sort of shock I could hardly have conceived it possible on a division in the House.' Nor was he the only one: Hepburne Scott saw many others who were so overcome that they were unable to speak.[29]

The Chamber of the House of Commons rapidly emptied as MPs

rushed to spread the news. In the small hours crowds were still thronging all through the corridors of Parliament waiting to hear the result.
Reporters ran to file their copy and coaches set out through the growing daylight for the provinces. Macaulay had a particularly satisfying
encounter with his cab driver as he left the precincts of Westminster
at four o'clock in the morning. The first thing the driver asked was:
'Is the Bill carried?' 'Yes, by one.' 'Thank God for it, Sir,' replied
this stout reformer. Macaulay reflected that the scene would probably
never be equalled in Westminster until the reformed Parliament itself
needed reforming; in an optimistic prediction he added, 'not till the
days of our grandchildren'. It was like seeing Caesar stabbed in the
Senate house or Oliver Cromwell taking the mace from the table, 'a
sight to be seen only once and never to be forgotten'.[30] Of the two
alternatives he was convinced faced the country, Reform or Revolution, it seemed for the time being that Reform had been chosen.

The reaction to the news in the rest of the country was predictably ecstatic. Alexander Somerville was a witness to the scene in Edinburgh. At this point he was nineteen or twenty, the youngest of eleven
children of an East Lothian farm worker, who had supported himself
by manual labour since the age of eight; later in the year Somerville
enlisted in the Scots Greys, and later still published his memoirs under
the title *The Autobiography of a Working Man*, an important testimony
since he had lived through many of the events of the Reform era in the
ranks of the Army.

Now he described how the Edinburgh crowd roared like a wild beast
roaming the streets.[31] 'It proclaimed itself the enemy of anti-reformers
– and of glass.' Somerville also sounded a cautious note. This was a parliament of popular commotion and at first even the sound of breaking
glass was 'not unmusical'; but as 'dash, smash, crash' went on towards
midnight, there were those who began to reflect seriously and severely
whether this was truly about Reform 'or was it popular liberty?' It was
a pertinent enquiry which would grow in strength as time passed. But
in the first happy reaction to the majority – however minuscule – this
question was less important than the general rejoicing.

There was 'a sort of repose from the cursed Bill for a moment', wrote Greville in London.[32] It was not however a repose which the two groups ranged on either side of the issue of Reform expected to enjoy as they entered the Committee stage of the Bill. Lord Grey in the House of Lords announced that he stood by the Bill and would not amend it. Reforming groups such as the Birmingham Political Union declared that their support was for the compact, which supposed the whole compact – in short the whole Bill and nothing but the Bill, as the *Spectator* had it. The support of the Irish Members led by O'Connell for Reform, at 56 votes, had been decisive – English Members voted narrowly by 3 votes against it. They were not in a mood to accept a watering-down of the Bill. Yet some kind of amelioration, as the Tories saw it, was what they were determined to secure. After all, many of them, including Peel himself, had talked of moderate Reform.

CHAPTER SIX

KING AS ANGEL

'The King has behaved like an angel.' –
Lord Grey to the Marquess of Anglesey

'The best dressed, the handsomest, and apparently the happiest man in all his royal master's dominions' – thus Creevey described Lord Grey standing in his own drawing room, alone with his back to the fire, on 25 March 1831, two days after the vote in favour of the second reading of the Bill: a considerable change from the doleful Grey of January. Lady Grey also looked as handsome and happy as ever she could be.[1] This was an exciting time for the Whigs as a whole and the Cabinet in particular. Of course, these were disparate men, ranging from the fanatical reformer 'Radical Jack' Durham and the sincere advocate of change 'Honest Jack' Althorp, to Stanley and Richmond, Tories who had entered the Cabinet to form a kind of coalition in favour of moderate Reform.

Brougham in particular could never have been expected to act Patient Griselda, Chaucer's long-suffering bride; his close relationship with the charismatic editor of *The Times*, Thomas Barnes, led to leaks which reflected whatever Brougham's current conspiratorial strategy was at the moment. That gossipy Tory, Mrs Arbuthnot, eagerly reported Brougham's indiscreet disparagements of his fellow Cabinet members: Grey was in his dotage, led by the nose by Durham, Althorp was a blockhead, Sir James Graham (at the age of twenty-six) a puppy and, in a flourish of malice, the Duke of Richmond had not enough brains to fill the smallest thimble that ever fitted the smallest lady's finger.[2] For all these internal difficulties – against the attacks from the Tories pledged at the very least to diminish the Bill, and the Radicals calling for something far more extreme – the Cabinet remained remarkably united.

Henry Hunt, MP for Preston, was a key figure in the protests of the Radicals. Now nearly seventy, he had aimed to restore his fortune by commerce after his release from prison following Peterloo. Hunt offered a series of products including tax-free Breakfast Powder and shoe-blacking, whose bottles were embossed appropriately enough with the slogan: *Equal Laws, Equal Rights, Annual Parliaments, Universal Suffrage and the Ballot.* Caricaturists were naturally happy with Hunt and his wildly bombastic manner of speaking: he was depicted as bursting a symbolic bottle of blacking in the Chamber of the House of Commons. Hunt had originally been supportive of Russell's unofficial earlier Bill, but increasingly felt that it had not gone far enough; now the Reform Bill proffered by the Whig Government lacked any proposals for what may be termed the shoe-blacking ideals.

Hunt turned against the Bill on 7 April in a crucial speech in Manchester.[3] He accused the Government of deliberately framing a measure to bind together 'the middle classes, the little shopkeepers and those people, to join the higher classes' who would raise yeomanry and support a standing army; in this way they intended to 'keep power out of the hands of the rabble'. It was the contemporary distinction between the people as rabble and the people as respectable individuals of the middling sort – except that Hunt, unusually, appeared to believe in the sacred rights of the rabble. Hunt suggested that the Government was bowing down before the illiberal determination of the Tories to avoid a 'democratical House of Commons'.

A week later Hunt made a speech on the floor of the House.[4] He did so in response to Sir Charles Forbes. The latter had been one of those who threatened never to sit in the House of Commons again if it became constituted according to the new Bill; now Forbes prophesied the decline of prosperity and destruction of property as a result of it: for why else was the country from one end to another 'in a flame'? Joseph Hume, the familiar burly Radical figure who specialized in interjections – he had made 4,000 of these, together with short speeches, since 1820 – now pointedly answered Forbes: yes, the country was in a flame, but it was the fire of 'illuminations' (indicating the country's joy at what was happening). Hunt's denunciation of the Bill which followed, as something that did not go far enough, was pouring cold water on these flames. Hunt, unlike Forbes, reported disillusionment throughout the country; the people thought they were deluded by the Bill and would not actually be any better off. Yet even Cobbett, declaring his support for the Ballot in the *Political Register* in February, thought that Hunt was wrong to oppose the Bill.

The fact was that the Whig Government combined genuine enthusiasm on the subject of Reform with attitudes to matters like Universal Suffrage and the Secret Ballot which were very far from the 'shoe-blacking' ideals of Hunt. This distinction between the rabble and the people was at the heart of it. Where Universal Suffrage was concerned, the brilliant Macaulay, for example, argued that the poor, in a state of distress, lost their judgement, and in consequence would fall prey to evil flatterers; a monetary qualification for voting was therefore fully justified. It was an attitude of mind well expressed by *The Times* in the preceding December, when it denounced Universal Suffrage in these terms: 'we are against all monopolies'. Universal Suffrage would introduce 'the mass, and with the mass, the dregs of the existing population'. Parliament would be monopolized by 'the numerical majority of the people' – in other words, by the mob. Furthermore it would result in the virtual exclusion of all influence derived from property.[5]

The Secret Ballot was another subject on which contemporary attitudes fought with what would be seen later as enlightenment. There had been calls for it as early as the seventeenth century. Jeremy Bentham had mooted it in the late eighteenth century, and it had been the subject of a long article by James Mill in the *Westminster Review* in 1830.[6] The genuine argument for a Secret Ballot was the need to terminate the fearful atmosphere of bribery and corruption which surrounded the polls. If the vote were to be secret, men could vote according to their convictions, not according to the orders of their masters – in other words their landlords or employers.

Edward Stanley had frankly criticized the idea of the Secret Ballot earlier in 1830 as depriving the higher orders of their legitimate influence. A further argument suggested that it was in fact *more* corrupt than open voting because the electors could happily take bribes from both sides.[7] Sydney Smith as usual had an original take on the subject: he was against secrecy because people would want to know 'who brought that mischievous profligate villain into Parliament. Let us see the names of his real supporters.' At the discussions before Russell's presentation of the Bill, Durham had, perhaps predictably, been in favour of the secret Ballot and Althorp also, although doubtful that it would actually take place. In contrast, the Whig grandees Lords Holland and Lansdowne had shown themselves remarkably indifferent to the subject. It had finally been struck out in view of the King's professed dislike: 'nothing should ever induce him to yield to it'.[8] The need for William's overall approbation was paramount.

The duration of Parliament was another question where Hunt's proposal of Annual Parliaments was avowedly hostile to Whig thinking. Since the Septennial Act of 1716 this duration had been fixed at seven years. In his previous incarnation as a young reformer, Grey had been in favour of Triennial Parliaments, just as Durham was now; but since Russell was against this, there was a compromise of five years.

The future might be with the Radicals – as true reformers must always believe – but for the moment the power of opposition was undoubtedly with the Tories; the question was just how much of it would be mounted in assault upon the Bill in the Commons and Lords. There was very little resignation to the inevitable in the Tory ranks and a great many predictions of fearful woe. It was at this point that the clever, eccentric Tory MP, Viscount Mahon produced his satirical piece *A Leaf from the Future History of England*.[9]

A Leaf had a melodramatic beginning as it purported to look back at 1831 in despair from the vantage point of history. At that point had begun 'that famous English revolution, so fatal a disaster to that country, so useful a warning to others'.* *A Leaf* continued: 'This unhappy

---

* Since the text purported to be written about a revolution 'now above a century ago', in theory this imaginary historian could have been looking back from 1945, a time when the actual coming of the Labour Government produced similar predictions of disaster.

restlessness was fanned by artful and designing men, and kindled into open flame by the second revolution in Paris.' There was mockery of the date of Russell's Bill, the first of March ('not of April'), before Mahon settled into a series of ghoulish descriptions. He placed the new House of Commons, for example, in February 1832: 'Instead of independent country gentlemen', sometimes prejudiced, perhaps, or sometimes stubborn, but always upright and high-minded – there came in 'a set of needy adventurers, cajolers and pot-companions of the multitude and still reeking with the fumes of their tavern popularity'. In this new Government, where Hunt would be Chief Secretary for Ireland, the post of Foreign Secretary had to be left vacant because no one understood French.

Where real-life politics were concerned, the atmosphere at Westminster grew increasingly tense, with the plottings at the London Clubs by both Whigs and Tories, the gossiping of the hostesses contributing the soprano voices to the choir of rumbling political basses. The Houses of Parliament went into recess for Easter shortly after the victory of 23 March and resumed sitting on 12 April. The Tory strategy was a matter of acute debate within their own circle: obviously one way to go was to propose amendments which would by degrees rob the Bill of any Radical character. Early on, an aged Ultra Tory MP, General Isaac Gascoyne, who had sat for thirty-five years through nine Parliaments, gave notice of one such amendment.[10] Gascoyne had been a Coldstream battalion commander in Ireland in 1798, and fought with the Guards in Flanders; he had opposed such causes as the abolition of slavery and Catholic Emancipation. Now he gave notice of a specific amendment which would prevent any reduction in the present number of MPs in England and Wales (although Gascoyne, MP for Liverpool, did support the enfranchisement of Leeds and Manchester, which was a different matter).

Lord Wharncliffe, a Tory peer, suggested a different course of action: the Tories should demonstrate themselves as capable of taking the tiller again, and guiding the national ship to a safe harbour of moderate, necessary Reform. As James Stuart Wortley, Wharncliffe had been an MP until 1826, when he lost his Yorkshire seat and was created

a peer. Intelligent and thoughtful, with independent views on matters like education and the controversial Game Laws, it was Wharncliffe in the House of Lords who had pressed forward the debate on
the Reform Bill in terms of the figures and the Census. In their need
to preserve the Bill itself, the Whigs proved accommodating to some
changes: the number of MPs to be abolished, for example, was reduced
by half, so that the new House would now contain 627 MPs; there
were also minor changes consonant with the Bill remaining the whole
Bill. But in the end, the crisis by which the Tories hoped to defeat the
Government was manufactured. A version of Gascoyne's amendment
was used, with Gascoyne himself as proposer and another Ultra Tory
as seconder.

On 20 April the Government was indeed defeated – there was a
majority of 8 for Gascoyne's amendment, in other words against the
Bill. The critical vote was taken even later on this occasion, approaching five o'clock in the morning. The lawyer Francis Jeffrey, who had
recently entered Parliament for the first time in his late fifties after
a distinguished career as Lord Advocate for Scotland, gave a vivid
description of the scene thereafter: 'It was a beautiful, rosy dead calm
morning when we broke up a little before five'... and I took three
pensive turns along the solitude of Westminster Bridge, admiring the
sharp clearness of St Paul's and all the city spires soaring up in a cloud-
less sky, the orange and red light that was beginning to play on the
trees of the Abbey, and the old windows of the Speaker's house, and
the flat green mist of the river floating upon a few lazy hulks on the
tide, and moving low under the arches. It was a curious contrast with
the long previous imprisonment in the stifling roaring House, amidst
dying candles and every sort of exhalation.'[11]

Nobody could be absolutely certain at this point what would happen
next. The Government had indicated in advance that they might seek a
dissolution if defeated – but that could be interpreted as a mere threat.
William IV had expressed himself so firmly only a few weeks ago that
from outside there could be no assurance on the subject. The royal
Court, as ever, with its fundamental Tory bias, was the source of disquieting stories from the Whig point of view. John Wilson Croker

heard on 29 March that the Duke of Gloucester, a profoundly right-wing figure, had told his cousin the King that the effect of Reform would be to deprive him of his crown. 'Very well, very well,' replied William 'pettishly'. At which Gloucester added with relish: 'But, Sir, Your Majesty's head may be in it.' The House of Commons was also a rumour factory. Typically, Le Marchant overheard someone else saying that William had promised his rabidly Tory brother the Duke of Cumberland on no account to dissolve; and that Sir Charles Wetherell had been authorized to say so in the House of Commons.[12] There was nothing to substantiate this; but people who wanted to believe it were glad to do so.

The next day, Althorp as Whig leader was defeated in the House of Commons on a bill for supplies, and as a result supplies were refused. This upset the Government plans: it had been hoped to get this bill through before going for a dissolution and the vital election which would follow it. The Opposition, on the contrary, were now keen for the Government to admit that they were seeking dissolution. Then they could promptly defeat them on a motion against it; thus there would be no dissolution and no General Election. It was, in short, a war of nerves.

In the meantime, extensive backstairs lobbying had continued. It is possible, as has been suggested, that the Whig Lord Chamberlain, the Duke of Devonshire, was the key voice in the King's ear at this point. 'Hart', as he was known after his original courtesy title of Hartington, son of Georgiana, was an important member of the Whig cousinhood. He had recently come out strongly for Reform in a striking speech at a city meeting in Derby, adjacent to his enormous, widespread estates.[13] How bad the present system had been for the image of the aristocracy! He reflected on the irony of a situation where the Duke's connection with his fellow countrymen was stronger through his Knaresborough burgage tenures – a form of enfranchisement based on rented land which meant that seats could be bought and sold like the land itself – than through 'the cordial and independent body . . . I now see before me, the yeomen of the county of Derby'. Devonshire's influence was obviously important. But there was also a general Whig campaign to inform the King of the Tory sneers on the subject of his prerogative. It was being questioned by some Tories whether the King really did have the right to dissolve Parliament against the wishes of the majority.

Another crucial character in this crisis – and in various crises which lay ahead – was Sir Herbert Taylor, the King's private secretary, and thus the conduit for his correspondence with the Prime Minister. In an age when royal servants occupied an important but largely unsung position, hung as it were between the heaven of the monarchy and the earth of its subjects, Taylor was supremely well qualified to fill the position. He was devoted to the interests of his royal masters but quietly interpreted these interests as encompassing those of the country as a whole, which would benefit from a popular, respected monarchy.

The son of a Kentish clergyman, Taylor had been educated abroad for ten years. He emerged as an excellent linguist, which enabled him to work for the Foreign Office for a period before joining the Army; there he encountered George III's second son, Frederick Duke of York. In 1795, at the age of twenty, Taylor became his ADC, and later his private secretary; Taylor rose by degrees to the rank of lieutenant-general in the Coldstream Guards, of which the Duke of York was Colonel. All these were excellent preparatory diplomatic and military experiences for the next vital appointment: as private secretary to George III in 1805.[14]

In this delicate position, Taylor won golden opinions for his tact and discretion, also his wisdom; later he became private secretary to Queen Charlotte. After her death in 1818, other positions of trust of a mainly military nature followed, including that of military secretary to the Duke of Wellington. Not all his missions were straightforward. It fell to Taylor, for example, to negotiate financially between the Duke of York and his mistress Mary Anne Clarke and it was Taylor too who helped suppress scandalous allegations about the parentage of Thomas Garth, illegitimate son of Princess Sophia. At the death of George IV, Sir Herbert was actually Surveyor-General of the Ordnance of the United Kingdom and Adjutant-General of the Forces when he was seconded to be private secretary to the new (and inexperienced) King.

Taylor's private correspondence with Grey during this period shows that he managed to bring royal diplomacy to a fine art. He was well aware of the need for secrecy over any possible dissolution, equally frank about his master's distaste for the 'obnoxious proposal', yet somehow managed to maintain a private sense of the true interests of the monarchy. Nevertheless the most tactful secretary in the world might bring the royal horse to the water but still would not necessarily be able to make him drink.

The crisis deepened as the state of the country indicated very clearly to the Tories that they might fare badly at any General Election held in the current climate. Fortunately there was a convenient theory that the dissolution of Parliament could not take place in the middle of unfinished business: this made the need for Tory action in the House of Lords all the more acute. A plan was evolved by which Lord Wharncliffe would propose a vote against dissolution in advance. According to this theory, such a vote would take precedence over the admission of the Commissioners of the Crown (to secure the dissolution).

At a Whig Cabinet meeting on 21 April, the resolution was taken to ask the King for a dissolution despite the King's adverse letter on the subject: 'Nothing but an imperative sense of duty' could have led them to propose a measure to which they were aware the King felt 'strong objections', ran the minutes of the meeting.[15] * Yet public expectation had been raised high; as a result, the effect of a disappointment was 'greatly to be feared, as likely to disturb the peace of the country'. In short, it was to prevent an agitation of 'so formidable a nature' that they had asked the King to dissolve Parliament. The King's reply was indicative of the lifestyle of a Hanoverian monarch: he had to receive the Prince of Coburg, he replied, at eleven o'clock in the morning, but he would see his Prime Minister at eleven-thirty and hold a Council at twelve noon. 'Everybody being in their morning dress', this Council would concern the dissolution.

When they reached St James's Palace the Ministers found a King hating dissolution as much as ever, in Brougham's words, but hating

* An important surviving witness to all this was Grey's son, then Lord Howick, who subsequently edited his father's correspondence with William IV: he reported the dismay when Wharncliffe's cunning plan of attack was discovered.[16]

even more the Tory interference with, or attempt to delay, the exercise of the royal prerogative. This is where the Duke of Devonshire and, one may suppose, privately, Sir Herbert Taylor had done their work. Caught on the raw, King William fired up: 'What! Did they dare meddle with the prerogative! He would presently show them what he could and would do.' In his impulsive, even rash way, William agreed at once to go down to the House of Lords (where the actual dissolution of Parliament had to take place). The old sailor declared: 'I am always at single anchor' – that is, ready to sail.[17]

The royal *cortège*, however, was not always at single anchor. It was a question of the necessary traditional pomp for such an occasion, august yet daring. By his own account, Brougham now informed the King that he had taken the liberty – which he hoped the King would forgive – of summoning any Horse Guards that happened to be stationed close by, since the Life Guards, who were generally in attendance, were in a distant barracks. 'Well, that was a strong measure,' commented the King. (In the future, William would make Brougham's action the subject of one of his repetitive jokes, which he at any rate found funnier each time he made them: with great good humour he would remind Brougham of his 'high treason' in ordering up the troops.)[18] Now Brougham had to dash home to put on the 'gold gown' of the Lord Chancellor.

Durham had a slightly different version in his report to his wife Louisa. 'All is right,' he wrote in ecstasy. 'The King has consented to a dissolution. Hurrah!' It was Durham who, having jumped into Brougham's coach, went to see the Master of the Horse, the Earl of Albemarle, who was having his breakfast.

'You must have the King's carriages ready instantly.'

'The King's carriages!' exclaimed Albemarle. 'Very well. I will just finish my breakfast.'

Durham told him that, on the contrary, he must not lose a moment.

'Lord bless me! Is there a Revolution?' asked the alarmed Master of the Horse.

The answer symbolized the urgency felt by the Whigs about Reform.

'Not at the moment,' replied Durham. 'But there will be if you stay to finish your breakfast.'

According to this story, Albemarle hastened to the Palace in alarm, with the news that the horses' manes needed time to be appropriately plaited. 'Then I will go in a Hackney carriage,' King William replied cheerfully.[19]

There was then enacted a scene which was 'never exceeded in violence and uproar by any bear-garden exhibition'. The House of Lords was crammed, including a multitude of peeresses as spectators. As Lord Wharncliffe was actually on his feet in the House of Lords speaking, with a view to moving to dismiss the idea of dissolution, the sound of cannon was heard. In the Commons it was Sir Robert Peel who was in mid-oration when the thunderous noise interrupted him, together with 'loud and vehement cries' (in Hansard's phrase) of 'To the Bar! To the Bar!' – the signal to go to the House of Lords.[20] Peel struggled to keep on speaking until the Usher of the Black Rod appeared at the bar of the House and said: 'I am commanded by His Majesty, to command the immediate attendance of the honourable House in the House of Lords.'

So the MPs flocked down the narrow passage between the two Houses, where glass from a broken watch led to at least one moment of jocularity. The MP John Campbell, crunching it underfoot between Peel and Russell, said that he hoped that there would be a clause in the Bill for better communication between the two Houses; to which Peel bantered back that there was surely a case for a compensation clause. The Tory MP Sir Henry Hardinge, a gallant soldier who had been Wellington's political and military ADC and lost his left hand at Quatre Bras, had a grimmer take on the proceedings: he told Sir John Hobhouse that the next time he heard those guns, they would be 'shotted', that is loaded, 'and take off some heads'.[21]

The MPs, some shocked, some excited, all surprised, were headed by the Speaker, Charles Manners-Sutton, who was said to be red-faced and quivering with rage at the King's unexpected and imminent arrival to dissolve Parliament. Lord Lyndhurst, recently the Tory Lord Chancellor, shook his fist at the Duke of Richmond, the Tory who had joined the coalition for Reform. The violent Ultra Tory the Marquess of Londonderry did not so much speak as scream abuse. As Jeffrey put it, it was a scene of 'bellowing and roaring and gnashing of teeth'.[22] Inevitably such extraordinary noise reached the ears of the King when the doors of the Chamber were thrown open. In bewilderment, he asked his Lord Chancellor what the noise was. This gave Brougham his chance. 'If it please Your Majesty,' he replied smoothly, 'it is the Lords debating.'

William IV himself was resolute in the face of the confusion; perhaps the sound of battle was rather more to his taste than the manipulative chicanery of party politics. There was some doubt as to whether a (so far) uncrowned king could properly wear the crown. William would have none of this. He turned to the courtier beside him and said: 'Lord Hastings, I wear the crown, where is it?' The crown was brought and Hastings was about to put it on his master's head when the King intervened. 'Nobody shall put the crown on my head but myself,' he declared, suiting the action to the word. In view of his innate reluctance to have a coronation in the first place on grounds of expense, William then allowed himself the barbed comment to Grey: 'Now, my Lord, the coronation is over.'[23]

This display of royal spirit behind the scenes was one thing. From the opposite point of view, the twenty-three-year-old Viscount Villiers, MP, heir to the Tory Earl of Jersey, shuddered at the sight of the King on the throne with his self-imposed crown loosely on his head and Lord Grey's tall, gaunt figure towering over him: 'It was as if the King had got his Executioner by his side'; the whole image was 'strikingly typical of his and our future destinies'.[24] In short, forty years of politics had turned the beautiful patrician youth admired by Byron that Grey had once been into a sombre figure of Fate.

King William's declaration was all that the Whigs (and the reformers in the country generally) could have wanted. He explained the coming dissolution: 'I have been induced to resort to this measure for the purpose of ascertaining the sense of my people, in the way in which it can be most constitutionally expressed, on the expediency of making such changes in the representation as circumstances may appear to require' – in other words, dissolution was intended to bring about a General Election on the subject of Reform. It was no wonder that Grey wrote to Lord Anglesey, following the period of doubt about the royal intentions: 'The King has behaved like an angel. There is no extent of gratitude that we do not owe him for the confidence and kindness with which we have been treated.'[25]

The City was similarly enthusiastic. When the news reached it, a Court of Lieutenancy was sitting at the Guildhall; those present included the Lord Mayor and directors of the Bank of England. Members of the Court of Common Council called for a general meeting at the Royal Exchange 'to express our sentiments on the occasion of His Majesty having so promptly and patriotically determined to exercise his Royal Prerogative' by dissolving Parliament. Subsequently the Lord Mayor ordered a general celebration by means of illuminations on 27 April.

Queen Adelaide's attitude to it all in her Diary was naturally rather different; it constituted an interesting indication of the way the Tory element at the Court was thinking. 'The Ministers prevailed on the King to prorogue the Parliament and dissolve it in his own person,' she wrote, adding, 'May God will that the step be not dangerous for the welfare of the Country.' As for her own reaction: 'I was very much moved and upset.'[26] At least she kept up her poise when questioned anxiously by William's twelve-year-old nephew, Prince George of Cambridge, who had gleaned that something exceptional had happened. 'What has the King done?' he asked anxiously. 'Has he not done something odd?' Queen Adelaide responded with dignity: 'The King can do odd things.'

The whole episode aroused the most passionate feelings in which families were divided and friends abused each other; there was 'heat, fury, discussion and battling', in Haydon's phrase. The Hon. Robert Smith, heir to the first Lord Carrington, a wealthy banker, had been Member for Buckinghamshire for the last ten years; he had presented petitions for the Bill from his constituents (as well as anti-slavery petitions) and voted against Gascoyne's wrecking amendment on 23 April. Lord Carrington was described by Maria Edgeworth as 'most amiable and benevolent' and he was certainly extremely philanthropic. On this occasion, his amiability was apparently stretched too far. He wrote to his son: 'My dear Bob . . . It would be as well for you not to come to this house for sometime as I would be tempted to use language which you would never forget, and [for] which I myself might never forgive myself.'[27]

The disgust of Lord Carrington was at least expressed in a letter. Among the Tories, General Gascoyne himself, whose amendment had wreaked this havoc, was hooted, hissed and pelted in his own constituency of Liverpool. An eyewitness recorded: 'When I saw him his face, his hair and his clothes were covered with filth and spittle . . . not from a mob of the lowest sort, but from men his own equals.' Gascoyne would in fact be defeated in the coming election.[28]

Certainly the incident added to the enormous popularity of William IV. The very different stages in his feelings were hidden from his grateful subjects as they hallooed their joy. Much was made of the happy coincidence of the King's nickname – 'Vote for the Two Bills' was a favoured cry. John Doyle produced an amusing drawing of the King, unmistakable with his stout figure and turnip-like face, gazing at a wall on which were the words: 'The Bill and nothing but the Bill.' William asked: 'Is that me?' At the Theatre Royal, Drury Lane, the actor-manager William Charles Macready scored great success with *Alfred the Great or the Patriot King* by James Sheridan Knowles. The play was announced within days of the dissolution and 'God Save the King' was incorporated into the text. Lines appropriate to recent events included the following:

> Thus to a people faithful to their King
> A faithful King an institution gives
> That makes the lowly cottage lofty as
> The regal dome . . .[29]

Unfortunately William's admirers celebrated not only with further illuminations 'sagaciously' ordered by the Lord Mayor – the phrase was Elizabeth Grosvenor's as she and her husband wandered down Regent Street 'dressed in plain clothes' – but by breaking windows.

This left Princess Lieven to record picturesquely that the Tories who refused to illuminate in honour of the dissolution were obliged to sleep 'in fresh air'.[30] The Lord Mayor's order found the crowds in no mood to tolerate dissent, which was freely interpreted as meaning any unlit window in a great house. For all that, Elizabeth and her husband, home at midnight, found it 'a very pleasant and entertaining walk' in their plain clothes, others were not so lucky. The Duke of Wellington at Apsley House was one of the victims. The Duke was not there; his house was in darkness and there was certainly no sign of the candles with which other grandees had lit up their windows (either with joy or in a bid to preserve them). As the mob swept up Piccadilly, Apsley House seemed to present an inviting target.

There was in fact a far more solemn reason for the darkness which mantled the great house than mere political disappointment. Kitty, Duchess of Wellington, the neglected wife, had died on 24 April and her body lay there in its coffin while the Duke made preparations for her funeral in the country. The Duke reported afterwards that his servant John had saved the house, or the lives of the mob – 'possibly both' – by firing gunpowder over their heads: 'They certainly intended to destroy the House,' he wrote, 'and did not care one Pin for the poor Duchess being dead in the house.'[31]

On the subject of Reform itself the Duke felt an equivalent gloom. He followed the current trend for looking for a disastrous precedent in the events leading up to the English Civil War: 'I don't believe that the King of England has taken a step so fatal to his monarchy,' he wrote of the dissolution, 'since the day that Charles I passed the Act to deprive himself of the power of proroguing or dissolving the long Parliament.'[32]

The representative of the banking house of Rothschild in London, Nathan Rothschild, also found his windows suffering from association: he was known to be a friend of the Duke. But it was his brother James in Paris who was almost as gloomy as the Duke, due to his recent experiences there of revolution in which stocks had fallen sharply. He compared events in the two countries. To start with, in France no one viewed the matter as giving cause for concern, 'but then we fell some

30 per cent and I hope To God this will not be repeated this time in England . . . Let us get down to the nitty gritty, I am not pleased with the situation in England.' It was high time for England to put a stop to the progress of 'the infamous liberal spirit'.[33]

Meanwhile that country itself, watched by the wary financiers, settled down to the joys – or dangers – of a General Election. It was less than six months since the Whigs had come to power but already the whole political climate had changed. Public opinion on the subject of Reform – 'the expectations of the people' – had just been quoted by that 'angel', the monarch himself, in justifying his dissolution of Parliament.

CHAPTER SEVEN

AWAY WENT GILPIN

'Away went Gilpin, neck or naught;
Away went hat and wig.
He little dreamed, when he set out
Of running such a rig' –

William Cowper, *The Diverting History of John Gilpin*, 1782

'The cause of Reform looks cheerily!' declared *The Times* on 29 April 1831, six days after the King had dissolved Parliament. 'Indeed it is triumphing. What Dryden called "The Royal Plant", the true British oak . . . is now seen to yield the fruit along with the blossom – fruition along with hope.' All the same, the Thunderer felt that there was a warning to be given: 'Let no man listen to any terms of compromise . . . A half Reform is no Reform.' In terms of the election, let the country be 'precise, rigid and memorable'. What was needed was a majority of 100.[1]

This note of caution following the initial triumphalism was understandable. Paradoxically, the General Election of the early summer of 1831, although fought on the issue of Reform, took place under exactly the same rules as that of July 1830, against which the angry protests had been mounted countrywide. At this time, there was no universal polling day: the returning officer for each constituency (or group of constituencies) worked out the timetable; if the election was contested, polling (which was of course held in public) might take place over several days. Thus the first voting took place on 28 April, only five days after William IV's dramatic dissolution, and the last on 1 June.

The total number of seats to be filled was as before 658, of which nearly 500 were in England, 24 in Wales, 45 in Scotland and 100 in Ireland. These were to be found in borough or burgh constituencies, which accounted for the vast majority, and included freeholds of

115

various types, so-called potwallopers (those residents who 'boiled a pot' in the district), soc-and-lot payers (those who paid the poor rates, the equivalent of the medieval 'pay lot and bear lot'), and so forth, esoteric descriptions indicating the ancient roots of the whole business. Then there were county constituencies and universities – four seats in total for Oxford and Cambridge.[2]

During the five weeks which followed, there were two strong trends in the country as a whole. On the one hand there was a surge of resolution that Reform should take place; on the other, there were those who felt the Whig Government was galloping to destruction in a manner and with a swiftness which had not been anticipated. John Doyle, vivid as ever, captured this contrast with spirit when he adopted William Cowper's rhyme concerning John Gilpin, that 'citizen of credit and renown' whose horse bolts with him and takes him on a hectic and unexpected journey. Just as the word 'Bill' for William lent itself to double meanings, so the adjective 'Grey' could be similarly employed for a runaway horse (as well as for a tailor's fustian).

In Doyle's image dated 13 May 1831, an unhappy-looking William IV is seen on the back of a galloping steed, whizzing past a shocked-looking John Bull. The unmistakable figure of the Prime Minister salutes him with his hat, but one spectator cries: 'I think the *Grey* is evidently running away with him.' Ladies of the Court in huge hats are watching and wailing on the balcony, headed by Queen Adelaide, who calls out: 'Good Mr Gatekeeper Stopham . . . he doesn't know where he's going.'

In real life two incidents in royal circles seemed to indicate the way the wind was blowing with regard to Reform – except that they pointed in opposite directions. On 4 June William IV's eldest son by the actress Mrs Jordan, George FitzClarence, was given the peerage he had long coveted as due to his semi-royal status; in the process of securing it, he had even made hysterical threats of suicide. The Earl of Munster, as he now became, was a professionally disgruntled character; much later Lord Melbourne suggested that it was perhaps that 'unfortunate condition of illegitimacy' which distorted the mind and feelings of men like Munster, rendering them incapable of 'justice or contentment'.[3]

On this occasion Munster felt deprived of the dukedom which the bastards of Charles II had received; but he now concentrated his efforts on securing the right to place the crown on his father's head at the coronation in September.[4]

There were more histrionics from the aggrieved son: 'Who is more fit than your own *flesh and blood*?' he pleaded. Munster entertained hopes that the Garter would follow as an appropriate acknowledgement of his new position. The King, feeling he had already rewarded his son adequately, reacted with anger.[5] But this did not stop him promoting the man who was indeed his eldest son to the position of Governor of Windsor and Constable of the Round Tower, making him in addition a member of the Privy Council. Munster also remained very much within the tight, affectionate circle in which King William – and the ever indulgent Queen Adelaide – liked to dwell. And Munster was a known, vociferous anti-reformer. Fears of the influence of the Tory Court were not allayed by Munster's elevation.

At the same season, the person who actually received the Garter was the Prime Minister, Lord Grey. This was a particularly marked honour, given that the ranks of the Knights of the Garter, designed to be limited to twenty-five, were in theory full.[6] There were even those who suggested that the King had no right to swell the ranks of the chivalric order in this manner. The Duke of Wellington (who had personally been nominated a Knight of the Garter nearly twenty years previously) described it to the Duke of Rutland as 'a gross impropriety . . . not justified by services or by precedent'. It hadn't even the 'merit', he complained, of being a grant from a Sovereign to a favourite; or, as Princess Lieven wryly commented, 'the Blue Riband [for Grey] is not at all to the taste of our hero'. It is fair to say that the 'hero's' temper at this time was not of the best; he had difficulty controlling it, reported Mrs Arbuthnot, and it was all the fault of this 'nonsensical Bill . . . so preposterous, so unjust'.[7] There were Tory rumbles that Grey was being given a pay-off for agreeing to the ennoblement of Munster; the royal Dukes of Cumberland and Gloucester pointedly stayed away from the ceremony of installation.

It was true that in recent years monarchs had laid down rules designed to limit the numbers of ordinary knights; while ordaining that royal (male) descendants should be received into the order by virtue of their blood. Yet *pace* the Duke of Wellington, Grey's elevation as an Extra Knight was not without precedent. In 1814 the Earl of Liverpool and Viscount Castlereagh were appointed for 'political expedience', bringing the number up to twenty-seven, even though the Prince Regent (the future George IV) agreed that numbers should thereafter be allowed to sink back. In a similar fashion William IV, while appointing Grey, once again reaffirmed the general principle of twenty-five: in short, this was a striking demonstration of his favour to his Prime Minister – at a time of political ferment. From the Whig point of view, the King did indeed show himself 'a prime fellow', in the words of Grey.

The monarch as father enhanced the status of his child (and as grandfather, for William adored his grandchildren, including Munster's newly ennobled seven-year-old son Viscount FitzClarence); the monarch as a political figure publicly elevated his Prime Minister. As rumours spread into the press of the persistent Tory tittle-tattle at Court, William IV was for the time being still exempted from criticism. On 23 May *The Times* reported that 'a certain Earl, connected with the Royal Household' – the reference was to Queen Adelaide's favourite, Earl Howe – 'has received a severe rebuke from the King on account of his continued meddling and incessant chatter about the Reform Bill'.[8] It remained to be seen whether the King would maintain this dignified posture of impartiality if it were the Queen herself who took part in the meddling and the chatter.

Since the General Election was fought under the same rules, the same extent of venality and its shadow, corruption, was to be expected, as was the astonishing cost of the whole business. In his bold attempt to bring about Reform (to soften the effects of Catholic Emancipation), the unabashed Ultra Tory the Marquess of Blandford had made the excellent point that corruption could not be justified by results. 'The thing retains the same character of corruption, whether it generates the venal statesman or the useful MP, the splendid fly that soars in this

House upon the wings of eloquence or the grub that feeds upon the vitals of the country – Corruption is the father of them all.' Certainly some of the sums spent at this period beggared belief, in terms of cost-effectiveness. The 1830 Liverpool by-election caused by the death of Huskisson found over £100,000 (£10 million today) being dispensed for the benefit of a mere 4,400 voters.* Three pilots who arrived by sea on the last day of the poll were said to have received £150 each for their votes.[9]

Leaving aside by-elections, the whole country had been submitted to the expensive electoral process only eight months previously. As Lord Althorp, standing for Northamptonshire, wrote to his father on 13 May 1831 in a matter-of-fact way: 'the votes are now becoming very expensive, for we must send so far for them'.[10] In this context, it was easy to see why pocket boroughs were regarded as property, since so much money had been spent in acquiring them. Earl Grosvenor had received the news of Lord John Russell's Bill in March with 'as much good humour', according to his daughter-in-law Elizabeth, as if he had gained £150,000 (roughly £15 million in today's money) instead of losing it – which was the sum he told her that he had spent acquiring the pocket boroughs.[11]

The future Marquess of Westminster remained very good-natured about his losses, determined to support the Bill 'for the safety of the country'; but others were not so high-minded, as when the Duke of Newcastle gave vent to that notorious expostulation, 'May not I do what I like with my own?' The Reform Bill, it should be noted, had not called for any kind of compensation to be paid to these owners, although this proposal had been made much earlier in suggestions for Reform in the late eighteenth century; this was in contrast to the £2 million compensation finally paid to slave-owners. There was a Welsh attorney named Williams who, having speculated in coal mines, invested the proceeds in buying the two seats at Great Marlow in Buckinghamshire, paying the voters £15 (£1,500) each at

---

* One is reminded of the sums of money dispensed in the American Presidential Elections in the twenty-first century; but these take place in a country with a huge population and covering a vast area.

election time; the indignation of such a man at being disappropriated is comprehensible.[12]

It could be said that the attitude of Whigs to payments belied their reforming views. Grey had not grudged paying out £15,000 (£1.5 million) for his son's attempt to secure the Northumberland seat – an attempt which actually failed.[13] The attitude of the grandees like Lord Lansdowne to nomination was equally relaxed: Macaulay was the most famous beneficiary, induced by his patron to do a little gracious canvassing for the look of the thing.

Meanwhile another whole group of middle-class reformers was gaining influence: the group headed by Thomas Attwood, whose attitude to violence was summed up by fervent chants such as this:

> See, see, we come! No swords we draw
> We kindle not war's battle fires,
> By union, justice, reason, law
> We'll gain the birthright of our sires.[14]

Members of the Birmingham Political Union were happily active during the election campaign with such a good cause to promote. Attwood himself made numerous personal appearances, during which he took care to praise not only the Whigs but also the King: indeed the authority of William IV was persistently invoked – that Patriot King who was being celebrated in the theatre in London. In consequence, all the candidates backed by the Union were successfully elected; whereupon the order was given for illuminations, accompanied by the victorious ringing of church bells.

Unfortunately, even if Attwood and his associates were determined not to draw their swords, there were others who found the sheer pleasure of physical protest irresistible. When the Revd Thomas Moseley of St Martin's refused to admit the bell-ringers, they climbed in through a belfry window, treating the clergyman roughly thereafter. This was just the kind of behaviour that Attwood deprecated. He met the clergyman's vociferous complaints with an excuse which was diplomatic even if it lacked chivalry: a few children and 'loose women' were responsible, not 'frenzied unionists'. But the violence was at least as much, if not more, due to the reformers as their opponents. The wind of change was blowing them forward, not always the softest of breezes. Edward Bulwer, future Lord Lytton, for example strongly urged his Tory mother to lie low on purely worldly grounds: 'I see great reason why for your own sake you should not even quietly and coldly oppose Reform. The public are so unanimous and so violent on the measure, right or wrong, that I do not hesitate to say that persons who oppose the Reform will be marked out in case of any disturbance. It is as well therefore to be *safe and neuter*, especially when no earthly advantage is to be gained by going against the tide.'[15]

And there were random brutal episodes, not specifically connected to the election, which led to the unease of the country as a whole. The punitive incident at Merthyr Tydfil in early June was a case in point. Despite the rise in population there due to the presence of steelworks, Merthyr had not actually been enfranchised. The violence occurred over the reduction of wages by the owner of the Cyfarthfa works. Strikes followed by riots ensued, in course of which soldiers shot over twenty of the demonstrators; a man who wounded a soldier was subsequently hanged. At least Merthyr was now granted a seat although it would be an ironmaster, naturally, not a steelworker who occupied it.[16]

Opponents of the Bill were keen to promote any dramatic stories of disturbance which suggested that the people – the rabble – were getting out of control, with the further hideous possibility of a successful popular rising. There was a rumour that groups of servants were declining to be hired for more than six months: after that the Bill would have been passed, and they would never need to work again.[17] It was significant that the celebrated Radical William Cobbett, put on trial for encouraging sedition among the rural classes, was acquitted in the summer of 1831 because the jury could not agree among themselves. (Thereafter he resumed his advocacy of the Bill.)

One young man who was 'misled' – as he said later – was William Ewart Gladstone, then twenty-two. During the autumn he had written to his father to the effect that the Whigs could make speeches, but they were not men of business. Now he argued with a certain man of the people along the familiar Wellingtonian lines that Reform meant

Revolution, citing the recent events in France and Belgium. His inter-locutor looked hard at the young Gladstone and responded fiercely: 'Damn all foreign countries, what has old England to do with foreign countries?' It was, Gladstone would reflect, an important lesson from a humble source.'[18]

In May 1831 the lesson had still to be learnt. There were three nights of debate at the Union in Oxford, where Gladstone was an undergrad-uate. In a speech of three-quarters of an hour, short by his future stan-dards but long by those of the Union, he argued that the Reform Bill threatened to change the form of British government and ultimately break up the whole frame of society. At the subsequent vote the under-graduates, influenced perhaps by this eloquence, divided 94:38 against Reform. This was along the lines of Wellington's reaction at the end of May: 'I don't in general take a gloomy view of things,' he wrote – not entirely accurately – 'but I confess that, knowing all I do, I cannot see what is to save the Church, or property, or colonies, or union with Ireland, or eventually monarchy if the Reform Bill passes.'[19]

The tide in the early summer of 1831 proved to be too strong for the opponents of Reform and certainly Lytton's advice to his mother was tactically correct. The new Parliament which was summoned for 14 June contained Members overwhelmingly in favour of Reform – in the House of Commons, that is. The hereditary House of Lords was another matter: what the Whigs called 'the frightful superior-ity of our enemy' – the inbuilt Tory majority in the Upper House, compounded by the Tory creations of George III – continued to be a source of anticipatory concern.[20] What would happen if this House absolutely refused to pass a Bill which had been endorsed by the Com-mons? There was one radical solution which Grey discussed with Lord Holland in a letter as early as 2 June. That was the creation of new peers by the Sovereign. That, of course, immediately raised the ques-tion of how many peers would be necessary to secure a majority; at this point Grey mentioned a mere half-dozen. This would be followed by the second – vital – question of King William's reaction to such a request. Would he refuse? *Could* he refuse and still expect to retain in his service a lawfully elected Government which had made the request?

Various calculations concerning the new Parliament have suggested that in the Commons there was a potential majority of between 130 and 140, although, as one authority has written, 'Figures are less precise than under a system of sharply defined parties.' The calculations of John Wilson Croker came up with 380 in favour and 250 against, with the rest undecided.[21]

There were casualties, of course. Lord Palmerston, the Foreign Secretary, was one of them. As one of those brought into Grey's Government to underline its character of coalition. Reform was not a personal preoccupation, although he believed in it. For the time being, he was able to pursue his patriotic agenda abroad without too much interference; in August 1831 he admitted that it might have been different if everybody had not been 'so entirely engrossed' in domestic affairs.[22] However, his detachment did not prevent him from losing his seat at the University of Cambridge. Although one voter talked of subversion of the Church and State, others acknowledged the need for Reform, but rather differently implemented.

With characteristic *hauteur* Palmerston described the upset after twenty years of tenure as 'a terrible bore'; he complained lightly that 'all the anti-reformers in England are concentrated in Cambridge; there is no end of them here'. By contemporary standards, it seemed convenient rather than ironic that he was found a seat at Bletchingley in Surrey, a rotten borough for which much money had to be paid – one of the seats on the list to be disenfranchised when and if the Reform Bill was passed.

On 24 June Lord John Russell introduced the Second Reform Bill in the House of Commons; he was now, like Edward Stanley, in the Cabinet.[23] This new Bill was only very lightly modified from the previous one, even though members of the Cabinet like Palmerston and Stanley would have been happy with further concessions. It remained sufficiently intact for it to be regarded still as nothing but the Bill. Counties would not now be divided and single-Member constituencies were not for the time being envisaged. One suggested modification concerning eligibility would have substantially reduced the number of voters in places like Birmingham. The £10 franchise voter was going to be limited to those who paid their rates at six-monthly intervals or longer. A letter of remonstrance from Attwood to Grey secured its deletion – an example of how seriously the Whigs took their middle-class supporters in the provinces.[24]

Russell moved, he said, a measure in the name of the Government which, 'in their opinion, is calculated to maintain unimpaired the prerogatives of the crown, the authority of both Houses of Parliament, and the rights and liberties of the people of this kingdom'. Among the possible obstacles he listed, with a hint of menace, were 'those most dangerous weapons, unwarranted and slanderous as they were, which imputed to the Sovereign . . . a will different from that of his constitutional advisers'. But he had nothing but praise for the people of England: 'the sacrifices made and the devotedness shown in the recent election'. Certainly this was an election in which passion had been displayed – but it was 'a noble passion', love of country.

If this was the point of view of the Government, that of the Opposition was expressed by Sir Robert Peel on 6 July.[25] He began with some general criticisms, denouncing the frequent use of quotations from this great authority and that, such as Bacon and Burke; whenever he heard these citations, 'I know that sometimes in the next page, and more frequently in the same, a passage might be found, which, if taken separately, might be relied upon as an authority for opposite doctrines': one example he gave was that of Clarendon on Cromwell, which could be taken in many different ways. But Peel's main message was this: 'I have been uniformly opposed to Reform upon principle, because I was unwilling to open a door which I saw no prospect of being able to close. In short, the advantages of such a measure were not sufficient to counterbalance the evil of altering the constitution of Parliament, and agitating the public mind on the question of Reformation.' Peel acknowledged that the feeling of the country was currently in favour of Reform, but questioned whether the excitement would not soon die down. As for Russell's reference to the Sovereign having the same will as his constitutional advisers, Peel showed his own hint of menace when he attacked 'the lavish use of His Majesty's name'.

This was an intense period of debate and late-night argument in the House of Commons, as the Bill went towards the Committee stage. Outside this narrow world, society had its own preoccupations. There was for example the chilling news of the arrival of cholera in the country – *cholera morbus* or Asiatic cholera – coming from Russia. It had made its first appearance during the previous November; by June 1831 there was general alarm at the idea of an epidemic. Although the capital was as yet untouched, Macaulay told his sister Hannah in July that the great topic in London was cholera, not Reform.[26] There, the vast population of British dog-lovers were also busy being concerned over the new edict of the royal Duke of Sussex, appointed King's Ranger of Hyde Park. In order to avoid disturbance to the deer, and preserve the does and fawns, all dogs found in Hyde Park were to be summarily shot by the keepers. The executions were said to be indiscriminate, from ladies' lapdogs to huge Newfoundland dogs. As a change from wrangles about Reform, there were protests in the House of Commons, emphasizing the danger from the shootings to the children playing there, to say nothing of the horses; Daniel O'Connell, that lover of liberty in all its forms, joined in the attack on the keepers.

This was a diversion. The country as a whole basked in magic weather; at one point the Tory Lord Ellenborough, a close friend of the Duke of Wellington, noted in his Diary that it was 'very hot and quite beautiful', adding a pointed reference to last year's French Revolution: 'It is the anniversary of the first of the *glorious* days which have produced so much mischief in Europe.' For the MPs conditions were much less idyllic as they argued on the great issue, seemingly without end, in the stifling heat of their cramped and old-fashioned abode. (In such conditions, predicted Stanley, MPs would start dying off – although in fact he underestimated the toughness of the breed and there were no deaths.)[27] Late-night – or rather early-morning – sittings were the norm; irritability grew to a new high as the parties took to drafting in fresh Members after dawn broke, who returned to the attack with zest, to the horror of their sleep-deprived opponents. The Bill passed on 7 July with a majority of 136.

Attempts to scupper the Bill from going to Committee had included the use of counsel arguing against the disenfranchisement of Appleby in Westmoreland in Schedule A (boroughs which lost all their Members). If this objection had been sustained, all the disenfranchised boroughs could have claimed the same privilege and the delay in going to Committee – the object of the exercise – would have been infinite. The argument was that the Reform Bill was a Bill of Pains and Penalties, to which Althorp sturdily replied that no bill could be so called with any show of justice, whose only aim was the public benefit. The Opposition queried any decision which was not based on hearing counsel. Nevertheless the motion was denied by a majority of 97 – at seven-thirty in the morning. It was in the spirit of these endless dawn wranglings that Sir John Brydges, an ancient Tory MP, threw ridicule on the whole drawn-out filibustering process by proposing simply to draw lots whether to adjourn or not. Sir Denis Le Marchant, who lived through it, certainly had a point when he described the process as 'this dreary warfare'.[28]

In all this Lord Althorp, stout figure of integrity that he was, played an important part as Leader of the House, while bemoaning the circumstances which kept him away from his country estate (and his prize bulls). Althorp's reaction to a performance by the great violinist Paganini at St James's Palace sums up his discomfort in London society. 'He certainly made every noise that could be made with a fiddle, and a great many more than I ever heard before,' but once was enough, wrote Althorp: 'I never wish to hear him again.' Regarding politics he told his father: 'I hate my situation more and more every day, and really go down to the House of Commons as if I was going to execution.' Yet Althorp confided to a friend that, although it was all he could do not to drive right away when his carriage came to fetch him, once in the *mêlée* of the House he recovered his spirits.[29] In a meeting of 350 Whigs held on 11 July at the Foreign Office, Althorp made his feelings about the relative importance of various procedures clear. He asked the MPs never to leave the House; they were there to support the Government with votes, not speeches.

Let us not forget that Althorp's sport of choice was prizefighting; in short he was an excellent example of that apparently reluctant English pugnacity captured in the music hall song written half a century later by G.W. Hunt: 'We don't want to fight, but by jingo if we do. . . .' In this way, he would sometimes find himself speaking twenty times in one night at the Committee stage; at which point physical resilience – which he certainly had – became at least one important quality for a politician. Althorp also cheered himself up with the optimistic thought that the Commons was slightly more bearable in the summer, because the windows were kept open for relief. Others simply shuddered at the hot, dirty, dusty air which wafted through them.

In the royal rituals of the summer, there was an outward semblance at least of that political neutrality which the Crown was supposed to maintain. On 25 July William IV visited Eton College to attend 'Election speeches' (the reference was to the school, not the national arena). One of those in attendance was the Whig Cabinet Minister Lord Holland, who had been at Eton for nine years. In his Diary he showed himself in the characteristic nostalgic mood of any visitor to his old school: 'the weather was fine, the scene was gay, and to us all [the many Old Etonians present including Lord Durham, Lord Melbourne and Lord Grey himself] the recollections a mixed emotion of pleasure and melancholy.' He was especially moved by the numerous portraits of himself and friends in early youth, 'some no more and some so altered'.[30]

Nostalgia apart, it could certainly be argued that at Eton the homogeneity of English society at the top was demonstrated. It was true that the Provost, Joseph Goodall, incumbent for the last twenty years and showing 'excessive and foolish delight' at the royal presence, was a pronounced Tory. But Lord Holland noted that 'the most remarkable feature was the dexterity and impartiality with which praise was distributed to Etonians, Whig or Tory, statesmen or warriors, and the ingenious choice of avoiding the appearance of party by clapping the names of Wellington and Grey, as the two living Premiers in one line.'* It was whispered to Holland that the head boy who achieved

---

* *Floreat Etona* – let Eton flourish, as the school's motto had it, whatever the administration.

this feat was a Tory; the Whig names had been inserted against his inclination at the request of the Masters. 'But a boy of Tory principles,' reflected Holland the lofty Whig, 'should learn, no doubt, to submit to authority.'

A week later there was a more public demonstration of that same 'excessive and foolish delight' evinced by the Provost of Eton at the royal presence. William IV, accompanied by Queen Adelaide, travelled by barge to declare the new London Bridge officially open. The fact that the royal couple scattered silver medals among the people certainly did not detract from the popular joy. However, on this occasion political prejudices did play their part. Wellington – 'somewhat uncourteously', as Lord Holland thought – refused to attend. The Whig story was that he did so, pretending the people might salute him in preference to the Sovereign; Lord Ellenborough was probably closer to the truth when he wrote that the Duke declined because 'he had been in November informed that his going into the City would endanger the peace'.[31] As it was, Sir Robert Peel, who was made of sterner stuff, did attend and in consequence was hooted at by the people. In general, 'the contrast of the poor old bridge with the magnificent new structure', according to Sir John Hobhouse, was very striking. William IV himself said he had never seen anything like it, as he looked down the long vista. John Doyle commemorated what was said to be an actual incident in one of his drawings ten days later.[32] The Duke of Cumberland, standing with a group of eminent right-wing Tories including Lord Londonderry and Lord Eldon, told the Duke of Devonshire that he had come to the wrong barge: 'All here are against you.' To which Devonshire was said to have replied: 'Well, if you all here are against me, all there are against *you*.' And he pointed to the huge multitude of spectators thronging the banks of the river, stretching as far as the eye could see.

The next day, 2 August, William came in person to the House of Lords to give his assent to the Queen's dower-bill. This made financial provision for the royal widow in the event of the King's death. (Constitutionally, it was not essential for the Sovereign to be present in the House of Lords in order to give his assent; as time would show, this mark of favour could not be taken for granted but on this occasion the King was determined to make a show of his approval.) Adelaide herself was conducted into the House of Lords, preceded by her Lord Chamberlain, Earl Howe. She sat on a chair of state covered in red velvet, to the right of the King's throne but level with it, and at the end made obeisance three times.[33] On this occasion the King was as usual much pleased by the degree of applause; it was little Prince George of Cambridge, he who had already questioned the Queen about the oddity of what his uncle had done, who cowered behind Lord Albemarle for protection, not realizing that he was hearing the sounds of acclaim.

There had been no need for any equivalent ceremony for seventy years since the days of Queen Charlotte, and Lord Holland at any rate found the whole occasion 'indelicate if not distressing', despite the popular enthusiasm for the monarch. It was a reaction which reminds one of the continuous concern about the King's health – based on his family record of survival as well as his father's long madness – for just as William had, for liberals, turned out to be a vast improvement on George IV, so it was feared that little Victoria, in the power of her baleful mother the Duchess of Kent, might blight their hopes of Reform. It was the same threat of the personal to the political as was experienced in a lesser way by the Whigs over the health of Earl Spencer; there were sinister reports of his deterioration in late July; his death would automatically elevate Lord Althorp in his father's title to the House of Lords, leaving the House of Commons without a popular figure of management at this vital moment.[34]

There were private stresses too: Durham's relationship with his father-in-law Grey was beginning to be profoundly affected by the piteous condition of Durham's elder son, Master Charles Lambton. The thirteen-year-old boy, immortalized in Lawrence's famous portrait 'The Red Boy', showing him in all his romantic innocence, was wasting away from tuberculosis; he spent the summer at Marine Square, Brighton, in a vain attempt to restore his unrestorable health. Grey alternated between presiding over the political ferment centred on Downing Street and visiting him at Brighton; the devoted grandfather was struck by the almost unbearable stoicism of the boy. Durham, a dedicated reformer, was also a frenzied and in many ways unbalanced character; already, as has been seen, he enjoyed the kind of troubled relationship with his father-in-law common to those who first designate an older man a father figure, and then proceed to resent his paternal authority. An element of emotional blackmail was creeping in as the poor boy grew ever sicker, yet the beneficiary, if any, was the cause of Reform about which Durham felt so passionately.

As the date of the coronation approached at the end of the first week of September, MPs were ragged with their debating in Committee, while the country simmered with enthusiasm for Reform. For all the forty separate sittings, the only major modification concerned the so-called Chandos clause. Lord Chandos, heir to the Duke of Buckingham, sat for a seat in Buckinghamshire. On 18 August he carried an amendment which enfranchised £50 tenant farmers in the county constituencies, thus enhancing the prospect of the landlords maintaining that influence which they had long considered their right.

Outside the narrow enclave of Westminster there was – not for the first or last time in history – the sound of apprehensive wailings in the financial sector; at the end of August one banker informed Ellenborough of the lack of confidence in the City, and the Tory peer had already heard that James Rothschild had withdrawn from English funds.[35] Nevertheless true reformers felt that conditions could and surely would be alleviated by the passing of the Reform Bill – that is, if the House of Lords permitted it.

On 26 August Althorp wrote gloomily to his father in the country that the Government had 'little chance' in the House of Lords, even allowing for those extra peers created, not for political reasons but according to custom, to mark the formal ceremony of crowning.[36] At a Cabinet meeting on 5 September, there was no unanimity on the subject: the Duke of Richmond argued forcefully against such a creation, backed by the 'timid counsel' of Stanley, also by Lansdowne, Goderich and Palmerston – in short, exactly that coalition element coming mainly from Canningite Tories which had been so valuable to the Whig Government. In this atmosphere of tension, even within the Cabinet, the Bill finally passed its prolonged Committee stage at seven p.m. on 7 September and the country gave itself up to the glories – economical glories – of the coronation. John Gilpin paused in his flight long enough to take the sacred oath, which even the reluctant William IV admitted was of vital importance in the contract between a sovereign and his people.

CHAPTER EIGHT

CONFOUND THEIR POLITICS

'Confound their politics
Frustrate their knavish tricks' –

Sung at a Whig dinner, 25 September 1831

On 8 September at long last that coronation, so much resented and criticized by the King, took place. Whatever William's private feelings, the rejoicing in the country was almost universal. For days beforehand newspapers had been advertising apartments with a view of the procession (there were also tickets available to the public for seats inside the Abbey). On the day itself, the cries of 'God Save the King' seemed endless, in the words of *The Times*, 'As far as the eye could reach, hats, hankies and flags were waving in the air.'[1]

The report added: 'It must not pass unnoticed that the word *Reform* mingled with the loudest shouts that greeted the monarch's ear.' The dark, boarded-up windows of Londonderry House, punished for its owner's hardline opinions, were another reminder that the issue was ever present. But in general the coronation was thought to demonstrate one salient fact about the national character: 'Of all people on the face of the earth, the people of England are a King-loving generation.' The vision of well-dressed young women in their best bonnets and frocks, gradually getting swallowed up by the crowd, where only their piercing screams saved them, was thought to add to the gaiety of the occasion; as the poor young things emerged, the sight of their crushed costumes and bonnets 'twisted into fantastic shapes' was greeted with good-natured laughter.

There was certainly a huge contrast between this delirious reception and the one which had greeted George IV ten years earlier. This time the hisses and groans which Peel had received at London Bridge were reserved for the Duke of Cumberland – which, given his well-known Ultra Tory views, was a good way of indicating approval for the Whigs. Enthusiasm was not limited to the capital: the Birmingham Political Union, for example, held a so-called monarchical dinner in honour of the occasion at the Globe Inn; under Attwood's expert management, expressions of opinion were limited to approval of the Sovereign.[2] The odd complaint about the cost was not anything that ruling systems must not inevitably endure. The barber who told his client, while cutting his hair, 'we want a cheap government like America and we will have it' was in this great tradition of popular grumbling. In the same way, Croker's suggestion that the young Princess Victoria might one day find herself to be plain Miss Guelph was in the equally great tradition of pessimistic upper-class prophecy. The fact that the Duchess of Kent wilfully kept the heiress presumptive to the throne away from the ceremony did more harm to the thirteen-year-old girl's image than any lavish stories of splendour.

In any case, when it came to the details William had not budged in his emphasis on economy. Only a few weeks earlier, he had expostulated once more on the subject: 'the Solemnity' of a coronation, as he put it, might have been useful in its time but was 'ill adapted to ours', and the expense it involved 'in the present circumstances of the country and those of Europe most idle and unnecessary'. The result was summed up by Greville as designed to 'cost as little money and as little trouble as possible'. Macaulay made fun of it all: 'The Archbishop mumbled, the Bishop of London preached well enough but not so effectively as the occasion required . . . and the King behaved very awkwardly, his bearing making the foolish parts of the ritual appear monstrously ridiculous.' It was the Whig grandee the Duke of Devonshire, commented Macaulay, who looked as if he came to be crowned, instead of his master.[3]

All the same, the cost was only just over £43,000 (roughly £4,300,000) as compared to that of his predecessor at more than five times that figure.[4] Peers wore their parliamentary robes, which undermined the opportunity for conspicuous consumption in ordering new ones. The ushers in Westminster Abbey were volunteers who paid for their own costumes. A single fiddler on a single string was thought the cheapest way of accompanying the anthem. The Tory press was in addition horrified when William insisted on doing away with the procession, which led to the abolition of some hereditary offices.

William IV's annotated copy of the proposed coronation ritual has been described by an authority as resembling 'a battlefield'.[5] The King felt particularly strongly on the subject of the anointing; he wanted no one to wipe away oil from his head: 'I will not be smeared,' he told Lord Holland. There were all sorts of simplifications and cost-cutting changes. George IV had aimed to eclipse Napoleon's coronation as Emperor in 1804; William IV on the other hand did not even have the crown itself remodelled – it was merely padded. (Queen Adelaide, however, scorned the idea of the crown once used for Mary of Modena, Catholic wife of James II, and announced she would have one made up for herself out of jewels belonging to the late Queen Charlotte.) The ceremony, termed the 'Penny coronation' or the 'half-crownation' by wags, was in direct contrast to that of George IV in another way: this time the Sovereign did not occupy his time ogling his mistress, Lady Conyngham, both in the Abbey and afterwards. On the other hand, William IV's lewd toast at the post-coronation dinner was gleefully reported by Greville, one of those less than happy incidents when the spirit of the old sailor took over from that of the new King. William toasted killing eyes and moving thighs, before celebrating another part of the body by rhyming *le cul qui danse* with *honi soit qui mal y pense*.[6]

During the more formal part of the day there was one significant new prayer, in contrast to the many cuts: 'The Lord give you a faithful Senate, wise Counsellors and magistrates, loyal nobility, dutiful gentry . . . ' it ran. One can easily believe that this prayer found a heartfelt echo in the royal breast. It remained to be seen in the coming weeks whether the Senate was indeed so faithful – especially that part of the Senate known as the House of Lords.

The third reading of the Bill took place on 21 September and the House of Commons finally passed it at five o'clock the next morning. The majority was unequivocal: 345 in favour to 236 against. The Tories were not however showing any signs of conceding the case.

Where the House of Lords was concerned, the destination of the Bill in October, this was ominous. Only the day before the vote, Sir Robert Peel had expatiated at length on the characteristics of tyrants through the ages, citing Napoleon under the name of 'Boney'; Cromwell, that ever popular source of historical parallel at this time, as Peel himself had pointed out earlier; and the French Assembly of 1791: in each case these tyrants had *pretended* to preserve the outward form of things, in order to transform the substance. And the Tory leader in the Commons proceeded to quote *Macbeth:*

> Upon his head they placed a fruitless crown
> And put a barren sceptre in his grip.

The reference was to the witches' prophecy that Banquo would be father to a line of kings, while Macbeth would have no heirs; Macbeth was mocked with the emblems of power but the reality was transferred away.[7]

Publicly, the triumphant Whigs and their allies were not disturbed by these fearful predictions. There were Whig dinners. One celebration of over 250 people was given in the Hall of the Worshipful Company of Stationers, to which all the various individuals who had backed Reform were invited. In the Chair was Sir Francis Burdett, in his kaleidoscopic character illustrating the various elements which made up the reforming movement at this time. Burdett, with a magnificent patrician nose to rival that of the Duke of Wellington, looked what he was: 'a thoroughly high bred gentleman' in the words of Sir Denis Le Marchant. He was a hereditary baronet, and after a dashing youth as the lover of Lady Oxford, had married Sophia Coutts, a member of the banking family (their daughter Angela Burdett-Coutts would be the celebrated philanthropist). First in a seat paid for by his Coutts father-in-law, and later as MP for Westminster, Burdett had been in Parliament for nearly forty years; but there were interruptions. Burdett was a born subversive, sacked from Westminster School when young, a frequenter of Paris in the early idealistic days of the Revolution, then imprisoned in the Tower of London for breach of parliamentary privilege, finally sent to the Marshalsea Prison after Peterloo for protesting about the massacres and the 'bloody Neroes' who were responsible.[8]

Perhaps Burdett summed up his own character best when he described its finest part as being 'a strong feeling of indignation at injustice and oppression and a lively sympathy with the sufferings of my fellows'. Naturally Burdett had been an early and passionate advocate of Reform. At the same time that paternalistic side of his nature, which made Whigs call him a Tory and Tories a Whig – as he himself joked – led him to see the Crown as the natural protector of the poor. This certainly made him an appropriate Chairman for this particular occasion. It was notable that 'God Save the King' was sung with particular vigour, with special emphasis on the lines concerning the scattering of his (and their) enemies:

> Confound their politicks
> Frustrate their knavish tricks
> On Thee our hopes we fix
> God Save the King!

Lord Althorp, he whose easy, unforced manner of management had been responsible for so much of the successful outcome of the 'dreary warfare', in Le Marchant's phrase, made various speeches to his colleagues. His style was to be brief: 'I have never been ambitious of power, or of high degree,' declared Althorp, one of the few Ministers who could say such a thing with conviction, 'but I have been, am still, ambitious of that popularity which is the true result of an honest and consistent discharge of public duty.' How, he asked, had the recent happy result been obtained? Certainly by the support of the men before him, but also by 'the support of the people of England'.[9] This was the Whig philosophy which needed to be emphasized, in case the cause of Reform, now officially sailing forward, was threatened by shipwreck some time in the future.

As for the people of England themselves at this juncture, much was anticipated with regard to the passing of the Bill – and much was feared by the men who were their rulers. In particular the rising number of trade unions were the subject of apprehension. The idea of

workmen combining to secure better working hours and more appropriate wages, together with limiting the right of entry to a profession,
went right back to the medieval craft guilds. It was in the eighteenth
century that the potentially dangerous – to the employers – idea of
combination among workers led to a series of so-called Combination
Acts. Repealed in 1824, they were replaced the next year by measures
intended to limit at the very least this kind of activity. In the autumn of
1831, therefore, it was not absolutely clear either to the authorities or
the uniting workers what might be legal and what was not. Although
the Birmingham Political Union, founded late in 1829, led the way
and continued to act as a template, there were many others, not all
necessarily with that commitment to non-violent protest on which the
charismatic Thomas Attwood insisted.

A significant figure in the Radical movement at this stage in his
ambivalence towards protest was Joseph Parkes. He had been born
in Warwick and moved to Birmingham in 1822, playing a role in the
earlier attempts to enfranchise it. On several occasions this 'shrewd
little fellow', in Carlyle's description, had acted as an election agent.
On the one hand Parkes, a disciple of Jeremy Bentham, regarded Francis Place as his 'political father' from whom he, as 'a raw miseducated
boy', learnt much that was '*sound* and *honest*'. He abandoned hopes of
a life at the Chancery Bar in London when his father's business failed,
but his air of erudite intelligence common to that profession remained;
that enabled a local paper to sneer at him in 1828 as possessing 'the
light of wisdom ting'd by folly's shade', in the words of a satirical
poem, *Chancery Court*, published shortly before.[10]

On the other hand Parkes had originally deplored the founding of
the Birmingham Political Union as 'ill-contrived and worse timed'. Sus-
pecting that Attwood rated currency reform above that of Parliament,
he described the Union as a 'burning lava of red hot radicalism' which
'devastated the fair field of reform'. Then he threw his energies and his
dissenting idealism into supporting it (and if necessary modifying it). In
May 1831 he wrote that, although he was a Radical and 'may be a Republican in the year 1900, if by the grace of God I so long live [he would
have been 104] I am a great advocate for the respect of caste and order'.

On 30 September Parkes organized a Birmingham meeting with the stirring declaration: 'if the Lords throw out the Bill, the question of the utility of the hereditary peerage will infallibly arise.'[11] The King's prerogative (to create peers) was not an ornament but something for use. There was a subtle change here – even a hint of a threat – from the loyal declaration of the previous December, when William IV was thanked for getting rid of Wellington, and 'entire confidence' was placed in his 'wisdom, patriotism and firmness'. But Parkes, with his lightly balanced scales dipping between a desire for progress and respect for the status quo, stood for many sincere men, both governors and governed, at this delicate moment.

From the opposite point of view, Lord Melbourne, as Home Secretary, had his own concerns. He was in touch with the King's secretary, Sir Herbert Taylor, immediately after the Bill passed through the Commons. 'So far as I can learn,' wrote Melbourne, 'the political unions are undoubtedly extending themselves, increasing their numbers and completing their arrangements' in case the Bill was defeated. He believed that plans to resist taxes while preserving the peace – an interesting challenge in itself – were constantly discussed. Melbourne, by no means an ardent reformer, reported 'the most serious fears' of those who knew the people well, of the consequences of rejecting the measure of Reform.[12]

As a matter of fact, Melbourne was indirectly in touch with Radical opinion: he used his younger brother, the MP George Lamb, to make contact with the agitator-cum-tailor Francis Place. In good Whig fashion, Melbourne had appointed Lamb Under Secretary at the Home Office and his spokesman in the House of Commons. Lamb was a rumbustious fellow – 'very diverting' in Macaulay's estimation – who had defended the use of force by the military at Merthyr in June on the grounds that it was necessary to maintain public order; but he was sound generally on the need for Reform.[13] Immediately after the Government was formed in November 1830, Lamb had been used by Melbourne to ask Francis Place to calm down the Swing rioters; that overture had not worked but the connection, via Lamb's own Private Secretary, Thomas Young, existed.

*

The great debate starting in the House of Lords on 3 October began inauspiciously with a squabble between two marquesses: Cleveland quarrelled with Londonderry over a petition from Durham for Reform.[14] Londonderry was sure the inhabitants of Durham at large 'by no means partook of these sentiments', to which Cleveland retorted that there was no counter-petition to be considered. But Londonderry was not done yet. The Duke of Sussex now presented a petition from merchants, bankers, traders and so forth of Bristol: nearly 26,000 names altogether. Care had been taken, the Duke reported, that none of those who had signed were under sixteen. Londonderry jumped up and announced that he had received certain knowledge from a correspondent that 5,000 or 6,000 of the signatures were fake. But the petitions rolled on: there were for example over 33,000 signatures from Manchester, and lesser amounts from towns throughout the country from South Shields in the north-east to Weymouth on the south coast. Finally the bickering ceased.

Lord Grey now rose to his feet and moved the second reading of the Reform Bill in the House of Lords. He was, however, a man only very recently pierced by the personal tragedy so long feared – none the easier to bear for that. On 24 September, Durham's son Charles Lambton, Grey's favourite grandchild, gave up his struggle to survive tuberculosis and died. Grey was devastated. To Princess Lieven he uttered the heartbreaking cry of the old who have survived the young: 'Why did the blow fall on this heavenly boy, while I and so many others who would be no loss to the world are spared?'

The pathetic funeral *cortège* of the thirteen-year-old boy was actually passing north as the devastated grandfather rose to speak. Perhaps it was appropriate under the circumstances that his 'grave and beautiful eloquence' was felt by the young Gladstone, intently listening to every debate for nine or ten hours a day, to be that of 'an older time';* there were surviving Members of the House of Lords who were

* This connection makes for an interesting historical link: the youthful Grey had listened to Pitt the Younger as Prime Minister when he was first in Parliament in 1786; Gladstone's last premiership ended in 1894.

reminded of their own youth as they listened to the rippling, majestic oratory emanating from the sixty-seven-year-old Prime Minister.[15]

'In the course of a long political life,' began Grey, a phrase he was certainly entitled to use, given that he had entered Parliament as MP for Northumberland forty-five years earlier. Then he had to sit down.[16] He was evidently labouring to master strong emotion – the consciousness of that sad little coffin travelling north was too much for him. Recovering, Grey described himself as the advocate of principles from which he had never swerved, and declared boldly that if Reform had sometimes appeared to 'slumber' – a convenient way of dealing with the twists and turns of its history, including his own participation – it had never slept. There were cheers and counter-cheers. Grey then reminded his audience of that 'imprudent declaration', Wellington's denunciation in principle of 'all Reform whatever', before pointing out that he himself had only accepted office from the King on condition that he could bring in 'a measure of peace, safety and conciliation' – in short, Reform.

Yet 'men of learning and character have actually been found elsewhere', continued Grey, who have 'gravely' told their audience that unless Members of the House of Commons were allowed to be 'the nominees of Peers, of loan contractors, and of speculating attorneys, rather than the Representatives of the people, all security for the happiness, the prosperity, and the liberty we enjoy, will fall from under us'. Was this really to be the case in modern times, 'in this hour – in the nineteenth century – when the schoolmaster is abroad, and when the growing intelligence of all classes of the community is daily and hourly receiving new lights?' Grey would have supposed that the mere mention of nomination would have brought about 'universal derision and contempt'.

In the course of a long speech, the Prime Minister made prolonged excursions into past history: the Spanish Netherlands, the execution of King Charles I, the deposition of James II, the loss of British America, the extinction of the old French monarchy under Louis XVI with 'the utter sweeping off of the French nobility as a power in the State' – all found mention, all were cited as examples of the tragedies which occurred when the will of the people was ignored. It was, wrote *The Times* afterwards, 'a grave, dignified, earnest and impressive speech', in other words 'a model of luminous statement'.[17]

Grey did not receive universal acclaim from his fellow peers, as he had hardly expected to do. When he touched on the suggestion, made by some Lords, that removing the nominations was 'an act of spoliation and robbery', there were loud cries of 'Hear, hear!' Grey responded swiftly: the right to nominate MPs was 'not property but a trust'. As to the argument that the present system worked well enough, there was one vital thing it had not achieved: it had not 'conciliated the affections and feelings of the people'. Witness the fact that petitions on the subject of Reform had been presented 'to an extent which, I believe, was never equalled on any other occasion'. If his opponents in the Lords still doubted the sentiments of the people, still imagined that this anxiety for Reform would pass away, he conjured them: 'do not lay that flattering unction to your souls!'

A particularly serious passage in Grey's speech – from the point of view of the future – was what he designated an address to 'the Prelates'. Bishops – the Lords Spiritual as opposed to the Lords Temporal – were by ancient historical tradition Members of the House of Lords, some *ex officio* such as the Archbishops of Canterbury and York, others by appointment; there was a long-standing connection between the Church of England and the Tory Party, parallel to the Whig connection to dissent. There were of course clerics who were 'good Whigs', in the revealing phrase of Lord Holland, drawing up a document for Lord Grey which discussed various clerical claims to preferment. (To be 'a thorough old Whig' was the highest praise and there was a conspicuous lack of emphasis on spiritual values.)[18] But once again it must be remembered how long the Tories had been more or less exclusively in office. During this period 'good Whigs' were not first in line for promotion. Under the circumstances, there had been dire predictions from some Tories that the Church of England as well as the monarchy – all part of the established order – would be threatened by Reform.

Contemporary attacks on the bishops were not infrequent, suggesting that they were a set of worldly men ignoring their pastoral function. From their point of view, the bishops upheld anti-revolutionary values to the general benefit of a hierarchical society. Critics of the Anglican Church took a different line: here was a politicized extension of the State (with the Sovereign as its supreme governor). Attacks ranged from the crude designation of them as 'black locusts', to Francis Place's more florid malediction – 'luxurious, rich, overbearing, and benumbing'. Then there was Sydney Smith's characteristic barb that the bishops deserved to be 'preached to death by wild curates'. The fact was that the need to pay Church tithes – literally a tax for the support of the Church – caused much unpopularity for obvious reasons at times of economic distress. One John Saville, thought by some to be Captain Swing himself, was responsible for such 'inflammatory' notices as this: 'Oh ye Church of England Parsons, who strain at a gnat and swallow a camel, woe woe woe be unto you, ye shall one day have your reward.' Among the lower classes, it was not forgotten that a clergyman had actually read the Riot Act at Peterloo.[19] And where the higher echelons of the Church were concerned, so many 'Prelates' had of course votes in the House of Lords.

The current Archbishop of Canterbury, William Howley, was in his mid-sixties like the King and Grey, and had been appointed in 1828. A strong opponent of Catholic Emancipation, as also of that repeal of the Test and Corporation Acts which allowed offices previously disbarred to dissenters, Howley was a man whose strong religious convictions made him highly conservative in his politics. For the Whigs his was not a reassuring presence on the ecclesiastical benches. No one could accuse Archbishop Howley of being a thorough old Whig, although his spiritual values, in the tradition of High Churchmen since the seventeenth-century Caroline divines, were not in doubt.

Addressing the prelates as he moved towards a conclusion, Lord Grey implored them to consider what would happen to their standing in the country if the Bill was demonstrably rejected by *their* votes. Were they not 'the ministers of peace'? So their actions should lead in the direction of peace. He ended not in the pastures of the Church, but where the true rocks of Reform lay. Grey announced fairly and squarely that he was not prepared to compromise, putting an end to the hopes of moderate Tories in that direction. Nor would he submit to them any 'delusive' measure of Reform. It was the Bill and the whole Bill. 'My Lords,' he said, 'I have now done.'

In Birmingham on the same day, the Union held a meeting on Newhall Hill. Shops and factories closed early for the event, bells rang and flags were to be seen in every hand with slogans such as 'William IV – the People's Hope' and 'Earl Grey – the just rights of our order secured, we will then stand by his order'. Newhall Hill, certainly a more salubrious setting than the crammed and claustrophobic Chamber of the House of Lords, was to prove a crucial environment for the all-important protests of the Birmingham Political Union; Joseph Parkes described it as 'a natural amphitheatre on twelve acres of rising ground', although a placard of sale three years later showed it to be something less than half of that. Parkes also erred on the side of generosity when he estimated the crowd on this occasion as 100,000; it was probably more like 30,000, although sceptics went even lower.[20] *

All the same, whatever the numbers, this was a cheerful crowd, dressed up as though for a gala day, with plenty of women present, some in bonnets, others in practical shawls. There was also loud patriotic music, which must have been easier for the crowds to hear than the actual words of the speeches, despite the favourable slant of the hill. *The Times* wrote that there never was 'we may safely assert, any previous occasion upon which such a deep and universal excitement pervaded the public mind of Birmingham and its neighbourhood'; it was the most important public meeting since 1688 (a report later copied in the *Birmingham Journal* and the *Scotsman*).[22]

In his speech, Attwood cited with a flourish the Marquis de Lafayette forty years ago: 'for a nation to be free, it is sufficient that she wills it.' He then asked the whole assembly, having bowed their heads,

---

* Such figures are a perpetual subject of debate between the demonstrators and the demonstrated-against; according to the formula of an experienced magistrate in Manchester, cited by one authority, under these circumstances 6,000–7,000 persons fitted to an acre. The peculiar geography of this historic place, rising ground virtually in the midst of a shopping district, can still be seen today, although unmarked by any memorial.[21]

to 'look up to the Heavens', where the just God ruled both Heaven and Earth and cry 'God bless the King'. Everyone present duly uncovered their heads and shouted out in enthusiastic acclamation of their Sovereign. All this was in line with the Radical medals now beginning to be struck: Thomas Attwood's fine profile might be on one side of the medal, but on the other the words 'God Save the King', with protestations of loyalty, would be found. The next day the Birmingham Political Union's petition to the House of Lords was presented by the Lord Chancellor, Lord Brougham, along with seventy-nine others.

The expressions of loyalty to William IV among the reformers were almost universal; as at the Whig dinner, the confounded politics of opposition were contrasted with loyalty to the Sovereign. Yet in Whig circles an uneasiness was beginning to be felt about the King's precise stance, as Grey reported privately. It was of course all a question of that cloud on the horizon, creation of peers for a particular political purpose, as opposed to the traditional coronation creations, which had gone off smoothly. *The Times* for one, with its excellent contacts (preeminent among them the indiscreet maverick Lord Brougham), picked up on this development.

As the debate itself was in progress, it ran a story expressing sympathy for the King as being in a difficult position. The 'female part of his family' were said to differ generally from him in opinion on the important question of reform. *'Heaven bless the amiable babblers!'* exclaimed the patriarchal newspaper, hoping they would all live to see the happy effects of that measure to which they now fancied themselves averse. In general, of course, 'petticoat politicians' were not to be heeded and *The Times* consoled itself with the thought that the King, as a sailor, was used to separating himself 'by whole seas' from the persons to whom he was most attached.[23] This begged the question as to what would happen when the King was not so much separated by whole seas from his family, as marooned in their midst.

In the meantime the importance of what was happening in the Lords was signified by 'a somewhat unusual circumstance', in the discreet terminology of Hansard. It had been usual for one or two, even as many as half a dozen peeresses, escaping the uncomfortable Ventilator above, to attend the actual Chamber, in a small part of the space below the bar, protected and screened by a curtain. But now a considerable number of peeresses, their daughters and relations, attended every evening, occupying a considerable portion of the space below the Bar, where chairs were placed for them. (The young Gladstone, who noted this phenomenon, thought Lady Grey the most beautiful of them all.) So far, so good but, 'as might perhaps be expected' went on Hansard, 'they displayed all the enthusiastic ardour of the sex in sympathy with the sentiments of different speakers'.[24]

As the atmosphere in the House of Lords came closer to that of Newhall Hill than might have been expected, there was at least one celebrated male visitor who knew how to behave: the 'Hindoo' Rammohun Roy occupying the space around the throne with Members of the House of Commons. Lord Ellenborough, who met him at dinner with the Director of the East India Company, noted in his Diary with innate English condescension that Roy spoke English well but slowly: 'He is great for an Indian, I dare say, but he would be nothing particular as an European.'[25] Roy was in fact more accurately a distinguished social and religious reformer who had challenged traditional Hindu culture (calling, for example, for the abolition of suttee); he was thus an appropriate witness to the English attempts to set their own house in order.

He listened to Lord Wharncliffe among others, who in effect led for the Opposition, since the Duke of Wellington's position was inevitably compromised by that blunt declaration against any Reform in the autumn of 1830. Wharncliffe took his stand on the apparent inflexibility of the Government. Why, he asked, were they to accept this particular measure and no other, and to declare that acceptance of the whole measure on the second reading? There was a slight kerfuffle in the Lords when Wharncliffe's method of dealing with the Bill was criticized. But in the end Wharncliffe made it quite clear: 'his great object was to have this Bill rejected'.

The next day the Earl of Harrowby accused Grey of trying to 'overawe' the House with threats as to what would happen if they did not pass the Bill. But he did admit to regretting Wellington's speech 'because it induced the country to think that no alteration would be paid to his wishes for a rational, moderate and well-tempered Reform'. Like Wharncliffe, Harrowby appeared to be hinting at a possibility of compromise if something 'rational' was proposed. This was more than their titular leader did; Wellington was unswerving when he called the Bill 'the most considerable alteration or change ever proposed'. It was indeed 'Radical Reform rather than Reform of any other description'.

On 5 October one Tory peer gave vent to a sentiment which under the circumstances was peculiarly optimistic: the Earl of Dudley declared that the Tories were entitled to be recognized as 'the true friends of order and liberty in future ages, and draw down on their memory the gratitude of the country'. The Marquess of Londonderry on the other hand struck a less elevated party political note. 'The details of the Bill,' he declared, 'were most ingeniously devised for the great object of its framers, that Whig supremacy should be eternal.' The Earl of Carnarvon chose to let rip with a colourful description of His Majesty's Ministers putting out to sea, in spite of all the dangers and perils with which their journey had been threatened. Subsequently they would cling to the sinking Ship of State till it went down, 'not as the Royal Standard which made her the envy and admiration of all beholders', nor as the rudder which had made her victorious in many battles, but 'they would cling to her as barnacles, yes, like barnacles to a vessel to impede her navigation . . . until she sank in depths unfathomable never to rise again'.

On Friday 7 October, the last full day of the debate, the veteran High Tory the Earl of Eldon began by referring to his feelings of infirmity – he was eighty and there were courteous requests to him to speak up – but announced that he would not go to his grave without giving his opinion that this 'most destructive measure' was calculated to reduce the country, 'which has hitherto been the most glorious of all nations upon earth, to that of misery which now afflicts all other countries in the world'.[26]

The Archbishop of Canterbury, William Howley, rose to his feet very late and cut short his speech for this reason: but its message was nonetheless clear – all the more so because he was the only prelate

William IV by Sir Martin Archer Shee, who came to the throne in July 1830, aged 65.

Adelaide of Saxe-Meiningen, wife of William IV, who was twenty-seven years his junior.

Mary Countess Grey with two of her daughters; Lord and Lady Grey believed in the education of daughters as well as sons.

Charles 2nd Earl Grey; his aristocrat appearance and demeanour made a marked impression on all his contempo-
aries, whether friends or foes.

Arthur Wellesley, 1st Duke of Wellington: the Hero of the Nation. Prime Minister at the accession of William IV in 1830.

Sir Robert Peel: the Tory Leader of the House of Commons during the period of the Reform Bill.

Old Sarum by John Constable: the famous 'green mound' which was represented in Parliament by two MPs, despite a total lack of inhabitants; it became a symbol of the corruption of the old electoral system.

High-street market, Birmingham; this bustling scene represents the extraordinary growth in the city's population although in 1830 Birmingham had no MPs.

Thomas Attwood, founder of the Birmingham Political Union, and a charismatic orator in the cause of Reform.

Captain Swing, c. December 1830, the mythical figure said to be behind the agricultural riots, made out of the materials for arson, including 'portable gas', gunpowder, pitch and tar, with lighted matches for fingers. The body is a corn-stack and the head a sheaf of corn.

The PRESTON Shoe Black in Parliament Showering a few of his Brilliant Ideas out at the Expence of Some of the Rotten Members

Cartoon showing Henry Hunt, the radical politician and MP for Preston, firing shoe-blacking at his opponents; this played on the fact that Hunt tried to sell shoe-blacking among other products to restore his fortunes.

Lord John Russell, nicknamed 'Lord John Reformer' by Sydney Smith, and Lord Holland; both prominent Whigs.

Lord and Lady Holland in the library at Holland House; Macaulay compared the imperious Lady Holland to Queen Elizabeth I.

William Cobbett, the Radical; etching by Daniel Maclise, 1835, when he was in his seventies.

Thomas Babington Macaulay at the time of his election for Leeds, aged 32; he dominated by his brilliance, not his appearance—Sydney Smith called him 'a book in breeches'.

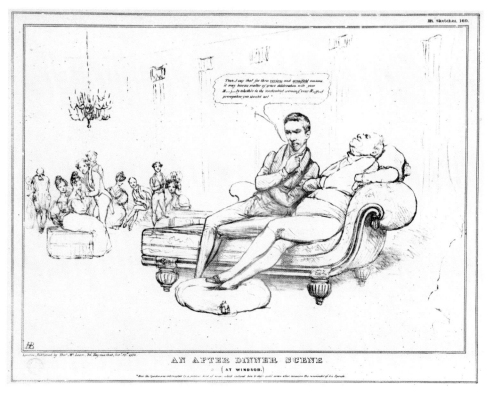

Lord Brougham mutters, out of hearing of the Court ladies and gentlemen, that 'for *various* and *manifold* reasons' the King may need to create new peers by the exercise of his royal prerogative; William IV slumbers.

William IV asks, 'Does that mean me?' when he sees the words 'Reform Bill!' on the wall. This play upon his nickname delighted contemporaries.

A view of the interior of the House of Commons, 1821.

The Reformers' Attack on the Old Rotten Tree; or, the Foul Nests of the Cormorants in Danger.

A cartoon in favour of Reform, showing a tree being cut down, with 'nests' on its branches which represent the rotten boroughs; May 1831. Brougham, in wig and gown with an axe, is prominent in the foreground.

THE CITY of BRISTOL,

As it appeared generally on Sunday night, &c. &c. &c. October 30th 1831. When the New Gaol, the Toll House, the Bishops Palace, two sides of Queen Square including the Mansion House, Custom House, Excise Office Warehouses with various other Buildings & other property to the Amount of upwards of One Hundred Thousand Pounds Sterling was totally Destroyed.

Bristol was the scene of riots over three days in October 1831, in which the centre of the city was set on fire. A number of people, including rioters, perished; subsequently many rioters were hung or transported abroad.

BOMBARDING the BARRICADES or the STORMING OF APSLEY HOUSE.

A cartoon of the storming of Apsley House (home of the Duke of Wellington) by rioters in favour of Reform. The Duke of Wellington, supported by a Bishop in a mitre, has his arms extended as he repels them; the rioters flourish tricoloured flags in reference to the French Revolution.

John Doyle caricatures the Duke of Wellington, in a bonnet as Dame Partington, who thought she could sweep back the Atlantic Ocean with her housewife's mop; 1831.

A fearful William IV looks out of The Reform coach while a series of politicians comment; O'Connell wishes 'I could set up such a Coach in Old Ireland'; Wellington, outside the coach, remonstrates: 'You are pretty felons to throw away your *drag chain* when you ought to have your wheels locked' while the Whigs rejoice: 'We'll make you a present of it old Boy, we want *no drags nor clogs* of any sort upon our wheels.'

THE DOG BILLY LED ASTRAY BY A GERMAN B——.

Printed and Published by G. Drake, 12, Houghton Street, Clare Market.

Satirical print of King William IV as 'the dog Billy' being led astray by 'a German b----'; one of the many attacks on Queen Adelaide, focussing on her German origin.

A banner of the Shoemakers celebrating the passing of the Great Reform Bill; St Crispin was the patron saint of the Shoemakers.

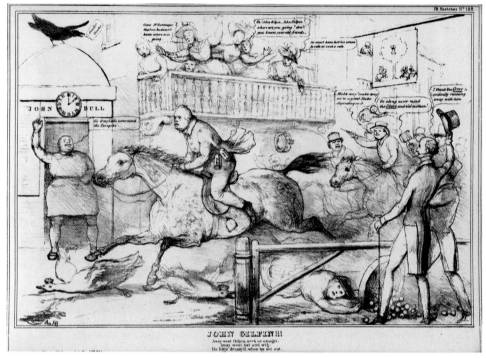

William IV depicted by John Doyle as John Gilpin on a runaway horse. John Bull cries out: 'Go to it my Lads never mind the Turnpike'. Other spectators exclaim in distress ('Don't you know your *old* friends') or encouragement ('Go along never mind the *Geese* and old women!'). Lord Grey wields a hat on the far right. Behind him a man exclaims: 'I think the *Grey* is evidently running away with him.'

Villagers rejoice at the passing of the Reform Bill, Scorton Green, North Yorkshire.

The banquet given in the Guildhall, 7 July 1832, to celebrate the passing of the Bill. Lord Grey is on his feet, speaking.

A memento of the Great Public Question of Reform: William IV is in the centre, surrounded by politicians, with Britannia below (right).

who spoke and, by virtue of his revered position, was deemed to speak for the clergy as a whole. He described the Bill as 'mischievous in its tendency' and extremely dangerous to the fabric of the Constitution. His hope for 'an union of men of all parties' in the future which would 'tranquillize' fears of agitation, which even he agreed might seem 'chimerical and futile', was sufficiently vague to please neither side while doing nothing concrete for the reputation of the Church of England.

Of all the speeches, there was no doubt that Brougham's extraordinary peroration on the final day eclipsed all others.[27] It did so partly due to his amazing eloquence, but partly, it has to be said, because of the eccentricity of his behaviour. His gestures, his craggy figure with the famous, much-caricatured bottle-nose – and perhaps the allusion to a bottle was justified – were in themselves almost as persuasive as his words. From the beginning, Brougham declared the stakes to be high, even the highest. He was, he said, 'now standing with your Lordships on the brink of the most momentous decision that ever human assembly came to at any period of the world'. There was then a long rhetorical digression as to how he would have prepared himself 'every day and every hour' of his life, if he had ever known he would bear such a responsibility as had now fallen to him. It was the next loosing of the riptide which only Brougham could have carried off.

The Lord Chancellor chose to focus on Lord Wharncliffe, a man in vain pursuit of *some* people, *any* people who hated Reform: 'Whither shall he go – what street shall he enter – in what alley shall he take refuge – since the inhabitants of every street, and lane, and alley, feel it necessary in self-defence, to become signers and petitioners as soon as he makes an appearance among them.' (This was a reference to Lord Wharncliffe's ill-fated reporting of Bond Street shopkeepers as being anti-Reform, at which point they immediately came up with a petition in favour.) 'If, harassed by Reformers on land, my noble friend goes down to the water, there one thousand Reformers greet him.' (Brougham had presented petitions from Lambeth that day.) 'If he were to take a Hackney-coach, the very coachman and their attendants would feel it their duty to assemble and petition.' Brougham went on in full flow: 'Wherever there is a street, an alley, a passage, nay a river, a wherry. . . .' The unfortunate Lord Wharncliffe could of course try the south side of Berkeley Square, where he will wander 'remote, unfriended, melancholy, slow' – the quotation was from Oliver Goldsmith's poem *The Traveller* – for there at least there were no inhabitants and thus no friends of the Bill to be found. Elsewhere, wherever he went, he would be pursued by cries of 'Petition! Petition! The Bill! The Bill!' In a happy touch, Brougham suggested that even in country inns Wharncliffe would not be safe, since the landlords would take care that the waiters who served him were reformers in disguise.

In conclusion Brougham struck a majestic note of warning: 'Raise not the spirit of a peace-loving but determined people – alienate not the affections of a great empire from your body. As your friend, as the friend of my country, as the servant of my sovereign, I counsel you . . . For all these reasons, I pray and beseech you not to reject this Bill' – there were cheers at this point – 'I call upon you by all that you hold most dear, by all that binds every one of us to our common order and our common country – unless, indeed, you are prepared to say that you will admit of no reform, that you are resolved against all change, for in that case opposition would at least be consistent – I beseech you, I solemnly adjure you, yes, even on bended knees, my lords' – here, according to *The Times*, Brougham slightly bent his knee upon the Woolsack – 'I implore you not to reject this Bill.' There followed a prolonged and heartfelt bout of Whig cheering.

Afterwards, there was some controversy about that modest genuflection in the direction of the Woolsack as reported by Brougham's ally *The Times*. Was it in fact an involuntary fall, not a genuflection at all? There was obviously some need to explain the incident. Lord Lyndhurst, he who had been put aside as a possible Lord Chancellor (although a Tory) in favour of Brougham, had this to say: 'He continued some time as if in prayer; but his friends, alarmed for him, lest he should be suffering from the effects of the mulled port he had demonstrably been imbibing, picked him up and replaced him safely on the woolsack.'[28]

There was certainly evidence that Brougham drank. Edward Littleton MP, an eyewitness who described the speech as 'one of the most splendid conceivable – flaming with wit and irony and elo-quence, and served with argument and admonition to a degree that made one tremble' – did not mention the fall. But he did record that in the course of a speech which was over three hours long, Brougham drank three immense soda water bottles full of hot negus (sweetened wine and water); at one point, getting agitated when he thought his refreshment was in danger from Lord Bathurst sitting next to it, he proceeded to remove the bottle to his own side amid some laughter. Lord Grey and Lord Holland, however, both assured Althorp that as a feat Brougham's speech was 'superhuman', uniting the excellences of the ancient with those of modern oratory.[29]

Lord Grey himself, speaking again at five o'clock in the morning shortly before the vote, struck rather a different note. 'I had no desire for place,' he said, 'and it was not sought after by me.' Only his sense of duty made him delve back into a world so inimicable to his whole being: 'I am fond of retirement and domestic life and I lived happy and content in the bosom of my family . . . What but a sense of duty could have induced me to plunge into all the difficulties, not unfore-seen, of my present situation.' And he quoted from Dryden's *Absalom and Achitophel*, written 150 years earlier at the time of the Exclusion Crisis, with Shaftesbury as Achitophel and Monmouth as Absalom:

> What else could tempt me on these stormy seas . . .
> Bankrupt of life yet prodigal of ease

So the House proceeded to the division. Lord Campbell recalled afterwards that at this point Grey was 'tranquil and smiling as if they had been dividing on a road Bill'. Mrs Arbuthnot, on the other hand, heard that he 'vapoured' – which was not quite the same thing.[30] At six-thirty in the morning the Government was defeated by a majority of 41 against the Bill: it was noteworthy that twenty-one bishops out of twenty-three voted against it. And the list of Not Contents was headed by two royal Dukes, Cumberland and Gloucester.

Perhaps it was the exhaustion of the night, the lateness of the hour. Sir Denis Le Marchant reflected that there was no sense within the House that a measure was being decided which might cause the land to be deluged in blood. Very different was the reaction of those, the thousands, the hundreds of thousands dedicated to the cause, who were outside. 'What *will the Lords do?*' That had been the question on every lip when friend met friend for several months, according to Alexander Somerville, the Scottish working man turned soldier. Now 'expressions of disappointment and indignation arose loudly, and ran swiftly through every street in London, and with every mail back out of it; along every turnpike road; into every bye-path in the kingdom and almost to every hearth, save in the houses of the fractional minority of the population, the anti-reformers.'[31] There was a feeling of thunder in the air.

Lord Althorp wrote to his father, Lord Spencer, in a spirit of despair: 'I think Reform will never pass the House of Lords, unless it is brought forward by its enemies', as Catholic Emancipation had been. In Paris, Harriet Granville, wife of the British Ambassador and a key figure in the new generation of the Whig cousinage, was quite clear about what the House of Lords had done. 'They have made their own 25 July,' she wrote, referring to the French Revolution – and the news made her shudder.[32]

CHAPTER NINE

WHAT HAVE THE LORDS *DONE*?

'What have the Lords *done*? The answer is that they have
done what they can never undo. The House of Lords will
never again be on the same foundations in the confidence
of the people' –

The Times leader, 10 October 1831

On 8 October the 'frightful majority' of 41 against Reform in the Lords
was published in the *Sun* newspaper, fringed in black. At the same time
it was known that Lord Grey had told the King that he would not
resign. A friend of Francis Place named John Powell, an attorney's
clerk who was subsequently sub-editor of the *Morning Chronicle*,
happened to take a steamer to Gravesend and Chatham that morning.
He wrote an account of events for Place two years later: 'Never shall
I forget the excitement that prevailed in the breast of everyone' when
the black-fringed newspaper was seen in his hands. The passengers
rushed towards him in order to hear an authentic account of what had
happened. Powell was instantly mounted on a chair and forced to read
aloud the whole debate, while all around him on board ship the
bishops were the subject of 'fearful' denunciations. When Powell
reached Grey's 'noble declaration' that he would not give up so long
as he could be of service to his King and his country – in short, the
Government was not going to resign – 'the very shores of old Father
Thames reechoed the reiterated shouts of applause'.[1]

Unsurprisingly, there were crowds of angry 'hooters' outside the
House of Lords itself; prominent Ultra Tories like Lord Dudley (who
had already boarded up his windows) found members of the mob
trying to grab the reins of his horse, until the spirited steed, named
Paris, gave a great leap and dispersed them. The remaining windows
of that familiar target, Lord Londonderry, were broken, as were those

of the Duke of Newcastle. The hated Duke of Cumberland was pelted with mud which totally covered his body.

In the provinces the bad news spread, and with the news came an ugly reaction, as incredulity and dismay gave way to physical manifestations of disgust. If Lord Holland was right, and the Reform Bill was not the cause of the danger – unemployment, low wages, general economic distress were fundamentals in the country – then certainly the prompt passing of the Bill had been the best hope of allaying it. Late at night on Saturday 8 October, a large mob came from Derby to the home of William Mundy, a local dignitary, and his wife Harriot; the household was in bed. The mob had just heard of the rejection of the Bill by the Lords. Now they surrounded the house, as Harriot Mundy wrote to a friend in a panic at eight o'clock the next morning, 'shouting and hallooing and smashed all our windows and broke in many doors and frames of windows'. Luckily quite a lot of manservants were in the house, and troops could be dispatched from Nottingham, a mere sixteen miles away. Mrs Mundy reported later: 'I have been four nights without undressing.' Nearer Nottingham at Colwick, a Mr Musters was not quite so lucky: known to be very unpopular locally, he found his pictures and furniture being carried out and burnt. Mrs Musters, her daughter and her mother-in-law, who was sick in bed, had to be smuggled out and laid down under the bushes.[2]

Significantly, popular acclaim for the monarchy was beginning to fray at the edges, despite the declared loyalty of the middle classes. The *Poor Man's Guardian* had been founded in July by Henry Hetherington, the son of a London tailor, who had become an apprentice printer at the age of thirteen at Hansard's printing works. Influenced by the reforming ideas of Robert Owen, he was responsible for a series of Radical newspapers including the *Penny Papers for the People* of 1830. Such a penny newspaper, paying no stamp tax, and selling in tens of thousands, was unabashedly matching popular will against the law.[3]

On 15 October the *Poor Man's Guardian* issued an article headed WHAT WILL WILLIAM GUELPH DO? – the crude use of the surname was hardly a promising start.[4] The paper then proceeded to call for the creation of peers, at least 100 of them, before pointing out that this watered-down peerage would constitute such 'paltry, common trash' that the people would no longer be at all afraid of them. As for William Guelph, a man 'who never did and never could think for himself', he probably needed his friends to point out that if the peerage went, the King would be next. 'If our advice is any use to him, we are but a Job's comforter; he cannot save himself; he must go sooner or later; but he may go with a good grace or a bad one: so let him do *more than all his predecessors together,* some *honest* work before he goes.' The solution of the *Poor Man's Guardian* was to dispense with the bishops altogether, and as for the noble Lords, why not enable them to carry the Bill by creating every £10 householder a peer . . .

In contrast to such fulminations, the Birmingham Political Union, according to its long-held policy, remained temperate. And the Government acknowledged the importance of this restraint when on 8 October a communication was sent from Lord John Russell – he who had been dubbed 'Lord John Reformer' by Sydney Smith – Lord Althorp and Sir George Skipworth, thanking Attwood for his public support. In Russell's words regarding the House of Lords: 'It is impossible that the whisper of faction should prevail against the voice of the nation.' Undoubtedly this straightforward declaration helped Attwood to preserve some kind of peace, and the Union continued to counsel, in the words of their address, 'Patience! Patience! Patience!' There were references to 'our beloved King' standing firm. Once again, the people were told that they had nothing to fear – nothing unless their own violence should rashly lead to anarchy. The motto was: be patient, be peaceful. But streets and pubs with signs not only of Wellington but of Queen Adelaide were pulled down. Alexander Somerville, then stationed in Birmingham, recorded later that the Queen's influence was thought to be behind the rejection.[5]

The mob had so far no overt reason to criticize the King. The Queen was another matter. In a disagreeable incident at Court, King William had felt compelled to side with his Government against his wife. One of the notable Lords who voted against the Bill was Earl Howe, the Queen's Lord Chamberlain – suspected of being unduly close to her. (Kindly observers like Lady Bedingfield thought the devotion was

actually all on his side; the Queen 'was so truly good and virtuous
that she has no idea that people would fancy she likes him too well'.)[6]
Howe's prominence was due to his particular public role rather than
the Queen's favour, but the latter was undoubtedly a complication.
Nor, for all her virtue, was Queen Adelaide particularly tactful where
her husband's Government was concerned: she had chosen all her coronation attendants from among 'our enemies', as one Whig put it. On
10 October Lord Grey urged that Lord Howe be dismissed from the
Royal Household, on the grounds that an official had no right openly
to disagree with the declared policy of the Government. Grey wanted
to carry out the dismissal himself; the only concession William made
to his wife's feelings was to insist that Howe resign instead.

The deed was done while Queen Adelaide was out riding. By her
own account, she had no conception of what lay in store, and was therefore 'very much surprised' when, shortly after her return, Lord Howe
brought her back his keys, declaring to her at any rate that he had been
dismissed. The Queen wrote in her Diary: 'I would not believe it, for I
had trusted in, and built firmly on the King's love for me.' She added:
'I fear it will be the beginning of much evil' before confessing that she
had had a hard struggle to appear at table after such a blow, 'which I
felt deeply as an insult, which filled me with "Indignation" [in English
in the original]'. In short, 'I felt myself deeply wounded both as wife
and queen, and I cannot conquer the feeling.'[7] Thereafter the Queen
certainly made no secret of her hostility to Lord Grey, ostentatiously
refusing to speak to him. When Princess Lieven commented to her
in German that the Prime Minister was very much mortified at her
behaviour, Adelaide replied stubbornly, also in her native language:
'Is he? I am glad of it; he shall continue to be mortified for he shan't
be spoken to.'[8] *

'What have the Lords *done?*' asked *The Times* in a leader on 10
October, before answering its own question: 'They have done what

---

* This was an early version of the so-called Bedchamber Crisis which would plague the
young Queen Victoria; once again the personal predilection of a royal personage clashed
with the notion of official responsibility. But Victoria was of course a Queen Regnant,
whereas Adelaide was only a Queen Consort.

they can never undo. The House of Lords will never again be on the same foundations in the confidence of the people.' It was a question of 400 people versus twenty-two million, the population of the country. 'The nation willed it. The Lords forbade it. Will the nation give way or will the Lords?' And *The Times* mounted yet another attack on the errant bishops who had helped to bring about this miserable state of affairs.[9]

Indeed, the prominence of the bishops' vote in the tally of the majority was something not missed in the country as a whole. One prelate had the words 'Bishop of Worcester Judas Iscariot' scrawled on his cathedral walls; other bishops were said to be confined to their episcopal palaces for fear of outrages. Prominent anti-reforming clerics like Henry Phillpotts, recently made Bishop of Exeter, a high-flown and colourful debater on conservative issues of social order, were beginning to attract public attention. Like the Bishop of Durham, the Bishop of Exeter could no longer proceed freely round his diocese.[10]

Of course there were other clerics, good Whig men in Lord Holland's phrase, of a very different turn of mind – Sydney Smith, for example. Lord Holland's verdict on him to Grey was eloquent: what could be and was said against Smith was 'all hypocrisy or at best trifling – founded on his own maxim that "no man can be pious who is not dull"'. It was in the spirit of enjoyment in a highly tense situation that, in a speech at Taunton on 11 October, Sydney Smith now evoked the character of Dame Partington. He compared Wellington to this sturdy lady who had attempted to repel the Atlantic Ocean with her housewife's mop: 'The Atlantic was roused,' he declared. 'I need not tell you that the contest was unequal. The Atlantic Ocean beat Mrs Partington. She was excellent at a slop or a puddle, but she should not have meddled with a tempest. Gentlemen, be at your ease – be quiet and steady – you will beat Mrs Partington.' And the elderly clergyman began 'trundling' an imaginary mop about the platform, to the great delight of his audience.[11]

Joyfully the cartoonists seized on the comparison. Wellington as Dame Partington, wearing a bonnet and a woman's dress but his hawk-like features and black eyebrows clearly recognizable, armed with his/her mop, became a favourite subject of caricature. The enormous waves certainly looked as if they were about to engulf not only the Dame but also her modest dwelling.

So far were the bishops in general identified with the Tories that *The Times* actually questioned whether they should have seats in the House of Lords in the first place.[12] Alas, Smith, recently made a Canon of St Paul's by Lord Grey, was not considered episcopal material; do anything else for Smith, Lord Milton told Grey, 'but it will not do to give him a mitre'.

In the Commons it was only a short while before the displeasure of the Whig majority was made known on the floor of the House. Macaulay's trenchant speech on 10 October was thought by some to sail somewhat close to the wind on the delicate subject of intimidation since he made references to Ireland: 'England may exhibit the same spectacle which Ireland exhibited three years ago – agitators stronger than the Magistrate. . . .'[13] The keynote was as follows: 'I know only two ways in which society can permanently be governed – by public opinion and the sword.' And he referred feelingly to the relative keeping of the peace in the two cities of New York and Milan: in the one by the assent and support of the people, and in the other by the bayonets of Austrian soldiers. Therefore he did not understand how peace was to be kept in England, 'acting on the principles of the present Opposition'. There was danger that fearful things like Democracy and Revolution would be unleashed. This allowed the Tory Sir Charles Wetherell to suggest that Macaulay was actually advocating a breach of the peace – otherwise why cite Ireland?

Viscount Ebrington, heir to Earl Fortescue, who had been a Whig MP off and on for nearly thirty years, did better. With a fine upstanding appearance, looking 'quite the model of an English nobleman', he had, according to his friend Le Marchant, 'one of the purest minds I have ever known' with advanced views on the subject of liberty, even if he had a tendency to carry conscientiousness to extremes.[14] A meeting of about 200 Whig MPs was held, and it was agreed to back Ebrington's resolution which called on the House to redeem its pledge to the country concerning Reform. Ebrington's subsequent speech did make the point that the country should remain 'orderly' – a subject on which he also felt strongly – but he declared his complete confidence that the Reform Bill would 'consolidate all the blessings which the British constitution can bestow upon a happy and united people'. The result was 'a most opportune triumph' – 329 in support and 198 against.

Such brave declarations left unsolved the question of Radicalism in the country and how – if it all – it could be harnessed to help the Government. Bodies like the National Union of the Working Classes, set up with elaborate rules in July 1831, were beginning to be more overtly revolutionary; it called, for example, for total equality before the law, which meant Universal Suffrage, although even here mention was made of the need 'to wait with patience, and cheerfully pay the public taxes'.[15] The middle classes were, however, still practising patience.

On Wednesday 12 October a huge march took place in London.[16] What was significant, in the opinion of Francis Place's friend John Powell at least, was the competent organization throughout: 'for young soldiers, we were not bad generals'. The files were six, eight or ten abreast and at each flank a man was stationed responsible for managing his own line. In order to avoid accusations of drunkenness, there were orders against alcohol. The consequence, wrote Powell, which was 'universally admitted', was that there was absolutely no disorder, unless you counted the groans which greeted the houses of known enemies of the Bill. Here were respectable people. Here were housekeepers, shopkeepers and superior artisans. The numbers were estimated from 70,000 to 300,000 – probably nearer the former – and the spectators included 'elegantly draped ladies'. There were cheers and the waving of handkerchiefs. Not only petitions, but flowers and cockades were 'fragrantly' showered on the marchers as they passed. The music varied from the 'Dead March' and church bells tolling to 'God Save the King' and 'Rule Britannia'.

The declared intention was to present a petition to William IV at St James's Palace, an intention which was not viewed at the palace itself 'without alarm'. In the end the various deputies were persuaded to abandon their plan of seeking admission to the King himself, but to wait prudently in nearby St James's Square while Joseph Hume and another MP presented their petitions. Equally prudent was the conduct of the Government, which, being apprised of the march, promised to keep the police – a potentially inflammatory symbol of authority – out of sight. Powell reflected subsequently that the whole episode taught him that 'to the energetic, determined and persevering nothing is impossible . . . few things more repugnant to the general habits, customs and prejudices of the middle classes of London than walking through the streets in a procession can scarcely be conceived'. Yet it had been a triumph.

At six o'clock that evening, a meeting of about 100 people was held at the Crown and Anchor Tavern in the Strand with the declared agenda of discovering the 'best means of giving effectual support to the King and Government and on the measures necessary to secure the peace and safety of the metropolis'. Two long tables down the centre of the large room, and chairs at the sides, were all full, and many other people were standing. Unlike the march, the mood of the meeting was not encouraging, as Francis Place made despondent predictions about the Government's intentions to modify the Bill.[17]

Later, 'past ten o'clock' at night, Place led a self-styled delegation of members of London parishes to Number 10 Downing Street. There was no appointment but Grey agreed to see them. The demand of the delegates was simple: Grey should pass the Bill in seven days by the expedient of peer creation. The meeting did not, on the face of it, go particularly well. Sir John Hobhouse for example thought the whole thing was a mistake; he implied that 'such ill-looking fellows' had no place in the Prime Ministerial dwelling. Nor was Grey himself at his best in this kind of situation with his lofty manner: his idealistic purpose evidently did not help him to communicate with clever, determined men from a different class (who were not his tenants in the north) such as Place. This was not the House of Lords, ready to hear a rolling peroration in which past and future were seamlessly evoked. Francis Place, who was absolutely determined that the Bill should not be watered down, went away with the impression that Grey intended to do exactly that.[18]

He described the occasion to Joseph Parkes in a letter written at seven the next morning.[19] Francis Place made it clear that Grey's florid Whig style was not his own; he told Parkes that he would not bother him with the various 'tedious and silly repetitions' which the 'polite and courtier-like conduct of the Noble Lord occasioned'. What Place did tell him was that the delegation had clearly put Grey on the defensive from the first. Grey uttered various hardline sentiments about popular uprisings: if the people rioted, they would be bayoneted, shot and hanged. Apparently Grey did not intend to propose the creation of peers. 'What say you now to your motto – Peers or Revolution?' enquired Place of Parkes. Place thought the clear implication of the meeting was that Parliament would be prorogued and 'a more conciliatory Bill' would be introduced. All this was fairly disastrous.

But there was another, more favourable side to the encounter. Despite the misunderstanding, Francis Place was deeply impressed by one thing and that was Grey's integrity; he was 'the most open and manly' of Prime Ministers, and thus Place had at the very least confidence in Grey's intention to do good, even if he questioned his judgement. A link had been forged which other, younger men – the genial Lord Althorp for example – might be able to exploit: this was a link between those in theory capable of provoking (or controlling) revolution and those in charge of the policies against which they reacted.

After this meeting Francis Place went on to enjoy the hospitality of the Philosopher Radical George Grote and his famously intellectual wife Harriet at their salon in Threadneedle Street, close by the Bank of England in the City.[20] Both were or would be writers – Grote was at work on an authoritative *History of Greece*; they were in their late thirties and childless. Grote was an independently wealthy banker whose inclination was to be a scholar; influenced by both James Mill and Jeremy Bentham, he was 'a zealous friend of liberty' and had given £500 to the Committee of the July Revolution in Paris 'for the beautiful cause'.

Harriet Grote's nineteenth-century biographer Lady Eastlake compared her to an English Madame de Staël; she was certainly a passionate reformer who in conversation at least did not shrink from advocating principles which might lead to civil war.[21] As for George Grote, in *Essentials of Parliamentary Reform*, published in 1831, he boldly compared public feeling to that in France before the Revolution of 1789, and called firmly for the Secret Ballot, although as a banker he was both more reticent about personal involvement and a great deal more wary about the merits of public disorder. Mischievous Sydney Smith summed up the Grotes thus: 'I like him, he is so ladylike and I like her, she's such a perfect gentleman.' Less delightfully he pretended the tall, striking, unconventionally dressed Harriet Grote was the origin of the word Grotesque; her family nickname of 'The Empress' gave a kinder impression of her general character.[22]

On this occasion, as Francis Place fulminated in Threadneedle Street about Grey's vacillation – as he saw it – the Grotes and their circle of intellectual reformers rejoiced in the developments which they saw in a far more favourable light. But the growing force was undoubtedly with the unions. This period marked the foundation of the National Political Union, under the inspiration of Place, in direct imitation, it was hoped, of the success of the Birmingham Political Union – and also with the indirect intention of securing the national leadership. While proposing to construct this Union as much as possible on the Birmingham plan, it was specified 'that such matters as related to the particular views of Mr Attwood respecting the currency' should be omitted.[23]

Meanwhile the West Country of England seethed. Mary Frampton, sister of James Frampton, Justice of the Peace and Colonel of the Dorset Yeomanry, wrote a vivid account of it all in her Journal.[24] The carriage of a sheriff and his assessor – Mr Davies of Milton Abbas and Mr Philip Williams – was attacked. Yeomanry did eventually rescue them but the town of Blandford and its neighbours still continued its 'lawless proceedings'; the High Sheriff stayed the next day at Dorchester, fearing to pass through Milborne. A young couple, the Tory MP Lord Ashley and his wife, the captivating Minnie Cowper, reputedly the illegitimate daughter of Lord Palmerston by his mistress Lady Cowper, had to choose 'an unlikely route' to their house at St Giles, Wimborne, and a secret one to get away; Lord Ashley kept a pair of loaded pistols handy (although this fact was kept from the newly married Lady Ashley).

Ashley, heir to the local grandee the Earl of Shaftesbury, had recently been elected MP for Dorset at a by-election, switching from Dorchester, which was left to his younger brother. Although he would be better known to history as the great philanthropist Lord Shaftesbury, after he inherited his father's title in 1851, it was more relevant to the would-be attackers that Ashley was at this point a persistent anti-reformer; he had voted against the measure in March, and again in September. His evangelical principles, the compassion which had its origin in the sight of a pauper's funeral when he was a schoolboy at Harrow, and caused him already to be described as 'a Saint', did not find expression in this particular cause; like the young Gladstone's denunciation of Reform (he thought the Lords' rejection highly satisfactory), it was an interesting reminder of the complex mosaic of society at this time where social issues were concerned.

At the town of Sherborne, matters began on 19 October with cries of 'Reform' from the rough types gathered for the traditional October Pack Monday Fair; the windows of those who had supported Ashley in the recent by-election for the Dorset seat were the main target. Then a considerable mob broke every pane of glass they could find at Sherborne Castle, home of Lord Digby, and even tried to force the great gates. Mary Frampton recorded in her Journal that there was a large house party within the castle itself, playing at some round game, when the first yell was heard and a volley of stones broke the windows. Troops of yeomanry were summoned but for a while could do little in view of the general disaffection of the place; several of the yeomen were seriously injured by stones and knocked off their horses.

James Frampton was in fact at the Quarter Sessions at Dorchester when the news came to him, but set off immediately back to Sherborne 'in full costume'. Tranquillity was eventually restored, although the vicarage of the Revd Mr Parsons was much damaged. Here, according to the *Sherborne Journal*, 'the doors were forced, the window-frames torn out, the furniture broken up, hogsheads of beer staved, spirits consumed and wasted, and in fact the most wanton acts of spoliation resorted to'.[25] The Revd Parsons, who was an acting magistrate, fared even worse than his house: he was knocked down by the mob, 'shamefully ill treated' and only saved by being taken to a neighbour's, where he lay senseless for some hours. One imagines that it was his attempt to read the Riot Act which provoked this brutality, rather than his role as a member of the Church of England – although the combination of a clergyman and the hated Act was always liable to inflame the populace.

Things were no better in the Midlands. There were riots in Derby on Sunday 9 October and an assault on the gaol to rescue prisoners taken the night before, which failed; one bystander was killed. The next day the Mayor refused permission for a public meeting but set up stalls so the public might organize their petitions to Parliament. Unfortunately matters had gone too far for such peaceful methods: the mob destroyed the stalls and the Riot Act was read. In the ensuing *fracas*, three more innocent men were killed.[26]

In Nottingham on 10 October a mob assaulted another castle – this time they were successful in getting inside and burning it down. This was a gleeful development, given that the proprietor was the Ultra Tory and enemy of Reform, the Duke of Newcastle. Several factories were also burnt. On 11 October the magistrates declared the town in a state of insurrections and the Riot Act was read. The Duke himself was not actually there; he admitted that he had to give the manufacturing districts a wide berth: 'I should either be murdered or raise a riot by appearing.'[27] He also accused some of the local magistrates of haranguing the crowds about the Lords and the Bill – in short, of being on the side of the mob rather than of law and order, as they should have been; they had 'indifferently' suffered all these things to take place.

In London, where accounts of countrywide violence were not slow in coming in, just as press reports of Parliament were rushed into the provinces, tension in the Government was still further racked up. No one could predict how and when the present effective deadlock would be resolved. On 15 October Sarah, Lady Lyttelton (née Spencer), went to see her brother Althorp: she told their father that he looked 'fagged and ill', adding 'I could fancy myself admitted to the Captain's cabin on the eve of a hurricane.' As for her children –'*les petits*' – ironically enough, they had been terrified by crowds shouting and banging on the door of the house; although these were in fact amiable if boisterous salutations from those who admired Lyttelton's reforming stand.[28]

Relations between the King and his Prime Minister were clearly entering a delicate stage. The question of creation of peers was so far the unspoken issue between them, although, as the obvious solution to what the Lords had done, it was being widely discussed in both political and Radical circles. John Doyle was not slow to seize upon the subject. In a cartoon issued on 12 October entitled 'An After Dinner Scene (at Windsor)' he showed a sinister-looking Brougham, whispering in the King's ear as he sits with him on a sofa, while the Queen and other ladies and gentlemen are nattering in the background. The bubble of words coming out of Brougham's mouth tails off with the unfinished phrase: 'whether in the undoubted exercise of your R–y–l prerogative, you should not. . . .' William however is stretched out on the sofa fast asleep.[29]

In real life the King was not able to practise avoidance so easily and was in fact concentrating on establishing his constitutional position (and rights). In correspondence on 17 October – handled as before by Sir Herbert Taylor – William IV chose to quote from Bolingbroke's *The Idea of a Patriot King*.[30] * This work, originally published in 1738, which had not featured strongly in the concept of kingship in the late eighteenth century, was enjoying a new vogue; it was republished in 1831 after a gap of fifty years (quite apart from being used as the subtitle of that play at the time of the March division on the Reform Bill). It was felt that there was something peculiarly appropriate, even exhilarating in its message with regard to the reign which began in 1830 – or, as Bolingbroke had written, a new King meant a new people.

A royal biography by John Watkins, published in 1831, emphasized the point: 'What the masterly hand of BOLINGBROKE sketched as an

---

* The point has been made that of the Hanoverian monarchs William IV was probably the only one who actually read *The Idea of a Patriot King*.[31]

ideal character and a vision of virtuous excellence, this nation happily enjoys in the reign of William IV,' he wrote.[32] It was a flattering picture of a paternalistic monarch, standing above his Ministers in order to put the interests of his people first, and as such calculated to appeal to William's image of himself, in contrast to that of his late brother.

Now Bolingbroke was brought to the aid of the current crisis: 'Every new modification in a scheme of government and of national policy was of great importance,' he had written. Such modifications required more and deeper consideration than 'the warmth, and hurry, and rashness of party conduct admit'. So the duty of a prince required that he should use his influence to render the proceedings more orderly and more deliberate, even when he actually approved of the objective at which they were aimed. It was an argument for a king as a well-intentioned arbiter rather than the pawn of his Ministers. As Bolingbroke had put it: 'To espouse no party, but to govern like the common father of his people, is so essential to the character of a Patriot King.'[33]

Grey replied the same day: 'In the quotation from Lord Bolingbroke,' he wrote, 'with which Your Majesty concludes your gracious letter, Edward Grey readily acknowledges that there is much wisdom,' but he hoped that the measures he was putting forward, with the approval of his colleagues, were not actually open to the censure of having been urged with the warmth, hurry and rashness of party conduct, in the King's words. Of course all proceedings should be orderly and deliberate but public opinion should also be taken into account.[34] In short, a policy for the restoration of public confidence should be pursued with consistency and firmness.

Back came the King on 18 October.[35] While not intending to apply the words of Bolingbroke to Grey himself, he disapproved strongly of a clash between the two Houses of Parliament. And he drew attention to that particular letter from Lord John Russell with its reference to 'the whisper of faction' in the Lords, which was causing scandal. That is, if it had been received with delight by Attwood and the Birmingham Political Union to which it was sent, it was condemned angrily by the Tories. Lord Wharncliffe denounced the letter as being 'subservient' to the Birmingham Political Union; to which Lord John

Russell replied smoothly that he was merely thanking the Chairman of a meeting, said to be of 150,000 people, for his support. It was true that Russell apologized to the King, describing his letter as having been written 'in the first moments of disappointment'.[36] But the phrase summed up the popular revulsion against the Lords' behaviour, its numerical weakness versus the national will.

The game continued: the Whigs put forward the popular demonstrations, hopefully non-violent, as evidence of the need for Reform, while the Tories exclaimed furiously that such hooligans were not to be trusted with representation in Parliament. The fundamental question was whether a Whig Government could possibly carry any bill in the existing state of the House of Lords, numerically so weighted in favour of the Tories, against its will. Obviously such a situation might have the effect of arousing scepticism about the whole system. The intelligent reforming journalist Albany Fonblanque had written on the day of the Lords' rejection: 'A reverence for a hereditary legislature seems properly contemporary with witches and wizards.'[37]

On 20 October William IV formally prorogued Parliament; in other words he brought the current session to an end, as opposed to dissolving Parliament, which necessitated a General Election, as had happened in March.[38] It was, in a sense, a cooling-off period, or what the King called 'an interval of repose', since MPs were able to return to their constituencies (and peers to their country estates). William, surrounded by the Sovereign's usual entourage on such occasions, came in person to the House of Lords, the Speaker, Lord Althorp and other MPs being present at the bar.

In his speech, the King referred to 'a session of unexampled duration and labour' and went on to say that he was sure it was unnecessary for him to recommend to them the 'most careful attention to the preservation of tranquillity in your respective counties'. He also referred, beyond touching on the various achievements of the session, to 'the anxiety which has generally been manifested by my people for the accomplishment of a Constitutional Reform' in the Commons. He trusted that in the future proceedings would be regulated by a due sense of the necessity of order and moderation. Parliament must of course return again to a consideration of this important question at the next session. The King declared that he himself had an 'unalterable desire to promote its settlement'.

Ten days later the worst and most influential riots so far broke out in the West Country. Whatever the Lords had intended to do, their massive rejection of the Bill had brought about a crisis which not only scaremongers and the professionally pessimistic saw as leading rapidly towards revolution.

CHAPTER TEN

A SCENE OF DESOLATION

'Then away to Bristol he quickly walked
T'indulge in meditation
And he gaily laughed as he slowly stalked
O'er a scene of desolation' –

Charles Dickens, 'The Devil's Walk', November 1831

On Saturday 29 October, nine days after the prorogation of Parliament, the lawyer Sir Charles Wetherell, in his judicial capacity as Recorder of Bristol, set out for the West Country to perform his official functions. Later there were many found to assert that the presence of such a notorious Ultra Tory – remembering his fulmination about 'a dose of Russell's Purge' in the House of Commons in March – was provocative. Bristol was not a naturally pliant city: there had been riots in 1793 over the removal of houses for an access road to a new bridge in which eleven people were killed. In fairness to Wetherell, one of the MPs for Bristol, the young Whig Edward Protheroe, held a different view. Descended from a prominent Bristol family of merchants and bankers, he believed that his own solid support for the subject of Reform had not so much allayed the local fever as calmed the inhabitants.[1]

Wetherell was speedily undeceived about the state of Bristol. Even before he reached the city itself, he was greeted by hostile demonstrators among whom, it was remarked, 'not a few were women of abandoned character, whose violent language seemed well fitted to urge on the desperate population'. He entered Bristol at eleven o'clock in the morning escorted by a large force of special constables and police. He found himself immediately 'amid the groans, hisses and execrations of thousands'. At Temple Street, his carriage was showered with stones and rotten eggs; the unfortunate Wetherell was 'screwed up in one corner' with an air of complete terror on his face. At the Bristol Bridge, large stones were flung; one policeman was struck and fell to the ground, apparently dead. All the time, the loud and continuous groaning of the crowd was 'enough to shake the stoutest heart'. When Wetherell's presence was made known, a huge and menacing group gathered round his lodging at the Mansion House. Then they proceeded to attack, not with guns but with bars, stones and sheer physical force – and, of course, fire, the undiscriminating weapon of the mob down the ages. Gradually, a change occurred in the personnel of the attack: what had been a body of working men and artisans turned into something manned by what a contemporary called 'the lower grades of society', some dressed in smocks, others in 'generally mean attire'.[2]

There was another interesting social contrast when some of the shopkeepers who went to chase their stolen goods penetrated the quarters inhabited by the Irish labourers: hitherto a world away from their comfortable lives – if not literally so. An accumulation of dirt a foot deep was reported, including dead cats, dogs and rabbits, pig dung and pools of stagnant water containing rotting vegetables. At least 100 houses were burnt including the Bishop's Palace, the toll house, the excise house, the customs house and three prisons. (Charles Kingsley, the celebrated Victorian novelist, then a schoolboy in Clifton, remembered for the rest of his life the devastation, including charred corpses, in Queen Square.)[3] The Mansion House itself was sacked before being burnt and Wetherell himself only escaped, like some Mozartian character, by dressing as a postilion and fleeing over the roof. When the cooks were driven out of the kitchen the feast they had prepared was left behind; so the rioters were able to enjoy turtle soup, turkeys and joints of venison, an interesting variation on their usual meagre diet. Other rioters, enjoying the involuntary hospitality of the Mansion House and elsewhere, were not so lucky: many fell to the ground blind drunk and were consumed by the fire they had created.

Grey would refer to what happened in Bristol as 'the melancholy events', but in fact they were a great deal rougher than this graceful phrase suggested. Matters were compounded by the reluctance of Colonel Brereton, at the head of the Dragoons, to fire on the crowd because he had spent three years there as a recruiting officer and felt attached to the place. Brereton was even observed shaking hands with the rioters, many of whom he knew personally. Ever since the disaster of Peterloo, there had been some confusion about the relative roles of military and civilians in maintaining order. Brereton made the mistake of withdrawing the 14th Dragoons because they were in his opinion inflaming the populace. There were undoubtedly inflammatory incidents with terrible consequences: Elizabeth Grosvenor heard from her neighbour of a Captain Beckwith of the 14th Dragoons who had been hurt by 'a great stone thrown in his face'. In a passion, Beckwith gave an immense sweep of his sword and lopped the offending man's head clean off his shoulders.[4]

The official estimate was of twelve killed and just under 100 wounded in the course of a battle which started from the moment of Wetherell's appearance, when he was greeted by cries of 'The King and Reform' and 'We'll give them reaction'. In fact, the number of rioters who died was probably more like 400, including those burnt to death drunk, even if it could not be accurately estimated. One hundred and two prisoners were taken, eighty-one convicted, thirty-one of them of capital crimes; four were executed and seven men transported overseas. Colonel Brereton was another casualty: he was subsequently tried for his well-intentioned humane behaviour, but shot himself before the trial was concluded.

Most of the destruction took place on the Sunday and Monday, 30 and 31 October. On 1 November *The Times*, with the aid of a local correspondent on the *Globe*, revealed that the work of devastation was still going on at a most fearful rate. It was not until 2 November that Lord Althorp was able to comment: 'Bristol is at last got under.' He was also able to report a great escape at the Post Office where £300,000 (about £30 million in today's money) happened to be lodged on the Sunday night, but was rescued by an enterprising man who hired an inoffensive-looking 'hack chaise' and took the money away to Bath.[5]

These were by far the most aggressive riots so far; the question on everyone's lips, whatever their political persuasion, was: where would it all end? Charles Dickens expressed the countrywide horror in a poem written in November, 'The Devil's Walk', in which the Devil determined to make a few calls 'to see if his Friends were well'. His first call was the House of Lords where, 'with mixed feelings of pleasure and hate', he found a few rich and proud nobles declaring war against 'the People and Prince', which reminded him of the Wars in Heaven long ago.

> Then away to Bristol he quickly walked
> T'indulge in meditation
> And he gaily laughed as he slowly stalked
> O'er a scene of desolation

The Devil honoured the hand that had done the deed before deciding to return to London at speed to see his old friend Sir Charles . . .[6] It was all very well for the Whig Government to take the position stoutly that the violence would end when Reform was carried; for all anyone knew at the beginning of November, the revolution regularly predicted by both sides, most notably by the Duke of Wellington, was on its way. Whatever their point of view, most serious people feared that the Devil would continue to find scenes of desolation for a long time to come as he walked about Britain.

The fact was that law and order was a serious problem for the authorities at this point. There were historic bodies such as the civil magistrates; but the police force was in its infancy and the country was by no means overrun with troops. The effective strength of the Army in Great Britain, including Ireland, at the end of 1831 has been estimated at just over 25,000, with about 3,500 officers in addition; the cavalry were something under 5,000, the footguards under 4,000, and the rest made up of infantry.[7] The result was that unusual activity in one district was liable to cause a famine of protection in another. As Sir Willoughby Gordon, the Quartermaster General, drily observed about the lack of disposable forces in and around London: 'We need not fear a Military Despotism at least.' This had been seen clearly during the October riots when General Bouverie in Manchester declined to dispatch troops for Nottingham and Derby, urgent as the need was, because he did not feel he could safely detach anything from his own district. Meanwhile Colonel Thackwell in Nottingham sent a detachment to Derby, only to find himself in need of troops as the rioters tore apart Nottingham (including the Castle).

There was a further complication: were the existing troops loyal? Loyal to the Government that is; Brereton's reluctance to fire, animated by feelings for the neighbourhood he knew, has been noted. A speaker at a meeting of the National Union of the Working Classes in Manchester in late November declared that the soldiers, 'though they did happen to have scarlet coats', had feelings in common with the people, as well as having fathers, brothers and friends among those standing before them. There were all kinds of rumours of muskets ordered by the rioters – one in particular concerning a gunmaker called Riviere convinced the Duke of Wellington, even if it proved to have no foundation when it was checked. Similarly stories of disaffection among the troops themselves were rife. The soldier Alexander Somerville reported these widespread rumours in his memoir, adding that there was no proof of their reliability.[8] But of course in a volatile situation it was what was generally believed that was important in guiding popular reaction, rather than the actual truth.

The great estates took precautions. The incendiarism of the previous year had been a frightening experience; now there was a new element in the destruction among the rioters, the feeling of political justification. Sir Robert Peel had expressed the best-case scenario from the Tory point of view: there was yet a hope that the propertied class, 'by diligently reading the lessons which have been written in blood at Bristol', might learn the risk – or rather 'the certain price' – of revolutions. He referred to the disgust which must be felt at the 'whole reptile tribe of spouters at public meetings' led of course by Thomas Attwood and his like. As it happened, Drayton Manor, the country seat of Sir Robert Peel, was in a peculiarly exposed position, centrally placed in the Midlands industrial district, with Derby to the north, Nottingham north-east and Birmingham only ten miles south-west. In a less optimistic mood, Peel imported carbines and announced that he intended to defend his home as long as he could. Sir John Hobhouse wrote to the Tory leader of the House of Commons, pointing to the domestic style of the country houses built within the last 300 years: none of the owners had ever dreamt of being obliged to provide against 'the attack of the mob'.[9]

At Belvoir Castle, home of the Tory Duke of Rutland, cannons and one 'long gun' were set up on the North East Terrace, which was specially paved for their reception, under the instruction of a Sergeant John Kirkby.[10] * A room in the Round Tower was fitted up as 'an Arsenal'. The team of estate carpenters were trained to operate the guns. These were not the first precautions on the Rutland estates in the Midlands: there were those staves bought for Special Constables in January and recently, in October, the watchmen had been provided with flints and gunpowder. But cannons set to dominate the surrounding countryside sent the clearest message yet: no one could attack this fortress with impunity even though some were expected to try.

There was another aspect to it all. Richard Norman, manager of the estates, made a report to the Duke on 6 November in which he stressed the connection of poverty to rioting.[11] Described as 'of tall and noble presence, elegant and dignified in manner', the 5th Duke of Rutland was 'singularly courteous to everyone he met'; this paragon of an aristocrat was also 'a philanthropist in his neighbourhood'. Thus the Duke had contributed generously to the treatment of the poor by the parishes, yet the allowances being made to them were dismally small – six shillings a week for a man and his wife, one shilling and sixpence per child per week. This meant that the administrators of the parish of Waltham, for example, were actually pocketing money.

As a magistrate Norman intended to allow twelve shillings per week, and he hoped the farmers would respond with similar generosity, whether they employed the men on the farm or the road, lowering their rents. 'And as you have nobly done Your Part,' Norman told the Duke, 'I trust You will stand by me in doing but Justice to the Poor.'

Nevertheless, for all this high-minded local charity Norman was clearly in a state of apprehension about 'the greatest Excitement prevailing in the Minds of the People'. Only 'a Spark' was wanting to

---

* The big gun is still to be seen today at Belvoir Castle.

cause a general combustion. He did however question whether the political unions might not actually be a force for good in suppressing tumult – given that the people enrolled as unionists had 'the security of Property at heart'. This was the Attwood message of peaceful protest making itself felt. All the same, Norman ended on a note which summed up clearly what the majority of the property-owners and their households were thinking: 'We cannot in this Moment, look forward a Week without Alarm.'

Guy Fawkes Day, celebrated with bonfires and the burning of effigies ever since the uncovering of the Gunpowder Plot in 1605, fell conveniently – from the point of view of the rioters – a few days later. Originally Parliament had focused on the Catholic elements in the conspiracy and its official Anglican prayers on the day were redolent of anti-popery, with references to 'Popish treachery' and the Royal Family (in 1605) being led 'as sheep to the slaughter'. In the 200-odd years which had passed since the death of Guy Fawkes and his Catholic co-conspirators, things had moved on; it had gradually become customary to burn effigies of current hate-figures rather than the original villains.[12] There was indeed some dramatic irony in the fact that it was now the Anglican bishops being execrated on 5 November, a day originally planned specifically to denounce the Pope of Rome and his accomplices.

As the freethinker Richard Carlile had pointed out concerning the twenty-one prelates who had voted to reject the Bill, that number voting the other way would have been enough to pass it, given the 41 majority for defeat. 'The Bishops have done it,' he declared sardonically. 'It is the work of the Holy Ghost.' Thus on 5 November 1831 bishops' mitres took the place of Guy Fawkes's traditional black hat crowning the stuffed figures on the bonfires. In Huddersfield, according to the *Poor Man's Guardian*, there was a ceremony of 'rather novel description' when around 15,000 or 20,000 people paraded with an effigy of a bishop '*as natural as life*', and it was said that no funeral was ever conducted with greater awe and solemnity. One man dressed up as a priest himself and declaimed: 'Ho! All ye people of Huddersfield ... For lo! and behold! Here is a great, fat, bloated, blundering bishop whom we have bartered for the poor, deluded, murdered Guy Faux [*sic*].' The only light note was struck by the 'rueful expression' on the face of the burning bishop. A subversive rhyme was chanted:

> Good Lord! put down aristocrats
> Let Boroughmongers be abhorred
> And from all tithes and shovel hats
> Forthwith deliver us, good Lord!

Yet it was noted that the streets cleared quietly after ten o'clock when the flames had died down.[13]

Taking advantage of the traditional date, there were many more such demonstrations countrywide where it was sometimes difficult to draw a line between a bout of popular disaffection, often for local causes, and some more violent intention connected to Reform. In Dorset Mary Frampton had noticed that during their demonstrations, 'the minds of the common people' were 'wickedly excited' by suggestions that Reform would give them meat as well as bread in abundance, all at a much cheaper price than normal.[14]

In Exeter, Bishop Henry Phillpotts was already a target by reason of his notoriously anti-Reform stance; now his effigy was ostentatiously burnt. A 'tall, finely formed' figure of a man, with an imposing, lofty forehead and 'dark hair like the quills of the fretful porcupine' in the words of the parliamentary journalist James Grant, this was one 'Guy' which was unmistakable to the people of Exeter. It has to be said for the Bishop's *sangfroid* under the circumstances that he explained his toleration of the burning to the Duke of Wellington as follows: far from being a sign of weakness, it was simply the most convenient way of getting rid of the effigy, which would otherwise have hung about awkwardly. Nearer home, the Duke himself, together with the Duke of Cumberland, was burnt in effigy at Tyburn, near Marble Arch. Phillpotts's efficiency was, however, matched by Wellington's composure. On 8 November he told the Deputy Governor of Dover Castle loftily: 'In respect to insults to me, those who wish to insult me are perfectly welcome.' He added: 'I defend myself if they attempt injury. . . .'[15]

*

Back in London the Cabinet were far from united on what should be done. It was the question, posed crucially by Lord Lyndhurst in the House of Lords, to which some answer had to be found. Could the Bill really not be moderated – that was the right soothing word – in some way so as to bring in enough peers to pass it in its (comparatively) new form? A little group of Tory peers was beginning to take shape who would be known as 'the Waverers'; prominent among them were Lord Wharncliffe and Lyndhurst himself. Given that you only had to 'turn' twenty-one votes (and of course they did not necessarily have to be bishops), there was a body of opinion in the Cabinet, including Lord John Russell himself, Melbourne and Palmerston, who believed this must be the reasonable way to go.

The first debate concerned the date of the next meeting of Parliament. Grey, the Duke of Richmond and Lord Palmerston thought 6 December – the date generally proposed – was too soon. They were defeated; Lord Althorp was impressed by Grey's dignified bearing in the face of his failure. In any case the state of the country meant that the arguments for urgent action had been mightily reinforced. The Prime Minister was frank about it in his communication with the King: the recall was against his own wishes or, as the Cabinet minute put it which was sent to William IV, the three dissenters, 'though they were of the opinion that it would have been better to continue the prorogation till the beginning of January', acquiesced in the advice 'which is thus humbly submitted to your Majesty'.[16]

There was also an appalling scene at the Cabinet dinner on the eve of Parliament when Lord Durham started to insult his father-in-law Grey in a way that bordered on the mad. Grief had not improved Durham's excitable, even morbid temperament. Only a week earlier he had written to Grey, thanking him for all his kindness to him over the death of his son. Now he issued the most brutal attack on him, wrote Althorp to his father, that he had ever heard in his life. Lord Melbourne, more crudely, said that if he had been Lord Grey, he would have knocked Durham down.[17]

Durham accused Grey of keeping him in London while his son was dying, saying that he, Durham, would be disgraced if there was any alteration in the move towards Reform. (This was quite unfair, commented Althorp, because the Bill was essentially the same.) The deeply mortified Grey responded that he would rather work in the coal mines than be subject to such attacks. 'And you could do worse,' responded the noble colliery owner. Then Durham left the room. If there were two Durhams, quite unalike, as Lord Holland once suggested, this was certainly Durham in his most terrible mood – however understandable. It was the measure of his instability at this time that, although Althorp believed he would instantly resign, Durham proceeded later as if nothing had happened.

Meanwhile the stately dance with and round the King – with side-steps in the direction of the Radicals – continued. In the general state of perturbation throughout the country, not everyone took the enlightened attitude of the Duke of Rutland's estate agent, Richard Norman, that the unions might be a force for pacification. There were rumours – more rumours – about the existence of armed bodies and menacing military organization. Guns, it was said, were being concealed in walking-sticks. The Tory-inclined newspaper the *Standard* suggested that the Birmingham Political Union had actually played some part in the recent 'melancholy events', in Grey's phrase, at Bristol. This was certainly not true; in fact it was the Bristol riots that prompted Thomas Attwood to suggest that military organization of some sort might be a sound plan for the Union, in the face of such hostility. In Birmingham, 10,000 or 15,000 men would be able 'to vindicate the law, and restore the peace and security of the town'.[18] No mention was made of arms – although of course they were not officially forbidden either.

Under the circumstances the Government decided to issue a Royal Proclamation on the subject. This was something that William IV was easily persuaded to do. On 22 November it was officially announced that all political unions were illegal which assumed power independent of the civil magistrates. On the face of it this was a direct rebuff to the unions, a challenge to their growing numbers which could cost the Government dear, given the existing attacks on their policies from the opposite side of the political spectrum. But several days previously

Lord Althorp, having persuaded Grey of the need for secret intervention, had written privately to Joseph Parkes asking him to intercede in Birmingham: Attwood should be dissuaded from incorporating any such military organization into his flagship Birmingham Political Union, otherwise it would inevitably be brought into conflict with the Government.[19] This important undercover initiative was successful, and any such militarization of the Union was now explicitly rejected.

In a leader on the day of the Opening of Parliament, *The Times* expressed the pious hope that His Majesty would mention 'the dreadful occurrences at Bristol'. They were satisfied: putting on his spectacles to read his speech from the throne, William IV sounded duly shocked by recent events: 'My Lords and Gentlemen, the scenes of violence and outrage which have occurred in the city of Bristol and some other places, have caused me the deepest affliction'; therefore, foremost in the coming session the King wanted 'a speedy consideration of the measures of Reform in the House of Commons'.[20]

Fortunately, the King was in one of his ebullient moods, according to Sir Denis Le Marchant who, as the Lord Chancellor's Private Secretary, happened to be near him in the robing room when he was putting on his crown. When Grey remarked that this would be one of the longest speeches ever delivered from the throne, the King boasted that his boyhood tutor had believed that 'no lesson could be too long for him to learn'. He confided to Brougham that since he usually learnt his speeches by heart, he was not afraid of being put out by any accidental interruption.[21]

Lord John Russell presented the new Bill on 12 December.[22] Perhaps his manner could never be heroic, given the limitations of his old-fashioned 'Whig' voice and his slight figure. Sydney Smith once wickedly suggested that when the electors were worried by Russell's small size, they should simply be assured that he began by being much larger, but had been worn away by the anxieties and struggles of the Reform Bill.[23] Nevertheless Russell's words were stirring and his message forthright: there was no one who had attended to 'this great question' and noticed the manner in which it has agitated the country, 'the agitation increasing with every returning period of distress', without being convinced that the time had now arrived when speedy and satis-factory settlement was of an importance 'very nearly equal to the Bill itself'.

It was not the identical Bill that was now presented. There had been small but distinct alterations, as for example a reworking of Schedule B, whereby the number of towns to lose one Member was reduced, including Bodmin, Guildford and Huntingdon, and ten of the newly enfranchised towns got an extra seat. These alterations were at the suggestion of the so-called Waverers; but it could be argued that the Tory restitutions were neatly balanced by the increased influence of the more Radical towns.[24]

Besides Lords Wharncliffe and Lyndhurst, the Waverers now included the veteran Earl of Harrowby. Just on seventy, Harrowby had originally been the Tory MP for Tiverton, and a personal friend of Pitt; later, as a peer, he had occupied various prestigious posts and acted as Lord President of the Council for fifteen years until 1827. Greville paid tribute to him in his *Memoirs*: Harrowby, he wrote, if he lacked imagination and eloquence, had 'a noble, straightforward, independent character' who in the course of a long political life never incurred any blemish or suspicion.[25]

Obviously it was in the best interests of the Government for the hostile majority to be gradually eroded by changes of mind before the next vote. Harrowby was just the kind of man whose presence in the voting lobby of the Lords would be most valuable to them. Although meetings with the Waverers were liable to be described as treacher-ous by both sides, Radicals and Ultra Tories, they were an obvious pacific route towards the progress of the Bill. The Whigs had an excel-lent natural conduit to them in the shape of Edward Stanley, the Chief Secretary for Ireland. In the way such things worked, he had been at Oxford with Lord Wharncliffe's son and visited North America with him. Then Stanley called at the Harrowby home at Sandon Hall in Staffordshire on his way to Ireland, allowing Harrowby to establish a discreet relationship with the Cabinet.

So the new Bill included various modifications. For one thing the Census of 1831 (as opposed to 1821) was used, the absence of which had always been a legitimate grievance on the part of its critics. The number of houses and the number of assessed taxes were employed to calculate Schedules A and B, rather than the population; also the number of MPs was not to be reduced – as General Gascoyne had demanded in his amendment back in April, leading to the famous dissolution. In this way, dozens of boroughs could be taken out of Schedule B, and other well-populated towns such as Rochdale could be enfranchised.

The changes enabled Sir Robert Peel in reply to refer to 'the great escape from the previous Bill' and to express his gratitude to those – the Lords and the objectors in general – who had brought it about. At this point, therefore, the result could well be described as a triumph for compromise; in other words there was more than one way of putting down the aristocrats in the House of Lords, other than violence and burning effigies. Cobbett and Hunt both approved the Bill, *The Times* thought it very little changed and Ultra Tories like Croker considered the details a great triumph for the fuss made by his own party. Baring Wall, the MP for Guildford who had cried out 'They are mad!' when he first heard the provisions of the Bill in March, took the line that the concessions were due not so much to the Opposition as to 'reason and justice'.[26]

However, Croker went on to point out more gloomily that the Bill left 'the great objection' – to Reform in the first place – just where it was: 'Nay, by removing anomalies and injustices, it makes the Bill more palatable and therefore more dangerous.' Sir Charles Wetherell, admirably undaunted by recent experiences in Bristol, gave one of his history lessons. He recalled the attack on the Anglican Church in 1641; once again bishops were being treated as 'malignants'. And he quoted the lines from *Hudibras*, the popular poem by the seventeenth-century Samuel Butler, which referred to the sectarian female dissidents of the time:

> When oyster women locked their fish up
> And trudged away to cry 'No Bishop!'

Wetherell was also keen to pour scorn on Russell's notorious reference to 'the whisper of faction', that is the House of Lords. Like Croker, he believed that the Bill had been defeated not by a whisper but by 'the well-grounded conviction of reasoning men'.[27]

Not all the five days of debate were on the highest level. Hunt and Lord Morpeth got into a squabble over an entry in the *Leeds Mercury* following Hunt's visit to the city. Lord Morpeth took the line that the *Mercury* had never advocated physical assault against Hunt's person, to which Hunt (not unreasonably) replied that the words 'cracking open his skull' were difficult to interpret otherwise; in an argument reminiscent of that of Portia in *The Merchant of Venice*, Hunt queried how this could take place without loss of blood.[28]

The speech of Lord William Lennox, MP for King's Lynn since 1831, was on a more elevated level. Brother of the Duke of Richmond, Lord William took a similar interest in colonial matters. The Duke had advocated giving votes to the colonies (the right types, as 'a sure counteraction to the force of popular clamour', were expected to emerge in the House of Commons as a result). It was a measure which, despite being argued 'very ingeniously', was rejected by his colleagues as too large and late. Lennox was a spirited fellow who really preferred the theatre and sport to politics – he had made an unwise marriage to a singer which ended in disaster – but during his short-lived occupation of a parliamentary seat, he spoke out boldly and critically on the subject of nominated Members. He saw no difference, he said, between 'the vested right of a West Indian planter over the body of his slave' and the vested rights of nomination; 'for I see no distinction between mental and corporeal enthralment'.[29]

There were two fine speeches which impressed all who heard them, both by men who were young in parliamentary terms – Thomas Babington Macaulay and Edward Stanley were thirty-one and thirty-two respectively.[30] Macaulay's speech, an extraordinary compound of 'deep philosophy, exalted sentiments and party bitterness', was said to have had 'a prodigious effect'. Physically unimpressive, Macaulay created a greater impression with his oratory every time he spoke. Now he waxed both eloquent and furious on the subject of the new Bill and refused to give an inch on the subject of the Lords' rejection: '. . . in truth, we recant nothing – we have nothing to recant – we support this Bill – we may possibly think it is a better Bill than that which preceded it. But are we therefore bound to admit that we were in the wrong – that the opposition was in the right – that the House of Lords has conferred a great benefit on the nation? . . . Is delay no evil? Is prolonged excitement' – the word generally used for crowds out of control – 'no evil? Is it no evil that the heart of a great people should be made sick by deferred hope?'

Macaulay then went on to dispose of the idea that the great Parliamentarians of the past had arrived via nominations; in fact the five largest represented urban districts – Westminster, Southwark, Liverpool, Bristol and Norwich – had produced among others Burke, Fox, Sheridan, Canning and Huskisson. There would, of course, always be some 'extravagances' at a time of change: the Anabaptists had flourished at the time of the Reformation. But the history of England was one of government 'sometimes peaceably, sometimes after a violent struggle, but constantly giving way before a nation that has been constantly advancing'.

Examples Macaulay produced were the forest laws, the law of villainage, the oppressive power of the Roman Catholic Church, the Protestant establishment subsequently, the prerogatives of the Crown and the censorship of the press. The Stuarts could not govern as the Tudors had, nor the Hanoverians as their predecessors the Stuarts had done; the age of the last four Hanoverian monarchs was also over. As so often at this period, the French Revolution was brought into play; the government of Louis XVI had been 'much better and milder' than that of his ancestor Louis XIV, but the latter had been admired and loved, while Louis XVI died on the scaffold. Why? Simply because the French government had not advanced as rapidly as the French nation.

Stanley, the future 'Rupert of Debate', began with a well-argued defence of the new Bill in detail, allaying the fears of his friends who knew he could do the stirring stuff, but worried that this political firebrand might be 'stranded in a studied speech'. The concessions, he said, were responsible and in answer to genuine grievances; and in order to avoid a crisis it was essential the Bill should be passed as soon as possible. But his speech was also remarkable for his intervention in the long-running intellectual battle between John Wilson Croker and Macaulay. This was a matter which had involved not only the staple of such conflicts, bad-tempered reviews, but also acid references in Parliament. (Croker never willingly let Macaulay forget that he entered the House of Commons, sitting for Calne, at the whim as it were of Lord Lansdowne.)

Now Stanley lashed into Croker, who had made what was, as it turned out, an unfortunate reference to Charles I and his Parliaments – another historical period constantly invoked at this time. 'In the course of his extraordinary misrepresentation of the history of the country,' declared Stanley, 'he has given us events for causes and causes for events. What he describes as a consequence had actually preceded it. What he represents as a cause . . .' and so forth and so on. The trouble was that Stanley was right. Having demonstrated the complete falsity of Croker's contention, Stanley memorably observed: 'Inaccurate reading is as dangerous as a little reading.' This public putting-down of Croker was not totally unwelcome to his own side. Edward Littleton was told afterwards that Peel had remarked: 'I wonder how our *biographer*, Croker, likes the dressing [down] he got from Stanley.' Croker for his part went very pale, and pulled his hat down over his eyes. An Irishman in the gallery, listening to Croker's violent declamations, had once described him as being 'like a hen on a hot griddle'. For now the 'hen' was quiet.[31]

On 17 December, the last day of the debate, Peel spoke again and made an important statement of his position for the future.[32] There was a conventional tribute to the Constitution 'under which I have lived hitherto, which I believe is adapted to the wants and habits of the people' followed by a declaration: 'I will continue my opposition to the last, believing as I do, that it is the first step, not directly to Revolution, but to a series of changes which will affect the property, and totally change the character of the mixed constitution of this country.' But at the end Peel added an important *caveat:* 'On this ground I take my stand, not opposed to a well considered Reform of any of our institutions which need reform, but opposed to this Reform.' There was a hint of flexibility here – very different from the inflexibility of his leader, the Duke of Wellington, in the Lords in November 1830 and ever since.

On the same day, voting took place: 324 MPs voted for the Bill and half that number against; the 162 majority made it clear that there were Tory abstentions. Parliament was adjourned. The landowners now went to their country houses, the Duke of Richmond to his Sussex palace whose name was beginning to be used for 'the Goodwood Set'. This comprised those, such as the Duke himself, Palmerston and Melbourne, who were uneasy about the direction that Reform was taking, and the whole subject of creation of peers in particular.

There was no escaping the decision which had to be taken in some form or other early in the New Year. Given that the House of Commons had once again passed the Bill, and given that it seemed inevitable that the Lords would reject it – in clear defiance of the popular will – the creation of new peers had to be considered. The aristocrats were not so much to be watered down as swamped with new Members. Otherwise, wrote *The Times* in its report of the passing of the Bill, Great Britain would be 'one scene of blood and terror'. Joseph Parkes put it succinctly in a letter to Harriet Grote: 'All say New Peers or d–m–n to Lord Grey and co.'[33]

CHAPTER ELEVEN

THE FEARFUL
ALTERNATIVE

'It was impossible, therefore, to delay looking to the fearful
alternative which was thus forced upon our consideration ...' –

Lord Grey to William IV, 4 January 1832

On 1 January 1832, Lord Holland wished his close friend the Prime
Minister a happy New Year. 1831 had been, he noted in his Diary, the
first full year of Whig rule for seventy years. To Grey he gave his
New Year wish regarding the recalcitrant House of Lords: 'I hope you
will prove yourself (pardon the blasphemy) a famous Creator.' And
on the subject of numbers to be created, Holland proceeded to make
merry with the rules of tennis, of which he was a veteran player; he
said that he liked that way of counting – fifteen, thirty, forty, Game.[1]
Unfortunately the subject was by no means so light-hearted as Lord
Holland's sprightly comments suggested. Nor was creation – the
question of enlarging the House of Lords in order to nullify the large
natural Tory majority – quite as simple as the Radical Joseph Parkes
had indicated in his letter to Harriet Grote on the universal demand
for 'New Peers'.

At a Cabinet meeting on 18 December, Grey raised the matter in a
voice which was rather faint: what would happen if the second reading
of the Bill was defeated once more in the Lords?[2] In November he had
quoted to Sir Francis Burdett a Latin tag on the subject: *quieta prius
tentanda* – first of all, a peaceable approach must be tried. There was
nothing however to suggest that a peaceable approach, when it came
to the vote, would prove effective. Nevertheless, Grey's evident diffidence masked a real difficulty which was felt by aristocrats themselves
where the enlargement of their class was concerned. It is too simple to
describe this as being purely a jealous sense of superiority. No doubt

that came into it in some cases, as such emotions generally do where exclusivity is apparently being threatened from outside. But the whole matter was more complicated than that.

There was also a sincere feeling for the aristocracy as a special caste which was certainly not dishonourable; this caste was part of the natural order of society, along with Crown and People, which, by its establishment and maintenance, prevented any kind of unnatural upheaval. Like any other class, they were expected to show a sense of responsibility commensurate with their privilege: in this case, a sense of responsibility towards the government of the country and the people in it, as Grey in particular had felt so strongly all his life. But then so had the traditional Tory aristocrats. This patrician feeling was an essential strand woven into the fabric of the time, as much part of it as the Radical feelings of a Parkes or an Attwood.

Of course it was understood that this caste would be enlarged from time to time, most recently by the traditional coronation creations. Grey's own earldom, for example, was only second-generation, although he came from a long line of landed gentry. The new entrants were expected to be worthy of their new estate, which at least partially meant in a material sense. These kinds of creations, however, were individual honours, and while political allegiances obviously came into it – after all, the famous Tory majority had come about during the stretched-out years of Tory government – that was a different matter from a large block of creations at one particular time for the sake of one political measure.

This had occurred 120 years earlier in the reign of Queen Anne in order to bring about the Treaty of Utrecht, which ended the War of the Spanish Succession. But this was not necessarily regarded as a good precedent. In 1711 twelve peers were hastily created by a reluctant Queen in order to assist the new Tory Government at the expense of the Whigs; among them were Samuel Masham, the husband of her favourite Abigail Masham. When she was warned by Lord Dartmouth that this measure would have 'a very ill effect in the House of Lords and no good one in the kingdom', the Stuart Queen replied that she liked it as little as he did, but no one had proposed 'a better expedient'.[3]

It remained to be seen whether her Hanoverian cousin William IV, faced with the same choice, would with similar reluctance make the same decision.

In short, the Constitution held that the creation of peers was a royal prerogative; less clear was the part that ministerial advice should play, and whether this advice was in itself mandatory for the monarch to take. The relatively small number of twelve was also significant and presumably influenced Grey when he had made a reference to it in July. Although in theory a vastly bigger number must also be covered by the royal prerogative, in practice an influx of, say, forty or fifty peers at one go, as the Radicals cheerfully demanded, would have the effect of transforming the House of Lords. And, incidentally, who were these new peers to be?

There was an obvious difference between the eldest sons of existing peers – many of whom, sitting in the House of Commons under their courtesy titles, were destined to inherit peerages sooner or later – and actual commoners. The first category was infinitely preferable to those who felt strongly on the subject of the caste: it enlarged the Government majority but did not in effect enlarge the aristocracy. One obvious example whose name was mentioned in this connection was the Marquess of Blandford, heir to the Dukedom of Marlborough, who had favoured Reform as a way to combat the evil effects of Catholic Emancipation, voting with the Government on 22 March 1831. (He said later that he had rejected the possibility.)[4]

Similarly, giving certain Irish or Scottish peers – such as Lord Palmerston – the right to sit in the British House of Lords, hitherto denied them, did not actually enlarge the aristocracy. There was a further possibility: the granting of peerages to older men without children (who could be trusted not to beget them in the future) would also leave the aristocracy untouched in the future. This enabled Lord Holland to make one of his jokes: 'I shall tell the candidates for peerages to imitate the housemaid who enhanced her qualifications for the job: "My Lord, besides all this I'm a barrener" – since many [new barons] are to be barren with an "e" as well as an "o".'[5]

Of course it was not to be expected that, in an age when satire was a popular recreation, witticisms on the subject of the new peers should be excepted. There was for example a story that one lord had simply nominated a waiter at White's Club – the only problem being that he didn't know the waiter's name. The seventy-five-year-old Lord Essex had been one of the 'beaux of that day' – the day being pre-revolutionary France, where he had known Marie Antoinette; he was famous for having his hair magnificently coiffed in Paris for a party, travelling all the way back to London with his head 'in a forced position', and then dazzling the English capital once again with the same *coiffure*. Now he suggested that the King ought to stop at the first stand of hackney coaches in Piccadilly and make all the coachmen in succession peers until the number was filled up.[6]

In answer to Grey's question on 18 December, important differences of opinion on this potentially vital subject began to emerge in the Cabinet.[7] Lord Brougham was in fine bombastic form as he summed up both sides of the question. Although, after a long speech, he finally came down on the side of 'a very large increase in the Lords' as opposed to the loss of the Bill, he was felt by some to have spent too much time on the objections to an increase, even exaggerating them; so Brougham, as ever, managed to be both helpful and unhelpful in the same swoop of eloquence. What did emerge was the fact that a very large creation would have the counter-effect of alienating some peers who had hitherto been friendly to the Bill.

Both the Marquess of Lansdowne and the Duke of Richmond deprecated 'most earnestly' what they termed the 'destruction' of the House of Lords. It was an unpleasant fact that King Louis-Philippe had abolished the hereditary upper house in France late in 1831. Such an event across the Channel could not help evoking a kind of general dread of change regarding hereditary legislature in England, in case here also it all went too far, too fast. Lord Palmerston took a different line. Rather than endorse creation, he favoured indirect concessions over parts of the Bill: the Government would accept having 'obnoxious' changes forced upon them in Committee if in return the vote in favour on the second reading would be guaranteed.

Lord Holland, as ever of a pragmatic turn of mind, suggested that the right course was to demand the creation of a few peers, in order to demonstrate their power with the King; it might also persuade those who were totally averse to any large increase on constitutional grounds that acceptance of the Bill was the least bad alternative. The Duke of Richmond then admitted that the Archbishop of Canterbury – 'if convinced we would make peers' – might prefer to lead his fellow prelates into voting for the Bill, rather than accept a large increase.

Vacillation was one characteristic of the Prime Minister that Lord Grey's critics often commented upon when his behaviour did not suit their own purposes (of course, apparent indecision was also a useful weapon of statesmanship). On this occasion Grey could certainly be forgiven, in view of the divided views of the Cabinet, in saying that he referred the question to them for their further consideration. It was left to Lord Durham, mercifully in a less combative mood – although he did still manage to show 'asperity' towards Palmerston – to sum up the three possibilities: whether to make peers sufficient to carry the Bill; whether to create a small batch with a view to avoiding the first option; or whether to trust to 'modifications, arrangements and understandings' in order to secure a majority in the Lords. Durham seemed to grow in belligerence once more as he contemplated this third option, which he described as 'neither reconcileable to honour or prudence, an evasion of Lord Grey's pledge' and furthermore an incitement to defeat. He declared that he himself (and surely others) would actually vote against this Bill, 'so mutilated and the offspring of such compromise and contrivances'.

Later Holland visited Grey in the bosom of his beloved family at his southern retreat of East Sheen; here Grey was always at his most 'natural and amiable'. The Prime Minister confided to him that Durham's temper was often more of a trial to him than any public or private grievances whatsoever; all the same Holland found Grey's desire to gratify his daughter Louisa Durham, the bereaved mother, very touching. Nevertheless, with whatever reluctance, Grey still believed that the creation of peers was a necessity. And Holland was relieved to find that Lady Grey, who in her quiet way had great influence with her husband, was manifestly for a vigorous measure rather than a second defeat.[8]

It was a reminder of the troubles of the wider world that, at that late December meeting, the Cabinet had passed from Reform to discussing events in Ireland. Only the day before Lord Grey had had to inform the King of 'an affray' in Kilkenny on account of tithes: the chief constable and sixteen police were killed 'and only three or four of the mob'.[9] The police were said to have been attacked in a road with high banks by about 2,000 people armed with pitchforks and stones, who rushed them before they could fire more than a few shots; this incident demonstrated that the apparent unassailable advantage of firepower did not always prevail where the other side had numbers, surprise and ferocity on their side. Now Stanley, as Chief Secretary for Ireland, confirmed the increasing violence to the Cabinet. There were calls, he said, not so much for reform of Parliament as for repeal of the Union which had subsumed the Irish Parliament into the English one thirty years earlier. As ever, agitation was met by counter-agitation. So Stanley also commented on the 'no less violent and factious' combinations of the Orangemen and Brunswickers 'on the pretence of protecting the Protestant Church'.

Throughout the following months, as the future of the English – or one should say British – Parliament was being decided in a series of intricate conspiracies, the spectre of insurrection in Ireland stalked the Government's imagination, with the King at least believing that O'Connell was 'stirring the fire'. William IV feared that more troops would be needed in Ireland since the example of violence, especially if it has been successful, was always contagious in that 'inflammable population'. Meanwhile the riots in England and Scotland continued; here was no nationalist agenda but demands for bread and jobs – and Reform. In the eloquent words of Macaulay: 'the far-spreading light of midnight fires, and the outrages of incendiaries have all but too often indicated wretchedness and despair, starvation and daring recklessness'.[10] It was the potential recklessness of those who had nothing to lose which perturbed both sides in the debate on Reform.

*

On 2 January 1832 a long Cabinet meeting took place at which Grey set forth what he called 'the great question of the day' by reading three letters.[11] Two, from Lord Brougham, painted 'in strong language' the need for creation, ten or twelve peers acting as 'a demonstration of our power and the King's determination to support us'. The third letter was from Thomas Coke, MP for Norfolk since 1807, who described himself with some justice as 'a very old reformer'; he was now seventy-eight and in the old days had been a strong supporter of Charles James Fox; he continued to correspond with Lafayette as a fellow 'Patriot'. Coke was a fervent Whig and an equally zealous improver of his agricultural estates centred on Holkham. As the Duke of Bedford once said to him, at Woburn and Holkham they were not plagued by demands for lower rentals: 'The reason is simple; neither you nor I screw our tenants up to high rents which they are unable to bear.'[12] Grey acknowledged Coke's distinguished philanthropic history when he read his letter aloud to the Cabinet; the veteran reformer called strongly for creation in accordance with the 'earnest expectations and wishes' of the people of Norfolk.

Yet Grey himself continued to express openly his reluctance for such an extreme measure. It was only the conviction that 'yet greater calamities' would follow that persuaded him. And it was the obvious sincerity of this position that would help Grey in his relations with William IV, when he went down to Brighton the next day for the crucial meeting. Grey had the backing of the Cabinet to tell the King that they wanted a *'demonstration'* of his confidence – *demonstration* was thought to be a 'very serviceable' phrase. But by no means could the Prime Minister be held to represent any kind of ardent anti-monarchical force. There were those who argued for Reform just because it was 'subversive of aristocracy, favourable to democracy [fearsome word] and partaking of a revolutionary character' – as the Marquess of Lansdowne had put it in Cabinet. Grey was evidently not one of them. He brought to his beleaguered Sovereign something more convincing: the belief of an honest man that worse, much worse, would follow if the King did not pledge creation.

The meeting on the morning of 4 January was extremely long; the

King had been prepared for it not only by previous correspondence but by a preliminary talk the evening before. According to Grey's minute of the conversation, written afterwards and passed to the King, he began by outlining how little security the Government had for believing they would carry the Bill, despite the increased majority in the House of Commons and the general expectation.[13] It was impossible therefore to delay looking to 'the fearful alternative' which was thus forced upon their consideration. Either they would face all the danger attendant upon the loss of the Bill or they must prevent such a defeat 'by use of the means which the prerogative of the Crown afforded' for just such an emergency: Grey meant, of course, the creation of peers.

William IV listened to it all 'with the greatest attention and with evident anxiety'. Naturally he was surrounded at Brighton by his large, loving and vociferous family headed by Queen Adelaide, and the Tory lords who were their friends; but he, like his Prime Minister, was an honest man struggling to do his best in the situation in which he found himself, even if he was not absolutely sure what that situation was. In reply William stressed his 'undiminished' concern about creation and then concentrated on the vexed question of who these putative new peers might be. Above all, the King wanted to change the permanent character of the House of Lords as little as possible – which meant in effect heirs to peerages, Irish peers and those 'barreners', as Lord Holland put it, who could be relied on not to enlarge the ranks of the Lords for more than one generation. Grey, by his own account, conceded to all this but did add that 'some creations of Commoners of high character and great property' might be desirable, but once again limited so as not to pillage the House of Commons unduly.

Grey ended by expressing the hope that 'a first partial creation' might produce the effect which would obviate a subsequent addition. Once again William IV listened 'most graciously'; then reiterated his point about the need to avoid augmenting the peerage. Suddenly he became more animated: 'His Majesty added that he trusted it would not be proposed to raise to the Peerage any of those who had been forward in agitating the country, as nothing could induce him to consent to the advancement of persons of that description.' He went on to express the greatest anxiety about the state of the country, trusting there would be no further encroachments tending to diminish 'the necessary power of the Government'. And he asked to see an account of their conversation in writing.

When he did so, the King acknowledged its 'perfect accuracy'.[14] But he made it clear that he did not consider himself pledged at this point to the adoption of any proposal or suggestion; for that he would need a more formal minute of the Cabinet. And he proceeded to declare it as a condition *inseparable* – his italics – to any proposal of creation, that the peers chosen should be *exclusively* – his italics again – eldest sons or collateral heirs to peerages where there was no direct heir. (There were two or possibly three exceptions of named men who had earlier been considered for coronation peerages.) He did not believe that even Irish or Scotch peers were necessary, looking at the lists submitted, although he would not actually have objected to them.

At the same time the King was positively against any policy of a partial creation, leading to a further *measure*: if twenty-one was the desired number, it must be twenty-one now 'instead of feeling the pulse and beating about the bush'. Having made it clear that his acquiescence was subject to the exclusion of all creations except those specified, William signed off with a renewed admonition about not rewarding the agitators.

His last paragraph was positively apocalyptic about the state of the country. This was a time of great peril, 'when the overthrow of all legitimate authority, the destruction of the ancient institutions, of social order, and of every gradation and link of society are threatened, when a revolutionary and demoralizing spirit is making frightful strides, when a poisonous press, almost unchecked, guides, excites and at the same time controls public opinion'. So the King hoped that, once Reform was happily settled, his Government would see to it that there was no further encroachment from the House of Commons, and above all no further diminution of the authority, influence and dignity of the Crown. He was not conscious of having shown any tendency towards an extravagant display of dignity and splendour – in contrast to the previous reign, was implied – or the exercise of despotic and arbitrary power. Therefore the various encroachments must be ascribed to something the King once again italicized: that growing fancy for *liberalism*. However fair its appearance, in itself it threatened the Constitution and form of government 'under which this country has so long prospered'.

On paper Lord Grey now had some kind of grudging royal assurance concerning creation, although it was so hedged around with conditions about the people suitable to be ennobled that it was doubtful if any large-scale creation would be possible. There were also disquieting clues to certain growing preoccupations of the Sovereign: that reference to a poisonous press, for example. Like many other royalties before him – notably Louis XVI and Marie Antoinette – the King was beginning to be stung by the gadflies.

In due course the official minute from the Cabinet was submitted.[15] With 'deep pain' the Cabinet confessed that it could have no confidence in securing a majority in the House of Lords. In such an extreme case, therefore, they believed that the exercise of the King's prerogative of creation could be justified. While paying lip-service to the King's known disinclination to augment the peerage in the long term, the Cabinet minute did not commit to any particular number until the Government should have received more accurate information about the state of opinion, as the Bill continued to go through the Commons.

The King replied at length on 15 January.[16] Many old arguments were rehearsed. He also allowed himself to compare the creation of peers at the Government's instigation for the avowed purpose of obtaining a majority in the House of Lords to the use of nomination, 'vulgarly called rotten boroughs'. Yet Reform was against this in principle. In both cases 'the independent voice' was being overpowered. Nevertheless there was a crucial passage buried in the extensive text, the kernel of the nut which the Cabinet sought. If necessary, the King would not deny to his Ministers the power of 'acting at once up to the full exigency of the case' – here he was ostensibly quoting from the Cabinet minute, but by inserting the word 'full', absent in the original, had inadvertently strengthened it.

*

Parliament reconvened on 17 January and then went into Committee. Before it did so, in view of the King's recent explosion on the subject of dignity and splendour, it was ironic that a lively debate took place over public expenditure on Buckingham Palace – ironic because King William, in his genuinely frugal way, had strongly objected to the proposal to move the royal residence there, and preferred to stay in St James's Palace.

The history of Buckingham Palace hitherto was not an encouraging one to a lover of economical living. Buckingham House had originally been built for the Duke of that name at the beginning of the eighteenth century; it was then altered into a private residence for Queen Charlotte, where most of her fifteen children were born, and known as the Queen's House. The transformation to a palace was, characteristically, the inspiration of George IV, with John Nash as his architect; Nash, however, was actually sacked for extravagance in 1829 and Edward Blore was substituted. Gamely, William IV continued to resist the move; in 1831 he hopefully suggested that 1,500 Foot Guards in need of a new home should have Buckingham Palace adapted to a barracks, only to have Lord Grey condemn that as too expensive.*

The debate which now took place, with protests about the large sums involved in further works and the methods used to raise the money, was therefore an additional irritant to the King where his faithful Commons were concerned. Lord Duncannon for the Government, a good man but a bad speaker because of his stammer, tried to hold the fort against the denunciation of John Cresset Pelham, the eccentric MP for Shropshire, and the attack of Henry Hunt. Joseph Hume's intervention was especially waspish: he would like to know on what authority the pledge concerning expenditure was given. They had had a pledge from the Chancellor of the Exchequer on a former occasion 'which turned out to be worth nothing'.[17] All laboured the question – the familiar question where public works are concerned – was this really enough or were there further demands to come?

The main work of the Commons, the wrangling over the Reform

---

* As a result of which the present barracks in Birdcage Walk were built.

Bill, was scarcely more to the King's liking, as he received his reports from his Prime Minister, daily when necessary. In William IV's comments, as relayed by Sir Herbert Taylor, the tone of despondency, that considerable anxiety noted by Grey, grows markedly with the passing of the weeks. Even the tactful Taylor admitted to Grey that the King was often low, not bothering to conceal it; after all 'in his own family (I mean among his children) there is much difference of opinion'. Others did not scruple to report the King's low spirits; they then went further, suggesting that some expression of his had 'betrayed his apprehension' about the political future. But Taylor himself was sure that his master had in fact never shown any want of confidence in his Ministers. It is true that William IV by his own account stood firm when Lord Londonderry paid a visit to Brighton on 27 January. The King told Taylor that the notorious Ultra Tory was very quiet at first, but grew warm and eager by degrees, 'and finally wound himself into a state of great excitement on the question of Reform, and addition to the Peerage'. William IV listened but said nothing.[18] The trouble was that in the present situation, silence was more likely to be construed as assent than dissent by a man of such passionate feelings as Londonderry.

The state of the country was, from a very different angle, quite as warm and eager as Lord Londonderry and there was no evidence to support the occasional statements of Tory optimists that interest in Reform was dying down. William IV attributed this to the newspapers; he could not lose sight, he wrote, of the growing influence of the press, nor of the extraordinary power which it unfortunately possessed of exciting popular feeling and producing prejudice and misconstruction.

Of course the press performed a useful – or dangerous, depending on the point of view – function of facilitating communications around the country, and spreading the news of demonstrations after they had happened. On the other hand, to suggest that it was the press which was actually responsible for the countrywide cries for Reform was to mistake effect for cause – as Stanley had memorably castigated John Wilson Croker for doing in terms of English Civil War history. According to the Tory *St James's Chronicle*, the Fellows of Trinity College, Cambridge, had voted unanimously to eject the pro-Reform

Times from their Combination (Common) Room, disgusted by its 'violent and unprincipled language and doctrines'; it was the last straw when *The Times* ascribed the recent riots in Derby, Nottingham and Bristol to the Tories. The *Morning Herald* was substituted.[19] But the Fellows were in the position of Dame Partington and her fabled mop, attempting to sweep away the Atlantic. Reform at this point could be watered down and it could be defeated. But it could not be swept away.

Memories of the recent riots remained vivid, if only because a special commission was set up by the Home Secretary, Lord Melbourne, to hand out exemplary punishments. The consequent executions and transportations overseas caused unease in Whig quarters – not with Melbourne himself however, nor with Grey. Yet in general there was an acceptance of the status quo where punishment was concerned; Reform was not considered to apply to judicial penalties. Sir John Hobhouse for example reflected on the fate of the Bristol rioters: 'if our criminal code awards death as a punishment for any crime, I could not see how these men could be saved'. Many of the people involved in unions thought differently. On Sunday 19 January there was a big meeting in protest in St George's Square in Manchester, which caused local fright; it also shocked respectable citizens because of the use of the Sabbath, despite the obvious fact that this was the only free day for most working people. Amid stories that the unions had been seen drilling by moonlight, magistrates ordered the meeting to be adjourned for ten days; it was subsequently broken up by soldiers and some of the organizers put in prison.[20]

On 2 February the National Political Union met under the presidency of Sir Francis Burdett, that outspoken veteran of protest. But the ensuing meeting did not run smoothly. Burdett and Hume both objected to the idea of a petition which would urge the Ministers to press on with Reform, in view of the tumultuous state of the country. On the contrary, the pair of them felt that the Government was actually doing all it could. So the meeting ended in uproar. Curiously enough, as the see-saw of stability on one end and riot on the other swung up and down, one of the strongest advantages of the pro-Reformers was the adamantine stance of the Duke of Wellington on the subject. Here

was no Londonderry, an eccentric considered by some of the charitable to be half mad (even if Queen Adelaide did not agree). This was
on the contrary the hero of the nation, as the Queen had noted sadly
in her Diary when he departed from office in November 1830, a former
Prime Minister as well as war leader; whatever faults Wellington had,
no one doubted seriously that he had the best interests of the country
at heart.

But Wellington did not even indulge in the kind of weasel words
of his Tory leader in the Commons, Sir Robert Peel. Where Peel
might concede the need for some Reform some day, while rigorously
denouncing this one, Wellington was obdurate. He had nothing but
contempt for the King's honest attempts at constitutional government.
On 2 January he wrote that 'the great mischief of all is the weakness of
our poor King, who cannot or will not see his danger, or the road out
of it when it is pointed out to him'. Ten days later he was prophesying
the destruction of the monarchy: 'we are governed by the mob,' wrote
Wellington to Lord Strangford, 'and its organ – a licentious Press.'
Wellington was convinced that if the Bill was carried, 'there was an
end to the constitution and government of this country'.[21]

The hero of Waterloo was not about to give up. He told Lord
Howe that he went down to the House of Lords every day, in order to
prove to the world 'that I am not dead or dying'. He informed Lord
Harrowby, the prominent Waverer seeking to tone down the Bill, that
he disdained all compromise. And his mournful predictions of the
destruction of the Constitution continued to rain down on his correspondents. Just as Wellington's original speech in the House of Lords
had led to the fall of the Tory Government, so his hardline utterances
– his 'high tone and impracticable spirit', in Lord Holland's words –
continued to provide convenient ammunition for his opponents.[22]

The Committee stage of the Bill might have provided another episode of 'dreary warfare', in the phrase Sir Denis Le Marchant had
used for the events of the late summer of 1831. But in fact the stakes
were much higher now. Most sensible Members of either House real-
ized that matters would soon come to a final crunch with a vote in
the Lords; defeat would surely mean the resignation of the present

Government – and what would that mean to the state of the country as a whole, since the popular will was so evidently in favour of Reform? The first twelve clauses were carried in three nights. On 26 January there was a bizarre scene in the Commons by any standards when Spencer Perceval, son of the assassinated Prime Minister of the same name, took the floor. Perceval had once been 'a sweet young boy' spotted at Harrow by William Wilberforce; then the protected orphan, made financially secure by award of Parliament; now he was a frenzied advocate of the particular evangelical religious sect associated with Edward Irving and Henry Drummond, sometimes known as Irvingite.[23]

Perceval, who had regarded the Reform Bill in March 1831 as the greatest act of folly committed by any Minister, had a particular preoccupation. This was the current epidemic of cholera and its causes. Increasingly dreaded since it arrived in England, the disease had now reached London and, as John Wilson Croker wrote: it was 'in full speed along the banks of the river' with alarming consequences such as the stagnation of trade. John Campbell remarked on the decline in the sale of fruit and vegetables so that thousands of little shopkeepers were ruined, together with the boycotting of hackney coaches where infection might be spread by strangers. (Great hostesses like Lady Holland refused to eat ices; only the stubbornly Tory Mrs Arbuthnot continued to think the Reform Bill the greater evil.) But of course not just London but all the new densely peopled industrial cities suffered fearfully from 'this messenger of death', as James Phillips Kay put it: 'the abodes of poverty . . . the close alleys, the crowded courts, the overpopulated habitations of wretches, where pauperism and disease congregate round the source of social discontent and political disorder in the centre of our large towns'.[24]

For Perceval the remedy was quite clear, and it was not so much medical as spiritual: a day of national fasting and humiliation. This must take place as a result of a motion of the House of Commons. He began by using a traditional phrase (which had not been heard for the last eighteen years): 'I perceive that strangers are in the House.' According to practice, observers, including reporters, were duly cleared out. He had done this, Perceval explained at once, to remove the temptation to blasphemy from his opponents. In the absence of reporters, Hansard was compelled to rely on the memories of those present for the speech which followed. That version was certainly long and astonishing enough, leaving the experience of the full text to the imagination.

For one thing, Perceval spoke holding a copy of the Holy Bible in his hand which he frequently flourished. He intended to speak freely, he said, in the presence of baptized men. (There had been recent efforts to admit unbaptized Jews to Parliament.) Then he proceeded to address the Members 'in the name of the Lord Jesus Christ, the Saviour of the world, who was exalted King of kings, and Lord of lords . . . in the name of God, the Highest, he appealed to the House'. Since it was given that anyone who despised the messenger was despising Him who had sent him, he that rejected him (Perceval) rejected his God.

Perceval's main message from God was a fearful one: the nation trembled on the verge of destruction. In every district there were disorders, respect within the ranks of society no longer existed, and there was also 'the frightful collision of the two Houses of Parliament'. Furthermore the houses of the nobility and gentry were entered and pillaged and one of the great cities of the nation (Bristol) had been plundered and devastated by the mob. What was to be done? He would read from the Holy Book, declared Perceval, about God's mercy and his judgements. And so he proceeded to do, long, long passages about Israel, its transgressions, its atonements, Ninevah, further transgressions, further atonements, summed up in Hansard by the cool phrase: 'The hon. Member read a number of extracts from the Bible to the same effect.'

By concentrating on the various biblical pestilences sent by God, Perceval pointed out the way ahead for the present nation. Just as it had been in the time of the Old Testament, when 'the curse of God was on the land, and it had overtaken the people', so now the pestilence was once again countrywide. Members ought to hasten to address the throne to proclaim a fast and day of humiliation in the land, 'that we might avert this dreadful wrath'. This was the truth: they had departed from God, and God had departed from them. When it came to detail, and it did, Perceval gave the destruction of Bristol as a sample of God's wrath. And he spent some time denouncing 'the liberal mind that is marching through Europe', adding that it was blasphemy to attribute power to the people, since all power came from God. Perceval finally drew to a close asking the Members to 'Beware of the wrath that went forth on the plain against Sodom and Gomorrah'.

It was left to Lord Althorp, at his best in defusing a situation like this, to declare calmly that discussion on such a topic was 'highly inexpedient'. It was in any case the intention of the Government to appoint a day of fasting. And that was that. Except that 'Orator' Hunt seized the opportunity to quote from the Bible himself. Had Perceval forgotten Isaiah? He proceeded to jog his memory with the words from Isaiah 58:6. 'Is not this the fast that I have chosen . . . Is it not to deal thy bread to the hungry, and that thou bring the poor that are cast out, to thy house?' What Perceval wanted, he said, was not a proper biblical fast; a real fast was one that would feed the hungry and clothe the naked.

It was left to Perceval to withdraw his motion, lest his opponents would be encouraged to further blasphemies, while observing that 'a fast of hypocrisy' (such as he maintained the Government would instigate to 'get rid of the question') was in no way acceptable to God. Acceptable or not, on 6 February the Government duly announced a day of fasting and humiliation to be held on 21 March.

Perceval was not alone in his manic invocations, if his expression of them was extreme. His views were merely one outstanding example of passionately held convictions against 'liberalism' and the power of the people, just as there were equally passionately held convictions on the Radical and reforming side. It would be a mistake therefore to suppose that all the idealism was on the side of Reform, as the dealings of the Committee in the House of Commons continued, and Lord Grey pursued his elaborate negotiations with the King about the 'fearful alternative' of creation.

The Tories were animated by patriotism even as the Whigs were (and of course both sides were also inspired by that healthy spirit of self-interest which may be regarded as part of politics, if by no means the only part). The Tories, however, paid fervent attention to the evil consequences of Revolution on the one hand, the merits of stability on the other. For those of a conservative turn of mind, these evil consequences had been fully demonstrated by the developing events of the French Revolution, as a result of which so many innocent people suffered. As for the merits of stability, these were obvious to numerous well-intentioned people who, with some justification, believed that society at every level was the better for it. This was not a philosophy to be treated with intellectual contempt even if supporters like Perceval, with his crazy denunciations of the liberal mind, made it easy to do so. William IV's apocalyptic passage in his letter to Lord Grey in January with its reference to 'a revolutionary and demoralizing spirit ... making frightful strides' did in fact express the legitimate terrors of many decent people, including politicians.

CHAPTER TWELVE

BOUNCING BILL

'What though now opposed I be?
Twenty peers shall carry me
If twenty won't, thirty will
For I'm His Majesty's bouncing Bill' –

Macaulay's parody of a nursery rhyme, March 1832

On 18 February 1832 a banquet at the Mansion House gave Lord Grey an important opportunity to declare his unalterable commitment to the cause of Reform.[1] He thus publicly contradicted rumours that he was weakening on the subject of the whole Bill and nothing but the Bill: in short, that he would make concessions rather than face up to creation. At present there had been remarkably few modifications agreed in Committee, mostly matters of detail. The vital clause enfranchising the metropolitan boroughs, although much debated, actually passed with a majority of 80. But the strain of these weeks was beginning to tell on all the Whigs in Government.

Despite his staunch public espousal of Reform, Grey certainly felt an 'extreme repugnance' for creation, and was consequently in a permanent state of anxiety; although his actual parliamentary ordeal – in the House of Lords – lay ahead. Then there was the question of the King holding fast. At the moment, as Creevey cheerfully put it in his Diary, 'King Billy hates peer-making, but as a point of honour to his ministers, he gives them unlimited power.'[2] Meanwhile William IV's health began to give cause for concern – never a good sign with any member of the House of Hanover. Worse, much worse, were the reliable signals of Queen Adelaide's ever-strengthening disapproval. Her freezing attitude to Lord Grey in the autumn, after the fiasco of Lord Howe's so-called resignation, was indicative of her general approach to matters of Court and politics. Her Diary contained frequent pious invocations to Providence in view of the difficulties of her high position; but in fact by upbringing and experience Queen Adelaide, Princess of a minor German duchy, was ill equipped to deal with a highly complex period when the lightest of royal female touches – or possibly restraint altogether – was what was needed. With revolutions all round Europe, with royalties ousted from thrones and even countries, surrounded by Tories prophesying woe, it was scarcely surprising that poor Queen Adelaide feared for her husband's crown. And yet to her it seemed that the Whigs were doing nothing to shore up the situation. On the contrary, they were siding with the forces of revolution . . .

The trouble was that these fears quickly made their way into the avid press. One of their contacts was Brougham; he did not help with his hostile references to the royal ladies as 'the Begums'. The mud-slinging of the press duly incensed the Queen – and inevitably as time went on, her loyal husband the King – still further against the forces of Reform. It was, literally, a vicious circle. By January 1832, cartoons of the Queen as patroness of the Opposition were beginning to appear. On 1 March one called *Un Tableau Vivant* adapted a picture by the distinguished Scottish RA Sir David Wilkie, *Calabrian Minstrels playing to the Madonna*. It showed well-known members of the Opposition, including the Duke of Wellington in the guise of an old peasant, gathered round their own Madonna, the Queen. Robert Seymour was the principal artist of the satirical magazine *Figaro in London*; on 1 February he delivered his cast of the people engaged to bring out the so-called New Opera of Reform. They included Signor Giovanni Bulli, a bull with papers Schedule A and B stuck on his horns and M. de Guelpho as the lessee of the theatre; but also Madam Queeno in the lead.[3]

Words underlined the damage. To some she was becoming 'Queen Addle-head'. Francis Place contrasted 'the Queen with her spare form, her sour countenance and her straight, stiff German back' with the jolly, good-natured King. There were references to 'a nasty German *frow*' in popular newspapers.[4] Adelaide was not nasty – nor, for that matter, was she strictly speaking a *frow* – but she was German. Not unexpectedly, she had a German accent at which the press jeered in its captions.

Yet for all their chauvinistic pettiness, perhaps the press were not entirely misdirected in their attacks. It is true that on one occasion early on, William had roared at his wife when she made some public comment: 'Madam, English politics are not to be understood by any German.'[5] But that was a mere husbandly explosion. The devotion of the King to the Queen, their happy conjugal private life, meant that the possibilities of private influence grew apace, parallel with the press attacks which enraged William. And there is evidence that Adelaide herself cautiously began to explore the possibilities open to the King other than creation: did he, for example, have the right to choose new Ministers?

Lord Howe was her chosen emissary. On 20 January 1832 he showed the Duke of Wellington 'in great confidence' a letter he had received from the Queen. He added that she was not aware her former Chamberlain was taking this step, a statement which may be treated with polite scepticism. 'Should you think it *right* to send me a few lines which might be shown to her and to the *unfortunate* master' – Howe's italics – he would welcome them. Otherwise he hoped the Duke would return the Queen's letter untouched. 'God knows whether the King is sincere or not,' exclaimed Howe, 'but is it not frightful to see him acting as he does, while at the same time he detests his agents.'[6]

The Queen's letter, dated 18 January, left her feelings in little doubt. Of the King she wrote: 'his eyes are open and see the great difficulties in which he is placed; he sees everything in the right light.' But she was afraid that he had the fixed idea that 'no other administration could be formed at present amongst your [Wellington's] friends'. The crucial question came next: 'How far he is right I cannot pretend to say for I do not understand these important things, but I should like to know what the Duke of Wellington thinks.' It was quite clear what answer the Queen wanted: a new administration was perfectly possible.

Amid all these tensions in this agitating spring, most of those concerned were deeply apprehensive. Even the most diehard Tories could see that defeat of the Bill, if secured in the Lords, would raise as many problems as it solved. Macaulay managed to divert his sisters Hannah and Margaret with a bit of light-hearted fun on the subject of the Bill, which was obsessing everyone they knew. Adapting the well-known nursery rhyme beginning 'Twenty pound will marry me', and making the usual play with King William's nickname, Macaulay declaimed:

> What though now opposed I be?
> Twenty peers shall carry me
> If twenty won't, thirty will
> For I'm His Majesty's bouncing Bill.[7]

But then Macaulay, although idealistic, was also young and ambitious, and these were evidently good days for the young and ambitious, as such times of stress tend to be. They were less propitious for those actually in charge of guiding the bouncing Bill through Parliament.

It was Lord Althorp who showed real signs of cracking. That jovial John Bull appearance had always concealed a far more sensitive nature than he chose to reveal, as witness his lifelong mourning for his young wife coupled with his refusal to remarry. As Leader of the House of Commons he was suffering from the intense bombardment of activity, talk, negotiation, speaking, working all day and very often all night. The concentration on the probable outcome of voting in the House of Lords meant that rumour and counter-rumour about personal predilections were the gossip of every person; then there were the Waverers such as Lord Harrowby, who were not above trading a vote for Reform for some subsequent amelioration. The secret desire of the unambitious Althorp to turn his carriage in the direction of his country home instead of Parliament, which he had confessed to his father, had hardly gone away.

A crisis came when Althorp felt he had shrunk from the prospect of future defeat in the Lords long enough. Unless there was an immediate creation of some sort, he was determined to resign. Lord Holland agreed with the need for immediate creation, without temperamentally feeling tempted to desert his friend Grey. Matters were not helped by Durham's behaviour in Cabinet: he had reverted to his bad old ways. At the end of one long debate in Cabinet, wrote Lord Holland, after looking 'as black as the night and preserving a sullen silence', Durham very offensively asked if he might now be permitted to speak. At home among the ladies of the family, Durham behaved no better, disputing vigorously with his father-in-law.[8]

According to Greville, the Duke of Richmond quarrelled with Durham, while 'Melbourne damns him and the rest hate him. But there he is, frowning, sulking, bullying and meddling, and doing all the harm he can.'[9] It is perfectly true that this disruption in the Cabinet by a passionate pro-reformer was highly unpleasant for all its members, in purely human terms. Yet Durham's unruly but consistent behaviour had one important consequence: it undoubtedly prevented Grey from gracefully backsliding under the influence of Melbourne and Palmerston. He had not lost his affection, sympathy and even his respect for his son-in-law. Spoilt child as he might seem to be in many respects, on the issue of Reform Durham had never deviated and that was more than many of the Cabinet could boast. At this crucial moment, therefore, the wayward Durham supplied the iron determination of which Grey evidently stood in need.

Althorp himself did not lack determination, but by March he was at the end of his tether. There was a troubling incident when he was found locking away his pistols for fear of having too easy access to them in a moment of madness. In a conversation with Sir John Hobhouse on the precise difficulties of the situation, he said:

'I do not know whether I might not, to make matters easier, shoot myself.'

'For God's sake, shoot anybody else you like,' replied Hobhouse robustly.[10]

To politicians of the time, such threats of suicide would not have come across as pure histrionics; the point has been made that there had been three suicides, led by Castlereagh, in the last seventeen years.[11]

Now Althorp reminded Grey of their conversation in 1830 in which he, Althorp, had told Grey that he would take office because Grey said he would not do so without him.[12] 'I have acted up to my word,' declared Althorp, 'and have sacrificed my happiness in doing so.' Grey now had a choice: to create peers at once, or face up to Althorp's resignation (leaving of course an ugly gap in the House of Commons, to say nothing of the blow to Whig morale). Rather touchingly, Althorp felt the need to resort to a letter to Lord Grey in declaring his intention. He gave the following explanation: 'I do so because when I feel a decided opinion different from yours, I find it impossible in conversation with you to express it as strongly as I feel it. It is always the same with regard to my father.' Then he went on to say that he felt his 'honour and character' so completely involved in the passing of the Reform Bill that he could not risk the calamity of rejection without making every effort against it. If the Bill was still rejected *after* creation, that was one thing, but to allow it to go forward without trying this expedient was intolerable to him.

Grey also replied by letter, dated 11 March from Downing Street.[13] It was an extremely long letter but the effective passage came at the end. If Althorp resigned, it would result in the breaking-up of the Government. Given that Grey had refused to come into Government without Althorp, 'I should now find it still more impossible to go on, without you.' Althorp's sense of responsibility – that belief in 'an honest and consistent discharge of public duty' he had described at a reformers' dinner in September – was too strong for him: 'Honest Jack' gave in. There was a further crisis a little later when Lord Durham threatened to resign, but in this case it was Althorp the conciliator who persuaded him back.

On 21 March there took place that fast instigated by the Government (not at the official request of the House of Commons as the evangelical Perceval, flourishing his Bible, had so urgently requested) to mark the epidemic of cholera. It was complicated in the first place by a renewed exhibition of fanaticism by Perceval himself. The debate on the third reading actually had to be adjourned because of the 'temporary derangement' of the MP, as Edward Littleton put it. He raved yet again about the ungodliness of the House, so that both Whigs and Tories walked out. The gallery was once again cleared of strangers, according to tradition. Still Perceval ranted on. Finally Perceval sat down, 'exhausted by his own frenzy'.[14]

Such days of national fasting and humiliation, taking place on a working day, dated in fact from the mid-sixteenth century and all kinds of rituals had developed around them.[15] They were ordained either to implore God's forgiveness and assistance, at a time when the nation was under threat, or to celebrate some triumph secured with God's support.* In this case, prolonged sufferings over cholera were the cause: 'particularly seeking God to remove from us that grievous disease', as the official wording had it. Theatres were closed, churches were open (for specially designed sermons) and the shops, according to one commentator, 'manage their shutters to hit the happy medium'. In the Royal Chapel, Bishop Blomfield drew attention to the failure of the rulers of society to 'increase the comforts and improve the moral character of the masses'. But it was hardly to be expected, in view of the disrupted state of the nation, that this particular fast would go smoothly with the masses themselves.

This was something laid down from above and in many quarters the requisite spirit of self-abnegation and humility was conspicuously lacking. Henry Hetherington in the *Poor Man's Guardian* took the firm line that ungodliness was not the problem.[16] 'The Cholera has arrived among us,' he wrote, 'and this among other blessings, we have to lay at the door of our "glorious constitution" for it is a disease begotten of that poverty and wretchedness which are occasioned by the wealth and luxury of the few, to whom only the constitution belongs.' The 'fasting' tradition of eating salted fish – allegedly a penitential dish but spiced up with egg sauce and mustard – he greeted with a mocking response. The rich and greedy smacked their lips at all this delicious cream, while the poor were on a perennial fast anyway.

It was the political unions who raised the most obvious objections. The Birmingham Political Union took the strong line delineated by Hetherington: Reform, not fasting, was the solution to the nation's woes. The National Union of the Working Classes had their own individual resolution: on the fast day or sooner, all sinecurists, placemen or extortionists, whether in Church or State, living in luxury, should give up their ill-gotten plunder. A suggestion of one member that a

---

* The tradition spread to North America; for example on 30 March 1863, during the struggle for the emancipation of slaves, Abraham Lincoln introduced a Day of National Humiliation, Fasting and Prayer.

feast should be held on the *fast* day was not, however, adopted.

The Union now embarked upon a prodigious march starting with a meeting in Finsbury Square. In essence it was a peaceful march and once again steps were taken to exclude drunken men (the bane of serious demonstrations). One rule book actually read: 'No person shall be allowed to enter any meeting of the Union or Committee who may be intoxicated' – the appearance of respectability was vital. The march gained strength as each street added numbers. Nor was it restricted to one sex: 'Hundreds of women followed in its train, each attaching herself to her friend or husband.'[17] Symbolic bread and meat were distributed to the poor, making the political point again that it was bodily sustenance not spiritual nourishment which was needed here. Inevitably the march degenerated and there were clashes with the police towards the end and some arrests. Nevertheless this march, like others in the provinces, attested to a strength of feeling in the 'middling classes' and the 'lower orders' which could scarcely be denied by their social superiors in Parliament.

On 23 March, at one o'clock in the morning, the third reading of the Reform Bill passed in the House of Commons. Three days later, the Bill was formally presented to a packed House of Lords, hopefully for its endorsement. The second reading being set there for 9 April, the atmosphere of tension which had been mounting all year deepened further. The game was on. On 4 April *The Times* ran an advertisement for the impending performance of the brilliant young actress Fanny Kemble as Lady Macbeth – 'her first appearance in the role' – at the Covent Garden Theatre; unusually for Londoners, the impending real-life drama at Westminster seemed more compelling. In a strong leader in the same issue, the editor defended in advance the King's right to create peers against Tories who might pretend he had no power to do so. The Tories had been adding to the House of Lords for seventy years, and now they were pretending that their King had no right to do the same! In a subsequent issue *The Times* suggested that seventy or eighty new peers might be needed if the Bill were defeated.[18]

In political circles, there was canvassing of the uncommitted peers

– known Waverers or potential Waverers – on all sides. Typical was the rueful entry of the Earl of Coventry in his Diary: 'I never before was fully aware of the usefulness of indecision. It has raised me quite to importance. I have received more invitations to dinner this week than I have had for years, and my hand has been squeezed by men who long scarcely condescended to notice me.'[19] Lord Coventry had voted against the Bill in October; he was hitherto best known for featuring as 'a most profligate nobleman' in the searing memoirs of the courtesan Harriette Wilson, published in 1825, but better things were evidently now hoped for from him, in every sense of the word. Francis Place had a cynical comment on the Peers as a class: he wrote that he had had communication with a considerable number on many occasions; and 'true it is that I never knew one that as a politician, was not a mean shuffler'.[20]

King William IV was certainly not a mean man – the people were not altogether wrong in their original perception of him as a bluff, honest fellow, basically on their side, in contrast to George IV. But his prolonged correspondence with his Prime Minister during this period was beginning to betray signs of something closely akin to shuffling. The King was displaying a certain 'soreness,' wrote Lord Holland, as a personal friend of William Duke of Clarence in the old days frequently at Court. Holland added an ominous rider: 'some of us, that is in the Cabinet' were beginning to wonder whether 'the moment of separation' was not approaching; by this Holland suggested a Government, foiled of its desire to effect parliamentary Reform by the means of creation, might find itself resigning.[21]

On 5 April the King responded to a minute from the Cabinet with a long letter, full of emphases, dictated as usual to Sir Herbert Taylor. Prevarication was evident: 'the hesitation which *he feels and shows, to commit himself to the extent which is now required from him* was not produced by any new view of the question'. On the contrary, the King was simply adhering to the principles he had stated all along. An extended recital of all his previous arguments followed. The conclusion was inconclusive: 'what His Majesty cannot help feeling is, that all that is now connected with this question and with the measure submitted for his consideration and decision is *speculative, and calculated to engage him and commit him in that which is uncertain in its nature, its extent and its issue.*'[22]

Poor Sir Herbert Taylor felt impelled to add a short note of his own apologizing for his terrible handwriting: the King had asked him, at eleven o'clock at night, to introduce an abstract of all the correspondence which had passed, connected with creating peers. He had to read the letters all over again, then make extracts and notes, then write this 'formidable' letter, and then copy it. 'I was up the greater part of last night, having been at work all this day, and am quite knocked up.'[23]

On 9 April Lord Grey rose to his feet in the House of Lords and, according to his devotee Sir Denis Le Marchant, opened the debate with 'a very fine speech, admirably adapted to the occasion, being clear, dignified, and eminently prudent and persuasive'. Here was Lord Grey showing himself once again the awesome elder statesman; Macaulay, nearly forty years younger, told Le Marchant: 'taking into consideration the time of the night, or rather of day, the exhaustion of the subject, the length of the debate, and Lord Grey's age, it was almost unparalleled.' Understandably, Lady Grey was apprehensive in advance, as she told her daughter. She wrote again while Grey was still speaking. 'Tuesday night – or rather Wednesday morning, one o'clock. Car [his family name] is not yet home, and I am in a state of extreme nervousness.'[24]

The Prime Minister began by reminding his listeners of the Bill's provenance: it came before their Lordships from the other House of Parliament 'supported by a large majority of the House of Commons, and by an equally large and decisive majority of the people at large'. Moving on, Grey felt himself compelled to speak once again of 'the great affection of the people for this measure' and he emphasized that by the people, the term constantly invoked, he was not speaking of the mob, nor of 'persons uninstructed and uninformed'. If the Duke of Wellington was going to persist in condemning all Reform, Grey was sure that few would support him in his desire 'to place a ban and an interdict on the wishes of the people of England'. Towards the conclusion of his speech, declaring that all change was not necessarily revolution, he pointed to 'the great affection of the people for this measure'. In modern terms, it would be called an appeal to democracy. But that was of course never a term Lord Grey would have used. He simply repeated the words 'the people', a concept which was carefully undefined – except by excluding the mob.

The Prime Minister ended magnificently: 'If, however, I should unfortunately sink in the struggle, I shall at least have the consolation of feeling that I did, to the best of my judgement, that which I thought right and fitting, regulating my actions according to the sincere dictates of my conscience, with one sole objective of effecting that which should be best calculated to promote the interests of my country.'

The ensuing debate lasted for four nights. Members of the Commons and strangers crowded into the narrow Chamber of the Lords. During the second night two MPs, members of the Government, Stanley and Sir James Graham, lay sprawling on the floor opposite the throne. All the time the people outside – the unenfranchised – thronged the streets, anxious to hear the latest news of the discussions while the Council of the National Union of the Working Classes sat in more or less permanent conclave in its new Committee Rooms in Great Charles Street, Westminster.

The Duke of Wellington did not emulate the composure of the Prime Minister. Basically he reiterated that prediction of disaster which he had first expressed in 1830, leading to the fall of the Tory Government. Certainly he continued to make the gloomier predictions about the future throughout the spring, as Princess Lieven reported, following one dinner party: 'he foresees the end of the world after the Bill is passed' and intended to vote against it 'in every particular'. *The Times* had sneered on the eve of the debate: 'our Conservatives entertain such horror of *innovation* that they will not even give us a *new* argument'; despite the newspaper's Whig bias, there was certainly something in what it said. Compared to Grey's heroics, Wellington's speech had something commonplace about it, 'dull but violent' in the words of one observer.[25]

Once again, as so often, he struck the anti-revolutionary note. Thus he denounced the July Revolution in France as having 'inflamed' the people – there had been no feeling for Reform before that took place. He also attacked the idea of the King himself favouring Reform: 'it was not to be supposed that the King took any interest in the subject'. And he argued that the French Republic, headed by the King of the French, now needed far more soldiers to maintain it than the realm of the previous Bourbon Kings, Louis XVIII and Charles X. He prophesied that a similarly expensive and military government would shortly be needed in this country. In sum, he asserted that the theme of this Bill was not actually Reform: when accomplished it would produce 'a complete Revolution'.

It was not to be expected that the diehard Bishop of Exeter, Henry Phillpotts – he who had accepted the burning of his Guy Fawkes– style effigy in a practical spirit – would back down on the subject now. Such a change, he declared, amounted to something very like revolution, and it followed therefore that the principle of the Bill was revolutionary, however disagreeable the mention of the word might be to the polite ears of the noble Lords near him.[26] 'I must remind them that some of the chief supporters of the Bill glory in it,' he said, just because it was a revolutionary measure and advocated it as such. He then quoted Milton on the glories of the British Constitution. And he questioned whether the King's Coronation Oath did not preclude him from assenting to the Irish Reform Bill.

This incident had at least the effect of positioning the King temporarily on the side of the Government against his Queen. At breakfast over the newspapers – a favourite time for Adelaide to exercise her influence, as with many wives of busy husbands – she expressed approval for the Bishop's speech. 'Madam,' exclaimed the King, 'it may be clever or eloquent, of that I am no judge; but though the *peers* may occasionally be factious, By God, the Bishops are in that house to defend my crown and not to follow vagaries of their own.'[27]

On 13 April Lord Durham tore into the Bishop in a passage in which he denounced him for 'coarse and virulent invective – malignant and false insinuations – the grossest perversion of historical facts

– decked out with all the choicest flowers of his well-known pamphleteering slang'.[28] This was the House of Lords, not the market place,
and 'Radical Jack' had gone too far, at least in the opinion of Lord
Winchilsea, who interrupted him with protests about his language.
(Even Holland admitted that it had 'rather exceeded the bounds'.) A
row followed over the precise phrase 'pamphleteering slang' in which
other peers, including Grey and Holland, got involved. When Durham
was back on his feet his anger was in no way diminished, and a further dispute followed about leaks to the press. The only light note was
struck when Grey said that he refrained from employing the phrase
– 'in a jesuitical way' – since he was aware that 'the right reverend
Prelate [Phillpotts] abhors Jesuits'. That did not stop young Edward
Strutt MP from reporting that Grey had given Phillpotts 'a complete
dusting'.

And yet Durham, for all his notorious splenetics, did manage to
include one passage which in its good sense and evident truth did
much to explain why 'Radical Jack' was an honourable title which he
deserved. Lord Ellenborough, a Tory, had complained about the low
class – that is, middle class – of the new MPs which would only be
increased by the passing of the Reform Bill. Durham hit back. When
the gentry are brought together with the middle classes at public
meetings and on political occasions, 'their superiority in learning or
intellect is no longer manifest – the reverse is the fact'. If Lord Ellenborough were to attend any of the meetings of the middle classes, and
enter into a discussion with them on political or scientific subjects, he
would have no reason to plume himself on his fancied superiority.
This being the case, demanded Durham, why should such people, possessed of talents, skill and wealth, be excluded merely because they did
not happen to be part of a particular class, the aristocracy – endowed
with privileges bestowed upon them in different times and different
circumstances?

The debate wound on. Lord Grey was able to refer in his final
speech, without fear of contradiction, to 'the exhausted state in
which their Lordships must feel themselves'. Between four and five
o'clock, when the daylight began to shed its blue beams across the

candlelight, according to Jeffrey, the scene was 'very picturesque' from the singular groupings of forty or fifty peers, sprawling on the floor, awake and asleep, in all imaginable attitudes and with all sorts of expressions and wrappings. The candles had been renewed before dawn, and now blazed on after the sun came fairly in at the high windows of St Stephen's. Grey rose to his feet at 5 a.m. and spoke for one and a half hours, from 'the kindling dawn into full sunlight'.[29]

Although Grey promised to refrain from 'making any long trespass on their indulgence' he did in fact rehearse certain vital issues all over again. Most importantly, he utterly refuted the idea that the current agitation on the subject of parliamentary Reform was to be attributed to the misconduct of the present Ministers. On the contrary, by October 1830 the feeling in the country was already so strong that Reform needs must be granted to avert further evils. Lord Grey also condemned Henry Phillpotts, the Bishop of Exeter, denying his claim that the King's Coronation Oath prevented him from assenting to the Irish Reform Bill.

On the subject of Phillpotts himself, however, Grey forsook his habitual temperate approach. 'The right Reverend Prelate threw out insinuations about my ambition. Let me tell him calmly, that the pulses of ambition may beat as strongly under [a Bishop's] sleeves of lawn as under an ordinary habit.' But, said the Prime Minister, he did not wish to pursue the subject any further as his feelings were too passionate. He then proceeded to declare that 'a speech more unbecoming the situation of a Christian Bishop – a speech more inconsistent with the love of peace – a speech more remote from the charity which ought to distinguish a Clergyman of his order – a speech more replete with insinuations and charges, calculated to promote disunion and discord in the community, never was uttered within the walls of this or any other House of Parliament'.

It was seven o'clock in the morning when the vote on the second reading was taken. The result was a victory for the Government. But it was a Pyrrhic victory. The Contents were in total 184 and the Not Contents 175, giving the Government a majority of 9. A number of proxies were used.* The Bill now passed into Committee, in the formal words of Hansard, 'to be there improved, if possible'. Nobody was under any illusion that this slender majority should give the Government – or the country – any confidence in the future. 'The House will adjourn on Wednesday and go into Committee after Easter,' wrote Greville in his Diary, 'and in the meantime what negotiations and what difficulties to get over!' The essential difficulty, he believed, was to bring 'these extreme and irritated parties' to any agreement as to terms.[30]

Peers who had voted Content would now feel free to haggle and hassle in Committee. They could change their minds – five was the minimum number of derelictions which would secure defeat. Wharncliffe, the well-known Waverer, was currently Content – how long would that last? Nine prelates – not of course including the Bishop of Exeter, but headed by the Archbishop of York – had voted Content but there was no guarantee they would not soon join their ten colleagues, headed by the Archbishop of Canterbury, who had voted against. The bouncing Bill of Macaulay's merry rhyme was more likely than ever to need created peers to carry it through.

* The use of proxy votes in the House of Lords could be dated from 1626 when it was laid down that proxies from Temporal Lords must go to Temporal Lords, and the same principle with the Spiritual Lords. Proxies could not be used in Committee.

CHAPTER THIRTEEN

SEVENTH OF MAY

'Seventh of May, Crisis Day' –

Placards in the London streets, 1832

In early May 1832, all parties were agreed that there was a crisis. But that was where the agreement ended. It was not as if all the reformers were totally united in themselves: there remained a Radical fringe which continued to criticize the actual clauses of the Bill. On 28 April in his *Political Register* Cobbett published an account of a conversation with an unknown gentleman in a London bookseller's.[1] The unknown had asked at random in the shop: 'What do you think now? You see the Second Reading is carried. . . .' The bookseller declared himself too busy to care, but Cobbett sprang in. He would rather the Bill be lost, he declared, than that the qualification to vote be raised higher, thus excluding poorer voters. At which the unknown was alleged to have replied: '*We ought to take as much as we can get, for it is impossible to get the whole.*' And when Cobbett denied this, the gentleman replied that he knew the difficulties only too well; 'for that *he had a great deal to do with them*'.

The unknown then revealed himself to hail from Birmingham, and the name of Joseph Parkes was supplied by the bookseller. Parkes himself later publicly denied all knowledge of this conversation; but the fact was that the sentiments were indeed those of the men in the middle, willing to settle for what was available, attacked from left and right in consequence. While *The Times* called repeatedly for Reform, further down the line politically the *Poor Man's Guardian* denounced the Bill as 'most illiberal'.[2]

The Cabinet met on the Sunday night before Lord Grey was due to speak, dining in Holland House in Kensington with its delightful leafy surroundings. It was decided to strike out the simple figure fifty-six for the disenfranchised, and introduce into the Bill the actual names of those who would be thus ejected. It was further agreed that any postponement of the first clause should be resisted to the utmost, since this would be to attack the very principle of disenfranchisement. There was general optimism that the Waverers, such as Wharncliffe, would share this resistance.

Monday 7 May was the day on which it all happened. On going into Committee in the House of Lords, Grey rose to make this point about the substitution of names for figures in the first clause of the Bill.[3] This would have the effect of enabling members of the Committee to raise a question about each separate disenfranchisement. At which point Lord Lyndhurst, the former Lord Chancellor and a famously keen debater, arose on a separate point of order which he said preceded that announced by Lord Grey. Lyndhurst was, wrote Lord Holland, 'as much agitated and nervous as his nature, destitute of shame ... could be'.[4] Put crudely, Lyndhurst proposed that both Schedule A, for total disenfranchisement, and Schedule B, for the elimination of one seat, should be postponed. In the course of an elaborate speech, Lyndhurst called the Bill an attack on 'Monarchy and property itself'. Even more significant than the fundamentalist nature of this language was the fact that Lord Harrowby supported Lyndhurst. This indicated that the Waverers were – contrary to the Cabinet's hopes – putting their weight on the other side of the scales.

There had been good news earlier. The royal Duke of Sussex, presenting a petition on the eve of the debate, denied that the proposed Reform militated against the King's Coronation Oath; the Oath, he said, was irrelevant to the situation, and he supported the Bill not only because it was expedient but because it would be of great advantage to the country as a whole. He also pointed out that the Crown could create peers but not MPs – why then should peers create MPs (by nomination)?

If the Duke of Sussex represented one force of the establishment, during the debate itself another even greater force intervened: Wellington produced one of his familiar pieces of invective. 'For his own part he was unquestionably a decided enemy of the Bill. He was an enemy because he was convinced in his conscience that, let their Lordships do what they would with it, it could never be made anything but an evil to the country.' That was plain enough. The Iron Duke hardly needed to add that he would do everything in his power to avert the evil which was impending since he had been demonstrably doing everything in his power to that effect for the last eighteen months.

On 7 May, the Opposition carried the day. Despite a further fine speech from Grey, the Government was defeated. The defeat was not a puny one: the majority was 45. This meant that the entire effort of the Government up till now, since the presentation of the First Reform Bill in March 1831, was in effect put on hold. That is to say, the elected Government of a country shouting for Reform – literally so in the case of many demonstrators – was unable to bring it about due to the action of an unelected Chamber. The placards in the streets of London which anticipated this vital debate were proved right: 'Seventh of May, Crisis Day'.[5]

To add to the woes of the Government, there was an element of disagreeable surprise in what had happened (there is an analogy to the surprise felt by the Opposition on 1 March 1831 when Lord John Russell introduced the first Bill). As Le Marchant wrote in his Diary: 'We went down to the Lords on Monday wholly unconscious of our fate.'[6] He had dined with Brougham, and together they agreed that things were going well. Lord Howick, Grey's eldest son and an MP, reported afterwards that his father too had not expected 'a serious collision' that night. A vague rumour that Lyndhurst would propose something to do with Schedule A had been discounted. Le Marchant was 'quite stupefied' to find the debate going on after dinner and so were many others, Whigs and Tories, who had come up from the country and stopped off at Parliament in their carriages in a routine sort of way, to see what was going on. As a result 'the majority was startling,' wrote Le Marchant. 'We had not counted on such hostility from Waverers or Bishops.'

On this very same day, before the news of the defeat of the reformers' cherished hopes could reach Birmingham, the biggest public meeting yet known took place at that celebrated point of protest, Newhall

Hill. The London placards featuring the Seventh of May could equally be applied to the provinces. The inspiration for the meeting was that of the Birmingham Political Union. On the previous Friday the National Political Union had had its own gathering in London, threatening the House of Lords with the non-payment of taxes, leading to the extinction of 'the privileged classes' if the Bill was not passed in its entirety. The Birmingham meeting was held under Attwood's presidency and representatives of thirty other unions from the Midlands were invited to take part. From late April onwards, Joseph Parkes collected money and visited local towns to urge participation – money for the movement was an increasing preoccupation of his, as funds ran low. Francis Place also toiled, as he told Parkes on 28 April: 'Dear Joe, I am "working like a devil in a mud wall" in all directions and in all ways for you. . . .'[7]

Throughout the preceding weekend, people flocked to the city. Harriet Martineau evoked the scene in her history of the period, published at the end of the next decade: 'From forge and furnace, from mine and factory, from loom and plough, from the cities of Staffordshire, Warwickshire, Worcestershire, they marched with banners.'[8] *The Times* estimated that there were a quarter of a million people at Newhall Hill by noon, with the numbers increasing thereafter. Of course these figures were contested – there was nothing new in that. A week later a clergyman wrote to the Duke of Wellington, telling him that he had been assured by a member of the military that the numbers had never exceeded 30,000. Attwood himself, when asking Brougham to present a petition to the House of Lords on behalf of the meeting, referred to 200,000 people in the course of the day – which was possibly the more accurate estimate.[9] *

£5 and £10 notes were handed about as subscriptions poured in; some of them were from members of the upper classes hoping to avoid

---

* The population of England, roughly estimated, was sixteen million at this point.[10] The figure of 200,000 adults would therefore be a substantial percentage of this, in excess of the total population of many of England's rapidly expanding industrial cities. What was unquestionable was that this great sea of people, washing over the sands of Birmingham, was the largest, most impressive demonstration in living memory. The crowd included members of 'The Sex', as the female population was termed.

molestation. The bonnets, shawls and dresses of female figures, as well as an elegant lady in a riding habit on a horse, can be seen in Haydon's preliminary depiction of the event. This, with the intention of securing a wide subscription for copies, was done by Haydon very soon afterwards, using the descriptions of actual participants to achieve verisimilitude.

The Bromsgrove Union arrived late. As they approached in force, the verses of the Hymn of the Union, so familiar to children in the streets, swung out over the waiting crowds:

> Over mountain, over plain
> Echoing wide from sea to sea,
> Peals, and shall not peal in vain
> The trumpet call of liberty!
> Britain's guardian spirit cries –
> Britons, awake! Arise, arise.

The penultimate verse made allusion to previous heroes of liberty such as the chiefs of glorious Runnymede (who were in fact barons – but 600 years later, what of it?) and John Hampden. The last verse, with reference to these heroes, was momentous – if it were to prove true:

> But not to war or blood they call,
> They bid us lift not sword or gun,
> Peaceful but firm, join one and all
> To claim your rights, and they are won.
> The British Lion's voice alone
> Shall gain for Britain all her own!

The answering song was equally emphatic:

> We kindle not war's fatal fires,
> By union, justice, reason, law
> We claim the birthright of our sires.

Then Thomas Clutton stepped forward and, taking off his hat, invited all those present to join him in a vow: 'with unbroken faith, through every peril and privation, we here devote ourselves and our children to our country's cause'. Many people wept.[11]

Fortunately for the guardians of public order, the military were not unprepared. There was to be no repetition of Bristol and Colonel Brereton's solicitude for the locals, considered unbecoming in a military man, and ending in personal tragedy. The order went out to 'rough-sharpen' the soldiers' swords. The purpose of this was to make the swords inflict a 'ragged' – that is, more lethal – wound. The swords of the Greys had not been submitted to this process since before Waterloo; now the old soldiers told the young ones anecdotes about it as the latter silently worked on their swords. Alexander Somerville, then serving in the Greys, described how they were 'daily and nightly booted and saddled' with enough cartridges in their possession for three days.[12]

In fact there was nothing aggressive about this huge assembly, according to the deepest conviction of Thomas Attwood that it was peaceful protest not violence which would lead to progress. As *The Times* put it in a somewhat breathless early report once the news of this vast demonstration had begun to filter in: 'The utmost harmony prevailed.' Later, having received fuller reports, the newspaper saw no reason to revise this judgement; the most magnificent meeting for its numbers and strength 'that was ever seen in England or the world' was also the most impressive for its 'order, discipline and resolution'.[13]

Otherwise the atmosphere was one of almost rural enjoyment, with the whole occasion treated as a gala outing. Then there was the music: 'the tunes of a thousand musical instruments thrilled through their hearts,' wrote Joseph Parkes of the spectators. In view of the crowds, silence for speeches had to be secured by the sound of a bugle above their heads. The meeting also had a religious connotation. Once silence had been secured with a bugle call, the Reverend Hutton took over with prayers. A native of Belfast, Hutton had graduated from Glasgow University, and acted as a Quaker minister; he was described by Haydon, who drew him, as 'highly powerful and intellectual' and confided to the artist how he had paced up and down his garden deciding whether to fight for Reform.[14]

Attwood's speech was an inspiring one even by his high standards of demagogic oratory. 'We have had but to stamp upon the earth . . .,' he said, 'and constantly from above the ground and from beneath the ground one hundred thousand brave men, besides the thousands of beautiful women I see before me, determined to see their country righted, present themselves at our call. . . .' He continued by confronting the dilemma of popular demonstration: 'If we hold no meetings, they say we are indifferent – if we hold small meetings, they say we are insignificant – if we hold large meetings they say we wish to intimidate them.' And Attwood made his own position completely clear: 'I would rather die than see the great Bill of Reform rejected or mutilated in any of its great parts or provisions.'[15]

As for the King, Attwood continued to lavish the praise upon him which had always been his custom, using what he considered to be appropriate naval terms. William IV, he said, 'has stood on the quarter deck with the waves of the political storm heaving around him; he has stood firm at the helm of the vessel of State; he has boarded the enemy when the occasion demanded'. Would he now throw himself from the topgallant mast of the vessel into the depths of the raging ocean? 'Oh no! my countrymen,' declared Attwood staunchly – with a confidence that those in London were no longer feeling quite so strongly. But perhaps his last declaration was the most important of all from the point of view of the political watchers. Attwood predicted a 'violent Revolution' if the Bill was not passed.

Although the reformers were in the main concentrated on their own domestic 'perilous question', they were not indifferent to events elsewhere in Europe, as witness the production at the meeting by Attwood of a striking foreigner he called – phonetically – Chopski. This was in fact the man born Count Joseph Kazimierz Czapski, a Pole who had taken the extra name Napoleon at his confirmation. The son of a general, Czapski was now in his mid-thirties; after a dispute with his uncle over the estates, he had dropped 'Count' and deliberately termed himself Joseph Napoleon Czapski, a peasant. Already a patriotic activist, believed by the governing Russians to be a dangerous revolutionary, Czapski was actually in Paris at the time of the Polish insurrection in

November 1830; he called for French aid for the Polish patriots. He then returned to the Prussian sector of Poland in January 1831, using a false French name while the Prussians attempted to capture him. Finally Czapski escaped on a British ship from Danzig and in January 1832 reached Ireland. Here he made speeches in favour of Polish independence, sometimes alongside O'Connell, which were widely reported in the English press, including the *Birmingham Journal*.

Czapski was actually on his way to London to present a petition of 5,000 names in favour of Polish freedom, when he was persuaded to step aside and visit Birmingham as part of the Wolverhampton Union's delegation. A banner reading 'A Tear for Poland' was presented to him: Czapski was visibly affected but admitted that he did not know what the word 'Tear' meant. He said later that his heart was more sensible than his head, for he had wept instinctively at the sight of it. Czapski, greeted with great acclaim by the crowds, instantly became a devoted adherent of the Birmingham Political Union. As the July Revolution, so frequently invoked, had been a political inspiration, so Polish Czapski became a symbol of outspoken political challenge, regardless of consequences.[16]

Tuesday 8 May was a day of ferment in political circles. After the voting there had been a hasty meeting late at night in the Lord Chancellor's room: a provisional decision was reached to resign unless creation was agreed. The full Cabinet met at the Foreign Office at eleven o'clock the next morning to discuss a minute to be submitted to the King. Following the defeat of the night before, the Government tendered their resignations 'as a natural consequence'. However, in view of 'the peculiar circumstances of the Country', the Government felt it their duty to state that the alternative of creating peers was one that His Majesty might consider, as it would enable the Bill to be passed without a change of government. In that case, the Government was willing to undertake the task. But it was thought 'prudent' that Lord Grey and Lord Brougham should go together to Windsor that afternoon to present the minute to the King; their task was to convey to him not only their determination to resign unless he consent to create, but also that such a creation – it should not be concealed – would have to number fifty or sixty new peers.[17]

So down to Windsor travelled the Prime Minister and the Lord Chancellor. These were positions they had held since November 1830, although it was not quite clear how long they would continue to do so. Grey and Brougham travelled in such haste, in fact, that, departing from Hounslow, they nearly upset the carriage of the unfortunate Lady Glengall, an Irish widow of a certain age. 'As it was they broke the pole of her ladyship's carriage and frightened her proportionately.' When they eventually arrived, it was not an agreeable meeting of Sovereign and his middle-aged Ministers. As Creevey wrote, the King did not care to preserve his usual civility: 'he did not even offer the poor fellows any victuals'.[18] It was not hard to gauge what the King's reaction was from all this, although what he actually promised Grey and Brougham was a letter on the day following.

Grey and Brougham returned together in a coach from Windsor. What happened next became the stuff of satirists. Starving, and no doubt needing a drink after all this, the two gentlemen stopped off en route at a public house in Hounslow. Here they dined on mutton chops. In Brougham's account: 'I insisted on a broiled kidney being added to the poor repast.' Grey laughed at him and declared that 'he cared not for kidneys'. Nevertheless he ate them when they came. As Brougham put it: 'And we were all in the print-shops in a few days.'[19] One cartoon was captioned 'Late Scene at Hounslow at the Sign of the Red Lion'. Brougham is depicted chomping away with the words: 'My Lord you don't eat your chops, I have already placed six in Schedule A and am about to discuss a seventh, while you have scarcely got through one.'

During this time of exceptional nervosity, Lord Althorp calmed himself – and perhaps showed where his real heart lay – by going to a nursery garden to buy flowers and shrubs. He brought home five enormous packages, and set about writing instructions where they were to be planted. He also cleaned and oiled his fowling-pieces for rough shooting on his estate, which he had neglected during the prolonged crisis.[20]

The promised letter from the King duly arrived the next day, Wednesday 9 May. William IV declined to make 'so large an addition to the Peerage' and in consequence he accepted the resignation of the Ministry. The King did however ask his present Ministers to continue 'in discharge of their official functions' until a new government was formed.[21] It was now Grey's duty to go back to the House of Lords.

Rising to his feet, the former Prime Minister made the announcement which everyone was awaiting. 'And now, my Lords,' he said, 'after the proceedings of Monday last, and after the result of that night's debate and decision, your Lordships are probably prepared for the information which I feel it to be my duty to communicate with you.'[22] After such a defeat, there were two courses: to resign at once or go to the King and ask him to create peerages. Then Grey made his dramatic announcement. After much consideration, he had taken the second course. And now: the King 'was graciously pleased to accept our resignation'. Grey and his Government were therefore holding office only until their successors were appointed. In the House of Commons, in contrast to the sullen Lords, Althorp was received with such a round of cheering as 'I never before heard', wrote Edward Littleton, as a result of which Le Marchant thought Althorp was on the verge of weeping.[23]

It was on 9 May that King William asked the Duke of Wellington, using the intermediary of Lord Lyndhurst, to form a new administration. If it was a chalice, it was certainly a poisoned one; for in the same breath it was made clear that the Duke was expected to bring sufficient measures of Reform to satisfy the country. Out of optimism – or political *naïveté* – the King did not seem to understand the extraordinary difficulties, both moral and practical, inherent in this demand. A courtier commented: 'The King appeared to think all this day, that he was done with the Whigs . . . for the next forty years.' William IV also hoped that Brougham and the Duke of Richmond might continue in office.[24]

Officially, while Wellington struggled with his paradoxical task, Britain was without a government; although the previous incumbents would continue to administrate, for what that was worth, Earl Grey still residing in Downing Street. The country was in a state of uproar. *The Times* on 10 May referred to 'the awful crisis in which the British empire is now placed . . . Every man without exception of age or calling, asks his neighbour the question: "What is to be *done*?"' William Cobbett put it more crudely: 'Every man you met seemed to be convulsed with rage.'[25]

As to that, the centre of attention was now well and truly focused on William IV. Here was a monarch, a man of sixty-seven, who, after a very different career, had reigned for one year and ten months – a period in which political crisis had become the norm. Rumours were rife, and none of them in Whig circles particularly favourable to the King (even if Attwood had maintained his position of loyalty at Newhall Hill). Creevey believed that he had been influenced by the defeat on Monday; as a result, 'Our beloved Billy cuts a damnable figure in this business.' He actually allowed the Duke of Cumberland to tell his friends that he would not create peers 'and then the rats were in their old ranks again at once'. This rumour was on a par with one Le Marchant heard concerning the fatal vote and the bishops: they had been swayed by the Archbishop of Canterbury who assured them that the King had no intention of creating peers.[26]

Then there was a *levée* or reception at Court, which might have been a grisly affair, given there was no government at the time, only some administrative caretakers. On this occasion, however, 'our perfidious Billy was the outside of graciosity' to Lord Grey. The King said that George II could not have felt more bitterly at parting with Walpole nor George III at parting with Lord North, than he did under the present circumstances.[27] But of course for a final parting it was necessary to secure the acceptance of office by a fresh lot of Ministers, and that was where the intrigues were now centred.

During these two days, people talked very openly of civil war, according to Edward Littleton. There was a further Newhall Hill meeting on 10 May and on this occasion it was thought seemly that those loyal medals with the words 'God Save the King' backing Attwood's profile should be abandoned. There was even talk of a change of dynasty – 'I never heard the like before,' wrote Littleton; it reminded him ruefully of a conversation he had had in Paris during the controversial administration of Joseph de Villèle. Then Littleton had assured a leading French politician: 'In England no one dreams of the removal of the monarch, one can be at no great distance from such an event when it becomes the subject of general conversation.'[28] Such complacency about the English Constitution was coming back to haunt him.

In this connection, there was a notable increase in attacks on the Queen in the press; an increase also in the degree of viciousness. If it was a question of who was to blame for the King's behaviour, then a German-born Queen presented an all too convenient scapegoat. Creevey was not the only one to refer to the Austrian-born Queen of France, Marie Antoinette, known sneeringly as *l'Autrichienne* from her first appearance in her new country at the age of fourteen. Of course the Habsburg Archduchess Marie Antoinette had been high-born, no one questioned that; it was where she was born that was the trouble. Adelaide of Saxe-Meiningen was not felt to have the same distinction; at a public meeting in Southwark, as reported in *The Times*, she was described as a tawdry foreigner – 'a woman raised from obscurity to the highest pitch of glory – raised from a state not so respectable or affluent as the lady of an English squire to be consort of the Monarch of the most enlightened kingdom on the earth'. Was it right, the speaker asked, for such a people to be ruled by the Tory despotism of a female? It was scarcely surprising that in answer to this question there were vehement cries of 'No, no'.[29]

On Wednesday 9 May the *Morning Chronicle* reported that the Queen and other royal ladies had in fact never ceased tormenting His Majesty with all manner of sinister reports and forebodings as to the evils which would result from Reform. The consequent verdict was even more damning: 'It is proper that the nation did know, without disguise or reserve, that the Queen has done more injury to the cause of Reform than any person living.'[30] William IV himself was no longer exempt from criticism. In line with the removal of the patriotic medals showing the royal visage was the fact that the King actually found himself being driven through a hissing crowd on his return from Windsor on 12 May.

*

The atmosphere in the House of Commons on 10 May was as different to that of Lords as it was possible to be, given that the social class of both Houses was not really very different, the Commons being choc-a-block with heirs to peers. Lord Ebrington MP, he who was considered quite the model of an English nobleman and conscientious to a fault, moved the Address to the King.[31] Pointing to the deep feeling in the country, he asked the King 'to call to his Councils only such persons as will carry into effect, unimpaired in all its essential provisions, that Bill which has already passed this House'. As for the recent Leader of the House, Lord Althorp, now apparently going into retirement, he would have the consolation of thinking how much he had done in 'the great cause of obtaining for the people a free Representation'.

The Address was seconded by Edward Strutt, the high-minded young MP for Derby. Strutt's manufacturing family had gained their fortune from an original partnership with Richard Arkwright, but along the way as successful businessmen had used their wealth, as the poet Thomas Moore put it, on 'elegancies' such as literature and music. Strutt began by emphasizing that he had the support of his constituents and then pointed out his own lack of prejudice, since he had had no post in the previous administration. 'Let this House come forward and place itself in its proper station at the head of the people,' he declared. After that, the people should not look elsewhere for leaders – a hint to the unionists, let alone the more violent demonstrators. As for the Tories, and the idea that they would now come into office: 'if indeed, the time shall ever come when we are willing to submit our victorious armies to the command of the officers of the enemy; if we shall ever call the culprits from the bar to the judgement seat,' then, and not till then, would he consent to entrust Reform to the 'avowed enemies of the Bill' or its reluctant and wavering supporters. The next day, in a packed House of Commons, Ebrington's motion was passed by a majority of 80 votes.

The focus of political attention now passed, naturally enough, to the Tories. Was it actually possible that the Duke of Wellington would consent to form a government which would bring about limited

Reform? Considering he had spoken publicly of Reform as an evil as recently as 7 May, there must be considerable doubt about the matter. Months before, Lord Althorp had suggested to his father that Reform would only be brought about by their enemies. And there was of course the vital, never-to-be-forgotten precedent of Catholic Emancipation. The Duke had chosen to carry through that measure, as part of his duty to his King and his country: was history about to repeat itself? And yet, if he did not, if Reform was abandoned at this stage, could the country be saved from violent disturbance, not to say uprising?

Not all the negotiations were with the Tories. Brougham was privately asked by King William to continue as Lord Chancellor; he declined. The King wept but Brougham refused to give way. Then Lord Lyndhurst, the obvious choice to return to the position he had once occupied, suggested on 11 May that there was a condition for his return: Lady Lyndhurst should be received at Court. On the surface an innocuous request, it referred to the fact that the skittish Dolly Lyndhurst was now openly the mistress of Lord Dudley, who presented her with some fine diamonds (which she presumably wished to flaunt at Court). Given Queen Adelaide's principles, this was a sacrifice on her part, in a cause that she at least felt to be a good one. There was a further mark against Dolly, in the opinion of the Tory ladies at least. She had in the past (to the general fury) exhibited Whig sympathies – if only to include Lord Grey among her admirers. Observers got used to a double act whereby Dolly praised Reform and her husband castigated it, 'like the old divisions of families in the Civil Wars', as Greville put it. But perhaps this was all part of the Lyndhurst plan for self-advancement.[32]

The key figure after the Iron Duke was, however, not Lyndhurst but Sir Robert Peel; he after all led the Tories in the Commons and would therefore have to guide any limited measure of Reform through that House. This supposed that such a thing was acceptable in any form at all to the Tories and, contrariwise, that the country would accept Reform in a strictly limited version. Yet Peel had told the Tory John Wilson Croker as early as 10 May that he would be reluctant to head any new government because he had sacrificed his own judgement over Catholic Emancipation; he would not now perform 'the same painful abandonment of opinion' on the question of Reform. And he talked to Croker of the advantage to the country 'that public men should maintain a character for consistency and disinterestedness'.[33] These were fine words. As opposed to them, it could be argued that what Peel – and Wellington for that matter – had done once, abandon principles, could be done again. But if Peel really did refuse to make a second 'painful abandonment' of his convictions, some extraordinary fate might threaten a country already thought by many to be on the verge of revolution.

Croker, the obdurate Tory, was outspoken in his response to Peel: how Peel's 'feeling' was obscuring his 'judgement'. He was even more outspoken in his predictions for the future, should the Tories fail to take their current opportunity so that Grey was allowed to return. Croker foresaw 'the King enslaved, the House of Lords degraded, the Bill passed, the Revolution, I may say, consummated'. Were Peel to allow the King and Constitution to sink under his eyes, without jumping in and trying to save them, his 'prudence and consistency' would be called less flattering titles in that 'black-edged page of history which will record the extinction of the monarchy of England'.

The Iron Duke himself took a different line. Not for him the heroics – sincere heroics – of Sir Robert Peel. On 10 May he listened to Lyndhurst's plea: 'It is our duty to try.' There was no inconsistency here, by his own standards of behaviour. Wellington announced himself ready to do whatever the King might command him to do. 'I am as much averse to the Reform as ever I was,' he declared. But no embarrassment of that kind, no private consideration would prevent him from making every effort 'to serve the King'.[34] It was, in its own way, an honourable position, because it was one that the grand old man had long maintained: his duty to the State, once achieved so triumphantly by force of arms, was now to be rendered by direct service to his Sovereign, and that included forming a government if he was asked to do so.

Other Tories were less happy at the prospect of bringing about limited measures of Reform, sharing the conscientious objections of Peel rather than the Wellingtonian concept of duty. There was the possibility that the Speaker of the House, a Tory, Charles Manners-Sutton, might prove an acceptable anodyne leader because, by the nature of his office, he was not tarred by the brush of his own anti-Reform declarations. Manners-Sutton was in his early fifties, and since his election in 1817 had proved popular enough as Speaker – a fine, friendly, genial figure, if inclined to pomposity (but that was a forgivable offence in a Speaker). The trouble was that at a crucial meeting of the Tories at Apsley House, Manners-Sutton spent three hours outlining his views on the whole matter at exhaustive and exhausting length. At the end of it, Lyndhurst, never one to flinch from excoriating a rival, flung back his chair and exclaimed that he refused to listen any longer to such 'a damned tiresome old bitch'.[35]

In the meantime the Whigs congregated at their beloved Brooks's Club in St James's. Due to the deft handling of Althorp and Stanley, the Whig MPs came to agree that they would permit the incoming – Tory – Ministry to pass the Bill themselves in the Lords, possibly with some additions of their own, and then proceed to defeat the Tories in the House of Commons, which their numbers permitted them to do. In private, Lord Grey was even beginning to believe, wearily, that the passing of the Bill by the Tories was the best thing that could happen to the country. At the same time he doubted whether the Tories could bring it off, and in a depressed communication to Holland on the same Sunday 13 May wrote: 'Can a new administration be formed? I begin to be *afraid* that the attempt will fail.' This want of spirit – after the long fight – was too much for Holland, and with his usual independence of mind he said so. Grey responded by comparing himself to a captive anxious to escape from prison before adding (ironically, in much the same language as Wellington): 'But I will do my duty.'[36]

While the politicians of both parties cogitated, argued, spoke much of duty but gave no appearance of reaching a conclusion, the country at large demonstrated a far more robust attitude. It was on Saturday 12 May that the decision was made in London among the Radicals, led by Francis Place, to attack the soft belly of any government – the finances of the country. Already the crisis was beginning to have the inevitable consequence of a loss of confidence in financial circles. As early as February, powerful financiers had been seeing their own particular kind of sense on the vexed topic of Reform. Charles Arbuthnot reported to the Duke of Wellington that Nathan Rothschild had visited him: 'He says that among the monied men, there is an alarm lest there should be such opposition to all Reform as would cause commotions. . . .' These worries among 'monied men' took a material form when, between 9 May and 12 May, consols fell from 85 per cent to 83.5 per cent. But in any case, the official historian of the Rothschild family has detected a change in the attitudes of some family members, including Nathan, despite his friendship with Wellington, veering from the Tories towards the Whigs; the Duke's opposition to Jewish Emancipation may have played some part in this.[37]

The meeting held at Francis Place's house, on Saturday 12 May, included deputies from Birmingham, among them Joseph Parkes.[38] This was in theory far from the privileged society of the Rothschilds. Nevertheless, those present were certainly not without connections. There had already been conversations, according to Place, 'in various parts of the metropolis . . . with merchants, bankers, traders, and Members of Parliament'. There was general perturbation among all of them at 'the no longer doubted intelligence' that the King had ordered Wellington to form an administration. Such was the alarm at this prospect that Wellington's vehement discourse in the Lords, made only five days previously, had already been reprinted, placarded and distributed – with a caution to the people against letting such a man and his party govern them in the future.

Now serious consideration was given to what should be done when – for it no longer seemed appropriate to say if – such an administration should be formed. Once again, any kind of violent demonstration was condemned: demonstrations yes, but of the orderly sort which would merely require the presence, not the intervention, of soldiers. (Nevertheless the need to be present would prevent the soldiers from moving about the country to obstruct other demonstrations.) The suggested financial manoeuvre was in a new and different category. In Francis

Place's own words, 'it was very clearly seen that if a much more open and general run for gold upon the banks, the bankers and the Bank of England could be produced, the embarrassment of the Court and the Duke would be increased.' In short, if a general panic could be produced, the Duke would inevitably be defeated.

An agitated and prolonged debate followed with many different suggestions as to how this general panic could be produced – the company included two bankers who, although likely to be 'inconvenienced greatly', entered heartily into the spirit of the thing. There were two possibilities. In the first place, such a general panic might prevent the formation of the administration in the first place; secondly, it might speedily bring about the defeat of the new government, if it did come to be formed.

It was during these discussions that someone had the wit to suggest: 'we ought to have a placard'. This placard would set forth all the consequences of permitting the Duke to govern the country, and call on the people to take care of themselves by collecting all the 'hard money' they could, withdrawing it from savings banks, bankers and from the Bank of England, and then hoarding it. So Joseph Parkes got to work drawing up a placard. Francis Place inspected his labours as he worked. Immediately the strong words 'WE MUST STOP THE DUKE' struck Place as containing, dramatically, the whole message they wanted to convey. Place therefore took a large piece of paper and wrote:

TO STOP THE

DUKE

GO FOR

GOLD

He then held up the paper and everyone acclaimed it; no more words were necessary. Money was quickly put on the table. The printer offered to work all night, and by Sunday morning six bill-stickers, each with a trusty aide at his side, saw to it that bills were posted all over London. Further parcels of posters were sent off that evening and the next day by coach to every quarter of England and Scotland. It was in this fashion that the poster — celebrated or infamous according to the point of view — came out of a Saturday night meeting in the Radical tailor's library.

CHAPTER FOURTEEN

PRITHEE RETURN TO ME

'Return, Lord Grey, I prithee return to me;
Return, Lord Grey, and bring the people with thee!' –

'Song of The King to Lord Grey', *The Times*, May 1832

Thus Monday 14 May, a week after the double Crisis Day, dawned with revolution in the air, calls for political action, posters everywhere, a run on the bank commencing – and no government as yet in place. The crescendo of attacks on the Queen did not help for stability, either in the minds of the people or, for that matter, in that of her husband. Typically, a bugbear of a paper aptly titled *The Satirist; or, the Censor of the Times,* issued a long, unpleasant poem on Sunday 13 May entitled 'The Royal Tabbies'.[1] The former Prime Minister was characterized as Grey Tom, 'a stern and stately cat' who cleared out every rat from the palace; whereupon the tabbies formed a base intrigue, led by their queen, 'a German tabby she (as Sour-krout better known)'. In the end the night-time squalling of the tabbies turned the poor King's brain until he dismissed Grey Tom. 'O woeful change! . . . This King undid all he had done / And was not worth a Crown.'

The Satirist in its prose articles on 13 May also questioned the very right of the 'House of Brunswick' to occupy the throne, describing their authority as nothing more than that of 'the poorest sausage-spinner in Germany'. And it went on to point out that a royal house which had been invited onto the throne could also be 'justifiably and patriotically' removed from it. Even if it meant that William IV had to 'take his chop' with Charles Dix at Holyrood – that is, in exile – 'we say, let England be free'. And this, the paper indicated, was likely to happen 'unless he can manfully surmount petticoat influence'. This was strong, unsubtle stuff, and the Tory Lord Stormont duly complained about it all as seditious in the House of Lords – a row which rumbled on, and of course enabled *The Satirist* enthusiastically to reprint all the material, together with Lord Stormont's complaints.

In the meantime the *Times* leader on 14 May, in a more elegantly literary fashion, made the same point.[2] The 'most regretted change' which had come about in the King's mind on the subject of Reform and creation had various causes, but 'it is asserted on all sides that domestic importunity has been one'. With the help of a ten-line Latin quotation from the *Aeneid*, citing the woes flowing from an ancient queen's behaviour, *The Times* reached the solemn conclusion: 'A foreigner is no very competent judge of English liberties, and politics are not the proper field for female enterprise and exertion.'

The reformers outside Parliament were less interested in Court intrigues than in the stark reality of the situation. Attwood had stated it clearly enough: if indeed the House of Lords could make and break governments at will, 'there was an end of popular power in England, and the spirit of the people would be utterly broken'. How was this so-called popular power to be expressed? Dr James Kay quoted Shelley at a meeting in Rochdale. He was a man who had personal experience of conditions in cotton manufacture and went on to write a book about them which would be quoted by Engels. Here he made a poetic suggestion, less crude than *The Satirist*'s verses, more contemporary than the classical allusions of *The Times*.

> Rise like lions after slumber
> In unvanquishable number
> Shake your chains to earth, like dew . . .
> Ye are many – they are few.

These lines were in fact taken from *The Masque of Anarchy* which Shelley had written thirteen years earlier following the massacre at Peterloo; the poem had not been published at the time as being too provocative, with its call for a great assembly 'of the fearless, of the free', and was only now being printed posthumously under the editorship of Leigh Hunt.[3]

The sentiments of the poem were all very well: it was factually true that the people outnumbered their rulers. What was much less clear was how they were to proceed once the chains had been shaken off, like the proverbial dew. Shelley's poem was in effect advocating passive resistance to violence. In 1832 was it to be revolution indeed? The word, so much dreaded, was used by the opponents of Reform as a nightmare threat of what might happen, but was not yet current among its advocates. Nevertheless, towards the end of his life Earl Russell looked back across a long career to the days when he had been 'Lord John Reformer'; the only moment of real peril that he could recall was the so-called 'Days of May'.[4]

In the meantime the Duke of Wellington was known to be struggling to carry out the commission given to him by the King when he accepted the resignation of Grey's Government: Wellington was to try to form an administration which would then provide some measure of Reform. The real problem for Wellington lay not so much in the personnel at his disposal but in the extraordinary nature of the about-turn he was expected to make, at the request of the King. As Holland wrote to Grey on the Sunday 13 May, if Wellington did move a bill, 'what is to be our tone? Silence, forbearance? Acquiescence and good wishes mixed with apprehension? Invective? Or ridicule?' Frankly, Holland felt that ridicule was the most appropriate emotion: 'for I can scarcely refrain from laughing when I think of a change' – of policy – 'beyond any farce, except perhaps a harlequin farce, exhibited in the grave assembly . . . and played by the great hero of the age'.[5]

The House of Commons filled up early on Monday 14 May. For all Holland's notional ridicule, it was assumed by many that the Tories were about to form an administration and that the cheerful 'new Ministers (expectant)' would soon be in place. Sir Henry Hardinge, Wellington's chief supporter there – he who had prophesied the loaded guns next time at the dissolution of Parliament in 1831, and was now a candidate to be Chief Secretary for Ireland – accosted Lord Althorp. He said he hoped that Althorp did not disapprove of Wellington forming an administration to pass a bill (which would not of course be that Bill put forward by the Whigs). Hardinge was too elated at the turn of events to notice Althorp's 'cold and unsatisfactory' answer.[6] He was also apparently too dedicated to the cause of Wellington to understand that the mood of the House in general – with its Whig majority – was not one of elation but of disgust.

The presentation of a petition from the City of London, praying that the House would not vote supplies until the Reform Bill was passed, provided the impetus for a debate of unparalleled rancour. Lord Ebrington rose to describe what was projected by a Tory administration as an 'act of gross public immorality' – given Wellington's unvarnished denunciations of the Bill.[7] It was a departure from every principle which had been expressed by the Tories throughout the discussions on the question. There could be no pro-Reform pledge given by Wellington which was stronger than 'repeated votes . . . speeches . . . solemn protests of an uncompromising hostility'. Wellington was the man who had called down 'the vengeance of Heaven on the principle of this Bill'. This, from Ebrington, was strong language indeed.

The Tory Alexander Baring went in for what one observer described as 'casuistry' when he tried to maintain that Wellington had actually come to the rescue of a King abandoned by those who should have been his servants. It was not to be denied, Baring said, that the country stood, at present, 'on the brink of a great crisis'. But it was all due to the Ministers who were refusing to perform their duties. As it was, the Government had resigned over 'a most dangerous and atrocious principle': it was being suggested that every time the Government disagreed with the Lords, the King had to create enough peers to enable them to win after all. And he also denounced Ebrington's use of language.

This was too much for Althorp. He insisted on clarifying what Ebrington had actually described as 'public immorality': his charges had been aimed at those individuals 'who, having opposed the Reform Bill in its principle and details, were nevertheless ready to accept office, with the view of carrying out the very measure they had strenuously resisted'. Under the circumstances, Althorp thought the language no stronger than was justified. It was left to Macaulay – the future historian – to provide the kindest gloss on Wellington's behaviour. He could not contemplate, said Macaulay, without the most acute pain 'the possible degradation of perhaps the most famous name in British history'.

This could be described as the exchange of high-level calumnies, when one party apparently loses and another gains, were it not for the behaviour of Sir Robert Inglis. It will be remembered that it was the ebullient Sir Robert who had vividly expressed the sheer amazed disgust of a certain kind of Tory when Lord John Russell first produced his Bill in March 1831. Now he issued an ominous preliminary to his speech: he, Sir Robert Inglis, 'never rose under a more reluctant and painful sense of public duty'. Then Inglis denounced the adoption of Reform by the incoming Government as 'one of the most fatal violations of public confidence that could be inflicted'. Sometimes one man who is unafraid can turn the mood of an assembly; the other Tories began to express their uneasiness and even disapproval.

For influence on the immediate future, however, the most significant speech was undoubtedly that which followed Inglis – by Sir Robert Peel, the Tory leader in the Commons. Peel began by describing the whole debate as 'injudicious'. He put it to the House whether 'declarations of determined hostility to a hypothetic Administration' were not somewhat premature. Then he used the fatal words – as many Tories and not a few Whigs instantly perceived – as follows: 'I feel unable to enter into the Service of the Crown . . .' Sir Robert added that he bitterly regretted that he was not able to accept office. Greatest of all was his regret that an opportunity was being given for sarcastic attacks on those who did accept office. And Peel was careful to emphasize that everything done by the Duke of Wellington 'will be dictated by the highest courage and the purest sense of honour'.

There can be little question that it was the refusal of Sir Robert Peel not only to head but even to join the new Government which proved in the end fatal to the Tory interest. In short, Peel could not make the about-turn which Wellington was apparently able to manage. At the start of Tuesday 15 May Lord Grey still thought that Wellington would 'persevere' and form an administration, as he told Lord Holland.[8] But in fact the time for Grey's task had come.

Wellington himself had already decided, given the past, that he should not actually head the Government. Peel had refused on principle. There was a third candidate, the verbose Charles Manners-Sutton, Speaker of the House. Along with a tendency to talk at inordinate length, he suffered from indecision: it was fatal to his prospects at a time when rapid action was necessary, and in the end he was understood to have declined.

It was in fact on 15 May that Wellington decided to abandon his attempt to serve his Sovereign – as he saw it – as impractical, since he could have no hope of controlling the Commons. The news was broken to Lord Althorp by the Duke of Richmond, in terms most likely to bring home the message to the passionate countryman who was also a reformer. 'Well, I have news for you,' said Richmond as he entered. 'No shooting this year. Pack up your guns again. I have the intelligence from the Palace, and knew it to be true. The Duke of Wellington has been with the King this morning, and given up his commission altogether.'[9]

Peel might have given the Tories at least a sporting chance of success with their chosen measure of Reform, but Peel, still mortified by his treatment over his final adoption of Catholic Emancipation, was not for turning this time. As Princess Lieven had noted in the spring, Peel did not foresee the end of the world if the Bill was passed, unlike Wellington; although he was strongly opposed to it. 'There you have the difference between forty and seventy,' she exclaimed, with a certain colourful exaggeration (Peel was actually forty-four to Wellington's sixty-three).[10] It was however certainly true that, coming from a different generation and being of a very different temperament, Peel could not emulate the Iron Duke's satisfaction in serving the King in peace as he had in war, with no regard to his very public declarations of conscience.

The Tory Party point of view was put by Lord Ellenborough in his Diary: 'I confess I do not think Peel's part creditable,' he wrote. 'He is afraid of being again taunted with inconsistency and so he exposes his country to peril.'[11] As against that, Peel could be sure that his 'pure and cold moral character', somewhat stained in Ultra Tory eyes in 1829, was once again intact.

The result was that, later on Tuesday 15 May, Lord Grey received a message from the King. Beginning with the phrase 'In consequence of what passed last night in the House of Commons', William IV expressed his hope that the Bill could now receive 'such modifications' as might appeal to those who held different opinions. This kind of arrangement would relieve the King from 'the embarrassment' which had been caused him by the proposal for large-scale creation.[12]

Negotiations had now started again. Given the backbench Tory distress at the idea of a Tory administration bowing to Reform, these negotiations were in fact welcome to many Tory MPs. One of them remarked that the King must either recall Grey, 'or start for Hanover'. From the Whig point of view, however, the situation was not so simple. This was hardly the moment to cave in to this new demand for 'modification', whatever that meant. A Cabinet minute of 16 May outlined the only two possible 'modes' which were acceptable to them. One was the 'cessation' of opposition to the Bill on the part of its adversaries; the other was 'such a creation of Peers as should give your Majesty's servants sufficient power to overcome that opposition'.[13]

In theory Grey was requesting no more than the King had already granted in his long – and rambling – letter of 15 January. Here William IV had apparently accepted, in a worst-case scenario, what the Cabinet had demanded in its minute: the power of 'acting at once up to the full exigency of the case', that is, creation and unlimited creation at that – for what else could the word 'full', which the King or Sir Herbert Taylor inserted into the language of the Cabinet minute, actually mean? Two things had happened since that grudging admission, in the middle of a long letter denouncing the Bill as stifling independent voices. First, the country itself had moved from being restive and disturbed on the subject of Reform to being angry and – in certain cases – violent. Second, and from the point of view of the Whigs vitally in the present instance, the attitude of William himself had substantially soured on the subject of Reform.

The satiric press was crude and even cruel in its attacks on Queen Adelaide and the other 'royal tabbies', but they were not necessarily for that reason wrong in the influence they attributed to her. Some of the tabbies were of course male – William's newly ennobled son, the Earl of Munster, or the High Tory Duke of Cumberland. A conservative figure by upbringing and by preference, Queen Adelaide showed no signs of understanding the niceties of the Constitution by which a consort did not interfere in politics – if only because such niceties were nowhere laid down, whereas the normal day-to-day intercourse of husband and wife was an established, socially approved routine. King William himself was not exactly a weak man: despite his late entry into the royal experience, he was determinedly conscientious, with a notion of his royal duty which he took extremely seriously. The *Bristol Mercury*, in a charitable assessment, called him 'not ill-natured but not very wise'; and suspected that sea life had taught him the valuable lesson that 'the poorer orders could feel'. At the same time, here was a man, old and infirm, with a love of domesticity – 'and he has a young wife!'[14]

What William did lack was the brilliance of a public figure who can assess a new situation adeptly and turn it to advantage; he was fundamentally inexperienced, and lack of experience made him easily frightened. Perhaps the monarchy really was under threat, as his family suggested, with all this talk of Reform: revolutionary events in Europe in recent times had made it all too easy to believe, to say nothing of the ominous presence of Charles X in exile in Holyrood. And it was Queen Adelaide the injudicious who, both in her speech and her writings, spread the news of the King's reluctance. As she told a friend of the Tory Lord Dover on Thursday 16 May: 'I don't despair yet.'[15]

In view of this developing obstinacy on the part of the King, it was clear to the Whigs, and to many conscientious Tories, that the first alternative outlined in the Cabinet minute was infinitely preferable. If the peers could be induced to drop their practical opposition to the Bill – while not being asked to express hypocritical approval of Reform – the 'fearful alternative' of creation could still be avoided. Obviously the attitude of the Duke of Wellington was of enormous importance, both as a moral and an actual political leader of his party. In this context, two speeches 'of extreme violence' on Thursday 17 May, from Lyndhurst and the Duke respectively, bade fair to wreck the whole tenuous process towards accommodation all over again, as Grey hastened to report to the King that very evening. 'He is sorry to inform Your Majesty, that nothing could be more unsatisfactory or embarrassing.'[16]

Wellington included his own apologia which, by implication, blamed the Whigs: he remained of the opinion that Reform would be 'most injurious' to the country. Be that as it may, 'I cannot help feeling, that if I had been capable of refusing my assistance to His Majesty – if I had been capable of saying to His Majesty "I cannot assist you in this affair" – I do not think, my Lords, that I could have shown my face in the streets from shame of having done it – for shame of having abandoned my Sovereign under such circumstances.' That was personal, and it was aimed at Lord Grey.

Lyndhurst added his own 'violent invective'. To this Grey responded with angry pride that he was fully justified in bringing in a measure consistent with the principles he had maintained 'through life'. The debate ended without any declaration regarding withdrawal of opposition, of the nature that the King had led Lord Grey to expect.

Lord Grey then told the King that the Cabinet would meet the next day, Friday the 18th, at twelve, after which he would be in touch with the King again. In a private letter to Sir Herbert Taylor, sent at the same time, Grey told the royal secretary that he had not yet recovered from his astonishment at what had happened in the Lords. To Princess Lieven privately he likened their attacks to something by Robespierre or Cromwell.[17] It was true that the recalcitrant peers had left the Chamber after speaking, which might be construed as an intention to pass on voting. Again, it might simply mean that they would reappear at a given moment and wreck the Bill. Later that night, Taylor hastened to reply. Purely in his capacity as a private individual, Wellington had assured the King that he would abstain from further discussion of the Bill; quite separately, many other Peers had made the same assertion.[18]

So the arguing went on, while the country appeared to be on the edge of incendiarism, if not actually in flames already. The *Morning Chronicle* declared that the debate in the House of Lords had been an 'open declaration of war' against the people of England. Harriet Grote remembered afterwards that in her political set in London, 'so intensely interesting was the crisis that we scarce did anything but listen for news and run from one house to another'.[19] Now rumours, which proved to be true, of Wellington's withdrawal spread rapidly.

Francis Place was up early on 18 May, reading *The Times* and the *Morning Chronicle* by seven o'clock. A stream of visitors followed, all of whom had come to the same conclusion: resistance to the Duke at any cost, and in every possible way. At half past eight he received a significant message from Sir John Hobhouse asking him to declare his intentions in a letter. At nine o'clock Francis Place duly replied, pointing out that the demand for gold – backed by Place and his allies – had ceased when news percolated of Grey's potential return. But Place added, while paying a tribute to the cool courage and admirable discipline of the people: 'We cannot however go on thus *beyond today*.' If the Duke came into power now, laws would have to be broken, barricades put up in towns. In short, 'Let the Duke take office as premier, and we shall have a commotion in the nature of a civil war.' The *Morning Chronicle* also chose to invoke the emotive word 'barricades' – shades of the French Revolution – which it feared would soon be erected.[20]

All along, the established connection of Place to Hobhouse provided an excellent conduit for discreet threats in the direction of the Cabinet, of the sort that could be employed usefully in campaigns which would one day be termed propaganda and, still later, spin. When Francis Place announced via Hobhouse, 'If the Duke comes into power now, we shall be unable to "hold to the laws"', he was well aware that this was a most helpful statement from the Whig point of view. The same applied to the various minatory public meetings of the National Political Union.

Meanwhile, in the central arena of politics, a riposte came from the King to Lord Grey, following his complaint of the previous evening.[21]

The King stated that various peers had intended to declare their abstention publicly during that debate so full of invective – but it was *Grey's* speech, 'so peremptory and unconciliatory', which had led them to abandon their intention.

Finally the King, very possibly on the gentle nudging of Taylor, gave way. There can be no certainty about Taylor's intervention at such a vital moment, only supposition based on Taylor's past record for discreet, tactful negotiation with the best interests of the monarchy at heart. Sir Herbert Taylor, the experienced royal servant of many years' standing, could see that from the King's point of view, the challenge of the current constitutional situation was best not confronted, but glided over; this diplomatic conduct of withdrawal from outright challenge would mean that the royal powers were far more likely to survive intact.

In this way, a further letter came from the King on 18 May, following his riposte.[22] William IV agreed that if there were continuing obstacles to the Bill, Lord Grey might submit to him 'a creation of peers' sufficient to carry the Bill. He did not fail to make his familiar point about the need to preserve the aristocracy, advocating heirs to peerages all over again; but in suggesting that this list must be exhausted first, the King did imply that the Government could also look elsewhere – Grey's people of substance and property, doubtless. It appeared that the mini-crisis – caused, one is obliged to conclude, by the outraged and outrageous feelings of the Tory peers on the subject of Reform, including Wellington and Lyndhurst – was over.

It was scarcely surprising that Grey felt himself unable to attend the Queen's Ball that night. He told Taylor in a private letter, 'I am quite knocked up with the fatigue of the last ten days', and was therefore obliged to send an excuse to Her Majesty. Grey added: 'Pray do what you can to prevent a wrong construction being put on my absence. I really am very unwell.'[23]

The next day, 19 May, in a calmer mood, Lord Grey was discussing with Taylor the technicalities of reinstating Ministers whose resignations had been accepted.[24] This applied especially to those, like the Duke of Devonshire, who had positions in the Royal Household.

But he could not resist commenting all over again on recent events in the House of Lords, which portended 'a very troublesome opposition', given the degree of passion which had been exhibited. He urged Taylor to do all he personally could to 'insure absence' on the part of the leading peers, even if it was impossible to procure positive support for the Government.

On the same day Lord Grey took part in his own exercise in the art of diplomacy. In a political situation which remained astonishingly delicate — as he had pointed out to Taylor, the intentions of the Opposition could not be guaranteed — Grey was determined to acknowledge his outside allies and, in so doing, confirm them in their vociferous but non-violent stance. So the Prime Minister, as Grey could be described once more, sent for Thomas Attwood. Already the reformers' hero of the hour was being fêted. Attwood told his wife in jocular fashion that if they stayed in London much longer, 'we shall have more to fear from the dinners than from the barricades and cannonballs'.[25]

Now he met Grey, together with Lord Holland, at the Treasury. Attwood and his companions wore the full regalia of the Birmingham Political Union, although, ever the aristocrat, Grey subsequently confided that he was irritated by the sight of all these badges and ribbons, 'knowing the misrepresentation that would be made of his reception of them in that character'. At the time, he displayed none of this irritation. Grey was in fact handsome in his acknowledgement of Attwood's role: 'we owe our situation entirely to you,' he said.[26]

This was a statement which could be accepted with equanimity by Attwood; at the same time it could not be contradicted by Attwood's opponents, since it was impossible to be certain how much the unionist thunder clouds, lowering over the country, had contributed to the restoration of the Whig Government. It had, thankfully from the point of view of most honest citizens, never been put to the test. Wellington had not formed his administration. The Bill remained the whole Bill and nothing but the Bill. *The Times* was able to salute the imagined sentiments of the King with a merry rhyme which it dedicated to that patriotic figure John Bull:

Return, Lord Grey, I prithee return to me;
Return, Lord Grey, and bring the people with thee! . . .
Too much Duke, I find, won't do, Lord Grey!
Too much Duke has turned my people away!
My spouse shall dance, and I will sing
Since Dukey is driven away:
For I'm sure I've done the wisest thing
I've done for many a day.[27]

At the same time Francis Place reported that the streets were full of placards 'of a most *indecent* description' featuring the King and Queen, designed in general to bring the Royal Family into contempt. Prints were selling publicly in the streets which showed the Queen in her room, having put the King in a corner with a fool's cap on his head. Another print showed the Queen wearing a crown, leading the King along by a halter round his neck. All through the country, there were 'terrifying' accounts of the lower classes with a strong desire to come to blows. Place told Sir John Hobhouse when he paid him a visit that 'there would, positively, have been a rising if Wellington had recovered power, yesterday. Everything was arranged for it.' To avoid apprehension, Place himself would not have slept at home.[28]

The people had indeed been turned away; it remained to be seen if the return of Lord Grey was sufficient to bring about tranquillity. And of course the Reform Bill had still not passed through the House of Lords.

CHAPTER FIFTEEN

BRIGHT DAY OF LIBERTY

'The bright day of our liberty and our happiness is beginning to dawn' –
Thomas Attwood, en route for Birmingham, late May 1832

During the tense period which followed the famous Days of May, the good news of Grey's return gradually spread throughout the country. At Liverpool, in consequence, 'all was joy and congratulation'. Three times three hearty cheers were given in the Liverpool Exchange, and from there the cheering spread, gaining still more strength, to the people outside. Early the following week, *The Times* chose to run a waggish advertisement headed 'DEATH EXTRAORDINARY'. What was said to have died on Friday 18 May 1832 'at an advanced age' was 'the Rt. Hon., the Rt. Rev., and Right Worshipful Tory Power'. This ancient gentleman had been born in the reign of Charles I, given over for dead in 1688, but would at last lie quietly in his unknown grave.[1]

Meanwhile the widespread feeling – which Grey had taken care to endorse – that Thomas Attwood and his associates had contributed a great deal with their mixture of strength and circumspection, led to positive reactions wherever their path took them. On 23 May Attwood was made a Freeman of the City of London; he pointed out that he was the first private individual to receive the Freedom. (There were a few objections to giving the honour to a member of an illegal society, but these were overruled.) A magnificent dinner in the Egyptian room in the Mansion House celebrated the accolade. George Grote declared that Attwood had 'divested the physical force of this country of its terrors and its lawlessness, and has made it conducive to the ends of the highest public benefit'.[2]

Attwood's return journey to Birmingham took on the character of a royal procession – except that royal processions were hardly the flavour of the day in a nation where William IV and Adelaide were being openly compared to Louis XVI and Marie Antoinette. A speaker in Newcastle upon Tyne had added insult to injury in a speech on 19 May by saying that Marie Antoinette had a fairer head than ever graced the shoulders of Adelaide, but that had not saved her from the scaffold, at the wishes of the people of France. In contrast to this were the lines of a broadsheet published in Coventry as the leading unionist passed through it on his way back to Birmingham: 'Hail PATRIOTIC ATTWOOD, hail! . . . Thou foe to the British slavish yoke . . . Thrice welcome Thou, REFORMING CHIEF.'

The crowds were so demanding that Attwood had to stop and make grateful speeches. Labourers and ladies wore blue ribbons; these were merely the forerunners of the plethora of Attwood souvenirs, including blue garters with the encouraging words 'Attwood for-ever' on them. Mugs and pipes displayed the image of 'King Tom', as once there had been 'allegorical' handkerchiefs of the friends and enemies of Reform, 'intended for the humbler classes', with the face of William IV depicted. The new King Tom – saluted just as the old King Billy was being insulted – certainly had a happy theme for his speeches: 'The final knell of despotism has tolled,' he declaimed on his route; 'the bright day of our liberty and our happiness is beginning to dawn.'[3]

There was still some time, it seemed, before full daylight. Grey's prophecy to the King of 'passionate opposition' in the House of Lords showed every sign of being fulfilled in the first week of the returned Whig Government – at least in words. On 25 May Lord Ellenborough recorded in his Diary that he was practically the only Tory who hadn't taken part in a 'violent tirade'.[4] For the Whigs, Lord Durham, fully capable of aggression himself in what he believed was a good cause, came up with an intelligent analysis of 'public excitement' in terms of the existing electorate. He pointed out that violence was in inverse ratio to parliamentary representation. That is to say, Marylebone was excitable but Westminster, with its freemen voters, was calm. The Tory Lord Kenyon on the other hand flew at Lord Grey in a verbal assault in which he described Grey's advice to the King on the sub-ject of creation as 'atrocious'. Grey reiterated the word and rejected it with 'contempt and scorn'. There was then a ding-dong between these two eminent gentlemen in which repeated words like 'atrocious', 'con-tempt' and 'scorn' were hurled to and fro. Lord Winchilsea chose to describe Lord Grey as being 'excessively sensitive', but it is hard not to sympathize with him under the circumstances.[5]

However, these public battles and tirades, by mainly insignificant Tories in an agony of disappointment, were one thing. The behaviour of the big beasts of the Tory Party was outwardly quiescent; Greville commented acidly that they saw out these events 'skulking in their clubs and country houses'.[6] Wellington had delivered his last public salvo on this issue in the House of Lords on 17 May. The battle over creation had been won by the Whigs; it was now up to the Tories to challenge this in public if they cared so to do.

But what would happen then? A massive enlargement of the House of Lords, by those who favoured the Whig interest, would follow. This was the last thing the Opposition wanted. In this war of nerves, the Tories had been outplayed. Wellington's attempt to form a gov-ernment following the Whig defeat had been a 'false move' which endangered his own party, as Creevey put it. Creevey further recorded a conversation with Lord Grey on 2 June: the Opposition, said Grey, had made a blunder in not believing that the Whig Ministry would resign over their defeat. 'Thank God!' commented Creevey, 'they did not know their man.'[7]

It was indeed the key point. If Grey had not resigned, but lumbered on, facing further defeat after further defeat in the Lords, in contradic-tion of the will of the Commons, the country would surely have been in flames – both literally and metaphorically. Over thirty years later, Lord Brougham would give his own version of events and suggest that Grey would never have actually carried through with creation.[8] But this is directly against the evidence of Grey's correspondence with the King, to say nothing of his own character; reluctantly but inexorably, Grey would have put the interests of the country above his own personal feelings and called for the King to fulfil his promise.

In the background, but highly articulate, there was always 'Radical Jack', the ardent reformer and thus creationist; in the family circle a further tragedy, the death of Durham's young daughter Harriet, also of tuberculosis, had not diminished his emotional hold on the Prime Minister.

As it was, quiet messages were passed: there was going to be no more official confrontation when it came to voting on the Reform Bill for the third time. One may suppose that some of Sir Herbert Taylor's discreet missives on the subject were not strictly authorized, and thus remain unrecorded – nevertheless they met their mark. This was particularly necessary in the case of outspoken peers who were seen, with justice, to be close to the King. William IV for his part remained sensitive to the principles of 'those who have dropped their reactions to the Bill, from a feeling of deference to him', in order to spare him from the cruel necessity of creation. The current 'disunion' in the House of Lords remained a sore point at such a crucial moment in the nation's history and he did not try to pretend otherwise.[9]

The event, so long desired, so long dreaded, finally took place on 4 June 1832. The House of Lords was thinly attended, a fact that *The Times* (in its report the next day) believed would be read by the public with disgust. It was Lord Grey himself who moved that the Reform Bill be read for the third time.[10] In view of his poor state of health – the Days of May had indeed taken its toll physically – Grey hoped not to have to make a speech. He had, after all, made so many in the fifteen months since Lord John Russell had first proposed the Bill in the House of Commons. What happened next left him no option. Even at this late hour, dramatically speaking, there was a tremendous rant – no other word will do – on the part of the Ultra Tory Marquess of Winchilsea, followed by another from the former Waverer, the Earl of Harrowby.

He suffered a pain greater than he could express, began Lord Winchilsea, in thinking that he had lived to that hour to witness the downfall of his country. He then proceeded to try to express the pain. 'This night would be the first act of the fatal and bloody tragedy . . . those who might live to witness the last act of the tragedy, would have to tell of the downfall of the Monarchy. In which case he trusted that the daring and wicked spirits with whom the Revolution commenced, might awaken to a sense of the ruin they had brought . . .' and so forth and so on. Winchilsea was also explicit on the subject of the existing Constitution which, until recent times, had enabled the country to survive that 'spirit of revolution and infidelity' which had been cherished in France. What else had enabled 'an illustrious Duke not then present' – for Wellington, along with the other Tory grandees, was conspicuously absent – to rescue France from 'the tyrant grasp' of Napoleon.

But it was Winchilsea's personal attack on Grey which was the most marked feature of his speech. He described himself as having been 'deceived' in Grey, whose career he had long followed. His friends had told him a different story but he had not listened to them – would to God that he had! It was Grey himself who had 'indirectly' encouraged the spread of 'seditious and revolutionary doctrines' – a remarkable charge, given the turbulent state of the country – and Winchilsea went further in quoting the late Prime Minister Canning: Reform, said Canning, was just a mask for the purpose of establishing a democracy. Coming from a Tory peer, this was a chilling if impotent accusation.

Lord Harrowby, venerable as he might be, honourable and straightforward as described by Greville, believer in compromise at the time of the negotiations with the Waverers, now launched his own attack in which he announced that he too had been 'grievously disappointed by the conduct of the noble Earl'. Grey and his Ministers had 'trampled' on the Crown and the House of Lords, but as a result they had now aroused a force which would trample on them. When Grey came to damn the torrent, he would find no workmen ready to help him. The disappointment of the former Waverer was underlined by the pronouncement of their erstwhile leader Lord Wharncliffe: he accused Lord Grey of 'wantonly' placing the country in its present dangerous state, in order that he might carry 'a favourite measure'. This equation of Grey personally with the revolutionary forces disturbing the country was manifestly unfair since he had so persistently advocated Reform as a means of bringing about peace. Nevertheless Grey felt he must reply.

In doing so, the Prime Minister mentioned his reluctance to speak in view of his state of health, adding that 'he was afraid his indisposition would be apparent to their Lordships' before he was through. Proudly (if not necessarily with total truth), Grey denied that he was speaking to rebut the personal attacks on himself: it was the general attack on his Government that he was there to answer. At the end of a long, justificatory speech, he stopped abruptly and had to sit down, as he had foreseen. But then his reward came.

The voting gave the third reading of the Reform Bill a majority of 84. Roughly 120 peers took part, in contrast to the far bigger figures of previous debates. Thirty or forty MPs came from the Lower House to witness the occasion. None of the great men of the Tory Party cast their vote among the 22 Not Contents; here was no Wellington and no Lyndhurst. The Duke wrote quite explicitly on the subject to the Earl of Scarborough: 'It is not my intention to go to the House of Lords for the Third Reading.' His explanation was made with characteristic brevity. 'This perilous measure, as all admit it to be' – here he echoed Lord Grey and the King – 'will pass this day.'[11]

No bishop was listed among the Not Contents – the Archbishop of York had even spoken out recently against the viciousness of the debates. In fact the list of their names included no one of particular distinction – unless you called the Ultra Tory Duke of Newcastle distinguished, for emphasizing his right to 'do what he liked with his own', his term for a rotten borough. The courtier Lord Londonderry did not vote. Nor did the favourite, Lord Howe. But at the end of the voting, a great number of peers immediately crowded round Lord Grey 'apparently to congratulate his Lordship upon the final success of the Bill', as Hansard put it.[12] A number of protests now issued under various peers' names over matters of electoral detail could not obscure the central fact: on its third reading, the Bill had been passed in the House of Lords.

'Thank God!' wrote Creevey, who was present. 'I was at the death of this Conservative plot, and the triumph of our Bill.'[13] It was the third great battle of his lifetime in which he had been involved, the first being Waterloo, the second the struggle over Queen Caroline's divorce, and now 'the battle of Edward Grey and the English nation for the Reform Bill'. And Creevey took sly satisfaction in the fact that the Master in Chancery, who carried the Bill from the Lords to the Commons, was 'our own Harry Martin', lineal descendant of Henry Martin the regicide. How shocked the Tory press would be to learn that!

A few days passed and the Reform Bill needed the Royal Assent. As has been noted, it was customary for William IV to signify his assent in person, although it was not strictly speaking essential. In this case there were to be no cannons, no processional military horses, as had been needed for that celebrated dissolution of April 1831. In what Sir John Hobhouse described as 'a fit of foolish spite', the King declined to honour the House of Lords with his presence. He wrote to the Lord Chancellor, Brougham, to this effect: 'he will not go down [to the House of Lords] to pass the Reform, for that after the Manner he and his Queen have been treated by the people he should feel himself disgusted and degraded by their applause.'[14] Lord Grey was annoyed to discover later that Brougham made another attempt to persuade the King, once again without success. But in this case, Brougham was acting in the King's best interests.

Given the fact that the venom of the press still spewed forth, William IV's reluctance is of course understandable on a human level. As Creevey noted: 'the King, the Queen, and the Royal Family are libelled, caricatured, lampooned and balladed by itinerant singers hired for the purpose to a degree not credible.' One typical flysheet ran: 'I'm a German stormer, I hate a reformer', suggesting that the Queen might return to her native land in a rage. In addition, Creevey emphasized the ceaseless, menacing allusions to the fates of 'Charles and Henrietta, Louis and Antoinette'. It was also perfectly true, as *The Times* put it on the day, that whether the King himself signalled his assent to the Clerk of the House of Lords or whether the Lord Chancellor did so on behalf of the designated Commissioners, 'matters to the validity of that law not a single farthing'.[15]

Nevertheless, in terms of William IV's royal reputation, to which his affable behaviour had contributed much in the early months of his reign, this sulky abstinence was a mistake. The King had managed to take the big decision – not without evident dismay, but in the end he had taken it; he had sent for Lord Grey to return to office, on the understanding that he would create a large number of peers if it proved necessary. But he could not manage to take the small one. Macaulay summed it all up in a letter to his sisters: 'I fear – I fear – that he has entered on the path of Charles and Louis. He makes great concessions: but he makes them reluctantly and ungraciously. The people receive them without gratitude or affection. What madness! – to give more to his subjects than any King ever gave, and yet to give in such a manner as to get no thanks.'[16]

William IV continued to rage impotently, as it proved, against the press. Prompted by the Queen, Royal Family and courtiers, William demanded prosecution. Given the level of vitriol, much of it very crude, some of it funny, most of it relentlessly anti-German – or anti-foreign – this was not surprising. Nor did the King's recent behaviour escape censure. One popular theme, because it lent itself to illustration, was that of King Canute. *Figaro in London* showed a bewildered, fool-ish man, vacant plump face beneath a crown, waving hopelessly at the sea. Wellington and Lyndhurst crouch malevolently behind him. The text described the so-called Modern Canute at the mercy of designing courtiers: 'Unfortunately, he was one day persuaded that the waves of Reform might be stilled, if he would only command them to become tranquil.' So the Modern Canute ventured down off his rock and tried his luck, only to find that the tempest of Reform raged more strongly than ever.[17]

Why would not the Attorney-General act with regard to such monotonous persecution? It was genial, worldly-wise Lord Althorp who pointed out the impracticability of such a step. The King com-plained that the 'revolutionary spirit of the day' meant that the 'most violent and treasonable attacks' levelled against the Sovereign were treated as though they were simply general criticisms, and thus immune from legal punishment. Althorp replied smoothly that no one could feel deeper regret or greater indignation than he did at such attacks. But there were two arguments against prosecution: in the first place it might not be successful; secondly, the names of the King and Queen would inevitably be dragged before the Courts of Law. That would be a most painful development for all loyal subjects. And it would be 'detrimental to the interests of the Monarchy'.[18] Perhaps we catch a note of respectful reproach behind these ultra-polite sentiments, given what the Whig Government had just endured.

On 7 June attendance in the House of Lords was even more sparse than it had been for the third reading. The precise timing of the Royal Assent was kept secret by the Ministers of the Crown – in the absence of the Crown itself – to avoid an appearance of triumphalism. A tepid atmosphere of anti-climax prevailed; but that was possibly welcome to the Government after the high drama of recent weeks. Neither the Duke of Wellington nor Lord Lyndhurst was present.

However, it is fair to say that it was Derby Day. The great national racing feast of the Derby, which happened to be run on 7 June, provided an excellent excuse for what Hobhouse called 'our gay and gambling world' to avoid the equally colourful contest, racing to a finish at Westminster. Perhaps there was some symbolism in the fact that the winner, St Giles, owned and ridden by Yorkshiremen, was subject to a tirade of objections at the end of the race, some concerning his real age and his dam's pedigree, together with accusations of jockeys being bribed not to compete too hard; there were even – shades of Francis Place! – placards with the message 'ST GILES NOT ENTITLED TO DERBY STAKES'. But in the end, despite all the difficulties, the Jockey Club found for St Giles and his northern team. In the same way the Reform Bill had become law.

One peer who was present in the Lords at the time of the assent was William IV's younger brother the Duke of Sussex, who had shown reforming sympathies all along; in fact the King had begun to see him as the *Philippe Égalité* of his own family, in reference to that infamous Bourbon (father of King Louis-Philippe) who had voted for the execution of Louis XVI. The Duke remained behind a curtain as the Commissioners, headed by the Lord Chancellor, including Grey, Durham and Holland, indicated assent on behalf of the King. Holland, as he sat with the others in his robes on the bench, reflected his satisfaction that he was among 'members of the old Opposition who uniformly maintained the principles of peace and reform'. When the brief ceremony was over, the Duke was heard to say loudly: 'Thank God the deed is done at last. I care for nothing now – this is the happiest day of my life.'[19] This at least provided some contrast to the current unpopular attitudes of the ruling House.

It is true that one old Tory responded to this by lifting up his hands in horror and exclaiming involuntarily: 'Oh Christ!' And shortly after the Clerk of the House of Lords announced the Royal Assent with the traditional words dating back to the Middle Ages, *le Roi le veult*, a note was handed to him. It read: 'Surely it would have been more appropriate to have said *La canaille le veult*.'[20] Here was another reference to the events of the French Revolution; but instead of citing the fate of Louis XVI and Marie Antoinette, as the people's protests did, it made a bitter allusion to a time during which the lowest class of people – *la canaille,* taking its meaning from the Latin for dog – had held sway. It was certainly a libel to describe Attwood, Francis Place and their respective followers as *la canaille.* Here were highly intelligent men, capable of intricate organization in the cause in which they profoundly believed, their idealism certainly matching that of the Whigs who came to work with them. Yet the snide comment, in its reference to the loudly expressed wishes of much of the population, had some truth in it. The role of public opinion – no need to designate the people as *la canaille* – had been crucial.

A correspondent in *The Times* the day after the Royal Assent was given, signing himself merely 'J.A.', called for a penny subscription to erect a triumphal arch.[21] This would commemorate the men who fought for 'the people's second Bill of British rights'. 'J.A.' suggested that the central focus should be on William the Reformer – who elsewhere in the paper was excoriated for his failure to go down to Parliament in person. *The Times* had called for the King to indulge his people 'with a spectacle of imperial state' which they could have applauded, thus wiping out the bad impression given by previous unruly behaviour; the august paper was duly shocked by the King's refusal to take its advice. In a more generous mood, 'J.A.' wanted

William the Reformer to be supported by statues of Grey, Brougham, Althorp and Russell – all of course lords, one way or another. It was not, however, suggested that statues of Attwood and Francis Place should be part of the group.

THIS GREAT NATIONAL EXPLOIT

'Thus ends this great national exploit. The deed is done.' –
Sir John Hobhouse, 7 June 1832

A vast celebratory banquet was held at the Guildhall on 11 July 1832. The great hall was hung with scarlet cloth, brilliantly lit, with musicians in the gallery. There was much clapping of hands, stamping of feet and thumping on tables. Lord Brougham made one of his speeches, in which he parodied 'the Bill, the whole Bill, and nothing but the Bill' by referring to 'the Law, the whole Law, and nothing but the Law'. Macaulay was among those present (he told his sisters that he had consumed two dishes of turtle soup).[1] Here were the Whigs in their hour of triumph, and happily they were recorded by Benjamin Robert Haydon, his second attempt at a great picture of the progress of the Reform Bill, and destined to be more successful than the Newhall Hill effort, for which he had not secured a subscription.

When Haydon called on Lord Grey, he was readily admitted into the presence of the Prime Minister. Grey showed considerable enthusiasm for the project of painting something connected to Reform, although he pointed out that it would not be 'delicate' for him to head the subscription list. It was Grey who suggested that Haydon painted the impending grand City Dinner, and instructed him to approach the Lord Mayor to give him a good place. Even if Grey passed over Haydon's sketch of Newhall Hill without comment – Haydon got the impression that he did not think the unions were suitable artistic subjects – he was lavish in his enthusiasm for this new project. He gave Haydon a commission for 500 guineas and told his wife: 'I mean this for Howick', to which Lady Grey replied that the picture would stay for ever in their family.* Grey was similarly generous with his time for his individual sitting, and at the end 'dear Lord Grey' shook Haydon heartily by the hand.

Later Grey called on Haydon, and showed himself 'unfazed' by the Haydon children running round; 'he seemed quite used to children' (which was of course perfectly true: Grey being that friendly *pater-familias* whose own children were allowed to call him by his name). In general Grey was delighted with the picture, and agreed that 'the most able supporters' of the Bill should be prominently displayed, without regard to their actual seating arrangements.[2]

In this way Haydon had a splendid time capturing the Whig heads: Melbourne, for example, was 'a fine head and looked benign and handsome'. Althorp he found 'the essence of good nature'; Palmerston had a good-humoured elegance; Lansdowne showed considerable knowledge of literature with great unaffectedness; Richmond had a deep-toned colour and a keen look. As for Brougham, with his startling, almost savage appearance, the artist would describe him as 'like a lion reposing in the possession of power, as years ago he had been a tiger in pursuit of it'. When it came to conversation, Haydon had the most significant exchange with Lord John Russell, 'an interesting, mild and determined creature', to whom he suggested that 'to be Reformers, now is the fashion'. Lord John agreed: 'People find out now they have been Reformers but never thought of it.' The finished picture is a splendid triumphalist affair, with flags and swords presiding over the vast array of banqueters. Appropriately enough Lord Grey, with his unmistakable appearance, the domed head and skull beneath that 'weighed down' the youth of the young reporter Charles Dickens, is on his feet.[3]

The picture of the Guildhall Banquet was not the only artistic work commemorating the Bill. A remarkable, bold assertion of the Bill's place in history was the marble relief commissioned from Francis Chantrey by the long-standing Whig MP Thomas Coke of Norfolk, to be installed at his great country house at Holkham. Coke, a personal

* It remains at Howick to this day.

friend of Lord Grey (as he had been of Charles James Fox) was now nearly eighty; always a keen reformer, he announced his retirement from Parliament on the actual day the Bill was passed, and a few years later was created Earl of Leicester.

Among the four 'Political Reliefs' at Holkham, including 'The Trial of Socrates', was to be 'The Signing of the Magna Carta', which actually depicted the signing of the Reform Bill of 1832, showing William IV as King John. Over him looms another close friend of Coke, Henry Bathurst, Bishop of Norwich, known as the Liberal Bishop because he had voted for Reform (as well as Catholic Emancipation). In a reference to Magna Carta, the Whigs were shown as barons and knights, with Grey once again prominent; Brougham, Durham, Althorp, Russell and the Duke of Sussex are also visible, as is Coke himself, looking flatteringly youthful, arm round a page in the shape of his son, born to a late second marriage and aged only ten in 1832.

As against this magnificent linking of heroic past and present, the many commemorative jugs, pots and basins appealed to a different public, but one which had contributed after all in its own way to the triumphant result. The rising use of printed decoration on ceramics meant that pottery firms in Staffordshire and London could respond quickly to the turn of political events. Jugs had the stirring words of the Union songs on them, such as 'Lo! we answer! See we come!' One plate referred to William IV as 'the only Royal Reformer since Alfred', while another plate with clasped hands symbolized the combining of the various political unions.[4]

The most popular depictions, taken from contemporary prints, were of Grey himself, Russell and Brougham. With his famous elongated truncheon of a nose, Brougham was considered an ideal subject for a stoneware cordial flask, made by skilled potters in Derbyshire, of which impressive examples survive; one has to bear in mind, looking at them, that the cordial which was the preferred beverage of the Lord Chancellor, making his torrential speeches in the House of Lords, was heavily laced with wine. With possibly less relevance, Althorp and Grey were made into gin flasks, and there were other images for toothbrush boxes.

Countrywide rejoicings involved village celebrations, larger gatherings on hills and heaths and other manifestations of popular pleasure. One typical dinner was held on Scorton Green in north Yorkshire, with booths and banners to enliven it. The local magnate, the Earl of Tyrconnel, commented feelingly in his Diary: 'A committee for the Reform dinner came this evening and screwed £20 out of me for expenses.' As a result of his generosity, about 400 people sat down to dinner, as well as 300 children and 150 'strangers'.[5] 'Reform' and 'Liberty' were the two watchwords. There were banners galore with simple legends like 'SEE THE CONQUERING HEROES! RUSSELL BROUGHAM GREY' and more complicated Shakespearean ones: 'THE BATTLES WON – BRITTANIA'S SONS ARE FREE AND DESPOTS TREMBLE AT THE VICTORY'. 'ST CRISPIN'. 'WE ARE ALL TRUE TO THE LAST'. The numerous medals often showed a variation on the date 7 June 1832, and mentioned the two majorities, 84 in the Lords, 116 in the Commons. The notorious rotten borough of Old Sarum was also commemorated: 'OLD SARUM DESERTED IN THE YEAR 1217, DISENFRANCHISED JUNE 7 1832'.

Only the office of the Lord Chamberlain remained lugubriously unenthusiastic where artistic celebration was concerned. Asked in June whether he would strike out the word 'Reform' in a work submitted to him, the Examiner of Plays replied that he would not. He would say instead: 'I think you had better omit it; I advise you to do it for your own sakes, or you will have a hubbub.' (He was apparently unaware that a good hubbub is exactly what many playwrights aim at.)[6]

On 23 June, in a letter to the Duke of Buckingham, Wellington pronounced quite definitely: 'The government of England is destroyed.' He added that a Parliament would be returned by means of which 'no set of men whatever would be able to conduct the administration of affairs, and protect the lives and properties of the King's subjects'. This was an extreme view, in line with Wellington as self-constituted Cassandra throughout this period. Of course he was not the only one with such an intense revulsion against Reform, but as a leading political figure he had been from the first in a position to affect the outcome.

A celebrated example of one whose views remained romantically obsessed with the past, to the detriment of this particular change, was William Wordsworth, now in his early sixties. In a letter of February 1832 he had written that 'Our Constitution was not preconceived and planned beforehand – it grew under the protection of Providence – as a skin grows to, with, and for the protection of Providence. Our Ministers would flay this body, and present us, instead of its natural Skin, with a garment made to order . . .' He went on to compare this garment to the Shirt of Nessus which drove Hercules to madness and self-destruction, and ended by suggesting that the Ministers had already gone far towards 'committing a greater political crime than any committed in history'.[7] *

The views of King William IV were not so extreme as either of these great men, but they were not particularly sanguine either. During the summer which followed the passing of the Reform Bill, he continued to shudder at the possibility of the Bill being a mere 'stepping-stone' to other reforms. William IV was encouraged in his fears by the declarations of Joseph Hume who, having openly disapproved of the Bill in its current state, now foretold further Radical reforms. From the other angle, the Duke of Cumberland preyed upon the royal imagination on the subject of the political unions, in a typically irascible communication in which he criticized Lord Grey strongly for defending them in the House of Lords. Enclosing a paper signed by Attwood, Cumberland wrote on 16 June that he felt certain that 'if some measure is not resorted to to put an end to these Political Unions, *they will destroy all government*'.[8]

In the House of Lords, Grey had kept a straight bat where the unions were concerned, as the Whig Minister Lord Duncannon, patron of cricket, would have said. Grey smoothly replied that nothing that was legal would be banned – and in any case he trusted to the good sense of the people of England. Grey's response to the King

---

* It was no doubt to tease his friend the poet that Dr Thomas Arnold nicknamed three roads near Dove Cottage in the Lake District where Wordsworth had lived, 'Old Corruption', 'Bit by Bit Reform' and 'Radical Reform'. 'Old Corruption' is now known locally to walkers as 'the coffin path'.

over Cumberland's objections showed in part, it must be said, a certain aristocratic *naïveté* ... Given that the Bill had been passed, 'he trusts and believes that, if not irritated by an injudicious interference, these Unions will die away'. He was on safer ground when he pointed out that nothing was more likely to unite people behind the unions than an 'impolitic' attempt to suppress them.[9]

The King's mood was not improved when a stone was thrown at him at Ascot races; he was only saved from actual physical harm by the padding in his hat. Nor did the attacks on the Queen, ranging from satirical references to the obliteration of her image over taverns, cease. At least the King could sympathize with his former Prime Minister the Duke of Wellington, who suffered attacks by the mob on 18 June. 'A strange day to choose,' observed the Iron Duke drily – for it was of course the anniversary of the Battle of Waterloo.[10]

Yet in general, the critical attention of the country had passed away from the Reform Bill itself in Parliament; this despite the fact that the separate Irish and Scottish Reform Bills, and the Boundary Bill (which Lord Lyndhurst had used to defeat the Government back in April 1831) were still going through Parliament. It was not until 27 June that the whole Reform Bill had been passed throughout the British Isles. The way was now clear for the first General Election to be held under the new rules.

Under the circumstances, an atmosphere of temporary contentment prevailed in both groups who could be roughly termed liberal. Joseph Hume was able to predict further reforms, including of the Church; the Whigs on the other hand were confident that Reform would produce an ideal House of Commons, representative of the people indeed – but not actually *of* the people. The Whigs believed that the stepping-stone of the Bill had led them safely over the abyss. Hume was equally sure that it was leading towards a more Radical future on the other bank. Francis Place shared Hume's view that further reforms, aiming at an actual republic, would surely follow.

Whig life resumed its characteristic round. Lord Grey's physical appearance, which had verged on the cadaverous in recent months, improved. Lord Althorp rushed to Wiseton for a precious three weeks with his prize bulls. He was visited by the Duke of Richmond and Sir James Graham and all three went on to Doncaster Races, riding there and back in four days, a distance of 100 miles, happily partridge-shooting in between. Lord Durham, however, was dispatched on a diplomatic mission to Russia to handle the Belgian question: revolutionaries are not always easy to deal with and it is possible that his dispatch owed something to Melbourne and Palmerston's desire to get rid of their awkward colleague. In view of his family tragedies, Durham had reason to be glad of the distance.

Durham confessed himself sick at heart to Grey and talked of his yearning to retire (although 'Radical Jack' would in fact go on to act with admirable energy as Governor General of Canada). Perhaps if he had not been so closely connected to Lord Grey, by affection as well as marriage, Durham would not have survived so long in the Cabinet or even been appointed there in the first place, given his reputation for truculence. And yet the lesson of history would show that Durham was right about Reform, and the more tepid Melbourne and Palmerston wrong. And without the stern application of Durham's conscience, perhaps Grey would not have stayed as firm as he did. Another difficult colleague, Lord Brougham, found that his trouble-making in the Cabinet imperilled and finally sank his actual political career. He ceased being Lord Chancellor in November 1834 when the Whigs went out of office, and held no further position in government. Yet his reforming zeal, his best quality apart from his native brilliance – so ably expressed in his flights of fierce oratory – continued unabated, as his agitation over the abolition of slavery and the need for public education demonstrated.

Parliament was dissolved on 3 December 1832, with the new Parliament due to meet on 29 January 1833. The General Election took place over a month – that long duration of the electoral period by modern standards had not changed – the earliest ballot taking place on 10 December and the latest on 8 January 1833; although voting in individual constituencies was now limited to two days.

Three symbolic elections showed the path of progress – and also lack of it. Thomas Attwood was returned unopposed as MP for the new borough of Bromsgrove, along with Joshua Scholefield, another Birmingham Political Union activist; although Attwood's subsequent parliamentary career did not flourish as he had hoped. His currency theories were, he discovered, no more welcome now than they had been before, and his long speeches, so effective at Newhall Hill, were much less so at Westminster. Nevertheless he survived to form part of the next surge of reforming energy, the Chartist movement, at the end of the decade; in 1838, for example, he was converted to the idea of Universal Suffrage.

It could be argued that Attwood's career ended in disappointment with both popular and parliamentary action; nevertheless he could be proud of the seminal part he had played in the events of the Reform Bill. His social philosophy, which led him to believe that the economic interests of master and man were tied together, spurred him on fruitfully to improve the electoral representation of the country. Much later he observed that there was no instance in history in which political movements had been successful without leaders, 'and in almost every instance these leaders have been men of wealth and influence'.[11] Attwood, the middle-class banker, could be proud of exercising that leadership.

In contrast to the new MP for the new seat, the Marquess of Blandford, the Ultra Tory, heir to the Duke of Marlborough, was now chosen without contest for the Marlborough family seat at Woodstock – he who had furiously and, as it seemed to his fellow Tories, perversely advocated Reform in order to prevent Roman Catholics, newly emancipated, getting hold of parliamentary power (and been rewarded by being made a member of the Birmingham Political Union). Thirdly, it seemed only right that Macaulay, once nominated for Calne by the grandee Marquess of Lansdowne, now transferred to Leeds. Here he was made happy by the vigour and intelligence of the men and women – he did not of course mention that the latter did not vote – in contrast to 'dumb agricultural workers': by his own standards, Macaulay had come to the right place.[12] The fact that the returning officer was called Dr Calne may have served to emphasize the contrast.

In terms of this General Election there was a fourth, less happy situation. Joseph Parkes did not secure a seat either in Birmingham or the new constituency of Dudley; lacking an independent income, he was obliged to return to the life of 'an obscure country attorney', as he put it to Edward Littleton in January 1833, 'sunk in the low and to me disgusting occupation of a county lawyer's office'.[13] Later, however, he played a prominent part in what had become Liberal electioneering, and the topic of municipal reform, in which his experiences in 1832 stood him in good stead. (Francis Place joined forces with him on this issue.) Parkes still hankered after a parliamentary seat, yet did not have the financial means to support the life – showing that not everything had changed with the Reform Act.

Joseph Parkes had toiled long and hard and, as he put it to Place after the election, 'I had rather go to the Swan River, or even Botany Bay, than go through the sacrifices and labour of the last eighteen months. I have read no books, I have not slept half enough, I have collected money, I have neglected my business.'[14] He spoke for many who were not so fortunate as the Whig grandees, relaxing at last on their country estates. Parkes signed off to Francis Place: 'Goodnight, old firebrand.' And it was true that Place continued his energetic Radical career, convinced that if enough action was taken 'king and lords will of themselves, if permitted, in time go quietly out of business' – a prophecy, like that of Lord Grey that the unions would now vanish with the passing of the Bill, so far unfulfilled.

When the new House of Commons met for the first time, it was gratifying to all reformers that the result was a large Whig majority – and, as Russell had pointed out, everyone was now discovering that they had been reformers all along. The Whigs were rewarded with 441 seats and the Tories not even half as many with 175; the Irish party secured 42 seats. The Whig majority over the Tories was 276.[15]

John Doyle duly saluted the occasion with a merry take-off of David Wilkie's celebrated picture *The Reading of the Will*, issued on 1 February 1833. Here an unmistakable William IV, looking distinctly disgruntled, is seen as an old lawyer reading the will of the late John Bull, Gent. As the widow, Lord Grey, recognizable beneath an appropriate white cap, is the chief beneficiary; but he looks worried at whatever malice the Duke of Cumberland is whispering in his ear. Perhaps the boy in the corner of the picture is intended as that enquiring youth, Prince George of Cambridge. A striking figure entering the door is the Duke of Wellington as John Bull's discarded mistress, the Marquess of Londonderry in attendance. Lord Brougham is also shown as a female figure – nursing the tiny baby Reform.

To subsequent generations, reared on a very different kind of franchise, something approaching Universal Suffrage, one obvious question occurs: how much had actually been achieved in practical terms? The House of Commons remained large, the idea of reducing it having been abandoned at an early stage, but the worst of the rotten boroughs had gone. There remained several oddities: one example has been cited of Rutland with 800 electors, controlled by two aristocratic families, compared to Westminster with around 50,000 electors, fought over by different local interests: both were represented by two MPs. Yet the overall size of the electorate was increased from 439,200 in 1831 to 656,000 in 1832 – a 49 per cent increase.[16]

Another estimate gives an approximate increase from 3.2 per cent to 4.7 per cent of the population.[17] This figure has to be matched against a population roughly estimated at 16,000,000. The franchise was still based on property, as all contestants had believed was desirable, although the use of a £10 freehold as a measure obviously enlarged it. The enfranchised were now about 18 per cent of the male adult population in England and Wales, and in Scotland about 12 per cent. The Irish electorate, already overhauled at the time of the Union, now had well over twice as many county votes at 61,000, and borough votes were also increased from 23,000 to 29,000.[18] There were also changes the importance of which would only be properly appreciated as time passed. One example was the need for voters to have their names registered in order to vote, officially introduced for the first time by the Reform Act. Registration of electors had the further consequence of developing party organization, hitherto a ramshackle affair, at the local level; just as the shortening of the polling period and the increase in the number of polling booths tightened control over corruption.

Yet the bare recounting of these details, fought over as they were, underestimates the truly radical nature of what had taken place. In 1835, the year before his death, James Mill reflected with wonder on 'the shortness of the time in which the spirit of Reform in this nation has grown to such a degree of strength', even if later generations may reflect with equal wonder at the slow pace of progress – but that is with the benevolent assistance of hindsight. The floodgates had been opened and, once open, could never be closed again. The Reform Bill was destined to be the first of such, spread forward across the nineteenth century and beyond, 1918 being a significant end date; although women were not fully enfranchised until 1928. As Mr Brooke, quizzical uncle of Dorothea Casaubon in *Middlemarch* was made to remark during the period of the Reform Bill (in a novel also benefiting from hindsight; it was published forty years later): 'This Reform will touch everybody by and by, a thoroughly popular measure – a sort of A, B, C, you know, that must come first before the rest can follow.'[19]

Could they have achieved more in 1832? The Whigs themselves never denied that there was a spirit of compromise about their Bill. From the first moment, it was specifically described as conciliatory. When Lord John Russell introduced it in the House of Commons on 1 March 1831, on that famous occasion when the amazed Tories felt that they had been ambushed, he stressed this middle position between 'Bigotry' on the one hand and 'fanaticism' on the other: 'we place ourselves between the two,' he declared. The Government did believe that Reform was necessary but it did not consider that Reform had to be limited to one particular type. The Whigs hoped to occupy 'firm and steadfast ground between the abuses we wish to amend, and the convulsions we hope to avert'.

It is fair to say that after many months of drama, anguish and violent disturbance, they did succeed in establishing themselves on this ground – firm for the time being, steadfast for the time being, but inevitably destined for development and improvement in the long term, as any historical measure must be. In the spirit of conciliation, it should be noted that the House of Lords did in fact emerge with its membership intact – the Whigs never did demand creation when they had the opportunity, despite the continuing hereditary Tory majority there. The Bill was considered to be enough. Sydney Smith wrote in the *Edinburgh Review*: 'all great alterations in human affairs are produced by compromise'. This was certainly true of the Great Reform Bill. One verdict which has stood the test of time is that of the Radical reformer John Bright. A young man in 1832, he remembered 'horses galloping and carriages coming at speed' as the thrilling news was conveyed from London to the provinces. Thirty years later, he declared in a speech at Birmingham: 'It was not a good Bill but it was a great Bill when it passed.'[20]

How much did character and personality matter? This perennial subject of debate, which can surely never be finally solved, leads to counterfactual questions. Lord Holland wrote in his Diary at the end of 1831 when matters were beginning to warm up: 'Improve and legislate as you will, how much the good government of Mankind depends on accident and individual character.'[21] What if the Duke of Wellington had been less savagely intransigent from the first? (Francis Place called it his 'blind courage'.) The Tory Party was already in disarray, thanks to the highly divisive effects of Catholic Emancipation in 1829, a factor which must never be ignored in this period. Undoubtedly his open, angry hostility led milder Tories to see how a more conciliatory course could be achieved, while his volte-face in May 1832, suggesting a Tory government might take on Reform, shocked the Ultra Tories. So it could be argued that, paradoxically, the great Duke of Wellington, by showing himself to be clearly unreasonable, helped the chariot of reason to drive forward.

Peel's principled refusal, during these same Days of May, to head this government if it meant introducing the Reform he had denounced obviously contributed to the eventual peaceful outcome. If Peel had agreed to head a Tory government in May, he would have had to deal with a hostile House of Commons, to say nothing of a hostile country; the resulting disturbances can only be conjectured but they can hardly have helped towards stability in such a turbulent situation. Peel's own take on the turbulence, and how to damp it down, is illuminated in a significant fashion by his attitude to the new National Gallery.[22] Like the triumphalist Whigs, but in a very different way, he too called in art in the interests of politics. The transference of the National Gallery from its previous overcrowded site in Pall Mall to a new building designed by William Wilkins at King's Mews, Charing Cross,* gave him the opportunity for speaking up on the subject in Parliament. The location was felt to be of especial importance because it was where the wealthy classes from the west of the city met the poorer classes from the east.

In the House of Commons at the end of July 1832, Peel quoted Dr Johnson on the subject of Charing Cross: this was where 'the great tide of human existence is fullest in its stream'. He also suggested that art might be invoked to calm the people down. 'In the present times of excitement,' he declared, 'the exacerbation of angry and unsocial feelings might be much softened by the effects which the fine arts ever produced upon the minds of men.' Such an institution, he suggested, cemented 'the bonds of union between the richer and the poorer orders of the state', on which subject no one felt more keenly than himself. It was William Cobbett who angrily rejected the idea of publicly funded galleries: 'If the aristocracy want the Museum as a lounging place, let them pay for it.' The poor wanted bread, he said, not an exhibition. Like other great matters in 1832, the perceived struggle between culture and welfare was not a debate which would end there. Nevertheless Peel's desire to bring back harmony to a disturbed nation by means of the arts did him honour by later standards, if his stance against Reform did not.

Figaro in London, the satiric paper, had printed an impertinent piece immediately after the passing of the Bill in June 1832: 'It is said that Ministers, having passed the Reform Bill, intend to try and bring the King to a better understanding. They must first bring a *better understanding* to his Majesty.'[23] Yet as in the case of Wellington, if not in such an extreme manner, it could be argued that the peculiar character of William IV, if it led to obstacles in the Bill – the crisis of the spring

* Site of the present National Gallery in what is now Trafalgar Square.

of 1832 was a real crisis – allowed him to be managed to good effect in the end. The stone thrown at him at Ascot was in a way an unfair stone, as stones often are. Rumbustious, sometimes crude as he might be, not innately intelligent, William IV was at the same time no tyrant, and took the responsibilities of his position, as he understood them, seriously. His consort, Adelaide, gave him a happy home life – never to be undervalued where royalty is concerned – but her peculiar Continental obsession against change, thanks to her upbringing, was an alarming element in the equation. Nevertheless, a great and beneficial transformation in the make-up of the country took place on his watch for which he deserved credit (even if he refused to take it at the last minute). The crown which his niece Victoria inherited five years later still shone brightly.

It is interesting that the Whig Lord Holland gave a highly favourable verdict on him at his death in 1837. William IV, he wrote, was 'the best King of his [Hanoverian] race and perhaps of any race we have ever had, and the one who has left the greatest name as a Constitutional Sovereign, and the first Magistrate of a free and improving nation'.[24] This was of course written just as Queen Victoria ascended the throne, the prolonged nature of whose reign contrasts with the brevity of her uncle's and casts it inevitably into shadow.

The character of Lord Grey, on the other hand, provided an inspiration to later generations. In 1834 Samuel Rogers saluted him in verse:

> Grey, thou hast served, and well, thy sacred cause
> That Hampden, Sydney died for . . .
> Scorning all thought of self from first to last

A hundred years later Winston Churchill would write sonorously in *A History of the English-Speaking Peoples*: 'It is given to few men to carry out late in life a great measure of reform which they have advocated without success for forty years.' When Thomas Coke of Norfolk wrote to congratulate Grey on the Reform Bill immediately after its passing, the Prime Minister replied: 'It is the unbidden approbation of men like you that I feel to be most valuable'; this was the approbation that was never denied to Grey during the agonized period of creation in the spring of 1832.[25] However much his opponents might hysterically denounce him for his reforming actions, it was impossible plausibly to depict Lord Grey as a dangerous revolutionary; and in that lay one of his great strengths, when combined with his true reforming zeal.

Alexis de Tocqueville, visiting England in 1833, noted from the French perspective that there was not at all the same hatred of the aristocracy in England as had, all too palpably, existed in late-eighteenth-century France.[26] For one thing the whole caste was far more porous than it was in France, with the middle classes never seeing desirable attainment of upper-class status as utterly beyond their reach. In de Tocqueville's words: 'The English aristocracy can therefore never arouse those violent hatreds by the middle and lower classes against the nobility in France where the nobility is an exclusive caste' offering no hope of joining their ranks. 'The English aristocracy has a hand in everything; it is open to everyone; and anyone who wishes to abolish it or attack it as a body, would have a hard task to define the object of his onslaught.' Where Reform was concerned, although the House of Lords in theory had made every effort to defeat the Bill, no one could deny that aristocrats had also led the charge in its favour: Grey was one manifestation of this, Althorp another. As a reforming pamphlet had it: 'If those who have most to lose appear to have least to fear, is this not rather a strong argument in favour of Reform?'[27]

Two years later, at the age of seventy, Lord Grey retired from Government: his return to his beloved north was saluted by a vast public dinner held in his honour in Edinburgh in September 1834, of nearly 3,000 people in a pavilion on Carlton Hill. He was also given the Freedom of the City. There were banners of 'O Happy Day!' and 'Welcome to the Champion of Reform'. In his speech responding to the toast, Lord Grey proclaimed: 'I desire no better remembrance for posterity, or any other inscription on my tomb, than that I have assisted in restoring the people of England and Scotland their fair, just, and necessary representation in Parliament.' Grey told his friend Lord Holland afterwards that his reception had exceeded 'everything I could have imagined'.[28]

Subsequently a statue of Grey was erected in Newcastle upon

Tyne at the top of Grey Street; the dedication referred to 'an arduous and protracted struggle safely and triumphantly achieved in the year 1832'.* A hundred years after the Bill, a further plaque was added with the words: 'After a century of civil peace, the people renew their gratitude to the author of the Great Reform Bill. 1932.' In principle, however, Lord Grey had the retirement of his dreams – remembering those yearnings often expressed during the difficulties of the Bill – that is to say, with his wife, surrounded by children and grandchildren. Creevey, who visited him, commented on his 'tranquillity and cheerfulness'; he said that Grey derived the same pleasure from winning half a crown at cribbage as he had from the Reform Bill.[29]

Lord Althorp, although younger, enjoyed a similar retirement following the death of his father Earl Spencer in 1834, when he inherited the superior title and had to leave the Commons for the Lords. In his case prize bulls and other agricultural pursuits stood in place of the children he had forsworn after the early death of his beloved wife (whose portrait he asked to be hung round his neck when he was dying in 1845). Macaulay's commentary on his political career, although apparently condescending, at the same time contained a great deal of the truth: he doubted whether anyone who had ever lived in England 'with no eloquence, no brilliant talents . . . with nothing in short but plain commonsense and an excellent heart had ever possessed such influence'.[30]

A very different fate awaited a large number of the prominent who had been involved in the two-year maelstrom of the Bill. No less than six of them would become Prime Minister: Wellington (again), Sir Robert Peel, Lord Melbourne, Lord Palmerston, Lord John Russell and the former Edward Stanley, now the Earl of Derby. The special circumstances of the maelstrom were demonstrated by the fact that Palmerston and Derby were both Tory Prime Ministers – leaders of a party becoming delineated as the Conservative Party, just as Whigs were transforming into Liberals.

* Still to be seen, and acting as a convenient local trysting-place for various activities, as well as – suitably enough – a focus for placards and protests. Sadly, the modern Metro sign reads 'MONUMENT', not 'GREY'S MONUMENT'.

There was one catastrophe – as it seemed at the time – which followed shortly after the passing of the Reform Bill which proved in the end to have a purgative effect, much like the Bill itself. This was the Great Fire which consumed the Houses of Parliament in October 1834. To the Tories and those of conservative inclinations, of course, it came as what has been described as 'a proper punishment for a craven legislature' which had surrendered to the double pressure of the mob and the middle classes in passing the Reform Bill. To the Whigs, and liberals generally, the fire came as a welcome cleansing element to sweep away the corrupt old order, symbolized by the ancient, stuffy, notoriously inadequate buildings. Some disaster in the antique structures, so ill-suited to their purpose (again there was a comparison to the electoral system of the country), had long been predicted. Sir John Soane observed the inherent dangers in such 'an extensive assemblage of combustible materials' and the want of security from fire, with so much timber covered in plaster.[31]

If Queen Adelaide, who had not forgiven the Whigs, believed with the Ultra Tories that the fire was divine retribution for the Reform Bill, King William, poking round the still smouldering ruins, appeared to be 'gratified as if at a show'. From his attitude to the remains, he obviously thought that what had begun should be completed. Ever anxious to escape incarceration in Buckingham Palace, he suggested hopefully that Parliament itself might be transferred there and occupy the space in place of the Sovereign: the combined Parliament and palace would be 'the finest thing in Europe'.[32] Once again his hopes were to be disappointed.*

Outwardly in the Whig world, it seemed that nothing had changed. And yet in reality nothing remained the same. There had been two confrontations of enormous moment during the last two years: between Lords and Commons, and subsequently between Crown and Ministers. In both cases, the reformers secured victory without the final bloodthirsty encounter which both sides dreaded; on the surface

---

* At the time of writing, the two fine things still remain separate.

politics, not physical force, secured the passage of the Reform Bill. Yet in the Europe of the 1830s, Crown, Lords and Commons were all grimly aware that riots which presaged revolution could not be so easily ignored. And there had been plenty of riots in Britain, from the early days of Captain Swing in the high summer of 1830 onwards. This was where economic distress played its part: as long ago as 1818, Thomas Attwood had declared that the Jacobins might as well clamour to the winds as to a well-fed and fully employed population, but the poor and unemployed were a different matter.[33] In the end we might reverse Wellington's famous *dictum* that the beginning of Reform was the beginning of Revolution: it was the apparent start of Revolution which led to the beginning of Reform.

The deft manipulation of popular outrage by unionists and Radicals, men like Attwood, Parkes and Francis Place – men who were in favour of Reform, even if for the time being it had to be limited – should never be underestimated in its contribution to the successful outcome of the Bill. Francis Place was certainly quite clear in his own mind about the part that popular fury – managed popular fury – had played. He gave his own verdict: 'But for these demonstrations, a Revolution would have occurred . . . we were within a moment of general rebellion.' This was the first time, he said, that the people ever combined of their own free will for a really national purpose. This was the fiercely held emotion of the time: a genuine dread of revolution which Sydney Smith recalled afterwards as a 'hand-shaking, bowel-disturbing passion of fear'.[34]

With the benefit of hindsight it is possible to wonder, of course, what kind of revolution would actually have taken place. Menacing comparisons to the 1640s and 1688, to say nothing of the frequent invocations of the French Revolution of 1789 (and 1830) – how valid would they have turned out to be if Wellington had returned to government? But in 1832, it was the passionate perceptions of the time – the real fears, not the calmer, dispassionate views of the future – which were crucially important and swayed the behaviour of all those involved.

When Lord Grey thanked Attwood for his help on 19 May 1832,

he may initially have seen himself as playing a diplomatic role; but he was also speaking the truth. 'The People' to whom Grey had referred so often in his own speeches, as did other Whigs, were beginning to emerge as a concept quite different from 'The Mob'. Attwood's own frequent emphasis on the need to avoid violence stood him in good stead since, like Grey, it made it impossible plausibly to denounce him as a revolutionary, one who yearned for those barricades. As it was, Macaulay was able to comment with truth that the changes produced by violence were often followed by reaction, whereas 'the victories of reason, once gained, are gained for eternity'.[35]

At the time of the Royal Assent, on 7 June, Sir John Hobhouse summed it up: 'Thus ends this great national exploit. The deed is done.' He added, with a sense of incredulity which reflected the tension of the whole long-drawn-out drama: 'It is difficult to believe that it is done.'[36] It was indeed a great national exploit. If the deed was not done for ever, it was at the very least a great beginning.

REFERENCES

Prologue: A new King, a new people
1. Arbuthnot, II, pp. 385–6
2. Gore, *Creevey*, p. 301
3. Haydon, p. 626
4. Broughton, p. 207
5. Wellesley, p. 16
6. Fraser, *Marie Antoinette*, p. 133
7. Greville, II, p. 345
8. Haydon, p. 561
9. Fonblanque, II, p. 95
10. Arbuthnot, II, p. 352; Robinson, p. 220; Edgeworth, p. 463
11. Times History, p. 267
12. Arbuthnot, I, p. xv
13. Croker, II, p. 70
14. Somerset, *William IV*, p. 104
15. Wakefield, *England*, I, p. 123; Hopkirk, p. 830
16. Aspinall, *Diaries*, p. xvi
17. Arbuthnot, II, p. 354; Aspinall, *Diaries*, p. xvi; Grey Correspondence, II, p. 464
18. Ziegler, *William IV*, p. 144
19. Somerset, *William IV*, p. 120; Trevelyan, *Grey*, p. 73
20. Queen Adelaide's Diary, p. 167, 16 December 1831; Hopkirk, p. 58
21. Edgeworth, p. 504; Greville, II, p. 333
22. Watkins, p. 486
23. Dino, I, p. 3
24. Greville, II, p. 3; Hopkirk, p. 103
25. *cit.* Armitage, 'Patriot', p. 415, note 78
26. Queen Adelaide's Diary, p. 53, 16 July 1830
27. Kelly, *Holland House*, p. 158
28. Trevelyan, *Macaulay*, I, p. 159, note 1
29. Mitchell, *Whig World*, p. 130
30. H. of C., VII, pp. 237–41; G.E.C., III, pp. 501–2
31. Innes, '"Reform"', p. 71
32. Evans, p. 52; Robinson, p. 232
33. BL Add. MS 51751 fol. 32; Times History, p. 269
34. Wallas, p. 243

Chapter One: The clamour
1. Briggs, 'Background', p. 317
2. Rutland MSS; Hansard, House of Lords 27 February 1812
3. Greville, II, p. 370
4. Foot, pp. 60 *et seq.*; Hansard, House of Commons 15 March 1832
5. Stirling, p. 193
6. Hilton, pp. 416–17; Wakefield, *Swing*, p. 7; Hamburger, p. 71; Hobsbawm and Rudé, pp. 16 *et seq.*
7. Hilton, p. 424
8. Bagehot, 'Althorp'; Cannon, pp. 29–30
9. Brock, p. 630
10. Pearson, p. 234
11. Hansard, House of Commons 4 March 1831
12. New, pp. 87–90
13. Clive, pp. 182–3; *Torrington Diaries*, p. 251; Hunt, p. 5

14. Hunt, p. 24; pp. 17–18; Dent, p. 430
15. Hansard, House of Lords 4 October 1831
16. Brock, p. 28; p. 22
17. Macintyre, p. 35; History of Parliament Online
18. Newbold, p. 47; Smith, *Grey*, p. 136
19. Creevey, II, p. 302
20. Foreman, p. 203
21. Holland Diaries, p. 121
22. Greville, I, p. 82; Briggs, 'Background', p. 299; Aspinall, *Diaries*, p. 48
23. Smith, *Grey*, p. 135; p. 237; p. 252; Hansard, House of Lords 2 November 1830
24. Greville, I, p. 258; Tocqueville, p. 43; Haydon, p. 570
25. *The Times*, 12 April 1832
26. Holyoake, p. 213; Longford, p. 267
27. Wallas, p. 295
28. Hilton, p. 411; Foot, p. 68
29. Gill, I, p. 203, note 1
30. Ellitson, p. 7
31. Briggs, 'Attwood', pp. 190 *et seq.*
32. Haydon, p. 119; Holyoake, p. 42
33. Buckley, pp. 57 *et seq.*
34. Moss, p. 185
35. Moss, p. 166; Croker, II, p. 100
36. *The Times*, 14 October 1830; Hobsbawm and Rudé, p. 106
37. Hobsbawm and Rudé, p. 103

Chapter Two: I will pronounce the word
1. Butler, p. 194, note 3; Grant, pp. 1–2; Shenton, pp. 5 *et seq.*
2. Lytton, p. 346
3. Grant, pp. 14 *et seq.*
4. Huxley, p. 82
5. *The Times*, 6 April 1832; Aspinall, 'Reporting', p. 232

6. Hague, pp. 27–8
7. Trevelyan, *Grey*, p. 303
8. Hawkins, p. 4; p. 32; p. 61
9. Howell-Thomas, p. 144
10. Rubinstein, I, p. 319
11. Lytton, p. 340
12. Stanhope, p. 185
13. Grant, p. 11; Russell, *Collections*, p. 160
14. Holland Diaries, p. 64; Haydon, p. 615
15. Russell, *Collections*, p. 157; Cecil, p. 294
16. Russell, *Collections*, p. 135
17. Stewart, p. 246
18. Byron, *Don Juan*, Canto XI
19. *The Times*, 2 November 1830; Smith, *Reform*, p. 23
20. Wallas, p. 148; p. 178
21. Wallas, pp. 246 *et seq.*
22. Tocqueville, p. 42
23. Trevelyan, *Grey*, p. 234, note 2
24. Hansard, House of Lords 2 November 1830
25. Cecil, p. 257; Smith, *Grey*, p. 16
26. Hansard, House of Lords 2 November 1830
27. Grey Correspondence, I, pp. 126–7
28. Hansard, House of Lords 2 November 1830
29. Butler, Preface to 1st edn
30. Longford, p. 228
31. Hamburger, p. 17
32. Arbuthnot, II, pp. 398–9
33. Lieven, II, p. 115
34. Wallas, p. 248, note 3; Granville, p. 67
35. G.E.C., X, p. 845, note c; Aspinall, *Diaries*, p. 224
36. Hansard, House of Lords 8 November 1830

37. Hansard, House of Commons 8 November 1832
38. Arbuthnot, II, p. 401
39. Brock, p. 125
40. Stewart, p. 190; O'Gorman, *Eighteenth Century*, p. 360; Croker, II, p. 75; Hawkins, p. 71
41. Aspinall, *Diaries*, p. 1
42. Robinson, p. 278
43. *The Times*, 22 November 1830

Chapter Three: Believing in the Whigs
1. Ziegler, *Dino*, p. 192; Rubinstein, p. 28
2. Dolby, *Cyclopaedia*, p. 215; Russell, *Collections*, p. 138
3. Stewart, p. 34; Howell-Thomas, pp. 54 *et seq.*
4. Greville, II, p. 248; Clive, p. 192
5. Aspinall, *Diaries*, p. li; Trevelyan, *Grey*, p. 302, note 1; Haydon, p. 648
6. Mitchell, *Whig World*, p. 17; Brock, p. 131
7. Mitchell, *Whig World*, p. 77; p. 80
8. Kelly, *Holland House*, p. 105
9. G.E.C., VI, p. 54, note b
10. Clive, pp. 210–12
11. Gash, *Politics*, pp. 393 *et seq.*
12. Wallas, p. 252; p. 261
13. Croker, I, p. 253; Gash, *Politics*, p. 393
14. Stewart, p. 249; Lee, p. 55
15. Lee, pp. 92 *et seq.*; p. 146; Creevey, I, p. 223; Edgeworth, p. 515; Greville, II, p. 91
16. Lytton, pp. 323–4; Aspinall, *Diaries*, p. 25
17. Times History, pp. 276–7; Martineau, pp. 49–50
18. Brown, p. 103

19. Russell, *Collections*, p. 167; Ziegler, *Dino*, p. 206
20. Brown, p. 140
21. Cecil, p. 32
22. Holland Diaries, p. 77
23. Grey Correspondence, I, p. 34
24. Hobsbawm and Rudé, p. 155
25. *Melbourne's Papers*, p. 121
26. Aspinall, *Diaries*, p. 30
27. Foot, p. 143
28. Althorp Letters, p. 87
29. Campbell, I, p. 483; Cockburn, I, p. 322; Spencer, *Spencer Family*, p. 199
30. Stewart, p. 258
31. Aspinall, *Diaries*, pp. 175–6
32. Russell Correspondence, I, p. 312
33. Lytton, p. 15
34. Howell-Thomas, p. 11
35. Grant, p. 281
36. Charmley, p. 234; Cecil, p. 290
37. Holland Diaries, p. 96; Butler, p. 147
38. Buckley, p. 67
39. Fonblanque, II, p. 69
40. Buckley, p. 69; Smith, *Reform*, p. 45

Chapter Four: The gentlemen of England
1. Trevelyan, *Grey*, pp. 275–6
2. Cannon, p. 218; PRO 30/22/1B-C465342
3. Grey Correspondence, I, p. 46
4. Grey Correspondence, I, p. 51
5. Grey Correspondence, I, pp. 54–5
6. Grey Correspondence, I, p. 139
7. Trevelyan, *Grey*, p. 275, note 1
8. Lieven, II, p. 151
9. Strong, p. 3
10. Hopkirk, p. 94
11. Queen Adelaide's Diary, p. 86, 22 November 1830

12. Queen Adelaide's Diary, p. 112, 9 March 1831
13. G.E.C., VIII, p. 114, note G
14. Greville, II, p. 92
15. Ward, pp. 101–2
16. Strong, p. 383
17. Aspinall, *Politics*, p. 4; pp. 25 *et seq.*; Croker, II, pp. 17 *et seq.*; BBC History
18. O'Gorman, *Eighteenth Century*, p. 362
19. Hamburger, pp. 8–10
20. Butler, p. 240
21. DNB 2004, Gordon Phillips, 'Barnes, Thomas'
22. Times History, p. 272
23. Trevelyan, *Grey*, p. 256
24. Hansard, House of Lords 3 February 1831
25. Huxley, p. 95; p. 97
26. Rutland MSS
27. Hansard, House of Commons 1 March 1831
28. Gash, *Peel*, p. 10
29. O'Gorman, *Eighteenth Century*, p. 364
30. DNB 2004, John Wolffe, 'Inglis, Sir Robert Harry'
31. Dent, II, p. 405; Aspinall, *Diaries*, p. 13; Robinson, p. 296
32. H. of C., VII, p. 314; Lyttelton, pp. 106 *et seq.*
33. Hansard, House of Commons 2 March 1831
34. Pearson, p. 201; Clive, p. 160; Aspinall, *Diaries*, p. 100
35. Creevey, p. 221
36. Campbell, I, p. 308
37. Hansard, House of Commons 2 March 1831

Chapter Five: Russell's Purge
1. Hansard, House of Commons 3 March 1831
2. Hurd, p. 148
3. Le Marchant, pp. 350–1
4. Trevelyan, *Grey*, p. 284; Lieven, II, p. 179
5. Wallas, pp. 25 *et seq.*
6. *The Times*, 2 March 1831
7. Douglas-Fairhurst, p. 73
8. Aspinall, *Diaries*, p. 14
9. Hawkins, p. 81
10. Grant, p. 97; Brock, p. 157; pp. 220–1
11. DNB 2004, Kenneth Baker, 'Doyle, John [H.B.]'
12. Grant, p. 90; Trevelyan, *Grey*, p. 283
13. H. of C., VII, p. 716
14. Creevey, II, p. 223
15. Creevey, II, p. 224
16. Newey, pp. 238–53; W.T. Moncrieffe, *Reform; or, John Bull*
17. *The Times*, 7 March 1831
18. Brock, p. 165
19. Macintyre, p. 23
20. Russell, *Collections*, p. 162
21. Somerville, p. 152
22. Grey Correspondence, I, p. 154
23. ibid.
24. Grey Correspondence, I, p. 176
25. Grey Correspondence, I, p. 179
26. Hansard, House of Commons 22 March 1831
27. Greville, II, p. 135
28. Clive, p. 152
29. H. of C., I, p. 356
30. Clive, p. 153
31. Somerville, pp. 92–3
32. Greville, II, p. 135

Chapter Six: King as angel

1. Creevey, II, p. 226
2. Arbuthnot, II, p. 417
3. Brock, p. 187
4. Hansard, House of Commons 12 April 1831
5. Hansard, House of Commons 2 March 1831; *The Times*, 9 December 1830
6. Wicks, p. 69
7. Wicks, p. 69
8. Grey Correspondence, I, p. 136
9. Mahon, Stanhope MSS, C305/1
10. Brock, p. 186
11. Cockburn, I, p. 317
12. Croker, II, p. 112; Le Marchant, p. 92
13. Brock, p. 182
14. DNB 2004, R.H. Vetch, rev. K.D. Reynolds, 'Taylor, Sir Herbert'
15. Grey Correspondence, I, pp. 237–8
16. Grey Correspondence, I, p. 234, note
17. Trevelyan, *Grey*, p. 295
18. *Brougham*, p. 116
19. Reid, I, p. 258
20. Hansard, House of Commons 22 April 1831
21. Broughton, p. 105
22. Cockburn, I, p. 318; Greville, II, p. 139
23. Trevelyan, *Grey*, App. F, pp. 382–4
24. Greville, II, p. 139
25. Ziegler, *William IV*, p. 187
26. Queen Adelaide's Diary, p. 123, 22 April 1831; Hopkirk, p. 110
27. Brock, p. 181
28. *Liverpool Chronicle*, 7 May 1831
29. Knowles, *King Alfred*, V. iii
30. Robinson, p. 300; H. of C., V, p. 266
31. Longford, pp. 267–8
32. WND, VII, p. 440
33. Ferguson, pp. 241–2

Chapter Seven: Away went Gilpin

1. *The Times*, 29 April 1831
2. Brock, p. 18
3. DNB 2004, K.D. Reynolds, 'First Earl of Munster'
4. Ziegler, *William IV*, p. 158
5. ibid.
6. Begent and Chesshyre, p. 74
7. WND, VII, p. 449; Lieven, II, p. 222; Arbuthnot, II, p. 420
8. *The Times*, 23 May 1831
9. H. of C., VII, p. 239; Hansard, House of Commons 18 February 1830; Brock, p. 149
10. Althorp Letters, p. 155
11. Huxley, pp. 97–8
12. Prest, p. 43
13. Brock, p. 49
14. Moss, p. 196
15. Wicks, p. 71; Sadleir, p. 160
16. Pearce, p. 156
17. Brock, p. 211
18. Morley, p. 70
19. WND, VII, p. 451
20. Holland Diaries, p. 17
21. Pearce, p. 151
22. Brown, p. 167
23. Hansard, House of Commons 24 June 1831
24. Moss, p. 197
25. Hansard, House of Commons 6 July 1831
26. Trevelyan, *Macaulay*, I, p. 223
27. Aspinall, *Diaries*, p. 110; Hawkins, p. 95
28. Le Marchant, p. 345

29. Le Marchant, pp. 325 *et seq.*
30. Holland Diaries, p. 17
31. Holland Diaries, p. 21; Aspinall, *Diaries*, p. 107
32. Trevelyan, *William IV*, no. xxi
33. Watkins, p. 695
34. Grey Correspondence, I, p. 310
35. Aspinall, *Diaries*, p. 126
36. Le Marchant, p. 340

Chapter Eight: Confound their politics
1. *The Times*, 5 September 1831
2. Moss, p. 198
3. Greville, II, p. 160; Trevelyan, *Macaulay*, I, p. 244
4. Strong, p. 372
5. Strong, p. 378
6. Greville, II, p. 197
7. Hansard, House of Commons 20 September 1831; *Macbeth*, III. i
8. Le Marchant, p. 120; H. of C., IV, pp. 426 *et seq.*; DNB 2004, Marc Baer, 'Burdett, Sir Francis'
9. Le Marchant, p. 347
10. DNB 2004, Philip J. Salmon, 'Parkes, Joseph'
11. Buckley, p. 73
12. Melbourne Papers, pp. 129–30
13. H. of C., VI, pp. 6 *et seq.*
14. Hansard, House of Lords 3 October 1831
15. Trevelyan, *Grey*, p. 306; Aspinall, *Diaries*, p. 135; Cecil, *Melbourne*, p. 257
16. Aspinall, *Diaries*, p. 140
17. *The Times*, 4 October 1831
18. Grey MSS, Box 34
19. Wallas, pp. 263–4; Hobsbawm and Rudé, p. 158; Trevelyan, *Grey*, p. 290
20. Moss, p. 202; Hamburger, pp. 132–9

21. Hamburger, p. 132, note 21
22. *The Times*, 6 October 1831
23. *The Times*, 5 October 1831
24. Hansard, House of Lords 5–6 October 1831
25. Aspinall, *Diaries*, p. 95
26. Hansard, House of Lords 7 October 1831
27. Ibid.
28. Lee, p. 134
29. Aspinall, *Diaries*, p. 143; p. 147; Trevelyan, *Grey*, p. 308
30. Trevelyan, *Grey*, p. 310; Arbuthnot, II, p. 430
31. Somerville, p. 152
32. Granville, p. 114; Le Marchant, p. 354

Chapter Nine: What have the Lords done?
1. BL Add. MSS 27, 790 fols. 39–47; Wallas, p. 275, note 2
2. Smith, *Reform*, p. 92; p. 97
3. O'Gorman, *Eighteenth Century*, p. 362
4. *Poor Man's Guardian*, 15 October 1831
5. Somerville, p. 157
6. Hopkirk, pp. 128–9
7. Queen Adelaide's Diary, p. 161, 10 October 1831
8. Arbuthnot, II, p. 431
9. *The Times*, 10 October 1831
10. Trevelyan, *Grey*, p. 317; p. 355
11. Trevelyan, *Grey*, p. 317
12. *The Times*, 7 October 1831
13. Hansard, House of Commons 13 October 1831
14. H. of C., V, pp. 185 *et seq.*
15. Brock, p. 167

16. BL Add. MSS 27, 790 fols 39–47; Vernon, pp. 212–13
17. Wallas, p. 275, note 2; Butler, p. 294; BL Add. MSS 35, 149
18. Broughton, p. 148; Butler, pp. 293–4; Wallas, p. 278
19. BL Add. MSS 35, 149
20. Clarke, *Grote*, pp. 37 *et seq.*; *Grote*, p. 64
21. Eastlake, *Grote*, pp. 72–3; p. 16
22. Buckley, p. 10
23. Wallas, pp. 280 *et seq.*
24. Frampton, pp. 300 *et seq.*
25. *Sherborne Journal*, October 1831
26. Butler, pp. 297–9
27. Hamburger, pp. 154–7
28. Lyttelton, pp. 264–5
29. Trevelyan, *William IV*, no. XXIII
30. Grey Correspondence, I, p. 381
31. Armitage, 'A Patriot', pp. 403 *et seq.*
32. Watkins, Introduction
33. *Bolingbroke's Writings*, p. 82
34. Grey Correspondence, I, pp. 381–2
35. Grey Correspondence, I, pp. 382–5
36. Russell, I, p. 26
37. Fonblanque, p. 122
38. Hansard, House of Lords 20 October 1831

Chapter Ten: A scene of desolation
1. Hamburger, p. 161
2. Eagles, p. 68; *The Times*, 1 November 1831; Aspinall, *Diaries*, p. 153; Trevelyan, *Grey*, p. 320
3. Brock, p. 253
4. Grey Correspondence, I, p. 394; Eagles, p. 79; Hamburger, p. 165; Huxley, p. 100
5. *The Times*, 1 November 1831; Le Marchant, p. 366

6. Tomalin, *Dickens*, pp. 46–7
7. Hamburger, p. 212, note 22; p. 216; Cannon, pp. 223 *et seq.*
8. Somerville, p. 152
9. Evans, p. 54; Gash, *Peel*, pp. 23–4
10. Rutland MSS
11. ibid.
12. Fraser, *Gunpowder Plot*, pp. 554 *et seq.*
13. Longford, p. 270; Smith, *Reform*, p. 108
14. Frampton, pp. 382–3
15. WND, VIII, p. 35; p. 42
16. Grey Correspondence, I, p. 431
17. Le Marchant, p. 374; Butler, p. 324
18. Moss, p. 205
19. Hamburger, p. 94
20. *The Times*, 6 December 1831; Hansard, House of Lords 6 December 1831
21. Le Marchant, p. 376, note
22. Hansard, House of Commons 12 December 1831
23. Russell, *Collections*, p. 13
24. Cannon, pp. 228–9
25. G.E.C., VI, p. 332, note e
26. Cannon, pp. 228–9; *The Times*, 13 December 1831; Hansard, House of Commons 17 December 1831
27. Hansard, House of Commons 17 December 1831
28. Hansard, House of Commons 14 December 1831
29. Holland Diaries, p. 86
30. Hansard, House of Commons 16 December 1831; 17 December 1831
31. Brightfield, p. 61
32. Hansard, House of Commons 17 December 1831
33. Buckley, p. 89

Chapter Eleven: The fearful alternative
1. Butler, p. 329
2. Holland Diaries, pp. 97–8
3. Somerset, *Queen Anne*, p. 463
4. H. of C., VII, p. 241
5. Butler, pp. 329–30, note 4
6. Russell, *Collections*, p. 44; Aspinall, *Diaries*, p. 171
7. Holland Diaries, p. 87; Butler, p. 329
8. Holland Diaries, p. 103
9. Grey Correspondence, II, p. 39
10. Grey Correspondence, II, p. 42; Clive, pp. 170–1, note 62
11. Trevelyan, *Grey*, pp. 331 *et seq.*
12. Stirling, p. 191
13. Grey Correspondence, II, pp. 68–73
14. Grey Correspondence, II, pp. 74–9
15. Grey Correspondence, II, pp. 96–102
16. Grey Correspondence, II, pp. 108–15
17. Hansard, House of Commons 17 January 1832
18. Grey Correspondence, II, p. 159
19. *The Times*, 10 December 1831
20. Pearce, p. 227; Butler, p. 338
21. WND, VIII, p. 144; p. 155
22. Holland Diaries, p. 127
23. Hansard, House of Commons 26 January 1832
24. Hunt, p. 14

Chapter Twelve: Bouncing Bill
1. Butler, p. 345
2. Creevey, II, p. 241
3. *Figaro in London*, 1 February 1832
4. Hopkirk, p. 111
5. Somerset, *William IV*, p. 140
6. WND, VIII, pp. 165–6
7. Trevelyan, *Macaulay*, I, p. 191

8. Holland Diaries, pp. 146–7
9. Butler, p. 349, note 1
10. Spencer, *Spencer Family*, p. 196; Broughton, pp. 189–90
11. Pearce, p. 234
12. Le Marchant, pp. 403–6
13. Le Marchant, pp. 407–13
14. Hansard, House of Commons 21 March 1832; Aspinall, *Diaries*, p. 213
15. White, pp. 362–3; Rowe, p. 73; Croker, II, p. 149
16. *Poor Man's Guardian*, 15 March 1832
17. Vernon, p. 216; Rowe, p. 76
18. *The Times*, 4 April 1832; 10 April 1832
19. Le Marchant, p. 414
20. Wallas, p. 294
21. Holland Diaries, p. 160
22. Grey Correspondence, II, p. 327
23. Grey Correspondence, II, pp. 327–8
24. Hansard, House of Lords 9 April 1832; Aspinall, *Diaries*, p. 222; Le Marchant, p. 418; Trevelyan, *Grey*, p. 335
25. *Lieven-Palmerston*, p. 35; *The Times*, 12 April 1832
26. Hansard, House of Lords 11 April 1832
27. Holland Diaries, p. 168
28. Hansard, House of Lords 13 April 1832
29. Reid, I, p. 284
30. Smith, *Reform*, p. 112

Chapter Thirteen: Seventh of May
1. Buckley, p. 91
2. *Poor Man's Guardian*, 19 March 1832
3. Hansard, House of Lords 7 May 1832
4. Holland Diaries, p. 176
5. Broughton, p. 218

6. Aspinall, *Diaries*, p. 240
7. Butler, p. 368; Buckley, p. 95
8. Martineau, pp. 464–5
9. *The Times*, 8 May 1832; Hamburger, p. 132, note 21
10. Hamburger, pp. 132–9; Hunt, p. 18
11. Dent, pp. 360 *et seq.*
12. Somerville, p. 155
13. *The Times*, 9 May 1832
14. Haydon, p. 620
15. Moss, pp. 215–16
16. Buckley, p. 96; Adam Zamoyski to author
17. Trevelyan, *Grey*, p. 339
18. Aspinall, *Diaries*, p. 240; Creevey, II, p. 245
19. Brougham, p. 192
20. Le Marchant, pp. 425–6
21. Grey Correspondence, II, pp. 395–6
22. Hansard, House of Lords 9 May 1832
23. Aspinall, *Diaries*, p. 247
24. Aspinall, *Diaries*, p. 246
25. *The Times*, 10 May 1832; Trevelyan, *Grey*, pp. 341–2
26. Creevey, II, p. 245; Aspinall, *Diaries*, p. 241
27. Creevey, II, p. 246
28. Aspinall, *Diaries*, p. 246
29. *The Times*, 16 May 1832
30. *Morning Chronicle*, 9 May 1832
31. Hansard, House of Commons 10 May 1832
32. Aspinall, *Diaries*, p. 246; p. 247; Lee, p. 97; p. 132
33. Croker, II, p. 153
34. Lee, p. 151; WND, VIII, p. 304
35. Lee, p. 152
36. Trevelyan, *Grey*, p. 342
37. Ferguson, pp. 244–5
38. Wallas, pp. 309 *et seq.*

Chapter Fourteen: Prithee return to me
1. *The Satirist*, 13 May 1832
2. *The Times*, 14 May 1832
3. Trevelyan, *Grey*, p. 342; DNB 2004, R.J.W. Selleck, 'Shuttleworth, Sir James'
4. Somerset, *William IV*, p. 163
5. Trevelyan, *Grey*, App. H., p. 389
6. Le Marchant, p. 430
7. Hansard, House of Commons 14 May 1832
8. Trevelyan, *Grey*, App. H., p. 389
9. Broughton, p. 226
10. *Lieven-Palmerston*, p. 35
11. Aspinall, *Diaries*, p. 254
12. Grey Correspondence, II, p. 406
13. Grey Correspondence, II, pp. 418–19
14. *Bristol Mercury*, 13 May 1832
15. Aspinall, *Diaries*, p. 260
16. Hansard, House of Lords 17 May 1832; Grey Correspondence, II, pp. 422–3
17. Grey Correspondence, II, pp. 423–4; Lieven, p. 352
18. Grey Correspondence, II, p. 425
19. Eastlake, p. 73
20. *Morning Chronicle*, 18 May 1832; Wallas, pp. 314–15
21. Grey Correspondence, II, p. 430
22. Grey Correspondence, II, pp. 434–5
23. Grey Correspondence, II, p. 436
24. Grey Correspondence, II, pp. 438–9
25. Moss, p. 224
26. Moss, p. 225
27. *The Times*, 16 May 1832
28. Wallas, pp. 321 *et seq.*

Chapter Fifteen: Bright day of liberty
1. *The Times*, 22 May 1832

2. Moss, pp. 225–6
3. *Birmingham Journal*, 2 June 1832
4. Aspinall, *Diaries*, p. 268
5. Hansard, House of Lords 22 May 1832
6. Longford, p. 277
7. Creevey, II, p. 247
8. Brougham, p. 276
9. Grey Correspondence, II, p. 450
10. Hansard, House of Lords 4 June 1832
11. WND, VIII, p. 356
12. Hansard, House of Lords 4 June 1832
13. Creevey, II, p. 247
14. Stewart, p. 276
15. Butler, p. 415, note 5; Creevey, II, p. 247; *The Times*, 7 June 1832
16. Smith, *Reform*, p. 139
17. *Figaro in London*, 2 June 1832
18. Le Marchant, p. 438
19. Holland Diaries, p. 190
20. Le Marchant, pp. 436–7
21. *The Times*, 8 June 1832

Epilogue: This great national exploit
1. Stewart, pp. 247–8; Clive, p. 216
2. Haydon, pp. 622–32
3. Tomalin, *Dickens*, p. 44
4. People's History Museum, Manchester
5. Tyrconnel Diary, 23 July 1832
6. Swindells, p. 1
7. WND, VIII, p. 361; Wordsworth Letters, V, pp. 500–1
8. Grey Correspondence, II, pp. 449–50
9. Grey Correspondence, II, p. 472
10. Ziegler, *William IV*, p. 277

11. Briggs, 'Attwood', pp. 205 *et seq.*; DNB 2004, Clive Behagg, 'Attwood, Thomas'
12. Clive, p. 221
13. DNB 2004, Philip J. Salmon, 'Parkes, Joseph'
14. Buckley, p. 114
15. General Election, 1832
16. O'Gorman, *Voters*, Table 4.3, p. 179
17. Hilton, p. 421
18. O'Gorman, *Eighteenth Century*, p. 388; see Salmon, App. 1, 'The Re-distribution of English and Welsh Seats in 1832', pp. 251–2
19. Hamburger, p. 48; George Eliot, *Middlemarch*, Ch. LI
20. Pearson, p. 150; Brock, p. 282; p. 332
21. Holland Diaries, p. 105
22. Hoock, pp. 254–70; Hansard, House of Commons 23 July 1832
23. *Figaro in London*, 9 June 1832
24. Kelly, *Holland House*, p. 212
25. Mitchell, *Whig World*, p. 152; Martin Gilbert to author; Churchill, pp. 34–43; Stirling, p. 200
26. Tocqueville, p. 67; pp. 70–1
27. Brock, p. 201
28. Smith, *Grey*, pp. 2 *et seq.*
29. Creevey, II, p. 301
30. Trevelyan, *Macaulay*, I, p. 242
31. Cannadine, 'The Palace of Westminster', p. 13; Hastings, p. 121, note 1; Shenton, pp. 101 *et seq.*
32. Shenton, p. 235; Ziegler, *William IV*, p. 251
33. Briggs, 'Attwood', p. 200
34. Rowe, p. 95; Hilton, p. 426
35. Clive, p. 182
36. Broughton, p. 242

SOURCES

This list gives bibliographical details of all books cited in the References.
Place of publication is London, and edition is hardback, unless otherwise stated.
The proceedings of the Houses of Parliament are given by dates of entry, which
   applies equally to hardback and online publication.

Allen, W. Gore, *King William IV*, 1960
[Althorp Letters] *Letters of Lord Althorp*, privately printed
[Arbuthnot] *The Journal of Mrs Arbuthnot 1820–1832*, ed. Francis Bamford and the
   Duke of Wellington, 2 vols, 1950
Armitage, David, 'A Patriot for Whom? The Afterlives of Bolingbroke's Patriot
   King', *Journal of British Studies*, vol. 36, 1997
Aspinall, Arthur, *Lord Brougham and the Whig Party*, Manchester, 1927
Aspinall, A., *Politics and the Press. c. 1780–1850*, 1949
Aspinall, A., ed., *Three Early Nineteenth Century Diaries*, 1952
Aspinall, A., 'The Reporting and the Publishing of the House of Commons'
   debates. 1771–1834', see Pares and Taylor
Auden, W.H., ed. and introd., *Selected Writings of Sydney Smith*, New York, 1956
Bagehot, Walter, 'Lord Althorp and the Reform Act of 1832', in *The Works and
   Life of Walter Bagehot*, vol. 7, 1915
Barlow, P.J., 'Benjamin Robert Haydon and the Radicals', *The Burlington
   Magazine*, vol. 99, 1957
[BBC History], http://www.bbc.co.uk/history/familyhistory/bloodlines/
   workinglife.shtml?entry=swing_riots&theme=workinglife
Begent, J. and Chesshyre, Hubert, *The Most Noble Order of the Garter: 650 Years*,
   1999
[BL] British Library MSS
Bolingbroke's Political Writings. The Conservative Enlightenment, ed. Bernard
   Cottret, New York, 1997
Briggs, Asa, 'Thomas Attwood and the Economic Background of the Birmingham
   Political Union', *Cambridge Historical Journal*, vol. 9, 1948
Briggs, Asa, 'The Background of the Parliamentary Reform Movement in Three
   English Cities', *Cambridge Historical Journal*, vol. 10, 1952
Brightfield, Myron F., *John Wilson Croker*, Berkeley, Calif., 1940
Brock, Michael, *The Great Reform Act*, pbk, 1973

[Brougham] *The Life and Times of Lord Brougham. Written by Himself*, vol. III, 1871

Broughton, Lord (John Cam Hobhouse), *Recollections of a Long Life*, ed. Lady Dorchester, vol. IV, 1910

Brown, David, *Palmerston. A biography*, New Haven and London, 2010

Buckley, Jessie K., *Joseph Parkes of Birmingham and the part he played in Radical Reform movements from 1825 to 1845*, 1926

Burns, Arthur and Innes, Joanna, eds, *Rethinking the Age of Reform. Britain 1780–1850*, Cambridge, 2003

Butler, J.R.M., *The Passing of the Great Reform Bill*, new imp., 1964

[Campbell] *Life of John, Lord Campbell*, ed. Hon. Mrs Hardcastle, 2 vols, 1881

Cannadine, David, 'The Palace of Westminster as Palace of Vanities', see *The Houses of Parliament*

Cannon, John, *Parliamentary Reform. 1640–1832*, Cambridge, 1973

Cecil, David, *The Young Melbourne & Lord M*, pbk, 2001

Chambers, *Palmerston. 'The People's Darling'*, 2004

Charmley, John, *The Princess and the Politicians. Sex, Intrigue and Diplomacy, 1812–40*, 2005

Churchill, Winston S., *A History of the English-Speaking Peoples*, vol. III, *Age of Revolution*, 1957

Clarke, M. L., *George Grote: A Biography*, Athlone, 1962.

Clive, John, *Thomas Babington Macaulay. The Shaping of the Historian*, 1973

Cobbett, William, *Rural Rides*, ed. and introd. Ian Dyck, pbk, 2001

Cockburn, Lord, *Life of Lord Jeffrey with a selection from his Correspondence*, 2 vols, Edinburgh, 1852

Colley, Linda, *Britons*, 1992

[Creevey] *The Creevey Papers. A selection from the correspondence and diaries of the late Thomas Creevey, M.P., 1768–1838*, ed. Sir Herbert Maxwell, 2 vols, 1904

[Croker] *The Croker Papers. The Correspondence and Diaries of the Late Rt Hon. John Wilson Croker*, ed. Louis J. Jennings, 3 vols, 2nd revised edn, 1885

Dent, R.K., *The Making of Birmingham. A History of the rise and growth of the Midland Metropolis*, 1894

Derry, John W., *Earl Grey. Aristocratic Reformer*, Oxford, 1992

[Dickens] *The Love Romance of Charles Dickens. Told in his letters to Maria Beadnell (Mrs Winter)*, introd. Walter Dexter, 1936

[DNB] Oxford Dictionary of National Biography, 2004, http://www.oxforddnb.com

Dolby, Thomas, *The Cyclopaedia of Laconics. School of reform in Church and State*, c. 1832–40

Douglas-Fairhurst, Robert, *Becoming Dickens. The invention of a novelist*, 2012

Duchesse de Dino, *Chronique de 1831 à 1862*, ed. Princesse Radziwill, vol. I, 1831–1835, 1909

[Eagles, John] *The Bristol Riots, their Causes, Progress, and Consequences. By a Citizen*, Bristol, 1832

Eastlake, Lady, *Mrs Grote. A Sketch*, 1880

Edgeworth, Maria, *Letters from England 1813–1844*, ed. Christina Colvin, Oxford, 1971

Ellitson, D.H., *The Chamberlains*, 1966

Evans, Eric J., *The Great Reform Act of 1832*, 2nd edn, Lancaster Pamphlets, 1994

Farrell, Dr Stephen, 'A First Step Towards Democracy', *History Today*, vol. 60, 2010

Ferguson, Niall, *The World's Banker. The History of the House of Rothschild*, 1998

Fitzgerald, Percy, *The Life and Times of William IV*, 2 vols, 1884

Fonblanque, Albany, *England under Seven Administrations*, vol. II, 1837

Foot, Paul, *The Vote. How It was Won and How It was Undermined*, 2005

Foreman, Amanda, *Georgiana, Duchess of Devonshire*, 1998

[Frampton] *Journal of Mary Frampton*, ed. Harriot Mundy, 1886

Fraser, Antonia, *The Gunpowder Plot: Terror and Faith in 1605*, pbk, 1997

Fraser, Antonia, *Marie Antoinette: The Journey*, 2001

Fraser, Flora, *Princesses. The Six Daughters of George III*, 2004

Fulford, Roger, *Hanover to Windsor*, 1960

Gash, Norman, *Aristocracy and People*, rev. pbk, 1994

Gash, Norman, 'English Reform and the French Revolution in the General Election of 1839', see Pares and Taylor

Gash, Norman, *Politics in the Age of Peel: A Study in the Technique of Parliamentary Representation, 1830-1850*, pbk, New York, 1971

Gash, Norman, *Sir Robert Peel. The Life of Sir Robert Peel after 1830*, pbk, 2011

[G.E.C.] G.E. Cockayne, *The Complete Peerage of England, Scotland, Ireland, Great Britain and the United Kingdom*, 13 vols, reprint 1982

[General Election, 1832] http://en.wikipedia.org/wiki/United_Kingdom_general_election,_1832

George, M.D., *Catalogue of Political and Personal Satires, preserved in the department of prints and drawings in the British Museum*, vol. XI, 1828–1832, 1954

Gill, Conrad, *History of Birmingham*, vol. I, Oxford, 1952

Gore, John, ed., *Creevey Papers*, Folio Society, 1970

[Grant, James] *Random Recollections of the House of Lords from the Year 1830 to 1836*, 1836

[Granville] *Letters of Harriet Granville, 1810–1845*, ed. the Hon. F. Leveson Gower, 2 vols, 1894

[Greville] *The Greville Memoirs, 1814–1860*, ed. Lytton Strachey and Roger Fulford, vols I and II, 1938

[Grey Correspondence] ed. Henry Earl Grey, *The Reform Act, 1832. The Correspondence of the late Earl Grey with H.M. King William IV and with Sir Herbert Taylor*, 2 vols, 1867

Grote, Harriet, *The Personal Life of George Grote*, 1873

[H. of C.] *The House of Commons 1820–1832*; *The History of Parliament*, ed. D.R. Fisher, 7 vols, Cambridge, 2009

Hague, William, *William Wilberforce. The Life of the Great Anti–Slave Trade Campaigner*, pbk, 2008

Hamburger, Joseph, *James Mill and the Art of Revolution*, New Haven, CT, 1963

[Hansard] http://hansard.millbanksystems.com/commons ; http://hansard.mill banksystems.com/lords/1830s

Hansard's Parliamentary Debates, Third Series

Hastings, Maurice, *Parliament House, the Chambers of the House of Commons*, 1950

Hawkins, Angus, *The Forgotten Prime Minister. The 14th Earl of Derby*, vol. I, pbk, Oxford, 2009

[Haydon] *The Diary of Benjamin Robert Haydon*, ed. N.B. Pope, vol. 3, Cambridge, Mass., 1963

Hilton, Boyd, *A Mad, Bad and Dangerous People? England 1783–1846*, pbk, Oxford, 2006

History of Parliament Online: http://www.historyofparliamentonline.org/volume/1820-1832/parliament/1830-0

Hobsbawm, Eric and Rudé, George, *Captain Swing*, pbk, 2001

[Holland Diaries] *The Holland House Diaries 1831–1840. The diary of Henry Richard Vassall Fox, 3rd Lord Holland . . .*, ed. Abraham D. Kriegel, 1977

Holland House Papers, BL MS 51635

Holyoake, George Jacob, *Sixty Years of an Agitator's Life*, 2 vols, 1893

Hoock, Holger, 'Reforming culture: national art institutions in the age of reform', see Burns and Innes

Hopkirk, Mary, *Queen Adelaide*, 1950

The Houses of Parliament. History. Art. Architecture, eds. Christine Riding and Jacqueline Riding, 2000

Howell-Thomas, Dorothy, *Duncannon. Reformer and Reconciler. 1781–1847*, Foreword by Earl of Longford, 1992

Hunt, Tristram, *Building Jerusalem, The Rise and Fall of the Victorian City*, pbk, 2005

Hurd, Douglas, *Robert Peel. A Biography*, pbk, 2008

Huxley, Gervas, *Lady Elizabeth and the Grosvenors. Life in a Whig Family, 1822–1839*, 1965

Innes, Joanna, '"Reform" in English public life: the fortunes of a word', see Burns and Innes

Jenkins, Roy, *Gladstone*, 1995

Kelly, Linda, *Holland House. The Salon of the Century*, 2013

Kelly, Thomas, *Radical Tailor. The Life and Work of Francis Place 1771–1854*, Birkbeck College, 1972

Knowles, James Sheridan, *King Alfred, or the Patriot King*, 1831

Le Marchant, Sir Denis, Baronet, *Memoir of John Charles, Viscount Althorp, 3rd*

Earl Spencer, 1876

Lee, Dennis, *Lord Lyndhurst. The Flexible Tory*, Boulder, CO, 1994

Liechtenstein, Princess Marie, *Holland House*, 2 vols, 2nd edn, 1874

[Lieven] *Correspondence of Princess Lieven and Earl Grey*, ed. and trans. Guy Le Strange, 3 vols, 1890

The Lieven-Palmerston Correspondence, 1828–1856, trans. and ed. Lord Sudely, 1945

Longford, Elizabeth, *Wellington. Pillar of State*, 1972

[Lyttelton] *Correspondence of Sarah Spencer, Lady Lyttelton, 1787–1870*, ed. Hon. Mrs Hugh Wyndham, 1912

Lytton, Rt Hon. Lord, *England and the English*, repr. 1874

Macintyre, Angus, *The Liberator: Daniel O'Connell and the Irish Party, 1830–1847*, 1965

Mahon, Viscount, *A Leaf from the Future History of England*, 19 April 1831, Stanhope MSS, Centre for Kentish Studies

Mandler, Peter, *Aristocratic government in the Age of Reform. Whigs and Liberals, 1830–1852*, Oxford, 1990

Martineau, Harriet, *A History of the Thirty Years' Peace, A.D. 1816–1846*, vol. III, 1877

[Melbourne Papers] *Lord Melbourne's Papers*, ed. Lloyd C. Sanders, 1889

Mitchell, L.G., *Charles James Fox*, Oxford, 1992

Mitchell, L.G., 'Foxite Politics and the Great Reform Bill', *English Historical Review*, vol. 108, 1993

Mitchell, L.G., *Lord Melbourne, 1779–1848*, Oxford, 1997

Mitchell, Leslie, *Holland House*, 1980

Mitchell, Leslie, *The Whig World*, pbk, 2007

Moncrieffe, W.T. Esq., *Reform; or, John Bull Triumphant. A Patriotic Drama*, 1831

Morley, John, *The Life of William Ewart Gladstone*, vol. I, 1903

Moss, David J., *Thomas Attwood. The Biography of a Radical*, Montreal, 1990

New, Chester W., *Lord Durham. A Biography of John George Lambton, 1st Earl Durham*, Oxford, 1929

Newbold, Ian, *Whiggery and Reform, 1830–41. The Politics of Government*, 1990

Newey, Katherine, 'Reform on the London Stage', see Burns and Innes

O'Gorman, Frank, *Voters, Patrons and Parties. The Unreformed Electorate of Hanoverian England, 1734–1832*, Oxford, 1989

O'Gorman, Frank, *The Long Eighteenth Century. British Political & Social History 1688–1832*, pbk, 1997

Pares, Richard and Taylor, A.J.P., eds, *Essays presented to Sir Lewis Namier*, 1956

Pearce, Edward, *Reform! The Fight for the 1832 Reform Act*, pbk, 2004

Pearson, Hesketh, *The Smith of Smiths. Being the Life, Wit and Humour of Sydney Smith*, introd. G.K. Chesterton, pbk, 2009

Prest, John, *Lord John Russell*, 1972

[PRO] Public Record Office, Kew

Queen Adelaide's Diary, Royal Archives, GEO/ADD 21/7 AC

Reid, Stuart J., *Life and Letters of the 1st Earl Durham, 1792–1840*, 2 vols, 1906

Robinson, Lionel G., ed., *Letters of Dorothea, Princess Lieven, during her Residence in London, 1812–1834*, 1902

Rowe, D.J., ed., *London Radicalism 1830–1843. A Selection from the Papers of Francis Place*, London Record Society, 1970

Rubinstein, William D., *Who were the rich? A biographical dictionary of British wealth-holders*, vol. I, 1801–1834, 1981

Russell, G.W.E., *Collections & recollections. By one who has kept a diary*, 1898

Russell, Rt Hon. George W.E., *One Look Back*, 1912

[Russell Correspondence] *Early Correspondence of Lord John Russell, 1805–1840*, ed. Francis Albert Rollo Russell, 2 vols, 1913

Rutland MSS, Belvoir Castle

Sadleir, Michael, *Bulwer: a Panorama, Edward and Rosina. 1803–1836*, 1931

Salmon, Philip, *Electoral Reform at Work. Local Parties and National Parties. 1832–1841*, Studies in History, Suffolk, 2002

Shenton, Caroline, *The Day Parliament Burned Down*, Oxford, 2012

Smith, E.A., *Lord Grey 1764–1845*, Oxford, 1990

Smith, E.A., *Reform or Revolution? A Diary of Reform in England*, 1830–32, Stroud, Glos., 1992

Somerset, Anne, *William IV*, 1980

Somerset, Anne, *Queen Anne*, 2012

Somerville, Alexander, *The Autobiography of a Working Man*, ed. and introd. John Carswill, 1951

Spencer, Charles, *Althorp. The Story of an English House*, 1998

Spencer, Charles, *The Spencer Family*, 1999

Stanhope, Philip Henry, 5th Earl of, *Notes of Conversations with the Duke of Wellington, 1831–1851*, Oxford, 1947

Stewart, Robert, *Henry Brougham. 1778–1868. His Public Career*, 1985

Stirling, A.M.W., *Coke of Norfolk and his Friends*, vol. 2, 1908

Strong, Roy, *Coronation. A History of Kingship and the British Monarchy*, 2005

Swindells, Julia, *Glorious Causes. The Grand Theatre of Political Change, 1789 to 1833*, Oxford, 2001

Taylor, Miles, 'John Bull and the Iconography of Public Opinion in England, c. 1712–1929', *Past & Present*, 1992

Taylor, Miles, 'Empire and parliamentary reform: the 1832 Reform Act revisited', see Burns and Innes

Thomas, William, *The Quarrel of Macaulay and Croker*, Oxford, 2000

[Times History] *The History of The Times. 'The Thunderer' in the making. 1785–1841*, 1935

Tocqueville, Alexis de, *Journeys to England and Ireland*, ed. J.P. Mayer, trans. George Lawrence and K.P. Mayer, 1958

Tomalin, Claire, *Mrs Jordan's Profession*, pbk, 1995

Tomalin, Claire, *Charles Dickens. A Life*, 2012

The Torrington Diaries. A selection from the tours of the Hon. John Byng (later the 5th Viscount Torrington) between the years 1781 and 1794, 1954

Trevelyan, G.M., *The Life and Letters of Lord Macaulay*, 2 vols, 1876

Trevelyan, G.M., *Lord Grey of the Reform Bill. Being the Life of Charles, Second Earl Grey*, 1920

Trevelyan, G.M., *The Seven Years of William IV. A reign cartooned by John Doyle*, 1952

Turner, Michael J., *The Age of Unease. Government and Reform in Britain, 1782–1832*, Stroud, Glos., 2000

[Tyrconnel Diary] Diary of the 4th Earl of Tyrconnel, Kiplin Hall Archives, Richmond, North Yorkshire

Vernon, James, *Politics and the People. A study in English political culture, c. 1815–1867*, Cambridge, 1993

Wakefield, E.G., *Swing Unmasked; or, the causes of Rural Incendiarism*, 1831

[Wakefield, E.G.] *England and America. A comparison of the social and political state of both nations*, 2 vols, 1833

Wallas, Graham, *The Life of Francis Place, 1771–1854*, fac. 1908, pbk, 2006

Ward, J.T., *Sir James Graham*, New York, 1967

Watkins, John, *The Life and Times of William the Fourth*, 1831

Wellesley, Jane, *A Journey Through My Family*, 2008

White, Jerry, *London in the Nineteenth Century*, pbk, 2008

Wicks, Elizabeth, *The Evolution of a Constitution*, Oxford and Portland, Oregon, 2006

[WND] *Despatches, Correspondence, and Memoranda of Field Marshal Arthur of Wellington, K.G.*, ed. his son the Duke of Wellington, K.G., vols VII and VIII, 1878–80

[Wordsworth Letters] *The Letters of William and Dorothy Wordsworth*, 7 vols, Oxford, 1967

Ziegler, Philip, *William IV*, 1971

Ziegler, Philip, *Duchess of Dino*, pbk, 2003

INDEX

Aberdeen, 4th Earl of, 42, 43, 61
Acklom, Esther, 62–3
Act of Union 1707, 16
Act of Union 1801, 15, 16, 30, 93, 189
Adams, John, 29
Adelaide, Queen
  marries William, 6–7
  children, 7
  domestic life, 6
  appearance, 7
  fears of revolution, 7, 203
  has dread of encouraging dissipation at
    Court, 7–8
  watches Opening of Parliament, 39
  and William's coronation, 71–2, 74, 134
  provisions made by the State for, 72,
    73–4, 128–9
  favours the Tories, 72–3
  relationship with Howe, 72, 153–4
  and Wellington's departure from office,
    72
  reaction to the decision to dissolve
    Parliament, 111
  in cartoons, 116, 163, 203
  attends opening of new London Bridge,
    128
  at House of Lords for royal assent to
    Queen's dower-bill, 129
  and Howe's departure from Royal
    Household, 154
  shows hostility to Grey, 154, 202
  general approach to political matters,
    202–3
  press attacks on, 203–4, 228, 236, 243
  unpopularity, 203, 228, 248, 250, 255, 265
  influence on William, 204, 228, 243

  letter to Howe, 204
  comments on Bishop of Exeter's speech,
    213
  permits Lady Lyndhurst to be received at
    Court, 230
  obsession against change, 273
  and 1834 fire, 276
  brief references, 44, 117, 118, 191, 197
Albemarle, 4th Earl of, 108–9, 129
Allen, Dr John, 53
Althorp, 54
Althorp, John Spencer, Viscount (later 3rd
    Earl Spencer)
  physical stamina, 33
  speaks about cancellation of royal visit,
    46
  meeting held at house of, 47
  wealth, 50
  and family relationships among Whigs,
    52
  and Brougham's appointment as Lord
    Chancellor, 55, 57
  and the composition of Grey's Cabinet,
    58, 99
  becomes Chancellor of the Exchequer as
    well as Leader of Commons, 58
  and formation of Committee of Four, 62
  background, interests and character,
    62–4
  presents budget to Commons, 76
  and O'Connell, 93
  Brougham's disparagement of, 99
  and Secret Ballot, 102
  defeated on a bill for supplies, 105
  comments on expensive electoral
    process, 119

INDEX

Althorp, John Spencer, Viscount (later 3rd
    Earl Spencer) (*continued*)
  and Committee stage of Reform Bill,
    126–7
  and concerns over his father's health,
    129
  not hopeful about the Bill's prospects in
    Lords, 130
  role in getting the Bill through
    Commons, 136
  comments after vote against Bill in
    Lords, 150
  and letter to Attwood, 153
  visited by his sister, Sarah, 162–3
  and riots, 169
  and Durham's attack on Grey, 175, 176
  writes to Parkes, 177
  and Perceval's speech, 200
  reaches crisis point and considers
    resigning, 205, 206–7
  calms himself, 225
  cheered in Commons, 226
  praised in Ebrington's Address to the
    King, 229
  and Whig plans if faced with new
    administration, 232
  encounter with Hardinge, 238
  speaks about the intentions of the
    proposed new administration, 239
  hears about Wellington's decision not to
    form new administration, 241
  comments on how to deal with press
    attacks on the King, 256–7
  Haydon's comment on, 261
  depictions of, 262
  spends time at Wiseton, 265–6
  lifestyle after inheriting title, 275
  Macaulay's opinion of, 275
  brief references, 16, 93, 149, 159, 165,
    230, 259, 274
American War of Independence, 3
Anglesey, 1st Marquis of, 5, 59, 111
Anglican Church; *see* Church of England/
    Anglican Church

Anne, Queen, 185
Appleby, 126
Apsley House, 44, 48, 77, 113, 232
Arbuthnot, Charles, 34, 233
Arbuthnot, Harriet, 1, 4, 23, 44, 47, 99, 117,
    149, 198
Arkwright, Richard, 229
Army, 170–1
Arnold, Dr Thomas, 264n
Ascot, 265, 273
Ashley, Lord (later 7th Earl of
    Shaftesbury), 160–1
Association movement, 10
Athenaeum, 55
Attwood, Thomas
  respect for Grey, 22
  founds Birmingham Political Union, 26
  character, gifts and beliefs, 26–8
  committed to non-violent protest, 27–8,
    60, 92, 120, 137, 222
  letter to Grey about proposed
    modification to Reform Bill, 124
  addresses meeting at Newhall Hill in
    1831, 143–4
  Russell's letter to, 153, 164
  suggests military organization, 176, 177
  at Newhall Hill in May 1832, 220, 223
  sums up stark reality of the crisis, 237
  meeting with Grey, 247
  thanked by Grey, 247, 277–8
  becomes Freeman of the City of
    London, 249
  return journey to Birmingham, 249–50
  subsequent career, 267
  important role of, 277–8
  brief references, 40, 43, 55, 133, 160, 171,
    227, 258, 259, 264
Austen, Jane: *Emma*, 18
Avington House, 61

Bagehot, Walter, 15–16
Baines, Edward, senior, 74–5
Baines, Edward, junior, 75
Baring, Alexander, 239

Baring, Sir Thomas, 68

Barnes, Thomas, 4, 75–6, 99

Barrington, George, 58

Battle, 28

Bathurst, 3rd Earl, 149

Bathurst, Henry, Bishop or Norwich, 262

Beardsworth, John, 26

Beardsworth's Repository, Birmingham, 26, 62

Beaumont, Thomas Wentworth, 18

Beckwith, Captain, 169

Bedford, Dukes of, 54, 89, 190

Bedingfield, Lady, 153–4

Belgium, 12, 40

Belvoir Castle, 13, 77, 172

Bentham, Jeremy, 101, 137, 159

Bessborough, Harriet Cavendish, Countess of, 21, 66

Birmingham, 18–19, 20, 26, 27, 124, 137, 171, 176, 177, 249, 271
  meetings in, 62, 138, 143–4, 219–24

Birmingham (racehorse), 21

Birmingham Journal, 143, 224

Birmingham Political Union
  founding of, 26
  dinner to celebrate recent French Revolution, 26, 27–8
  growing numbers in, 28
  Blandford as honorary member of, 28, 267
  petitions the King to dismiss his Ministers, 43
  and the growth of unions, 60, 137
  expresses confidence in William IV, 68
  supports Reform Bill, 92–3, 98
  active during 1831 election campaign, 120
  holds dinner in honour of William's coronation, 133
  meeting at Newhall Hill in 1831, 143–4
  petition to House of Lords, 144
  letter from Russell to, 153, 164
  National Political Union founded in direct imitation of, 160
  and Bristol riots, 176
  Attwood's suggestion concerning military organization for, 176, 177
  response to suggestion for national fasting, 208
  meeting at Newhall Hill in May 1832, 219–24
  Grey meets leaders of, 247
  members elected to Parliament, 267

Black, John, 76

Blackfriars Bridge, London, 44

Blackstone, William: Commentaries on the Laws of England, 75

Blandford, 160

Blandford, Marquess of (later 6th Duke of Marlborough), 10, 11, 28, 33, 118–19, 186, 267

Bletchingley, 123

Blomfield, Bishop, 208

Blore, Edward, 194

Bodmin, 178

Bolingbroke, 1st Viscount: The Idea of a Patriot King, 8, 163–4

Bolton, 89

Boundary Bill, 265

Bouverie, General, 170–1

Bowood, 54

Bradford, 19

Brereton, Colonel, 168–9, 171, 222

Bright, John, 26, 271

Brighton, 71, 129, 190, 191, 195

Bristol, 139, 167–70, 176, 177, 181, 196, 200

Bristol Mercury, 243

Bromsgrove, 267

Bromsgrove Union, 221

Brooks's Club, 54, 232

Brougham, Henry, 1st Baron Brougham and Vaux
  elected to Parliament in 1830, 20–1
  earlier career, 35
  appearance, 35
  character and intelligence, 35–6
  views about reform, 36–7
  becomes Lord Chancellor, 5, 57

Brougham, Henry, 1st Baron Brougham
and Vaux (*continued*)
close relationship with Barnes, editor of
The Times, 76, 99
and Tory response to Reform Bill, 86
disparaging remarks about fellow
Cabinet members, 99
and William IV's dissolution of
Parliament, 107, 108, 110
presents petition to Lords, 144
speech in debate about Reform Bill, 147–9
in cartoons, 163, 225, 269
and creation of new peers, 187, 190, 251
hostile reference to royal ladies, 203
does not anticipate defeat in Lords, 219
asked by Attwood to present petition to
Lords, 220
meeting with William IV, 224–5
at public house in Hounslow, 225
and possibility of continuing in office
under new administration, 226, 230
and William IV's decision not to attend
Lords, 255
speaks at Guildhall Banquet, 260
Haydon's description of, 261
popular depictions of, 262
later career, 266
brief references, 46, 47, 51, 58, 177, 259
Brydges, Sir John, 126
Buckingham, Duke of, 61, 263
Buckingham Palace, 44, 194, 276
Bulwer, Edward (later Lord Lytton), 121
Burdett, Sir Francis, 135–6, 184, 196
Burdett-Coutts, Angela, 135
Burke, Edmund, 80, 181
Bushy Park, 4, 6, 8
Butler, J.R.M. 41n
Butler, Samuel: *Hudibras*, 179
Byng, Captain the Hon. John (later
Viscount Torrington), 18
Byron, Lord, 13, 22, 37, 60

Cabinet
composition of, 57–60, 99
resolution concerning response to civil
disturbance, 61
remains united in spite of internal
difficulties, 99
asks the King for dissolution, 107
discussions about creation of peers, 130,
184, 187–8, 190
discussions about possibility of
moderating Reform Bill, 175
debate about date of next meeting of
Parliament, 175
Durham attacks Grey during dinner,
175–6
discussions about Ireland, 189
William IV requests a formal minute
from, 192
official minute concerning creation of
peers is submitted to William, 193
Durham's behaviour in meetings, 205–6
meeting on evening before Grey's
speech to Lords, 217–18
minutes submitted to the King after
defeat of Bill in Lords, 224, 242
see also names of Cabinet members
Caledonian Mercury, 94
Calne, 82, 89, 182
Cambridge, Prince George of, 111, 129, 269
Cambridge University, 59, 64, 116, 123
Trinity College, 195–6
Campbell, 1st Baron, 149
Campbell, John, 84–5, 109, 198
Canning, George, 9, 181, 253
Canningites, 33, 58, 59, 130; *see also* names
of individuals
Canterbury, 28, 37
Canterbury, William Howley, Archbishop
of; *see* Howley, William, Archbishop
of Canterbury
Carlile, Richard, 173
Carlisle, 61
Carlisle, 6th Earl of, 68
Carlton Club, 54
Carnarvon, 2nd Earl of, 146
Caroline, Queen, 9, 72, 76, 254–5

Carrington, 1st Baron, 111–12

Castlereagh, Viscount, 73, 118, 206

Catholic Emancipation, 9–10, 15, 17, 24, 45, 56, 81, 90, 103, 142, 186, 230, 231, 241, 271

Cavendish, Lady Georgiana, 68

Census
    1821, 89
    1831, 178–9

Chandos, Marquess of (later 2nd Duke of Buckingham), 90, 130

Chandos clause, 130

Chantrey, Francis: marble relief, 261–2

Charing Cross, 272

Charles I, King, 2, 113, 140, 182

Charles II, King, 73, 117

Charles X, King of France, 3, 11, 83, 95, 243

Charlotte, Queen, 3, 72, 106, 129, 134, 194

Charlotte, Princess, 6, 57

Chartist movement, 267

Churchill, Winston: *A History of the English-Speaking Peoples*, 273

Church of England/Anglican Church, 141–2, 147, 179

City, 44, 111, 130, 239

Clarence, William, Duke of; *see* William IV

Clarke, Mary Anne, 106

Cleveland, Marquess of, 139

Clutton, Thomas, 221–2

Cobbett, William
    on the link between poverty and riots, 13
    visit to Battle, 28
    and Hansard, 32
    on stamina and health needed by MPs, 33
    addresses crowds at the Rotunda, 44
    founds *Poor Man's Guardian*, 75
    and Reform Bill, 87, 101, 179, 217
    tried for encouraging sedition, 121
    on public anger, 227
    rejects idea of publicly funded galleries, 272

Cobden, Richard, 26

Cockburn, Henry, 59, 63

Coke, Thomas (later 1st Earl of Leicester of Holkham), 54, 190, 261–2, 273

Colwick, 152

Combe Florey, 17

Combination Acts, 137

Committee of Four, 62–7, 69, 76, 79

Commons, House of
    system of representation, 15–20
    conditions in, 30–3, 127
    debate in November 1830, 46–7
    Government defeated in a vote, 47–8
    Althorp is leader of, 55, 58, 63
    budget presented to, 76
    Grey announces that Reform Bill will be presented in, 76
    Reform Bill introduced by Russell, 77–80
    reaction to Bill in, 80–2, 83–4
    Peel mounts official attack of Tories in, 85, 86–7
    debate on the Bill, 88–9, 95
    vote on the Bill, 95–7
    Hunt makes speech against the Bill, 100, 101
    rumours in, 105
    Althorp defeated on bill for supplies, 105
    called to attend House of Lords for dissolution, 109
    majority of members in favour of Reform, 122, 123
    Second Reform Bill introduced, 123–4
    Peel gives Opposition's response to Bill, 124–5
    debate and vote on Bill, 125
    third reading and vote on Bill, 134
    speeches after rejection of Bill in House of Lords, 156–7
    Third Reform Bill presented in, 177–9
    debate, 179–83
    vote in favour of Bill, 183
    debate over public expenditure on Buckingham Palace, 194
    wrangling over Reform Bill continues, 194–5

Commons, House of (*continued*)
  Perceval's speeches in, 198–200, 207
  third reading of Bill passes in, 209
  cheering for Althorp in, 226
  Ebrington's motion in, 229
  fills up early on 14th May, 238
  speeches, 239–40
  and results of 1832 General Election, 268
  remains large, 269
  Peel's speech about National Gallery,
    272
Constable, John, 19
Conyngham, Elizabeth, Marchioness, 4, 134
Copley, John Singleton 56
Cornwall, 19
Court of Common Council, 111
Coutts, Sophia, 135
Coventry, 250
Coventry, Earl of, 210
Cowper, Earl, 69
Cowper, Emily Lamb, Countess, 51, 59, 160
Cowper, Minnie, 160–1
Cowper, William, 116
Creevey, Thomas
  on Brougham's wife, 36
  on Grey, 40, 91, 99, 275
  and Lady Grey's reflections on marriage,
    21
  on Lady Lyndhurst, 56
  on Queen Adelaide, 228, 255
  on railways, 1
  on Reform Bill, 84, 254–5
  on the Tories, 251
  on William IV, 202, 225, 227, 255
Croker, John Wilson
  and Government defeat in House of
    Commons, 47–8
  on the struggle between Whigs and
    Tories, 51
  and the Athenaeum, 55
  conversation with Palmerston, 59
  and the press, 74, 75
  speech during debate following the
    introduction of Reform Bill, 89

hears about conversation between
  William IV and Gloucester, 105
calculations about voting in new
  Parliament, 123
comment about Victoria, 133
comment on new Reform Bill, 179
battle with Macaulay, 182
attacked in Stanley's speech, 182, 195
on cholera epidemic, 198
conversation with Peel, 230–1
brief references, 28, 94
Cromwell, Oliver, 16, 39, 135
Crown and Anchor Tavern, the Strand,
  87–8, 158
Croxteth, 1
Cumberland, Ernest, Duke of, 6, 56, 90,
  105, 117, 128,132–3, 149, 152, 174, 227,
  243, 264, 269
Czapski, Count Joseph Kazimierz, 223–4

Dalrymple, General, 2
Dartmouth, 1st Earl of, 185
Davies, Colonel, 46
Davies, Mr, 160
Dawson, George, 58
Derby, 105, 152, 162, 170, 171, 196
Derby Day 1832, 257
Devonshire, 6th Duke of, 50, 52, 105, 108,
  128, 133, 246
Devonshire, Georgiana Spencer, Duchess
  of, 2, 21, 22, 28
Devonshire House, 52
Dickens, Charles, 2, 88, 261
  'The Devil's Walk', 169–70
Digby, Lord, 161
Dino, Duchess of, 59
Disraeli, Benjamin: *Endymion*, 48
Doncaster, 21
Dorchester, 160, 161
Dorset, civil disturbances in, 160–2, 174
Dover, 1st Baron, 243
Downton, 89
Doyle, John, 90, 91, 93, 112, 128, 163,
  268–9

Drayton Manor, 171

Drummond, Henry, 198

Dryden, John, 115
 Absalom and Achitophel, 149

Dublin University, 94

Dudley, 1st Earl of (later 4th Earl of
  Bessborough), 56, 146, 151, 230

Duncannon, Viscount, 51, 52, 62, 65–6,
  194, 264

Dunwich, 19

Durham, 139

Durham, John George 'Radical Jack'
  Lambton, 1st Baron (later 1st Earl of
  Durham)
  and 1826 Northumberland county
    election, 17–18
  description of Graham, 34
  and defeat of Tory Government, 48
  and family connections among Whigs,
    52
  included in Grey's Cabinet, 58
  and formation of Committee of Four,
    62, 66
  temperament and background, 66–7
  relationship with Grey, 66, 129, 130,
    175–6
  Committee begins to meet at house of, 68
  in favour of Secret Ballot, 102
  and dissolution of Parliament, 108–9
  as Old Etonian, 127
  and his son's illness, 129, 130
  and his son's death, 175
  insults Grey at Cabinet dinner, 175–6
  sums up options to ensure passing of
    Bill, 188
  difficult behaviour in Cabinet, 205–6
  threatens to resign, 207
  speech in Lords, 213–14
  analysis of 'public excitement', 250
  and death of his daughter, 252
  and Royal Assent, 257
  after passing of Reform Bill, 266
  brief references, 56, 71, 99, 262

Durham, Louisa Grey, Lady 52, 188

East Anglia, riots in, 15, 29

Eastlake, Lady, 159

East Retford, 19–20

East Sheen, 188

Eaton Hall, 77

Ebrington, Viscount (later 2nd Earl of
  Fortescue), 156–7, 229, 239

Edgeworth, Maria, 3–4, 7, 56, 111–12

Edinburgh, 97, 274

Edinburgh Review, 17, 35, 51, 59, 271

Eldon, 1st Earl of, 90, 128, 146

Eliot, George: *Middlemarch*, 270

Elizabeth, Princess, 7

Ellenborough, 1st Baron (later 1st Earl of
  Ellenborough), 22–3, 56, 57–8, 89,
  125, 128, 130, 145, 214, 241–2, 250

Ellice, Edward, 58

Ellis, Georgiana, 68

English Civil War, 2, 113

Essex, 5th Earl of, 187

Eton College, 127–8

Examiner, 68

Exeter, 174

Exeter, Henry Phillpotts, Bishop of; *see*
  Phillpotts, Henry, Bishop of Exeter

Ferrers, 8th Earl, 8

Figaro in London, 203, 256, 272

FitzClarence, George, later Earl of
  Munster; *see* Munster, George
  FitzClarence, Earl of

FitzClarence, Viscount, 118

Fitzwilliam, 4th Earl, 54

Fonblanque, Albany, 67–8, 165

Forbes, Sir Charles, 100

Fox, Charles James, 2, 12, 51, 54, 64, 87–8,
  181, 190

Frampton, James, 160, 161

Frampton, Mary, 160, 161, 174

France, 7, 39, 74, 113–14, 187, 213, 274
  revolutionary events in, 3, 11–12, 26,
    41, 52, 95, 160, 181, 201, 213, 250, 253,
    258, 277

French Assembly, 135

French Revolution
  1789, 11, 52, 160, 181, 250, 258, 277
  July 1830, 3, 11–12, 26, 41, 95, 201, 213, 277

Gambier, William Henry, 28–9
Garth, Thomas, 106
Gascoyne, General Isaac, 103, 104, 112, 179
Gatton, 19
General Election
  1830, 13, 15, 20–1
  1831, 114, 115–16, 118–20
  1832–33, 266–8
George II, King, 227
George III, King, 2, 3, 6, 106, 122, 227
George IV, King, 2, 3–4, 5, 6, 8, 9, 21, 71, 72, 106, 129, 132, 134, 194
Germany, 7
Gladstone, William Ewart, 2, 121–2, 139, 145, 161
Glasgow, 19
Glengall, Countess of, 225
Globe, 169
Glorious Revolution 1688, 2
Gloucester, HRH Prince William, Duke of, 57, 105, 117, 149
Glynne, Sir Stephen, 77
Goderich, Viscount (later 1st Earl of Ripon), 58, 130
Goodall, Joseph, 127
Goodwood, 29, 45
'Goodwood Set', 183
Gordon, Sir Willoughby, 170
Gorgon, 75
Graham, Sir James, 34, 46–7, 58, 99, 212, 266
Grant, Charles, 58, 73–4
Grant, James, 30, 31, 32, 66, 174
Granville, Harriet Cavendish, Countess, 44–5, 150
Great Fire 1834, 276
Great Marlow, 119
Great Reform Bill; *see* Reform Bill
Greville, Charles

on Durham, 206
on Grey, 22
on Harrowby, 178, 253
on Lady Lyndhurst, 56
on the Lyndhursts' different views about Reform, 230
on Macaulay, 82
on Queen Adelaide, 6, 7, 72
on Reform Bill, 96, 97–8, 216
on Richmond, 45
on severe weather, 13
on Talleyrand, 2–3
on Tories, 251
and Wellington, 24, 25
on William IV, 6, 8, 134
on William's coronation day, 133, 134
on William's illegitimate children, 73
Grey, 2nd Earl
  and Fox, 2
  and Georgiana, Duchess of Devonshire, 2, 22
  and death of George IV, 4
  disliked by George IV, 9
  early supporter of Reform, 10–11, 23
  happy family life, 21–2
  appreciation of female company, 22
  appearance, 22–3
  nepotism, 23, 52, 57–8
  believes the time has come for Reform, 23–4
  conversation with Brougham, 35–6
  political leadership is untried, 37
  speech after Opening of Parliament, 40–1
  comments on Wellington's 'blind presumption', 44
  and the vote against the Government, 47
  asked to form a government by the King, 48
  wealth, 50
  forms a government, 55–60
  and appointment of Lord Chancellor, 56–7
  and appointment of Foreign Secretary, 57

concerned about 'large assemblages', 60–1

and formation of Committee of Four to consider Reform, 62

relationship with Durham, 66, 129–30, 175–6, 188, 206, 266

reads draft of proposals of Committee of Four, 69

correspondence with William IV about Reform, 69–71

shows Reform Bill to William, 71

remains confident, 87

Creevey remarks on renewed vitality of, 91

backed by Birmingham Political Union, 93

decides to proceed with Reform Bill in spite of defeat on Timber Duties, 94

is informed of the King's opposition to dissolution, 94–5

announces that he will not amend the Bill, 98

described by Creevey, 99

private correspondence with Taylor, 106–7

the King agrees to see, 107

at dissolution of Parliament, 110

gratitude to the King, 111

becomes Knight of the Garter, 117–18

and payments, 120

letter to Holland about creation of new peers, 122

and Eton, 127

and his grandson's illness, 129–30

moves second reading of Bill in House of Lords, 139–41, 142–3

and death of his grandson, 139

accused of trying to 'overawe' the House, 145

speaks in House of Lords shortly before the vote on Bill, 149

urges dismissal of Howe from Royal Household, 154

Queen Adelaide is hostile towards, 154, 202

meets delegation led by Place, 158–9

correspondence between William IV and, 163–4

and Bristol riots, 168

and date of next meeting of Parliament, 175

scene caused by Durham, 175–6

issue of creation of peers raised in Cabinet by, 184–5, 187, 188

visited by Holland, 188

informs the King about events in Ireland, 189

reads letters to Cabinet about creation of peers, 190

meets the King to discuss creation of peers, 190–2

the King sends written response to, 192–3, 201

kept informed about the King by Taylor, 195

declares unalterable commitment to Reform, 202

Althorp writes to, 206–7

letter to Althorp, 207

and debate in House of Lords, 211–12, 214–15

speaks in Lords on 7th May, 218

presents Cabinet minute about resignation to the King, 224–5

at public house in Hounslow, 225

announces Government resignation, 226

at Court reception, 227

and the Tory attempt to form new administration, 232, 240–1

communications between the King and, 242, 244, 245–6

and speeches of Wellington and Lyndhurst, 244

discusses reinstatement of Ministers, 246–7

thanks Attwood, 247, 277–8

news of his return spreads, 249

angry exchanges in House of Lords, 250–1

Grey, 2nd Earl (*continued*)
  comments on the blunder made by the
    Opposition, 251
  and debate in House of Lords on third
    reading of Bill, 252, 253–4
  congratulated on the success of the Bill,
    254
  and the King's refusal to attend House of
    Lords, 255
  and Royal Assent, 257
  and Haydon, 260–1
  depictions of, 262
  on the unions, 264–5
  in Doyle's cartoon following General
    Election, 268–9
  inspirational character of, 273–4
  retirement, 274–5
  brief references, 25, 39, 54, 76, 81, 84–5,
    102, 124, 144, 151, 155, 156, 177, 194,
    238, 248, 256, 259
Grey, Lady Georgiana, 69
Grey, Lady Hannah, 58
Grey, Lady Louisa; *see* Durham, Lady
Grey, Mary Ponsonby, Countess, 6, 21, 39,
  69, 99, 145, 188–9, 211, 260–1
Grosvenor, Earl (later 2nd Duke of
  Westminster), 77, 119
Grosvenor, Elizabeth Leveson-Gower,
  Countess, 77, 112, 113, 169
Grote, George, 159, 160, 249
  Essentials of Parliamentary Reform, 160
Grote, Harriet, 159–60, 183, 184, 245
Guildford, 88, 178
Guildhall Banquet 1832, 260
  painting of, 260–1
Gunpowder Plot 1605, 173
Gurney, Hudson, 88–9
Guy Fawkes Day 1831, 173–4

Hansard (Hansard's *Parliamentary
  Debates*), 32, 144, 145, 199, 216, 254
Hansard, Thomas, 32
Harborne, 26
Hardinge, Sir Henry, 109, 238–9

Harrowby, 1st Earl of, 145–6, 178, 197, 205,
  218, 252, 253
Hastings, 2nd Marquess of, 110
Haydon, Benjamin Robert, 2, 19, 24, 27, 35,
  51, 60, 111, 221, 222, 260–1
Hepburne Scott, Henry, 96
Hetherington, Henry, 152, 208
Hobhouse, Sir John (later 1st Baron
  Broughton)
  reaction to 1830 Revolution in France, 12
  and Russell's introduction of Reform
    Bill, 79, 81–2
  at meeting in Crown and Anchor
    Tavern, 88
  and voting on Reform Bill, 95
  comments on the new London Bridge,
    128
  and the meeting between Grey and
    Place's delegation, 158
  and attacks on country houses, 171–2
  reflects on the fate of Bristol rioters, 196
  conversation with Althorp, 206
  asks Place to declare his intentions, 245
  Place visits, 248
  and the King's decision not to attend
    House of Lords, 255
  comments on 'this great national
    exploit', 278
  brief references, 2, 109, 257
Holkham, 54, 190, 261, 262
Holland, Elizabeth Vassall, Lady, 52, 53,
  65, 198
Holland, 3rd Baron
  response to 1830 Revolution in France,
    12
  admits that Grey is susceptible to
    women, 22
  and Brougham, 35, 149
  wealth, 50
  criticizes the self-educated, 51
  devoted to his wife, 53
  appearance, 54
  turns down Foreign Secretaryship, 57
  and Durham, 67, 205–6

and Secret Ballot, 102
and creation of new peers, 122, 184, 186, 187–8, 188–9
at Eton, 127–8
and occasion of royal assent to Queen's dower-bill, 129
verdict on Sydney Smith, 155
visits Grey at East Sheen, 188
and William IV, 210, 273
comment about Lyndhurst, 218
responds to Grey's depressed communication, 232
writes to Grey about possible reactions if Wellington were to move a Bill, 238
meeting with Attwood and companions, 247
in the Lords for Royal Assent to Reform Bill, 257–8
writes in Diary about impact of individual character on government, 271
brief references, 2, 59, 65, 134, 141, 152, 176, 197, 214, 241, 274
Holland House, 6, 17, 52–4, 217
Holyoake, George, 25, 27
Holyrood Palace, 11, 83, 243
Hounslow, 225
Houses of Parliament
  1834 fire, 276
  see also Commons, House of; Lords, House of
Howe, 1st Earl, 72, 118, 129, 153–4, 197, 202, 204, 254
Howick, 21, 35, 260
Howick, Viscount (later 3rd Earl Grey), 17–18, 58, 219
Howley, William, Archbishop of Canterbury, 142, 146–7, 188, 216, 227
Huddersfield, 173–4
Hume, Joseph, 100–1, 158, 194, 196, 264, 265
Hunt, G.W., 127
Hunt, Henry 'Orator', 13–14, 38, 44, 85, 100, 101, 102, 179, 180, 194, 200

Hunt, John, 68
Hunt, Leigh, 68, 75, 237
Huntingdon, 178
Huntly, 8th Marquis of, 2
Hurst Green, 28
Huskisson, William, 119, 181
Huskissonites, 33, 43, 47; see also names of individuals
Hutton, Revd, 222
Hyde Park, 125

Industrial Revolution, 18
Inglis, Sir Robert, 80–1, 83, 87, 240
Ireland, 10, 15, 59, 66, 156, 189, 224, 269
Irish MPs, 16, 66, 93–4, 98
Irish peers, 16, 186, 192
Irish Reform Bill, 213, 215, 265
Irving, Edward, 198
Itchen Abbas, 61

Jacobite Rebellion 1745, 2
James II, King, 2, 140
Jeffrey, Lord, 51, 59, 63, 104, 110
Jersey, Sarah Fane, Countess of, 48, 91
Jordan, Mrs Dora, 6, 73, 116

Kay, Dr James, 237
Kay, James Phillips, 198
Kemble, Fanny, 209
Kensington, 52
Kent, civil unrest in, 14, 28–9
Kent, Duchess of, 129, 133
Kent, HRH Prince Edward, Duke of, 6, 8
Kenyon, 2nd Baron, 250–1
Kerry, Knight of, 44
Kilkenny, 189
Kingsley, Charles, 168
Kirkby, Sergeant John, 172
Knaresborough, 105
Knights of the Garter, 117–18
Knowles, James Sheridan: *Alfred the Great or the Patriot King*, 112

Lafayette, Marquis de, 143, 190

Lamb, Lady Caroline, 60

Lamb, George, 138

Lamb, William, Lord Melbourne; *see* Melbourne, William Lamb, Lord

Lambton, Charles William, 129–30, 139

Lambton, Harriet, 252

Lambton, John George 'Radical Jack', Lord Durham; *see* Durham, Lord

Lansdowne, 3rd Marquess of, 54, 57, 82, 89, 102, 120, 130, 182, 187, 190, 261, 267

Lansdowne House, 52

Lascelles, Caroline, 68

Lawrence, Sir Thomas, 19
    'The Red Boy', 129

Leeds, 19, 36, 103, 267

Leeds Mercury, 74–5, 180

Leicester, 37

Le Marchant, Sir Denis, 64, 86, 87, 88–9, 105, 126, 135, 136, 149–50, 156, 177, 197, 211, 219, 226, 227

Lennox, Lord William, 180

Leopold, Prince, 57

Leveson-Gower, Elizabeth, 32; *see* Grosvenor

Lieven, Princess
    and Durham, 67
    and France, 11
    and George IV, 3, 4
    and Grey, 22, 44, 47, 56, 57, 71, 139, 244
    and Peel, 241
    and Queen Adelaide, 154
    and Reform Bill, 82
    and Wellington, 44, 48, 117, 212
    and window-breaking by the crowds, 113

Littleton, Edward, 83, 148–9, 182, 207, 226, 227–8, 268

Liverpool, 112, 119, 181, 249

Liverpool, Lord, 9, 79, 118

Liverpool-Manchester Railways, 1

London
    cholera epidemic, 198
    civil disturbances, 43, 44–5, 46
    Clubs, 54–5
    concerns about shooting of dogs in, 125

    gathering of National Political Union in, 220
    great Whig houses in, 52
    march takes place in, 157–8
    meeting of Radicals in, 232–5
    police force founded in, 1
    see also names of locations in London

London Bridge, 128

Londonderry, 3rd Marquess of, 45, 72–3, 110, 128, 139, 146, 151, 195, 197, 254, 269

Londonderry House, 132

Lords, House of
    Byron's maiden speech in, 13
    seats in, 16
    the King's speech at Opening of Parliament, 39–40
    Grey's speech on need for Reform, 40–1
    Wellington's speech, 25, 41–2
    Richmond states his position on Reform, 45–6
    and assassination attempt on Wellington, 61–2
    Grey announces that Reform Bill will be presented in Commons, 76
    members listen to presentation of Bill in Commons, 78
    Grey announces that he will not amend the Bill, 98
    William IV agrees to go to, 108
    dissolution of Parliament, 109–11
    inbuilt majority of Tories in, 122
    possibility of creating peers to get Reform Bill through, 122–3, 130, 144, 152–3, 158, 159, 163, 183, 184–9, 190–3
    William IV attends to give consent to Queen's dower-bill, 128–9
    Althorp pessimistic about Bill being passed in, 130
    debates on Reform Bill, 139–41, 142–3, 144–9
    bishops in, 141–2, 156
    petition of Birmingham Political Union presented to, 144

vote against the Bill, 149–50
situation after the vote in, 151–62, 166
Bill formally presented to, 209
canvassing of uncommitted peers,
209–10
debate on the Bill, 211–15
vote on second reading, 215–16
debate on 7 May, 218–19
Government defeated in, 219
Attwood asks Brougham to present
petition to, 220
Government resignation announced in,
226
speeches of Wellington and Lyndhurst,
244–5
angry speeches following the return of
Whig Government, 250–1
debate on third reading of the Bill, 252–4
vote in favour of the Bill, 254
the King declines to attend, 255–6
Royal Assent given, 257–8
emerges with membership intact, 270–1
Louis XIV, King of France, 52, 181
Louis XVI, King of France, 7, 140, 181,
193, 251, 257, 258
Louis-Philippe, King of the French, 3, 11,
39, 53, 187
Lovat, Lord, 2
Lulworth Castle, 11
Lyndhurst, Lady, 22, 56, 230
Lyndhurst, 1st Baron
and post of Lord Chancellor, 55, 56
background, 55–6
and his wife, 56, 230
and dissolution of Parliament, 109–10
and Brougham's fall/genuflection, 148
asks about possibility of moderating the
Bill, 175
as one of the Waverers, 175, 178, 218
proposes changes to the Bill, 218
acts as intermediary between William IV
and Wellington, 226
sets condition for returning to post of
Lord Chancellor, 230

Wellington's response to, 231
reaction to listening to Manners-Sutton,
232
speech on 17 May 1832, 244
absents himself from vote in Lords, 254
absent from Lords for Royal Assent,
257
brief references, 219, 246, 256, 265
Lyttelton, Sarah Spencer, Lady, 162–3
Lytton, Edward Bulwer, 1st Baron, 30–1,
34, 57, 65, 83, 93

Macaulay, Hannah, 125, 204–5
Macaulay, Margaret, 205
Macaulay, Thomas Babington
on Industrial Revolution, 18
and Lady Holland, 53
and journalists, 67
and Calne constituency, 82, 89, 182
brilliance, 82–3
speech during debate on first Reform
Bill, 83–4
Mahon's response to, 84
Hunt's attack on, 85
and the vote on the Bill, 96, 97
views on Universal Suffrage, 101
and cholera epidemic, 125
on William IV's coronation, 133
speech following defeat of second Bill in
Lords, 156
speech in debate on third Bill, 180–1
Croker's long-running battle with, 182
comments on public disorder, 189
writes to his sisters on the Bill, 204–5
on Grey's speech in Lords, 211
on Wellington's behaviour, 239–40
on William IV, 256
at Guildhall Banquet, 260
transfers to Leeds constituency, 267
on Althorp, 275
comments on 'the victories of reason',
278
brief references, 2, 120, 216
Macready, William Charles, 112

Mahon, Viscount (later 5th Earl Stanhope)
84
*A Leaf from the Future History of
England*, 102–3
Maidstone, 28
Manchester, 19, 26, 60–1, 80, 100, 103,
139, 170, 171, 196; *see also* Peterloo
Massacre
Manchester Guardian, 75
Manners-Sutton, Charles, 78, 109, 232, 241
Marie Antoinette, Queen of France, 2, 7,
74, 187, 193, 228, 250, 258
Martin, Harry, 255
Martineau, Harriet, 58, 220
Marx, Karl, 52n
Marylebone, 250
Masham, Samuel, 185
Meiningen, 7
Melbourne, 2nd Viscount
description of cities, 19
on Whigs' family ties, 52
becomes Home Secretary, 58
appearance, 60
private life, 60
earlier career, 60
view on appropriate response to civil
disturbances, 61
comment relating to Munster, 116–17
as Old Etonian, 127
concerns about plans of political unions,
138
in indirect contact with Radical opinion,
138
and disagreements among Cabinet
members, 175
and 'the Goodwood Set', 183
sets up special commission to hand out
exemplary punishments to rioters, 196
and Durham, 206, 266
Haydon's description of, 261
later becomes Prime Minister, 275
Merthyr Tydfil, 121, 138
Midlands, 13, 15, 162, 171, 172; *see also*
names of places

Milborne, 160
Mill, James, 75, 101, 159, 270
Milton, Viscount (later 3rd Earl
Fitzwilliam), 156
Moncrieff, W.T.: *Reform, or John Bull
Triumphant*, 91–2
Moore, Thomas, 73, 229
Morning Chronicle, 67, 75, 76, 151, 228, 245
Morning Herald, 196
Morning Post, 63
Morpeth, Viscount (later 7th Earl of
Carlisle), 180
Moseley, Revd Thomas, 120
Mundy, Harriot, 152
Mundy, William, 152
Munster, George FitzClarence, 1st Earl of,
73, 116–17, 243
Musters, Mr, 152

Napoleon, 134, 135
Nash, John, 194
National Gallery, 272
National Political Union, 160, 196, 220,
245
National Union of the Working Classes,
157, 171, 208–9, 212
Nelson, Admiral, 4
Newcastle, 4th Duke of, 16, 119, 152, 162,
254
Newcastle upon Tyne, 250, 274–5
Newhall Hill
meetings at, 143–4, 219–24, 227
Haydon's depiction of, 221, 260
Newtown, Isle of Wight, 17, 88
Norfolk, civil disturbances in, 61
Norfolk, 12th Duke of, 9
Norman, Richard, 172–3, 176
North, John Henry, 91
Northumberland, 17–18, 120
Norwich, 181
Norwich, Henry Bathurst, Bishop of, 262
Nottingham, 162, 170, 171, 196
Nottingham Journal, 75
Nottinghamshire, 13

O'Connell, Daniel, 2, 10, 20, 66, 93, 98, 125, 189, 224
Old Sarum, 19, 80, 263
Owen, Robert, 152
Oxford, Countess of, 135
Oxford University, 81, 116, 122

Paganini, Nicolo, 126
Palmerston, Henry Temple, 3rd Viscount
  relationship with Emily Cowper, 51, 59
  becomes Foreign Secretary, 57
  believes in need for Reform, 59–60
  and Queen Adelaide's outfit allowance, 74
  loses seat at Cambridge University, but is found a seat at Bletchingley, 123
  and Cabinet disagreements, 130
  and discussions about date of next meeting of Parliament, 175
  and 'the Goodwood Set', 183
  and Cabinet discussions about creation of new peers, 187
  painted by Haydon, 261
  and Durham, 266
  later becomes Prime Minister, 275
  brief references, 16, 160, 186, 206
Panshanger, 69
Parkes, Joseph
  expresses hopes about Reform, 67
  background, 137
  involvement in Birmingham Political Union, 137–8, 220
  description of Newhall Hill, 143
  estimates size of crowd at Newhall Hill in 1831, 143
  Place describes meeting with Grey to, 159
  Althorp writes private letter to, 177
  letter to Harriet Grote about creation of new peers, 183, 184
  and Cobbett's conversation in bookseller's shop, 217
  fund-raising efforts, 220
  at meeting at Newhall Hill in May 1832, 222

attends meeting at Place's house, 233, 234
  subsequent career, 268
  important role of, 277
Parliament; see Commons, House of; 1834 fire; Lords, House of
Parsons, Revd, 161–2
Partington, Dame, 155
Peel, Edmund, 58
Peel, Jonathan, 58
Peel, Sir Robert
  and Catholic Emancipation, 9–10
  and 1830 Revolution in France, 11
  Stanley and Graham make secret approach to, 34
  background and character, 34–5
  speech in Commons (November 1830), 46
  conversation with Princess Lieven after Government defeat in Commons, 48
  and promotion of relatives, 58
  speech after Althorp's presentation of budget, 76
  and Tory discussions before the presentation of Reform Bill, 77
  and the introduction of Reform Bill to Commons, 79, 84
  and loss of Oxford University seat, 81
  attack on Reform Bill, 85, 86, 87
  and dissolution of Parliament, 109
  responds to second Reform Bill, 124–5
  attends opening of new London Bridge, 128
  speech in Commons on the day before vote in Lords, 135
  concerned about public riots, 171
  response to third Bill, 179, 182–3
  reluctant to head new administration, 230–1
  refuses to head new administration, 240, 241–2, 271
  views on how to calm public unrest, 271–2
  later becomes Prime Minister, 275
  brief references, 33, 90, 98, 197

Peel, William, 58

Pelham, John Cresset, 194

Penny Papers for the People, 152

Pepys, Samuel, 31

Perceval, Spencer, 198–200, 207

Peterloo Massacre 1819, 13–14, 75, 76, 81, 85, 100, 135–6, 142, 237

Phillpotts, Henry, Bishop of Exeter, 155, 174, 213–14, 215

Place, Francis
   reaction to 1830 Revolution in France, 12
   background, 37–8
   avidity for learning, 38
   on Duke of Wellington, 38–9
   and popular violence, 43
   hostility to cliques, 54
   Parkes expresses hope of Reform to, 67
   enthusiasm for Reform Bill, 87
   regarded as 'political father' by Parkes, 137
   Lamb in contact with, 138
   view of Anglican Church, 142
   meeting with Grey, 158–9
   enjoys hospitality of the Grotes, 159
   founds National Political Union, 160
   on Queen Adelaide, 203
   on the peers as a class, 210
   letter to Parkes about his work, 220
   and decision to take financial action, 232–3, 233–4
   and the possibility of Wellington's return to power, 245, 248
   hopes for further reforms, 265
   subsequent career, 268
   important role of, 277
   brief references, 40, 51, 151, 157, 258, 259, 271

Poland, 224

Political Register, 101, 217

Ponsonby, George, 58

Ponsonby, Mary; *see* Grey, Mary, Countess

Poor Man's Guardian, 75, 152–3, 173–4, 208, 217

Powell, John, 151, 157, 158

Protheroe, Edward, 167

Radicals, 12 and n, 38, 40, 51, 75, 87–8, 99, 100, 102, 137, 138, 144, 152, 157, 159, 217, 232–5, 277; *see also* names of individuals

Radnor, 3rd Earl of, 62, 89

Reform Bill
   political and social context, 1–29, 33–9
   differing views on subject of Reform, 33, 36–7, 38–9, 40–2, 43, 44, 45–6, 47
   Government defeated over Whig motion about Reform, 47–9
   Committee of Four formed to consider Reform, 62–7, 68
   expectations of Reform, 67–8
   draft proposals, 69
   correspondence between William IV and Grey before introduction of, 69–71
   shown to William, and approved, 71
   announcement of forthcoming presentation of, 76
   Tories meet to plan response to, 77
   presented to Commons by Russell, 77–80
   reactions to, 80–5
   and Radicals, 85, 87–8
   Peel mounts official Tory attack on, 85, 86–7
   supported by *The Times*, 88
   debate in Commons on, 88–9, 90–1
   discussed in fashionable London, 91
   supported by Birmingham Political Union, 92–3, 98
   supported by Irish MPs, 93–4, 98
   debate on second reading summed up by Russell, 95
   Commons vote in favour of, 95–7
   enters Committee stage, 98
   Cabinet remains united about, 99
   Hunt turns against, 100, 101
   Tory opposition to, 102–4
   Whigs agree to make some changes to, 104

Government defeated over Gascoyne's
amendment, 104
dissolution of Parliament after defeat of,
107–11
1831 General Election fought on issue of
Reform, 115–16, 118–20
Gladstone's views on, 121–2
majority of Commons in favour of, 122,
123
concerns about possibility of House of
Lords refusing to pass, 122, 130
idea of creating new peers expressed by
Grey in a letter, 122–3
introduction of Second Bill into
Commons, 123–4
response of the Opposition expressed by
Peel, 124–5
passes in Commons, 125
attempts to prevent Bill from going to
Committee stage, 126
Committee stage, 127, 130
Chandos clause, 130
passes Committee stage, 131
passes in Commons, 134
Tories remain opposed to, 134–5
success celebrated at Whig dinner, 135–6
fears expressed about consequences of
rejecting, 138
debated in House of Lords, 139–43,
144–9
Lords vote against, 149–50
aftermath of Lords vote, 151–66, 167–74
William prorogues Parliament, 165–6
Cabinet discussions on the way ahead
for, 175
introduction of Third Bill to Commons,
177–9
debated, 179–83
passed by Commons, 183
creation of peers considered as solution
to problem of getting through Lords,
184–9, 190–3
remains topic of concern to the public,
195–6

Wellington maintains opposition to,
196–7
Committee stage, 197–8
reasons for opposition to, 200–1
Grey declares unalterable commitment
to, 202
tensions and apprehensions, 202–9
third reading passes in Commons, 209
formally presented to Lords, 209
canvassing of support of uncommitted
peers, 209–10
prevarication of the King, 210–11
debate in House of Lords, 211–15
vote on second reading in Lords, 215–16
passes into Committee stage, 216
and disagreements among reformers, 217
Cabinet agrees changes to, 217–18
debated in Lords, 218–19
Government defeated over, 219
public meeting in Birmingham in
support of, 219–24
Government resigns after defeat of,
224–5
days of crisis between Government
defeat and the return of Grey, 226–48
Tory reactions after Grey's return, 250–1
no further official confrontations over,
252
debate at third reading of, 252–4
passes in House of Lords, 254
the King refuses to attend House of
Lords for Royal Assent, 255–6
Royal Assent to, 257–8
crucial role of public opinion, 258
triumphal arch proposed to celebrate,
258–9
celebratory banquet at Guildhall, 260
artistic depictions to commemorate,
260–2
countrywide rejoicing about, 263
misgivings about, 263–4
whole Reform Bill eventually passed
throughout British Isles, 265
General Election under new rules, 266–8

Reform Bill (*continued*)
  achievement of, 269–71
  impact of character and personality on
    events, 271–4
  avoidance of revolution, 276–8
Reform Club, 55n
Richmond, 5th Duke of
  Goodwood estate attacked by rioters, 29
  background, 45
  views about Reform, 45–6
  included in Grey's Cabinet, 58, 99
  Brougham's comment on, 99
  Lyndhurst shows anger towards, 109–10
  and disagreement in the Cabinet, 130
  and discussion about date of next
    meeting of Parliament, 175
  and colonies, 180
  and 'the Goodwood Set', 183
  and Cabinet discussions about creation
    of new peers, 187, 188
  and Durham, 206
  possibility of continuing in office under a
    new administration, 226
  informs Althorp of Wellington's
    decision not to attempt to from new
    administration, 241
  painted by Haydon, 261
  visits Althorp, 266
Riot Act, 162
Riviere (gunmaker), 171
Robespierre, Maximilien de, 52
Rochdale, 179, 237
Rogers, Samuel, 36, 273
Rothschild, James, 113–14, 130
Rothschild, Nathan, 113, 233
Rotunda, Blackfriars Bridge, 44
Roy, Rammohun, 145
Royal Coburg Theatre, 91
Royal Hospital, Chelsea, 61
Russell, G.W.E., 35
Russell, Lord John (later 1st Earl Russell of
    Kingston Russell)
  own bill for Reform, 11, 100
  and East Retford, 20

emotional courage, 33
  voice, 33, 65
  lack of independent wealth, 50, 65
  as member of Committee of Four, 62
  background, 3, 64–5
  determination and intelligence, 65
  and draft proposals of Committee of
    Four, 69
  Grey's announcement of presentation of
    Reform Bill by, 76
  presents Reform Bill to Commons,
    77–80, 270
  speech reported in *The Times*, 88
  Croker's attack on, 89
  sums up debate on second reading of
    Bill, 95
  introduces second Reform Bill, 123–4
  letter to Attwood, 153, 164–5
  and Cabinet discussions about
    moderating the Bill, 175
  presents new Bill, 177–8
  perceives real peril in 'Days of May', 238
  conversation with Haydon, 261
  depictions of, 262
  later becomes Prime Minister, 275
  brief references, 26, 84, 86, 90, 179–80,
    219, 240, 252, 259, 268
Rutland, 269
Rutland, Duchess of, 9
Rutland, 5th Duke of, 13, 37, 77, 117, 172,
    176

St Giles (racehorse), 257
St James's Chronicle, 195–6
St James's Palace, 43–4, 107–8, 126, 157,
    194
Sandon Hall, 178
Satirist, The, 236–7
Saville, John, 142
Saxe-Meiningen, Duke of, 7
Scarbrough, 6th Earl of, 254
Scholefield, Joshua, 26, 267
Scorton Green, 263
Scotland, 15, 19, 59, 269

Scotsman, 143
Scottish peers, 16, 186, 192
Scottish Reform Bill, 265
Secret Ballot, 87, 88, 101–2, 160
Sefton, 2nd Earl of, 24
Septennial Act 1716, 20, 102
Seymour, Robert, 203
Shakespeare, William
  Coriolanus, 82
  Macbeth, 135
Sheffield, 19
Shelley, Frances, Lady, 37
Shelley, Percy Bysshe, 14
  The Masque of Anarchy, 237–8
Sherborne, 161–2
Sherborne Castle, 161
Sherborne Journal, 161–2
Sheridan, Richard Brinsley, 181
Sidmouth, 1st Viscount, 81
Skipworth, Sir George, 153
Smith, Hon. Robert, 111–12
Smith, Sydney, 17, 52, 53, 65, 83, 102, 142,
  155, 156, 160, 177, 271, 277
Soane, Sir John, 276
Society of the Friends of the People, 23
Somerville, Alexander, 97, 150, 153, 171,
  222
Sophia, Princess, 106
South Shields, 139
Southwark, 181, 228
Spectator, 92, 93, 98
Spencer, 2nd Earl, 54, 62, 129, 150
Spencer, John, Viscount Althorp; *see*
  Althorp, John Spencer, Viscount
Spencer, Lavinia Bingham, Countess, 52
Standard, 176
Stanhope, Lady Hester, 84
Stanhope, 5th Earl, 34
Stanley, Edward (later Lord Stanley and
  13th Earl of Derby)
  on the buying and selling of boroughs,
    17
  background and career, 33–4
  becomes Chief Secretary for Ireland, 59

speech in debate following introduction
  of Reform Bill, 89
and O'Connell, 93
criticizes idea of Secret Ballot, 101–2
and conditions in House of Commons,
  125
enables Whig contact with Waverers,
  178
speech in debate about new Reform Bill,
  180, 181–2
reports on events in Ireland, 189
during Lords debate, 212
subsequent career, 275
brief references, 99, 130, 195, 232
Stormont, Viscount (later 4th Earl of
  Mansfield), 82, 236–7
Strangford, 6th Viscount, 197
Stratfield Saye, 47
Strutt, Edward, 82, 214, 229
Suffolk, 61
Sun, 151
Sussex, civil disturbances in, 28, 29
Sussex, HRH Prince Augustus, Duke of,
  57, 73, 78, 125, 139, 218, 257, 262
Swing, Captain, 14–15, 29, 277

Talleyrand, Prince, 3, 39, 53
Taunton, 155
Tavistock, 89
Taylor, Sir Herbert, 41, 74, 108, 138, 163,
  210, 211, 242, 246, 252
  communications with Grey, 70–1, 94–5,
    106–7, 195, 244, 246–7
Temple, Henry, Viscount Palmerston; *see*
  Palmerston, Henry Temple, Viscount
Temple Bar, London, 44
Test and Corporation Acts, 65, 142
Thackeray, William Makepeace, 90
Thackwell, Colonel, 171
Theatre Royal, Drury Lane, 112
Timber Duties, 94
Times, The
  on George IV, 4
  and Catholic Emancipation, 9

Times, The (*continued*)

makes donations to 'necessitous Parisians', 12

on Wellington, 24

on civil disturbance, 28, 37, 169

complains about conditions for reporters in House of Commons, 32

on resignation of Tory Cabinet, 48–9

and Grey's nepotism, 58

Fonblanque on staff of, 67

pays stamp tax, 75

Barnes as editor of, 75–6, 99

complains about inaudibility of Russell's voice, 79

on first Reform Bill, 82, 88

on Universal Suffrage, 101

on prospects for Reform, 115

on Howe, 118

on William's coronation day, 132

on Grey's speech in Lords, 141

on meeting on Newhall Hill in 1831, 143

picks up on Whig uneasiness about the King's stance on creation of peers, 144

on Brougham's speech, 148

on the vote against Reform Bill in Lords, 154–5

questions whether bishops should have seats in Lords, 156

and William's speech at Opening of Parliament, 177

on passing of third Reform Bill in Commons, 183

Fellows of Trinity College disgusted by, 195–6

on creation of peers, 209

comments on lack of new arguments from Tories, 212

on meeting at Newhall Hill in 1832, 220, 222

on crisis in May 1832, 227

reports on a description of Adelaide, 228

on Adelaide's influence on William, 237

response to return of Grey's government, 247–8, 249

on poor attendance at House of Lords, 252

on Royal Assent, 255

correspondent calls for subscription to erect triumphal arch, 258–9

brief references, 179, 217, 245

Tocqueville, Alexis de, 24, 39, 274

Tories

Government in power at William IV's accession, 9

divisive effect of campaign on Catholic Emancipation, 9–10

party designation, 20

perceived as party of government, 21

differing views on Reform, 33, 47

and Whig philosophy, 50–1

Grey's Cabinet includes, 58, 59–60, 99

favoured by Queen Adelaide, 72–3

meetings before announcement of terms of Reform Bill, 77

official attack on the Bill by Peel, 85, 86–7

during interval between readings of the Bill, 94

brings about defeat on Timber Duties, 94

determined to secure changes to the Bill, 98

powerful opposition to the Bill, 102

discussions about the Bill, 103–4

manufacture a crisis to defeat the Government, 104

cast doubts on the King's right to dissolve Parliament, 106, 108

evolve a plan concerning dissolution, 107

inbuilt majority in Lords, 122

continuing opposition to the Bill, 134–5

and Church of England, 141

convictions about Reform, 200–1

the attempt to form a new administration, 229–32, 238–42

outwardly quiescent, 251

and voting on third reading of Reform Bill, 254

and General Election in 1832, 268
impact of Wellington's attitude on, 271
and 1834 fire, 276
see also Canningites; Huskissonites;
    Ultra Tories; Waverers; names of
    individual politicians
Trafalgar, Battle of (1805), 1
Trevor, General, 14
Trinity College, Cambridge, 195–6
Turner, J.M.W.: *The Fighting Temeraire*, 1
Tyburn, 174
Tyne, the, 61
Tyrconnel, 4th Earl of, 263

Ultra Tories, 9, 10, 20, 33, 47, 151, 179, 271;
    see also names of individuals
Universal Suffrage, 15n, 41, 87, 101, 157,
    267, 269
Union, Act of (1707), 16
Union, Act of (1801), 15, 16, 30, 93, 189
Utrecht, Treaty of, 185

Vane-Tempest, Frances, 73
Vassall, Elizabeth; *see* Holland, Lady
Victoria, Princess then Queen, 1, 2, 6, 7,
    129, 133, 154n, 273
Villèle, Joseph de, 228
Villiers, Viscount (later 6th Earl of Jersey),
    110
Vyvyan, Sir Richard, 95, 96

Wakefield, E.G.: *Swing Unmasked*, 14–15
Wall, Charles Baring, 82, 88, 179
Waltham, 172
War of the Spanish Succession, 185
Waterloo, Battle of (1815), 1, 11
Watkins, John, 163–4
Waverers, the, 175, 178, 205, 210, 218, 219,
    253; *see also* names of individuals
Webster, Sir Godfrey, 53
Wellington, Duke of
    on George IV, 4
    as leader of Tory Government, 9, 24–5,
        41–2, 48

and defeat of the French at Waterloo, 11
on Grey, 23
character, 24–5
views on dealing with riots, 25
on Peel, 34
Place writes to Hunt about, 38–9
speech against Reform, 41–2
reactions to speech of, 43–5, 46–7
fire at country residence of, 47
and the vote against the Government, 48
resignation, 48–9, 72
and political unions, 60
assassination threat to, 61–2
and Tory discussions before the
    presentation of Reform Bill, 77
hears first reports about contents of
    Reform Bill, 82
in cartoons, 90, 155–6, 203, 256, 269
and Wetherell, 90
remains firmly opposed to Reform,
    94, 122, 146, 183, 196–7, 211, 212–13,
    218–19
house attacked by rioters, 113
and death of his wife, 113
angry when Grey becomes Knight of the
    Garter, 117
refuses to attend opening of new London
    Bridge, 128
compared to Dame Partington, 155–6
effigy burnt, 174
and Adelaide's letter to Howe, 204
speeches in Lords during debates on
    third Reform Bill, 212–13, 218–19
and the attempt to form a new
    administration, 226, 229–30, 231, 233,
    234, 238, 239–40, 240–1, 251
speech in Lords on 17 May 1832, 244, 251
rumours of his withdrawal spread, 245
does not attend House of Lords for vote
    on Reform Bill, 254
absent from House of Lords for Royal
    Assent, 257
expresses his views after the passing of
    Reform Bill, 263

Wellington, Duke of (*continued*)
  attacked by mob, 265
  impact on events, 271
  later becomes Prime Minister again, 275
  brief references,, 1, 2, 10, 21, 33, 35, 40–1,
    68, 84, 106, 127, 140, 145, 153, 170, 171,
    220, 246, 247, 253, 277
Wellington, Kitty Pakenham, Duchess of,
  113
Wentworth Woodhouse, 54
West Country, civil disturbances in, 160–2,
  166, 167–70
Westminster, 38, 181, 250, 269
Westminster Abby, 132, 133–4
Westminster Review, 101
Wetherell, Sir Charles, 90–1, 105, 156,
  167–8, 169, 179–80
Weymouth, 139
Wharncliffe, James, 1st Baron, 103–4, 107,
  109, 145, 147–8, 164, 175, 178, 216, 218,
  253
Whigs
  earlier movement towards parliamentary
    Reform, 10–11
  pro-French sympathies, 11–12
  party designation, 20
  lack of experience in government, 20–1
  perceive possibility of fruitful overtures
    to Tories, 33–4
  and Brougham's ideas on Reform, 36–7
  traditional party of peace, 40
  feeling that time has come to move
    forward on Reform, 47
  motion concerning Reform causes
    Government defeat, 47
  characteristics of the party, 50–1
  family connections among, 52
  houses, 52–4
  and Club system, 54–5
  formation of Government, 55–60
  presentation of Reform Bill, 77–80
  optimism about the Bill, 84, 87
  relieved that Tories do not call for
    immediate vote, 86

  alleged bias in Reform Bill, 89
  and O'Connell, 93
  concerned about possible defeat of Bill,
    94
  and the vote in the Commons on the
    Bill, 96
  agree to make changes to the Bill, 104
  attitudes to Universal Suffrage and
    Secret Ballot, 101–2
  make changes to Reform Bill, 104
  attitude to payments in electoral process,
    120
  celebration dinners, 135–6
  uneasiness about the King's views, 144
  resignation of Ministers, 224–5, 226
  meeting at Brooke's Club, 232
  and renewed negotiations, 242
  celebratory banquet, 260–1
  depictions of, 261, 262
  confidence, 265
  win majority at General Election in 1832,
    268
  spirit of compromise and conciliation,
    270–1
  and Great Fire, 1834, 276
  see also Reform Bill; names of individual
    politicians
White's Club, 54–5, 187
Wilberforce, William, 198
Wilkes, John, 32
Wilkie, Sir David, 3, 203, 268
Wilkins, William, 272
William III, King, 2
William IV, King
  succeeds George IV, 4, 8
  naval career, 4–5
  character, 5–6
  domestic life, 6
  relationship with Mrs Jordan, 6
  marries Adelaide, 6–7
  appearance, 7, 8
  concerns about health of, 8, 129, 202
  reassures Wellington, 9
  sets out for Opening of Parliament, 29

at Opening of Parliament in November
  1830, 39–40
fear of democracy, 41
advised not to attend Lord Mayor's
  Banquet, 43
fears concerning public riots, 43–4
remains supportive of Wellington, 47
asks Grey to form a government, 48
visits to Holland House, 52–3
beginning of Grey's correspondence
  with, 69–71
shows wariness about Reform, 70–1
approves Reform Bill, 71
planning of coronation of, 71–2
and crisis over Adelaide's outfit
  allowance, 74
The Times remains supportive of, 76
referred to favourably in a play, 92
against dissolution of Parliament, 94–5,
  104
rumours about, 104–5
right to dissolve Parliament questioned
  by some Tories, 106
agrees to dissolution, 107–9
dissolves Parliament, 110–11
decision adds to popularity of, 112
in cartoons, 112, 116, 163, 268
and his eldest son, 116–17
appoints Grey as Knight of the Garter,
  117, 118
and Birmingham Political Union, 120
and the creation of peers, 122–3, 144,
  152–3, 163, 191, 192, 193
visits Eton, 127
declares new London Bridge open, 128
gives assent to Queen's dower-bill, 128–9
coronation, 131, 132–4
Parkes comments on prerogative of, 138
expressions of loyalty to, 144
and Howe's departure from Royal
  Household, 153–4
petition of Radicals presented to, 157–8
correspondence with Grey in October
  1831, 163–4

prorogues Parliament, 165–6
Cabinet minute about date of next
  Parliament is sent to, 175
issues Royal Proclamation about
  political unions, 176
at Opening of Parliament in December
  1831, 177
and situation in Ireland, 189
meeting with Grey, 190–2
states his position in writing, 192–3
Cabinet minute about creation of peers
  is submitted to, 193
responds to Cabinet minute, 193
and Buckingham Palace, 194
and the continuing difficulties about
  Reform Bill, 195
Wellington's comments on, 197
and Adelaide's influence, 204, 228,
  243
prevarication, 210–11
and Bishop of Exeter's speech, 213
Attwood has confidence in, 223
Cabinet minute about possible
  resignation is presented to, 224–5
accepts resignation of Ministers, 226
asks Wellington to form new
  administration, 226
rumours about, 227
antagonism towards, 228, 236, 250
and Lord Chancellorship, 230
The Times leader on, 237
communications between Grey and,
  242, 244, 245–6
fears and obstinacy, 243
agrees to creation of peers, 246
The Times salutes imagined sentiments
  of, 247–8
mocked in prints, 248
and the avoidance of confrontation over
  the Bill, 252
refuses to attend House of Lords for the
  Royal Assent, 255–6
demands prosecution of the press, 256
Althorp's reply to, 256–7

William IV, King
   and the suggestion of a triumphal arch, 258–9
   continuing fears after passing of the Bill, 264
   stone thrown at, 265
   role of, 272–3
   and 1834 Great Fire, 276
   brief references, 21, 57, 68, 102, 186, 201, 215, 218, 262
Williams (attorney), 119–20
Williams, Philip, 160
Wilson, Harriette, 210
Wimborne, 160
Winchester, 62
Winchilsea, 10th Earl of, 214, 251, 252–3
Windsor, 5, 6, 8, 224, 225
Wiseton, 63, 265–6
Woburn, 54, 190

Wolverhampton Union, 224
Wood, Charles, 58, 96
Wood, Thomas, 72
Woodstock, 267
Worcester, Bishop of, 155
Worcester, Marquess of (later 7th Duke of Beaufort), 48
Wordsworth, William, 264
Worshipful Company of Stationers, Hall of the, 135
Wortley, James Stuart; *see* Wharncliffe, 1st Baron
Wyvill, Christopher, 10

York, Archbishop of, 254
York, HRH Prince Frederick, Duke of, 4, 8, 106
Yorkshire Agricultural Society, 63
Young, Thomas, 138

ANTONIA FRASER has written several historical biographies which have been international bestsellers, since *Mary, Queen of Scots* published in 1969. These include *Marie Antoinette*, *The Six Wives of Henry VIII*, and *Cromwell*. Other historical works include *The Weaker Vessel: Woman's Lot in Seventeenth Century England*, and *Faith and Treason: the Gunpowder Plot*. Antonia Fraser was president of English Pen, the world-wide writers' organization for free speech, and is now a vice-president. She has received many prizes, including the Wolfson History Award, the Norton Medlicott Historical Association Medal, the Franco-British Literary Prize, and the St. Louis Literary Award. She was made a D.B.E (Dame) in 2011 for services to literature. She was married to the Nobel Laureate, Harold Pinter, who died in 2008.